Up and Running with Autodesk® Inventor® Professional 2017

PART 1 – Stress and Frame Analysis

Wasim Younis BEng (Hons), MSc CAE, CEng MIMechE, Cert Ed
Autodesk® Authorized Author

Copyright ©2016 Wasim Younis. All rights reserved.

No part of this publication may be reproduced or transmitted in any form or by any means, electronic or mechanical, including photocopying, recording, or any information storage and retrieval system, without permission in writing

DEDICATION

To all the designers and engineers out there who are using Inventor Stress and Frame analysis as part of their design process to help them create innovative products.

CONTENTS

Acknowledgements IX
About the Author X
Preface XI
How to access training files XII

SECTION 1 - 1

THE STRESS ANALYSIS ENVIRONMENT 3

The Finite Element Method (FEM) - An Overview 3
Types of Finite Element Method (FEM) Elements 4
Methods to enhance Finite Element Method (FEM) Results 7
    H-P convergence 8
Linear and Nonlinear analysis 9
    Linear analysis 9
    Nonlinear analysis 10
Static analysis - an overview 10
    Stress singularities 11
Modal Analysis - an overview 14
    Natural frequencies – Basic theory 15
    Preloaded modes 16
Stress Analysis Workflow 17
Stress Analysis User Interface 17
    Stress analysis browser 18
    Stress analysis graphic window 18
    Stress analysis panel 19
Manage tab 20
    Create Study 20
        Static Analysis 21
        Modal Analysis 23
        Shape Generator 24
        Contacts 30
    Parametric Table 32
Material tab 35
Constraints tab 37
    Fixed constraint 37
    Pin constraint 37
    Frictionless Constraint 38

CONTENTS

- LOADS TAB 38
  - General loads 38
  - Face loads 39
  - Body loads 39
- CONTACTS TAB 40
  - Types of contacts 40
  - The process of creating contacts 42
- PREPARE TAB 43
  - Find Thin Bodies 43
  - Midsurface 44
  - Offset 44
  - Example 1 – Thin Elements 45
- MESH TAB 47
  - Manual mesh refinement 47
  - Example 2 – Mesh Settings 48
  - Automatic mesh refinement (or automatic convergence) ... 51
  - Example 3 – Automatic Convergence 52
  - Example 4 – Manual Convergence 54
- RESULTS TAB 55
  - Animate 56
  - Probe 56
  - Convergence plot 57
- DISPLAY TAB 57
  - Apply uniform scale 58
  - Color Bar 58
  - Show probe labels 59
  - Show Maximum and Minimum values 59
  - Show boundary conditions 60
  - Display results 60
  - Adjust displacement display 61
- REPORT TAB 61
- GUIDE TAB 63
- SETTINGS TAB 64

SECTION 2 - 65

CONTENTS

DP1 – CYCLIC SYMMETRY ANALYSIS 67

KEY FEATURES AND WORKFLOWS INTRODUCED IN THIS DESIGN PROBLEM 67

INTRODUCTION 67

WORKFLOW OF DESIGN PROBLEM 1 68

Idealization 68

    Cyclic symmetry – Split model into a single blade 69

Boundary conditions 70

    Apply load and constraints 71

    Specify symmetry conditions 72

Run simulation and analyze 73

    Manual convergence of results 74

Optimization 78

    Investigate the effect of the thickness of the fan blade 78

    Change material 81

DP2 – ASSEMBLY OPTIMIZATION 83

KEY FEATURES AND WORKFLOWS INTRODUCED IN THIS DESIGN PROBLEM 83

INTRODUCTION 83

WORKFLOW OF DESIGN PROBLEM 2 85

Idealization 85

Boundary Conditions 87

Run simulation and analyze 92

Optimization 96

DP3 – BOLTED CONNECTION 99

KEY FEATURES AND WORKFLOWS INTRODUCED IN THIS DESIGN PROBLEM 99

INTRODUCTION 99

WORKFLOW OF DESIGN PROBLEM 3 100

Idealization 101

Boundary conditions 103

Run simulation and analyze 108

DP4 – PROPSHAFT 113

KEY FEATURES AND WORKFLOWS INTRODUCED IN THIS DESIGN PROBLEM 113

INTRODUCTION 113

WORKFLOW OF DESIGN PROBLEM 4 114

Idealization 114

Boundary conditions 115

CONTENTS

Run simulation and analyze..117

DP5 – WELDMENT ANALYSIS 121

Key features and workflows introduced in this design problem.....................................121

Introduction 121

Workflow of Design Problem 5 122

    Idealization *122*

    Boundary conditions..*122*

        Rerun simulation as assembly and compare results.................................125

    Run simulation and analyze..*130*

DP6 – ASSEMBLY ANALYSIS WITH BUILT-IN WELDS 135

Key features and workflows introduced in this design problem.....................................135

Introduction 135

Workflow of Design Problem 6 136

Part 1-Chassis design with Welds and RHS Channel Radii 137

    Idealization *137*

    Boundary conditions..*138*

    Run simulation and analyze..*142*

    Optimization...*144*

SECTION 3 - 145

DP7 – WIND LOAD ANALYSIS.. 147

Key features and workflows introduced in this design problem.....................................147

Introduction 147

Workflow of Design Problem 7 148

    Idealization *149*

    Boundary conditions..*152*

    Run simulation and analyze..*154*

DP8 – FABRICATION ANALYSIS 157

Key features and workflows introduced in this design problem.....................................157

Introduction 157

Workflow of Design Problem 8 158

    Idealization *159*

    Boundary conditions..*160*

    Run simulation and analyze..*164*

CONTENTS

DP9 – SHEET METAL ANALYSIS 169
Key features and workflows introduced in this design problem 169
Introduction 169
Workflow of Design Problem 9 170
    Idealization *171*
    Boundary conditions *172*
    Run simulation and analyze *175*

DP10 – 20G ACCELERATION 179
Key features and workflows introduced in this design problem 179
Introduction 179
Workflow of Design Problem 10 180
    Idealization *180*
    Boundary conditions *185*
    Run simulation and analyze *186*

SECTION 4 - 191

DP11 – MOTION LOAD TRANSFER ANALYSIS 193
Key features and workflows introduced in this design problem 193
Introduction 193
Workflow of Design Problem 11 194
    Idealization *194*
    Boundary conditions *195*
        Export motion loads 195
        Apply fixed constraints 197
    Run simulation and analyze *198*
        Analyze safety factor results 198
        Modify boundary conditions 198
    Optimization *200*

DP12 – MULTIPLE MOTION LOAD TRANSFER 201
Key features and workflows introduced in this design problem 201
Introduction 201
Workflow of Design Problem 12 202
    Idealization *203*
    Boundary conditions *203*
        Export motion loads 204
    Run simulation and analyze *206*

CONTENTS

    Analyze results 207
    Perform automatic convergence of results 209
  Further Exercise *210*

SECTION 5 - 211

DP13 – MODAL ANALYSIS 213

KEY FEATURES AND WORKFLOWS INTRODUCED IN THIS DESIGN PROBLEM 213

INTRODUCTION 213

WORKFLOW OF DESIGN PROBLEM 13 214

  Idealization *214*

  Boundary conditions *215*

  Run Simulation and Analyze *217*

  Optimization *219*

SECTION 6 221

THE FRAME ANALYSIS ENVIRONMENT 223

FRAME ANALYSIS OVERVIEW 223

FRAME ANALYSIS WORKFLOW 224

FRAME ANALYSIS USER INTERFACE 225

  Frame Analysis Browser *225*

  Frame Analysis Graphic Window *225*

  Frame Analysis Panel *227*

MANAGE TAB 227

  Create Simulation *227*

BEAMS TAB 228

  Update *228*

  Properties *228*

  Material *229*

CONSTRAINTS TAB 230

    Fixed constraint 230
  Pinned constraint *231*

  Floating pinned constraint *231*

  Custom constraint *233*

LOADS TAB 234

  Force *234*

  Continuous load *235*

CONTENTS

    Moment *236*

    Moment (general) *236*

    Bending Moment *237*

    Axial Moment *237*

    Example 1 – Cantilever model results compared with hand calculations *237*

    Example 2 – Simply supported beam created with custom constraint *238*

CONNECTIONS TAB *240*

    Release *240*

    Example 3 – Releasing moments in Structure using Beam Release *241*

    Custom Node *242*

    Rigid link *242*

    Example 4 – Simple frame in which beams are connected without using rigid links *244*

    Example 5 – Frame Generator in which beams are connected using rigid links *244*

RESULT TAB *247*

    Beam detail *247*

    Animate *247*

    Diagram *248*

    Probe *249*

DISPLAY TAB *249*

    Color bar *249*

    Beam and node labels *250*

    Display results *251*

    Probe Labels *251*

    Adjust displacement display *252*

    Max and min values *252*

    Boundary conditions *253*

    Local systems *253*

    Load values *253*

PUBLISH TAB *254*

    Report *254*

    Export *255*

FRAME ANALYSIS SETTINGS TAB *256*

DP14 – FRAME ANALYSIS USING CONTENT CENTRE STRUCTURES 259

KEY FEATURES AND WORKFLOWS INTRODUCED IN THIS DESIGN PROBLEM *259*

CONTENTS

Introduction 259

Workflow of Design Problem 14 261

    Idealization *261*

    Boundary conditions *261*

    Run simulation and analyze *265*

    Optimization *267*

DP15 – FRAME ANALYSIS USING FRAME GENERATOR STRUCTURES 271

Key features and workflows introduced in this design problem 271

Introduction 271

Workflow of Design Problem 15 273

    Idealization *273*

    Boundary conditions *274*

    Run simulation and analyze *277*

DP16 – FRAME ANALYSIS USING ADVANCE SETTINGS 283

Key features and workflows introduced in this design problem 283

Introduction 283

Workflow of Design Problem 16 284

    Idealization *285*

    Boundary conditions *285*

    Run simulation and analyze *292*

Acknowledgements

I would also like to thank all the companies, mentioned below, for allowing me to use their innovative product designs and models, without which none of this would have been possible. I would also like to thank Vince Adams, Autodesk.

Ian Parker – Halifax Fan Limited
Lee Chapman – Unipart Rail
Chris Tait - Destec Engineering Ltd
Jonathan Stancliffe – British Waterways
Philip Wright – Wright Resolutions Ltd
Mark Johnson - Variable Message Signs Ltd
Alex Ferguson - Croft Ltd
Adrian Hartley – Simba Great Plains Ltd
Adrian Curtis – In-CAD Services Ltd
Kevin Berry – Triple Eight Race Engineering Ltd
Adrian Oaten – Aerospace Design Facilities Ltd
Carl Geldard – Planet Platforms Ltd
Brian White – KONE plc (Escalators, Keighley)
Stephen Bennett - James Alpe Ltd
Mike Smith - Swire Oilfield Services Ltd
Dennis Fellows – GKN Land Systems

Finally I would like to thank my wife Samina, daughter Malyah and son's Sami and Fasee for their unconditional love, support and source of inspiration.

Cover image courtesy of Destec Engineering Ltd (http://www.destec.co.uk)

About the Author

An Autodesk simulation solutions manager with more than 20 years of experience in the manufacturing field, including working at Rolls Royce, British Aerospace and Nuclear Electric. Has been involved with Autodesk simulation software when it was first introduced, and is well-known throughout the Autodesk Simulation community, worldwide.

He also presents annually at Autodesk University, a prestigious event held annually in USA, including contributing articles, whitepapers, tips and tricks and tutorials to various forums. He also runs a dedicated forum for simulation users on LinkedIn –Up and Running with Autodesk Inventor Simulation

Wasim has a bachelor's degree in mechanical engineering from the University of Bradford and a master's degree in computer- aided-engineering from Staffordshire University.

Currently he is employed @ Symetri (http://www.symetri.com) – an Autodesk value added services provider across UK and Northern Europe.

Contact Details:

Email: younis_wasim@hotmail.com
Support: Forum http://www.linkedin.com/groups?mostPopular=&gid=2061026

PREFACE

Preface

Welcome to the sixth edition of *Up and Running with Autodesk® Inventor® Professional 2017 – Step by step guide to Engineering Solutions.*

I hope you found the previous editions of my books very useful and interesting. I thank you very much for your feedback/suggestions, which have helped me again to make this edition of the book even better. This edition of the book includes one new design problem, introduction to shape generator and a complete revision of most design problems.

This book has been written using actual design problems, all of which have greatly benefited from the use of Simulation technology. For each design problem, I have attempted to explain the process of applying Stress Analysis using a straightforward, step by step approach, and have supported this approach with explanation and tips. At all times, I have tried to anticipate what questions a designer or development engineer would want to ask whilst he or she were performing the task and using Stress Analysis.

The design problems have been carefully chosen to cover the core aspects and capabilities of Stress and Frame Analysis and their solutions are universal, so you should be able to apply the knowledge quickly to their own design problems with more confidence.

The book basically comprises of six sections: Stress Analysis Environment (Chapter 1), Design Problems using Solid Elements (Chapter 2-7), Design Problems using Thin and Solid Elements (Chapter 8-11), Design Problems using Motion Loads (Chapter 12-13), Modal Analysis (Chapter 14) and Frame Analysis (Chapter 15 – 18). Chapters 1 & 15 provide an overview of stress, frame, Shape Generator and the user interface and features so that you are well-grounded in core concepts and the software's strengths, weaknesses and work around. Each design problem illustrates a different unique approach and demonstrates different key aspects of the software, making it easier for you pick and choose which design problem you want to cover first; therefore, having read chapter 1 and 15, it is not necessary to follow the rest of the book sequentially.

This book is primarily designed for self-paced learning by individuals, but can also be used in an instructor-led classroom environment.

I hope you will find this book enjoyable and at the same time very beneficial to you and your business. I will be very pleased to receive your feedback, to help me improve future editions. Feel free to email me on **younis_wasim@hotmail.com**

HOW TO ACCESS TRAINING FILES

How to access training files

All files necessary to complete the exercises can be accessed from;

Download Exercises from
http://vrblog.info/

The Book exercises are available on the bottom of the blog page (available on all pages/posts). You may need to scroll-down a little to see the exercise-files available via Box.net
NB: datasets for version 2010, 2011, 2012 2013 and 2014 are also available from here.

Alternative links to download 2017 version exercises for this edition of the book.

https://goo.gl/6nPrPY
https://goo.gl/xbZiUr

Section 1 - STRESS ANALYSIS *Essentials*

The Stress Analysis Environment

The Finite Element Method (FEM) - An Overview

The finite element method (FEM) is a mathematical/computer-based numerical technique for calculating the strength and behavior of engineering structures. Autodesk Inventor Stress– and much other analysis software - are based on the FEM, where, simply, a component is broken down into many small elements, as shown below.

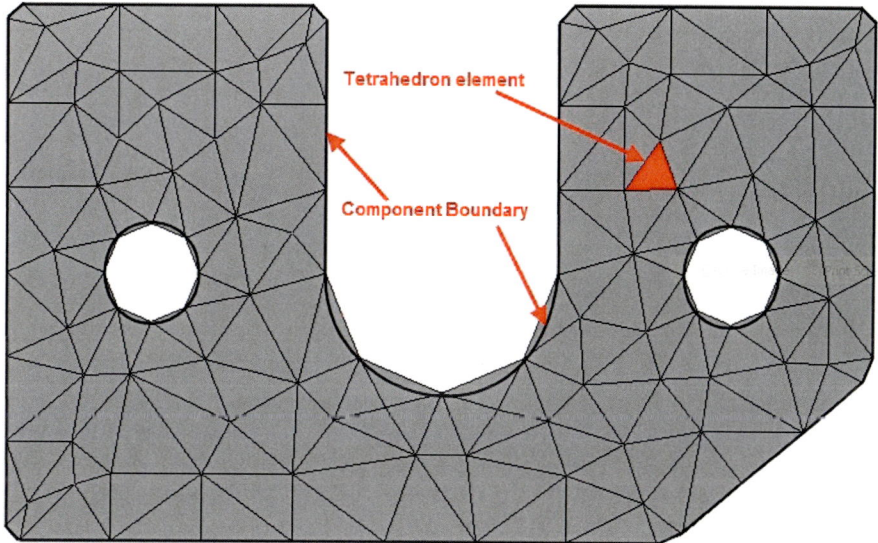

Discretization of a component into a number of Tetrahedron finite elements

Let's assume that we need to determine the displacement of the component. This displacement (unknown quantity) acts over each element in a predefined manner – with the number and type of elements chosen so that overall distribution through the component is sufficiently approximated. This distribution across each element is commonly presented by a polynomial- whether it's linear, quadratic or even cubic. It is important to note FEM is always an approximation of the actual component and is by its very nature will have errors due to discretization - particularly around curved boundaries (as shown above) or geometrically complex components.

These errors due to discretization can be reduced by either specifying more elements or using higher order polynomials to approximate the distribution of the unknown quantity over the elements - also referred to as polynomial interpolation function. Most finite element software uses the former method, specifically known as the H refinement process, in which the software goes through an iterative process of reducing the number of elements at each iteration until the results have converged. The latter method, of using higher order polynomials, is called the P-refinement process, in which the software increases the order of the polynomial at each iteration starting from 1(linear) to 2(quadratic), 3(cubic) and so on.

CHAPTER 1
The Stress Analysis Environment

Another approach to reduce errors due to discretization is to use higher order elements; this is discussed in the next section in more detail.

Types of Finite Element Method (FEM) Elements

Autodesk Inventor Stress Analysis uses first and second order tetrahedron and thin elements, as shown below.

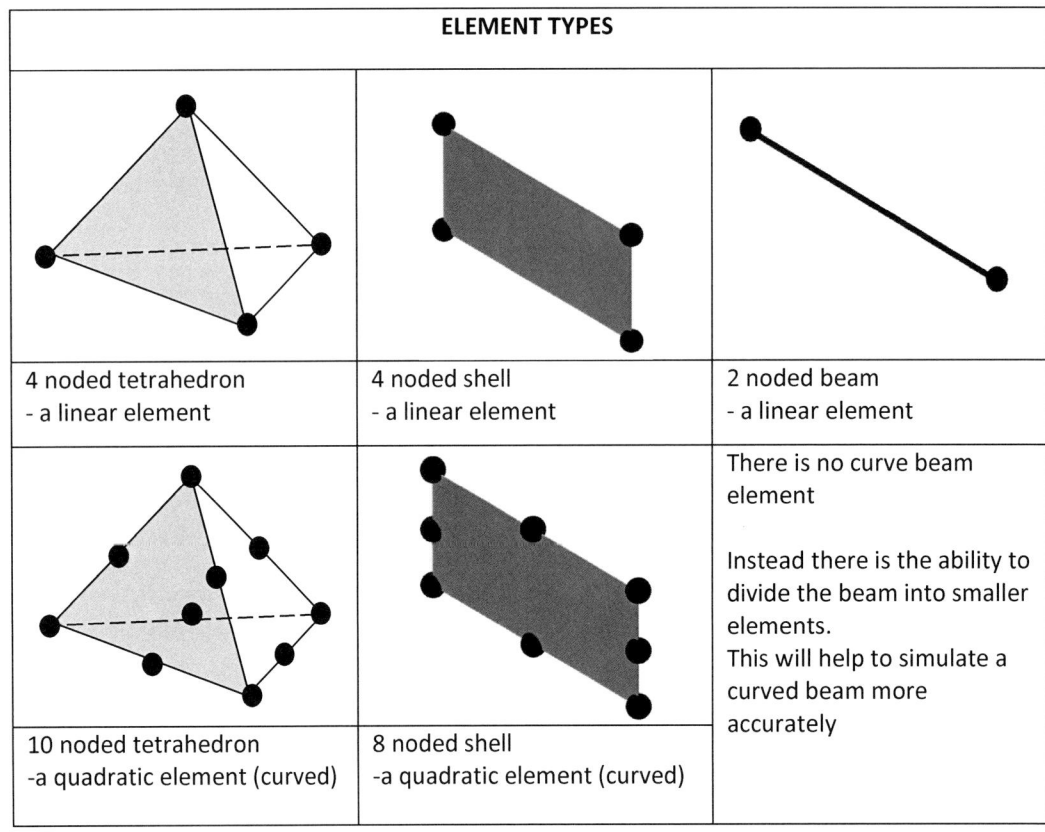

The following tube example will be used to demonstrate the results obtained by using different element types.

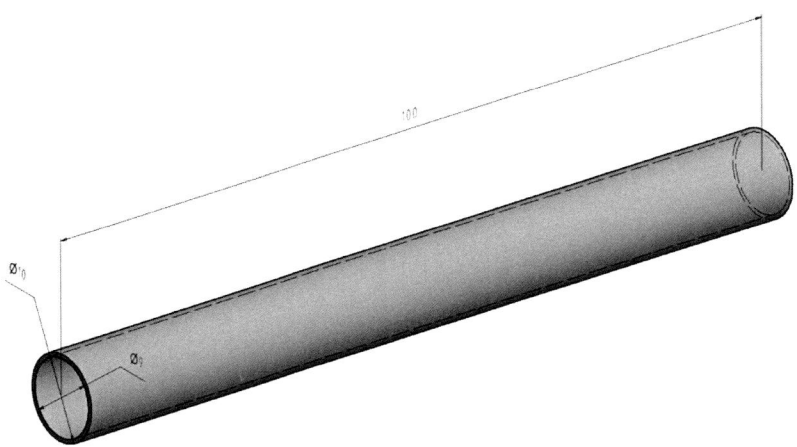

CHAPTER 1
The Stress Analysis Environment

Initially we will determine theoretical results for the tube. We will fix the tube at one end and apply a load of 100N at the other end

Tube data to be used is as follows;

Length   = 100mm
Diameter = 10mm
Thickness = 0.5mm
Material   = Mild Steel

Using the classical Bending Stress Equation:

$$\frac{M}{I} = \frac{\sigma}{y} = \frac{E}{R}$$

We can determine maximum stress (at fixed end)

M_{max} = Total length x Load = 100 x 100 = 10,000Nmm

y = 5mm

$$I = \frac{\pi}{64}(\varnothing_{outside}^4 - \varnothing_{inside}^4) = \frac{\pi}{64}(10^4 - 9^4) = 168.8 mm^4$$

$\sigma max = \frac{My}{I} (10000 \times 5)/168.8 = 296 \text{ N/mm}^2$

Stress Analysis Results - using 10 noded tetrahedron elements – 315.5 N/mm² or (315.5 MPa)

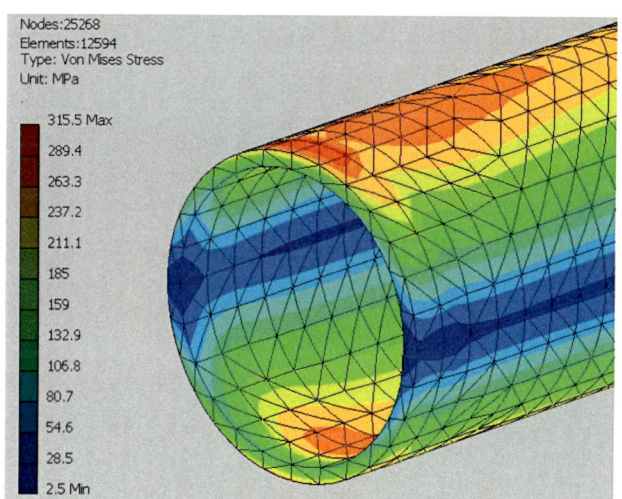

% difference = 6.59 based on using von mises stress and average element size of 0.025, for comparison purposes. Although this value is acceptable (within 10%) the difference is primarily due to stress singularities as refining the mesh around the high stress area will result in higher stresses. This is discussed later in the chapter.

CHAPTER 1
The Stress Analysis Environment

Stress Analysis Results - using 8 noded shell elements – 283.4 N/mm²

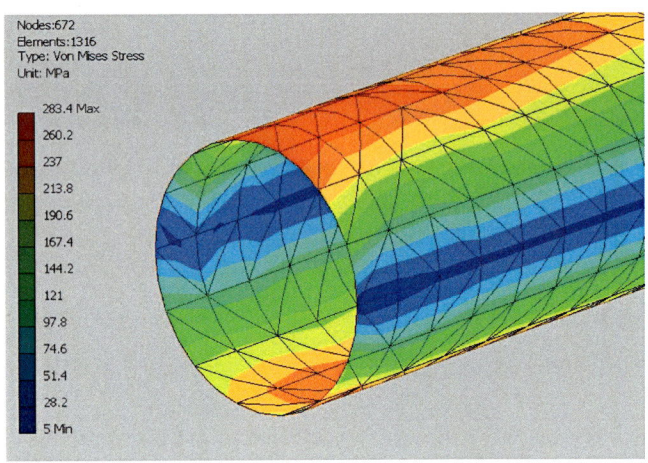

% difference = 4.25% based on using von mises stress and average element size in shells of 0.025, for comparison purposes. This indicates that shell elements are better than solid elements for thin structures, plus the element number count is a lot less than using solid elements.

Frame Analysis Results - using beam elements – 296.2 N/mm²

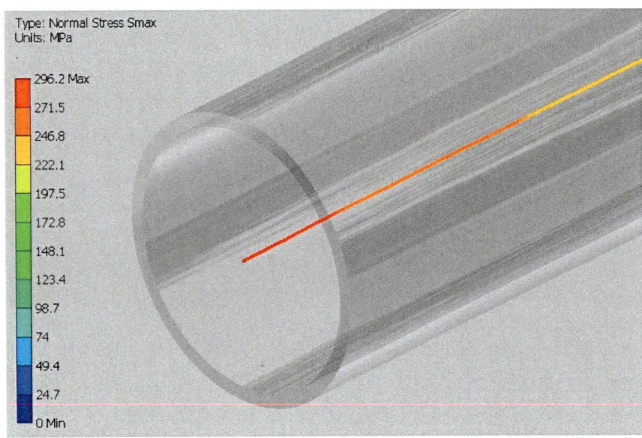

% difference = 0%. This is because frame analysis does not have the stress singularity issues as in stress analysis.

 Use beam analysis for structures with a uniform cross section that also have a length to cross section ratio generally above 10.

Frame analysis is discussed in detail in chapters 15-18. In the next section we will discuss how to improve stress analysis result.

CHAPTER 1
The Stress Analysis Environment

Methods to enhance Finite Element Method (FEM) Results

In summary there are three methods within Inventor Stress that can be used to enhance the accuracy of the results:

1. P-refinement
2. H-refinement
3. Higher order elements (quadratic – also referred to as curved elements)

There are pros and cons of using both P and H refinement.

	H-refinement	P-refinement
Results convergence	Slower – polynomial rate of convergence	Faster – exponential rate of convergence
Analysis time	Faster - in comparison to P-refinement	Slower – especially as P order increases
Stress singularities	Can converge – with careful consideration to settings	Never convergences

 P-refinement is automatically controlled by the software.

 For complex shapes it is always advisable to use higher order (quadratic) elements.

The following diagram illustrates that one quadratic element around a 90° circular arc is like having two linear elements. The quadratic element tries to match the 90° arc more closely and can also improve the accuracy of results.

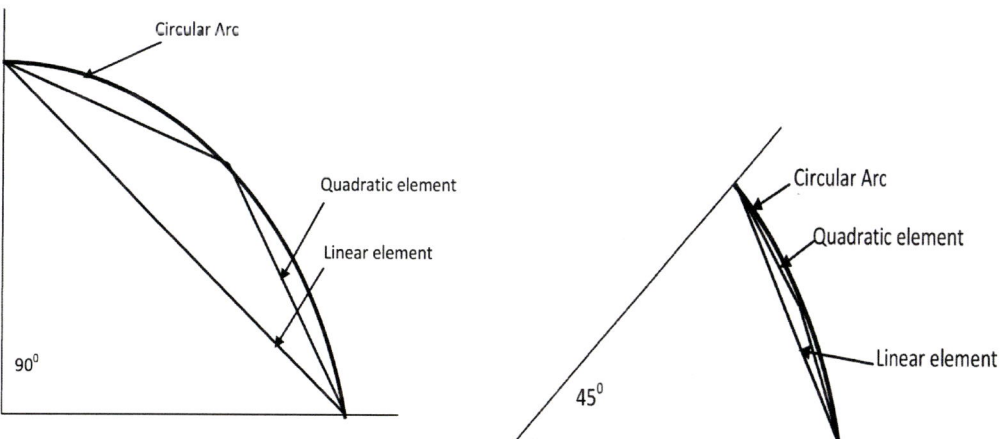

Also it is worth noting that the quadratic (curved) element almost matches the true profile of a 45° curved object (< 1% geometrical error). Therefore, it is advisable to have at least two quadratic elements around a 90° arc, whereas for linear elements there should be at least three elements, preferably four, around a 90° circular object.

CHAPTER 1
The Stress Analysis Environment

Furthermore Inventor Stress overcomes the pros and cons mentioned earlier by using an H-P refinement approach, with some benefits being:

1. Exponential convergence in practical problems (with the exception of problems with stress singularities).
2. Potential of maximizing sparseness of the stiffness matrix.

Inventor Stress takes this H-P refinement approach one step further by making the H-P approach adaptive. This means that the software will only refine the elements around the high stress areas - rather than the whole model - meaning that the results convergence process will be further enhanced. This process is explained in the next section

H-P convergence

Within Inventor Stress, the user can only control H-refinement part of the H-P refinement convergence process. The software automatically increases P-order from one to three for every part analysis and from one to two for assembly analysis. The assembly analysis does not use a P-order of three because, as P –order gets higher than two, the analysis time can get exponentially longer - especially when there are a lot of parts to analyze.

If the user has specified two iterations for H-refinement in the Convergence dialogue box, the software will perform the following H-P refinement:

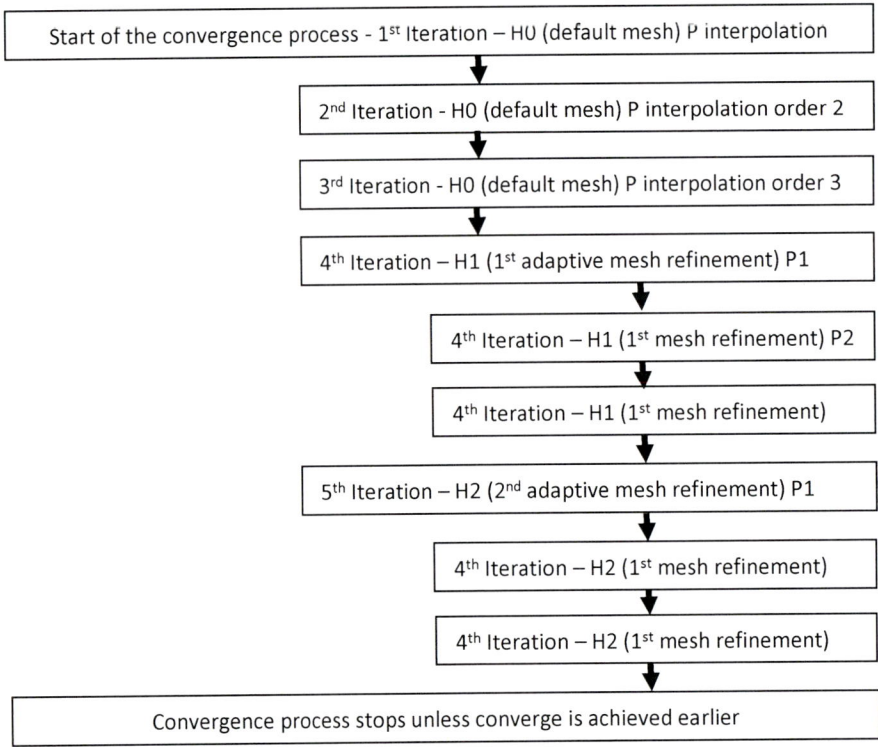

This H-P convergence process is very efficient, except when the model does not have stress singularities present. Stress Singularities and methods to overcome them are explained later.

SECTION 1 -Stress Analysis Essentials

CHAPTER 1
The Stress Analysis Environment

Linear and Nonlinear analysis

Inventor Stress Analysis is only capable of performing linear analysis where components have small deformations, under operational loading conditions. On the other hand, nonlinear analysis is typically associated with components that experience large deformations in addition to permanent deformation.

Linear analysis

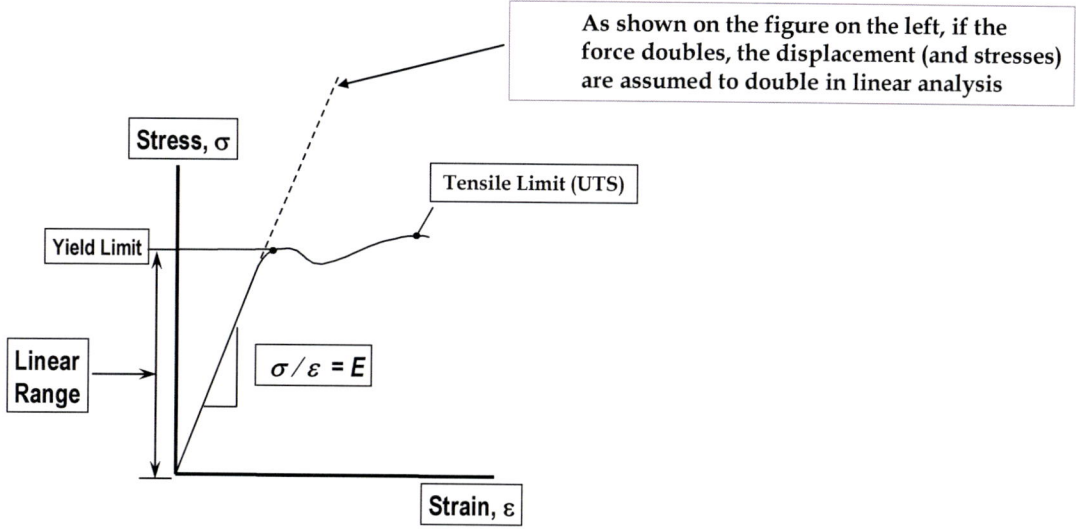

Young's Modulus provides the stiffness of the material; for example the higher Young's Modulus the stronger the material will be.

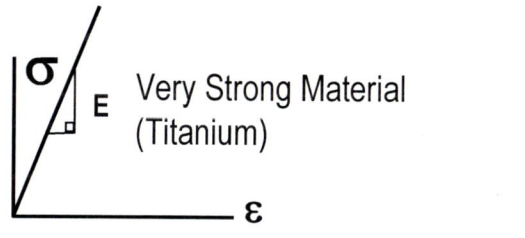
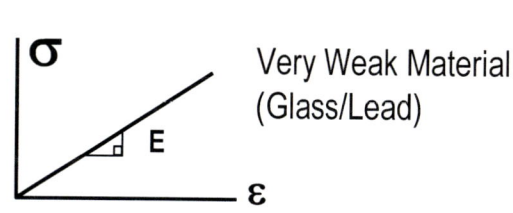

Strain = $\dfrac{\text{Change in Length}}{\text{Original Length}}$ & **Stress** = $\dfrac{\text{Force}}{\text{Area}}$

	Assumptions normally made when conducting a linear analysis
1	The material properties of the component remain linear after the yield limit. Hence, results beyond this limit are not valid using Inventor stress analysis.
2	The deflections of components are small compared to overall component size.
3	The components are rigid and ductile like metal (not rubber).
4	The components deform equally in all three directions; that is, the material properties are isotropic.

SECTION 1 - Stress Analysis Essentials

CHAPTER 1
The Stress Analysis Environment

Nonlinear analysis

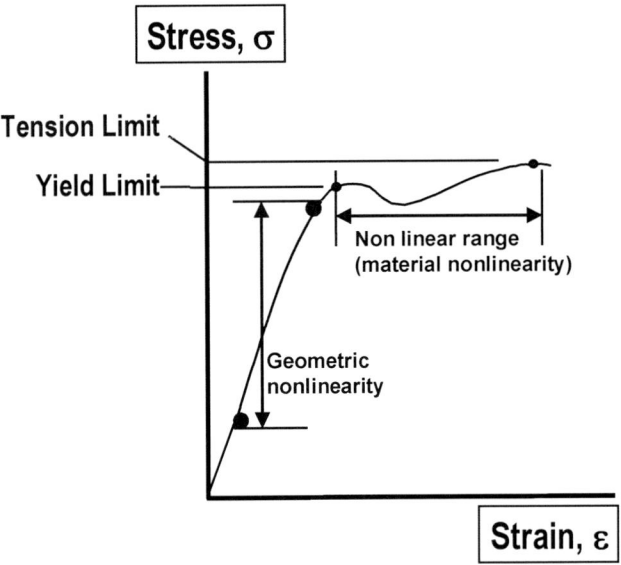

Non-linear Analysis generically falls into the following three categories;

Geometric nonlinearity – Where a component experiences large deformations and as a result can cause the component to experience nonlinear behavior. A typical example is a fishing rod.

Material nonlinearity – When the component goes beyond the yield limit, the stress/strain relationship becomes nonlinear as the material starts to deform permanently.

Contact – Includes the effect of two components coming into contact; that is, they can experience an abrupt change in stiffness resulting in localized material deformation at region of contact.

Autodesk Inventor stress analysis is only capable of performing linear static stress and modal analysis.

Static analysis - an overview

Static analysis is an engineering discipline that determines the stress in materials and structures subjected to static or dynamic forces or loads. The aim of the analysis is usually to determine whether the element or collection of elements, usually referred to as a structure or component, can safely withstand the specified forces and loads. This is achieved when the determined stress from the applied force(s) is less than the yield strength of the material. This stress relationship is commonly referred to as factor of safety (FOS) and is used in many analyses as an indicator of success or failure in analysis.

$$\textbf{Factor of Safety} = \frac{\text{Yield Stress}}{\text{Calculated Stress}} = \frac{\text{Ultimate Stress}}{\text{Calculated Stress}}$$

Factor of Safety can be based on either Yield or Ultimate stress limit of the material. The factor of safety on yield strength is to prevent detrimental deformations and the factor of safety on ultimate strength aims to prevent collapse.

CHAPTER 1
The Stress Analysis Environment

Below are some examples of where static analysis can be useful.

The canal bridge is a typical example of static analysis. Here, one will be interested to know whether the bridge will withstand a load of a vehicle when it crosses the bridge. This will help to identify weak parts of the structure, ultimately allowing us to design a bridge to carry the maximum physically possible load.

In this example one might be interested in the maximum deflection of the fan blade, which can have an impact on the efficiency of the fan. With the help of static analysis, the blade can be studied and analysed to reduce deformation, for example by using different materials, increasing the thickness, or adding structural stiffeners.

One of the major obstacles when conducting static analyses is stress singularities, which can significantly distort results and can reduce confidence in the results, as illustrated and discussed in the next section.

Stress singularities

Stress Singularities are a major concern when analyzing results as they considerably distort results. They are also a main cause for non-convergence of results. So, the first question - what is stress singularity? This can be best explained by the following example.

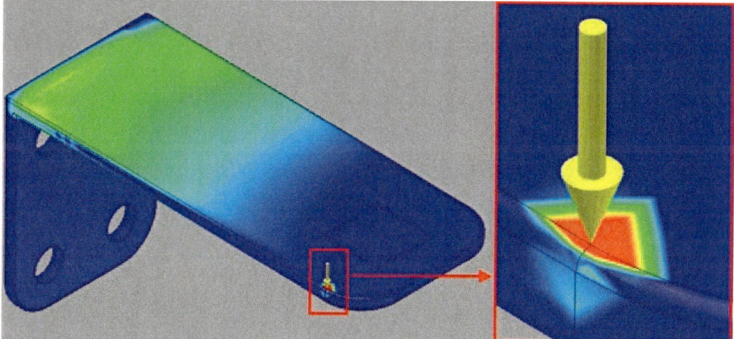

This bracket has a high localized stress around the force applied on a point. This stress can be considerably higher than the operational stress and applying a more dense mesh around this simply leads to a much higher stress. This phenomenon is known as stress singularity where the stress can become infinite, as illustrated by the following formula:

SECTION 1 -Stress Analysis Essentials

CHAPTER 1
The Stress Analysis Environment

$$\textbf{Stress (infinite)} = \frac{\text{Force}}{\text{Area of point (almost = 0)}}$$

Therefore, to avoid stress singularities when applying loads, it is recommended ***not to apply loads at points and small edges***.

Stress Singularities can also occur ***by applying constraints on points and small edges*** – even faces with sharp corners as illustrated below.

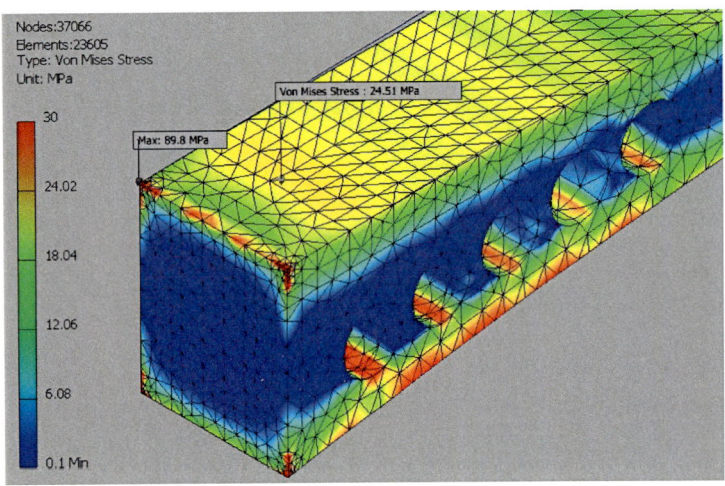

In the above example, stress singularities resulted from using automatic convergence, whereas the image below of the same model is showing very little change in stress in the area of interest by using the default mesh and no automatic convergence. Therefore, interpret results with care.

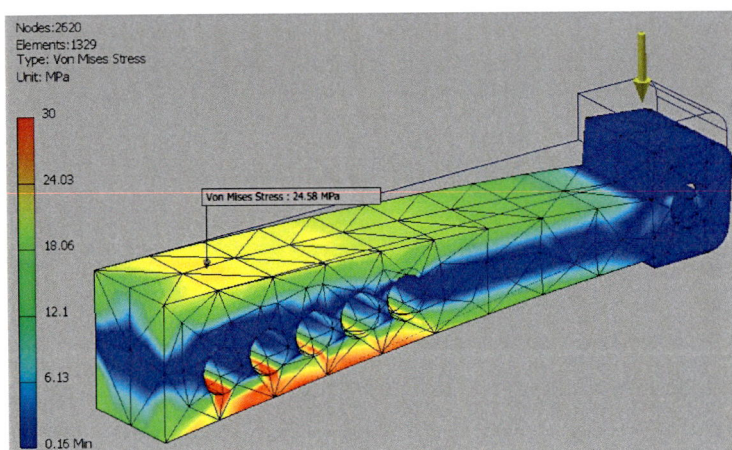

 Gain further confidence in your results by using manual convergence, mentioned later in this chapter, where models have stress singularities present.

CHAPTER 1
The Stress Analysis Environment

Finally, another cause of stress singularity *is over-simplification of components*. Let's look at the following example.

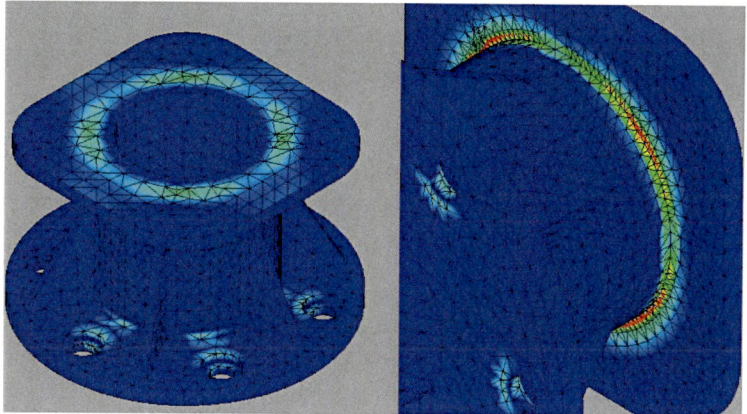

In this example, the fillets have been removed to simplify the analysis; however, when using automatic convergence, the maximum stress value does not converge as all the stress is concentrated around the edge, as shown. In this scenario it would advisable to unsuppress the fillets (or, in cases when fillets are not modeled, use fillets to help distribute loads).

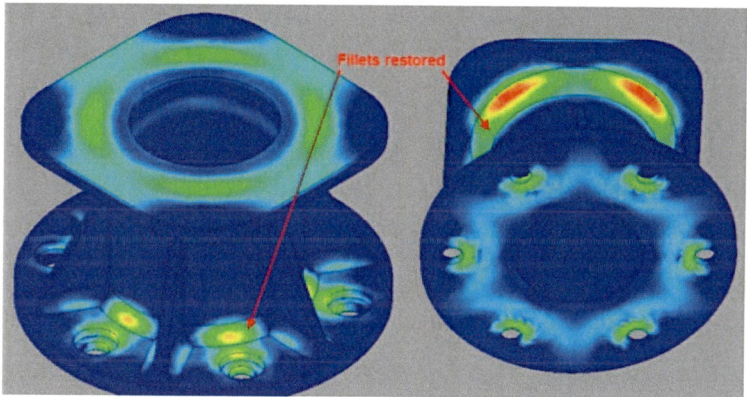

So in brief to avoid stress singularities within models do:

1. Avoid applying loads on points and small edges.
2. Avoid restraining faces with sharp corners, including points and small edges.
3. Apply fillets and chamfers to evenly distribute loads.

 Use linear elements when a model has stress singularities present, as they can capture stress singularities much better than the curve elements.

In some cases it is impossible to remove stress singularities, in which case careful interpretation of results is very important. One approach to this is detailed in Chapter 6.

CHAPTER 1
The Stress Analysis Environment

Modal Analysis- an overview

Modal analysis determines modes to better understand the behaviour of components and structures under free vibration. Modes are inherent properties of a structure, and are determined by the material properties and boundary conditions of the structure. Each mode is defined by a natural frequency and a mode shape. Frequency is defined as cycles/s; for example 10 cycles/s is equivalent to 10 Hz. It is these frequencies that cause vibrations in components and structures. All engineered products have natural frequencies that when excited can cause vibrations for example; the vibration felt through the steering wheel from an unbalanced wheel, the vibration felt through the floor when a passenger train goes past and vibration in airplanes especially at take-off caused by revving of the aero-engines. By analysing these modal shapes and frequencies, one can try to minimise these vibrations as they can cause failure in products by weakening the components and structures - due to fatigue. Another cause of failure due to vibrations is resonance - this is where a components natural frequency matches the operational speed of a connecting component, resulting in excessive vibration and ultimately leading to destruction. Following are some examples of structures that have been affected by resonance and in some cases, leading to destruction or excessive vibration.

The Tacoma Bridge in Washington, USA, is a famous example of bridge failure due to resonance induced by wind. The bridge was completely reconstructed to better withstand variations in the wind speed and with better damping to minimise and isolate vibrations in the bridge.

The Millennium Bridge in London, is another example, in which the lateral vibration in the bridge was caused by pedestrians walking over it. The greater the number of people walking on the bridge, the greater was the lateral movement. The problem was rectified by using a damping solution to absorb the movements, as stiffening the structure would have meant considerably altering the bridge.

Washing machines, which are used in many households, today can lead to excessive vibration of the drum induced by a full load, or partial load, particularly at max cycle spinning speeds. This in some extreme cases can lead the door to open, or even the machine to move from its original position, particularly in older machines.

Helicopter Design is another area where vibration and resonance are critical issues. For example, if any of the components of a helicopter have natural frequencies that are close to the rotational

CHAPTER 1
The Stress Analysis Environment

speed of the rotors, then resonance of a component could occur, leading, for example, to a possible fatigue failure.

Thus, modal analysis is instrumental in helping us to better understand the structural flexibility and potential vibratory issues related to noise, fatigue, and resonance failures.

Natural frequencies – Basic theory

Theory for vibrations of continuous beams can be found in standard engineering textbooks. The natural frequencies of a simple cantilever can be determined theoretically using the following equation:

$$\frac{K^2}{2\pi}\sqrt{\frac{EI}{\rho A L^4}}$$

Where the K values for the first four modes are
1 – 1.8751
2 – 4.6941
3 – 7.8547
4 – 10.9955

And
E – Young's Modulus
I – Area moment of inertia
ρ – Density
A – Area
L – Length

For a simple plate, 30mm x 10mm x 300mm, made out of nylon 66, the first two calculated natural frequencies are 5.75Hz and 36.04Hz. The following is a summary of results carried out in Inventor Stress Analysis using modal analysis

	Theoretical	Modal analysis (mesh size 0.1)	Modal analysis (mesh size 0.05)	Modal analysis (mesh size 0.025)
Mode 1	5.75 Hz	6.33 Hz	5.9 Hz	5.85 Hz
Mode 2	36.04 Hz	43.87 Hz	37.09 Hz	36.67 Hz

 Mesh size refers to average element size. Plus Enhanced accuracy and Curved elements options were also selected

For modal analysis, the mesh size can have impact on the accuracy of the results. An average element mesh size of 0.025 produces results within 2% when compared with theoretical results.

CHAPTER 1
The Stress Analysis Environment

Preloaded modes

In some situations, however, the loads will affect the natural frequencies. An example would be a guitar string: as tension is applied, the frequency changes. Loads that produce membrane stresses will affect the natural frequency of the object. Tensile member stresses will increase the natural frequencies and compressive membrane stresses will lower them, whereas pure bending stress will not affect natural frequency.

Suspension bridge designs are classical examples of where extensive use is made of tensile members (cables) suspended via towers to hold up the road deck. The weight is held by the cables via the towers, which in turn transfer the weight to the ground. Tension within cables also provides rigidity to the structural integrity of the bridge.

Let's look at a simple tie rod example in which the tie rod is not prestressed; the first mode and shape of the rod are shown below, giving a natural frequency of 32.63 Hz.

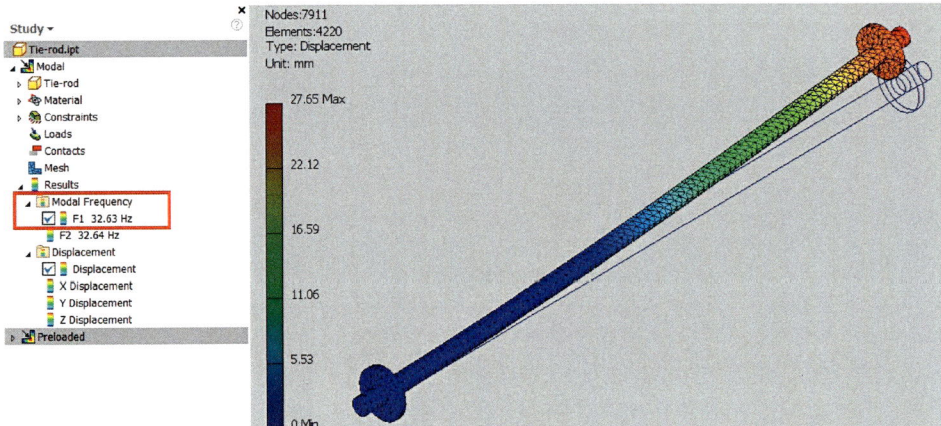

On the other hand, if a tensile load of 1000 N is applied to prestress the tie rod, the natural frequency of the first mode almost doubles to 60.20 Hz.

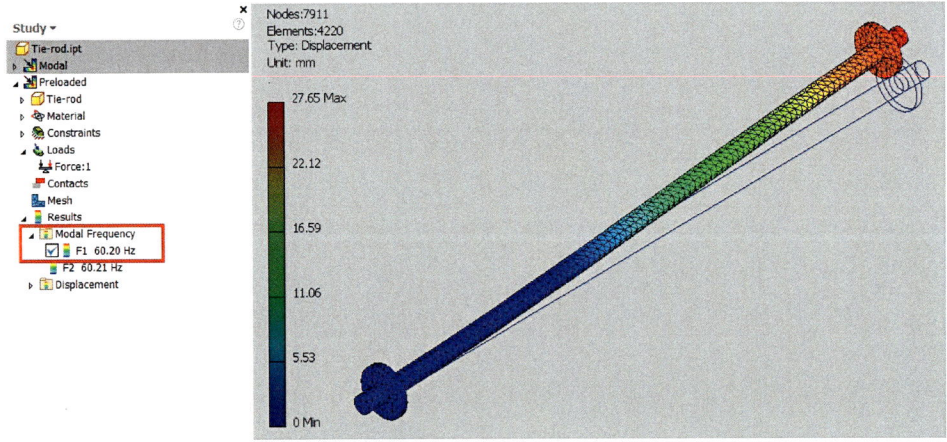

As we have now covered the basics of stress and modal theory, we will now go over the user interface of Autodesk Inventor Stress Analysis.

CHAPTER 1
The Stress Analysis Environment

Stress Analysis Workflow

The process of creating a stress analysis study involves four core steps:

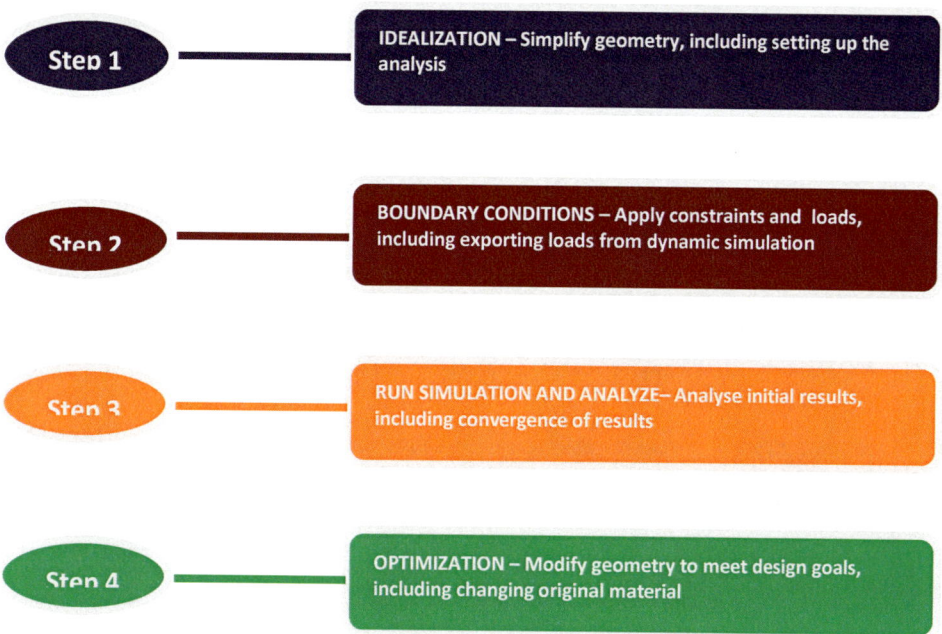

Step 1 — IDEALIZATION – Simplify geometry, including setting up the analysis

Step 2 — BOUNDARY CONDITIONS – Apply constraints and loads, including exporting loads from dynamic simulation

Step 3 — RUN SIMULATION AND ANALYZE – Analyse initial results, including convergence of results

Step 4 — OPTIMIZATION – Modify geometry to meet design goals, including changing original material

Stress Analysis User Interface

Stress Analysis can be accessed from both the Part and Assembly environment via the Environments tab.

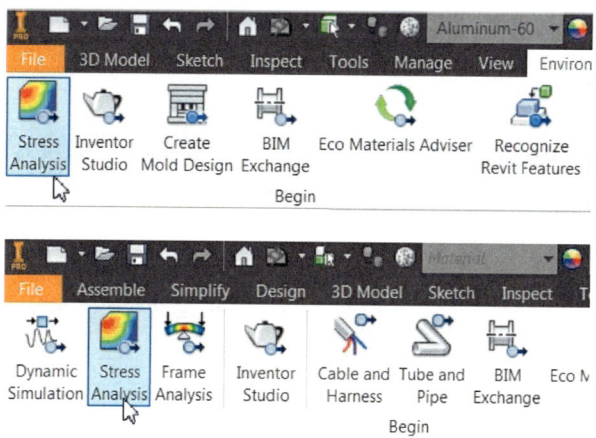

SECTION 1 - Stress Analysis Essentials

CHAPTER 1
The Stress Analysis Environment

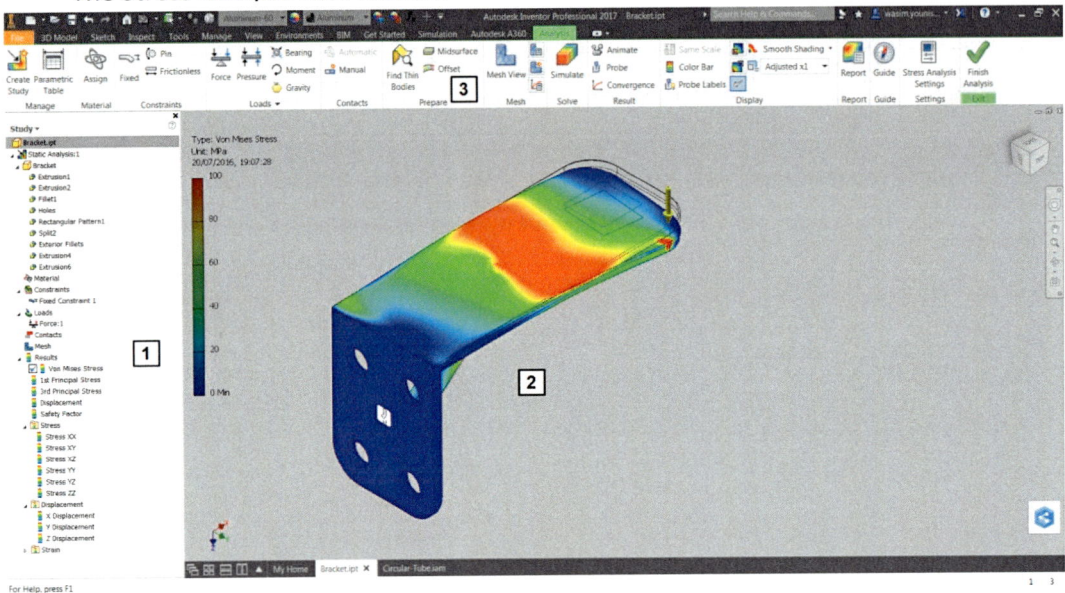

1. Stress Analysis browser
2. Stress Analysis graphic window
3. Stress Analysis panel

Stress analysis browser

Displays the study with part or assembly information and simulation parameters in a hierarchical view with nested levels of feature and attribute information. You can:

1. Copy whole simulations or simulation boundary conditions between simulations
2. Expand the folders, select the nodes, and see the selection cross-highlighted in the graphic region.

Stress analysis graphic window

Display's the model geometry and simulation results. Updates to show the current status of the simulation including applying boundary conditions and loads with the help of view manipulation tools.

CHAPTER 1
The Stress Analysis Environment

Stress analysis panel

Stress Analysis tab	Workflow stage	Description
Create Study, Parametric Table — Manage	Step 1	**Create Study** – Here you decide whether you need to create a stress, modal, or a parametric analysis.
	Step	**Parametric Table** – Define design constraints including mass, stress, deformation, etc.
Assign — Material		**Material** – Create and apply material for the components if not already defined in the Part environment.
Fixed, Pin, Frictionless — Constraints		**Constraints** – Represent how a part is fixed or attached to other parts in reality, and thus restricting their motion.
Force, Pressure, Bearing, Moment, Gravity — Loads		**Loads** – Represent the external forces that are exerted on a component. During normal use, the component is expected to withstand these loads and continue to perform as intended.
Automatic, Manual — Contacts	Step	**Contacts** – Create contacts between components automatically or manually. There are seven types of contacts including bonded.
Find Thin Bodies, Midsurface, Offset — Prepare		**Prepare** – Tools to create surfaces specifically for thin parts. Find Thin Bodies command automatically detects components suitable for midsurface creation
Mesh View — Mesh		**Mesh** – Preview and create mesh, including global and local mesh refinement.
Simulate — Solve		**Solve** – Run the study to analyze the results as a consequence of defining materials, constraints and loads.
Animate, Probe, Convergence — Result	Step	**Results** – View the stress and deformation results to help make an informed decision on whether the component will function under the defined loads and constraints.
Same Scale, Color Bar, Probe Labels, Smooth Shading, Adjusted x1 — Display		**Display** – Modify color plots, including displaying max and min values.

SECTION 1 - Stress Analysis Essentials

CHAPTER 1
The Stress Analysis Environment

Stress analysis panel continued

Stress Analysis tab	Optional Workflows	Description
Report	-	**Report** – Generate an html report of the results to share.
Guide		**Guide** – Provides guidance, when activated, on how to best set up and run a study.
Stress Analysis Settings	-	**Settings** – Can predefine initial settings, including contact tolerance and mesh settings.

Manage tab

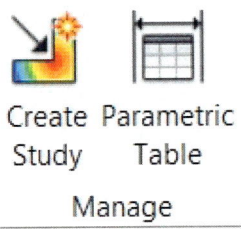

This is the first step in creating a stress analysis study.

Create Study

Here you can define whether you want to carry out single static analysis, modal analysis or a parametric study, including the option of selecting different levels of detail.

CHAPTER 1
The Stress Analysis Environment

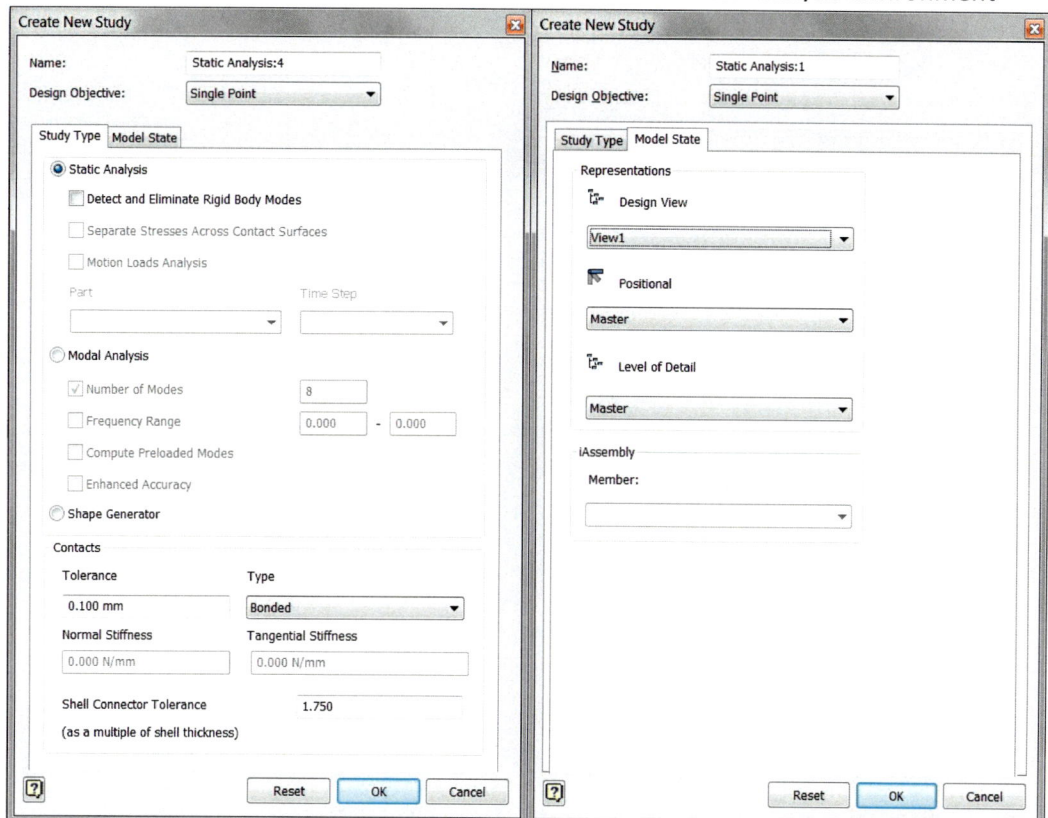

Design Objective – Here you define whether you want to carry out a single or parametric optimization; this is discussed in the next section.

Study Type - Here you define whether a stress, modal or shape generator analysis is to be carried out.

 Shape Generator only available for single part.

Model State – For an assembly, you can choose any design View, positional view or level of detail on which to perform analysis.

 Use level of detail with all parts suppressed except one when there is a need to analyze a single component, which has loads exported from Simulation.

Static Analysis
There are three settings when performing stress analysis.

Detect and Eliminate Rigid Body Modes - It is possible that a model may not have enough structural constraints to fix it completely in space. For example, imagine a cube with the top face loaded with normal pressure, and the bottom face which is constrained by a frictionless constraint. One frictionless constraint is not enough to uniquely define the position of the cube; it can slide sideways as a whole, and we call such movement a rigid body mode. For such cases of incomplete constraints we have a special algorithm that eliminates rigid body movements from displacements,

CHAPTER 1
The Stress Analysis Environment

if detect and eliminate rigid body modes is selected. The cube illustrated below will compress and expand sideways, but its center of mass will stay in place.

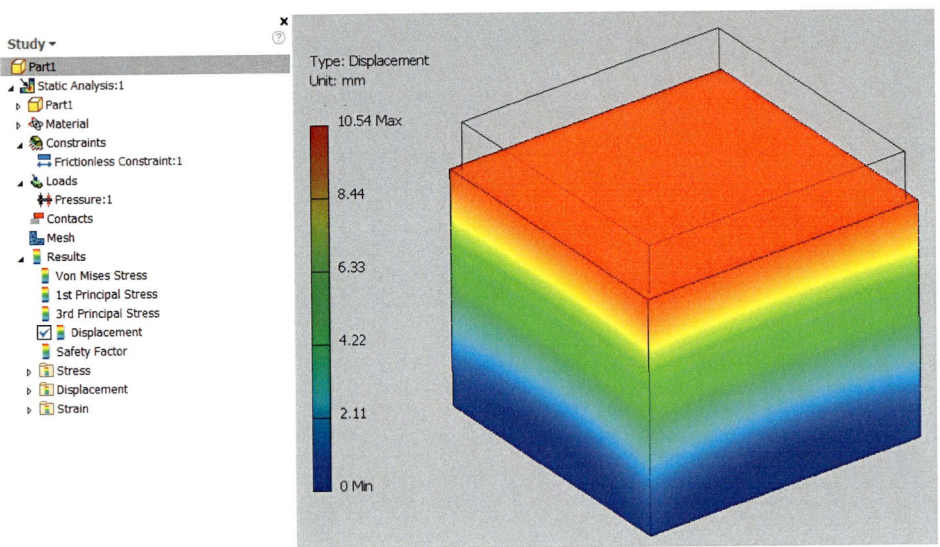

 Select detect and eliminate rigid body modes if you intend to use frictionless constraints only.

Separate Stresses Across Contact Surfaces - If two bodies have the same material and are connected by the bonded contact, theoretically both displacements and stresses should be continuous across the boundary. In FEA solution, because the meshes on the bodies do not exactly match, we may end up with different stresses on different sides of the boundary. By default, we compute average of the two sides and show it as the stress at both sides of the boundary. However, when elements on one side are substantially smaller than on the other, and the distribution of the stress on the contact is important, the user can turn the separate stresses across contact surfaces option on, and have each side's stress computed, resulting in differing stress plots on adjacent contact faces.

 This option only applies to bonded contacts and same materials.

Motion Loads Analysis – This option will only be available if the part to be analyzed has its loads transferred from the dynamic simulation study. If multiple time steps have been transferred then the user can select the specific time to be used for the stress analysis.

 You can copy and edit the first simulation and select another time step to compare the results with the first.

SECTION 1 -Stress Analysis Essentials

CHAPTER 1
The Stress Analysis Environment

Modal Analysis

When performing modal analysis there are four settings which can be defined.

Number of modes – Here you define how many modes you want the software to calculate. You can specify any value between 1 and 200, with 8 being the default value. The following shows one mode, as one mode was chosen.

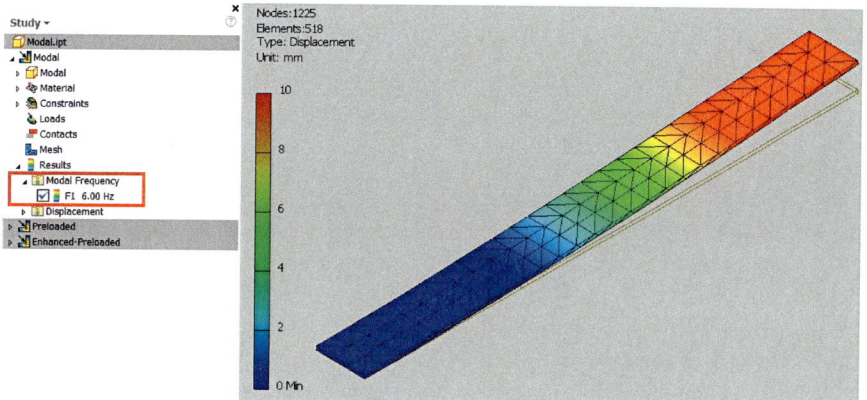

Frequency Range – Here you can specify the natural frequency range you want the software to calculate. If you have not constrained your model then you can specify a higher value than zero for your initial value as this will not calculate the first six modes, which will be zero due to rigid body motion reflecting the six degrees of freedom, with no distortion of the body shape.

Compute Preloaded Modes – Select to compute stress on the model and then compute modes for the pre-stressed condition. The following example illustrates that natural frequency increases from 6.00 to 105.10Hz as a result of applying a tensile force of 1000N.

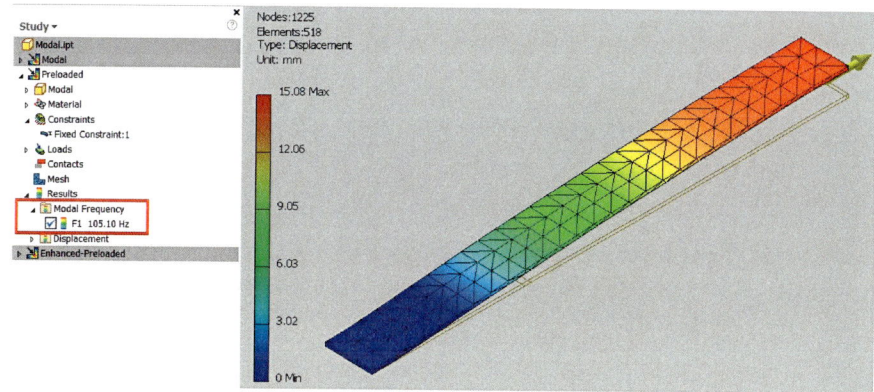

You cannot run a preload modal analysis if you apply a compressive or bending load within Inventor Stress Analysis.

SECTION 1 - Stress Analysis Essentials

CHAPTER 1
The Stress Analysis Environment

Enhanced Accuracy – This option, if selected, increases the accuracy of the calculated frequency values by an order of magnitude (10). The following example illustrates that the frequency is very similar at 104.4 Hz less, than 1% difference, however in some cases the difference can be higher in results.

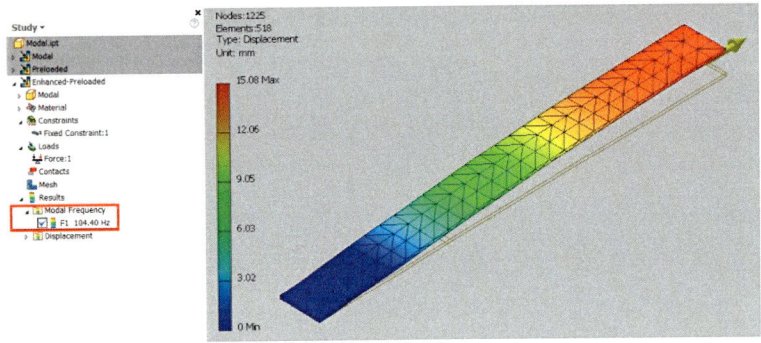

Shape Generator

Is a conceptual design tool which allows designers to create structurally efficient parts. Shape Generator is not available for assemblies and can only be accessed from the part modelling environment.

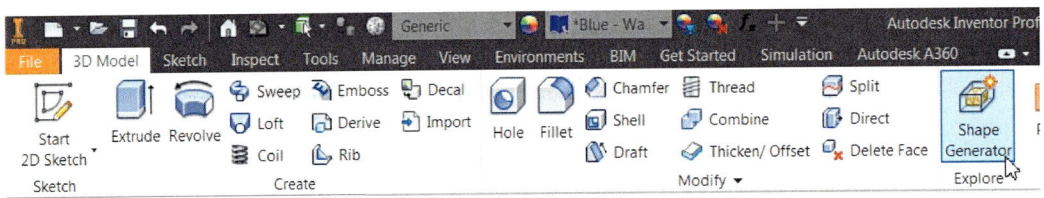

Shape Generator Environment

Within the shape generator environment you can apply materials, constraints and loads just like stress analysis. For further information on constraints and loads refer to the relevant sections. Density is the main material property needed for Shape generator as this is the value used to determine the initial mass of the component, which is the basis for setting mass target reductions within shape generator.

CHAPTER 1
The Stress Analysis Environment

Preserve Region

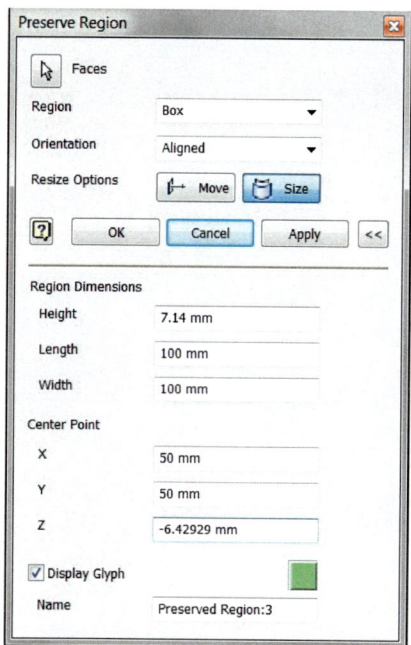

Only single faces can be selected to define cylindrical, rectangular or square volumes to be preserved when removing elements during the simulation, to meet mass targets. If a planar face is selected whether it's horizontal or angled the resize dimensions will be aligned to that face. At present the orientation can only be defined by aligned or global XYZ.

 When faces are selected to define constraint and loads then these faces will automatically be preserved for the 1st element layer. So if the mesh element size is 2 mm then 2mm will be preserved.

Region and Orientation
Will define shape of the model geometry you wish to keep. Currently you can only define a box or cylindrical shape. Switching between the two Region types will adjust the region dimension inputs. If you choose a flat face, region will be a box. If you choose a cylindrical face, region will adjust and change to cylinder. If this assumption is not what you want, you can change to either.

Region Dimensions
Controls the size of the preserving shape. The box region option will use values defined by the X, Y and Z vectors whereas the cylinder region option will use radius and length dimensions.

Center Point
Will control the region position with respect to Global XYZ coordinate systems or aligned with the geometry you have selected.

Display Glyph
You can also display and change the color of the transparent preserved region volume.

CHAPTER 1
The Stress Analysis Environment

Below is an example illustrating how shape generator preserves regions.

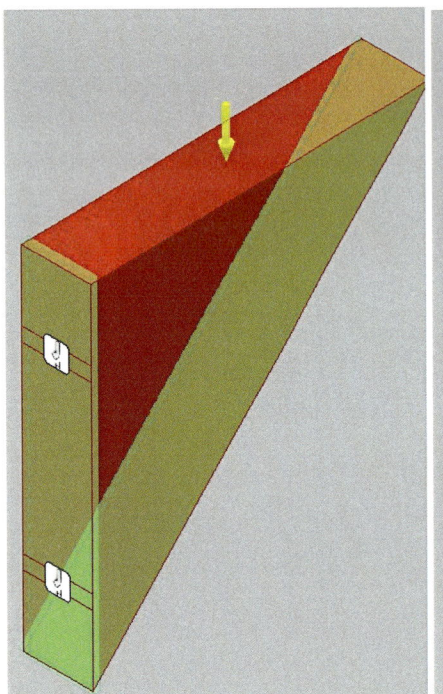
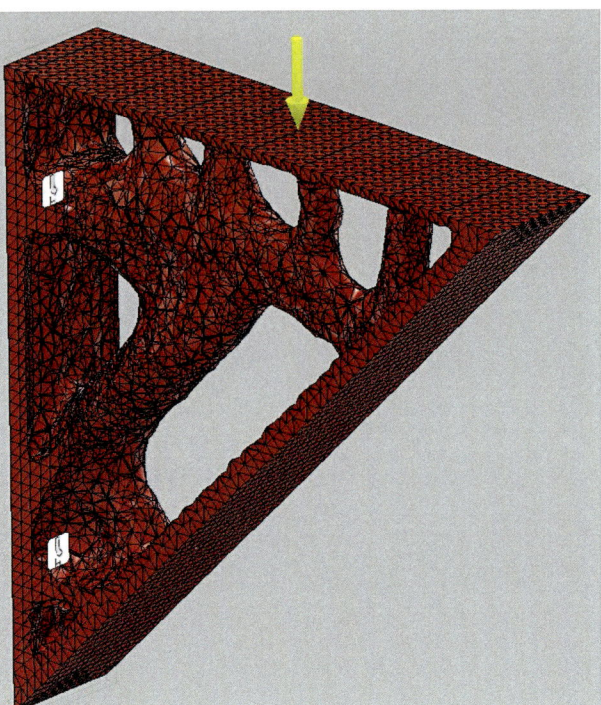

TRY IT! – Open Shape-generator1.ipt

Symmetry Plane

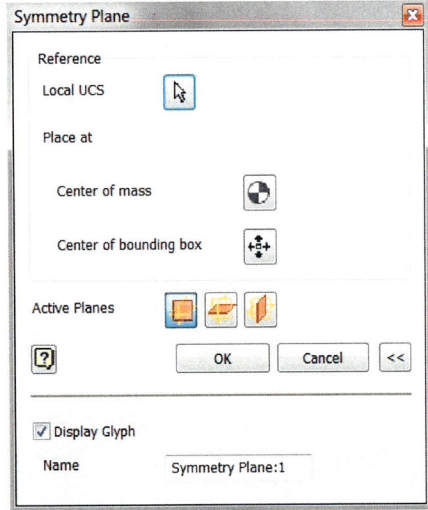

CHAPTER 1
The Stress Analysis Environment

Shape Generator will use symmetry planes to remove material (elements) such that they are symmetrical about the plane. You can define three symmetrical planes within shape generator.

Local UCS

The symmetry planes can be oriented using the default global axis or any user defined local user coordinate system illustrated by the following example.

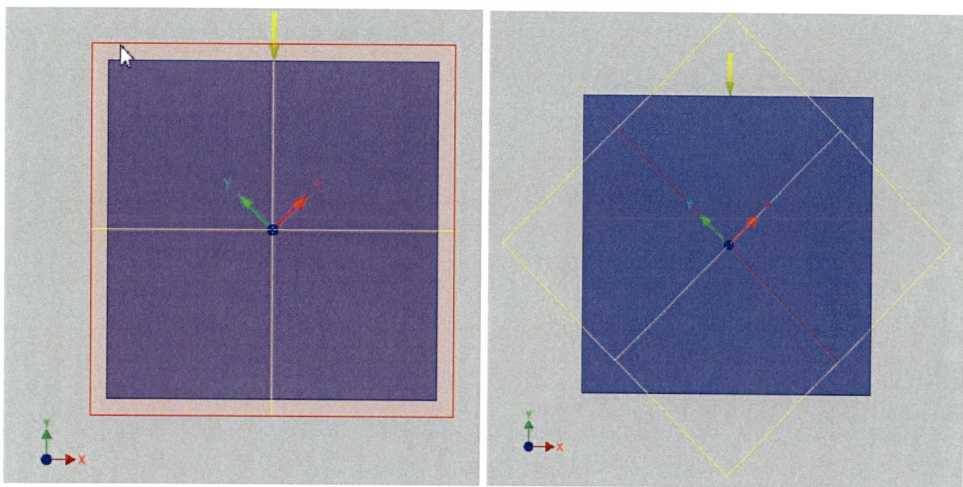

Below is an example of a result based on defining a symmetry plane.

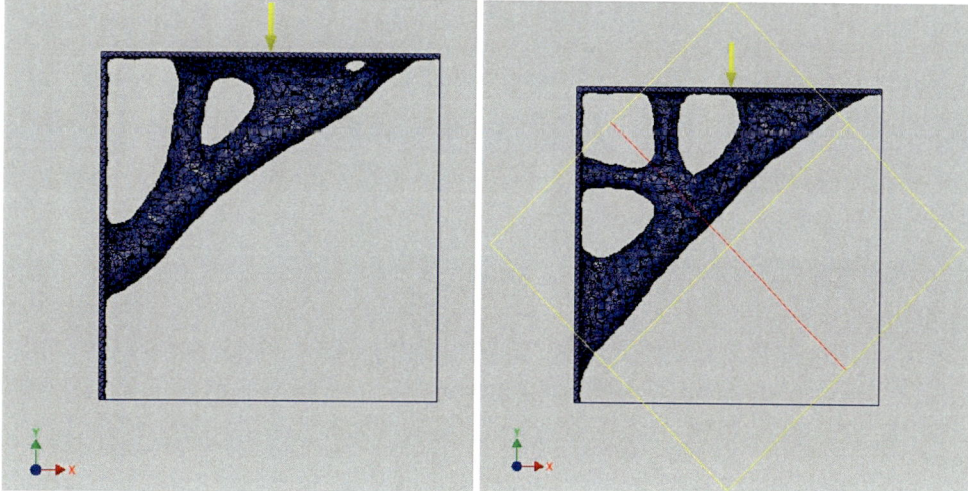

Center of mass
This allows us to place the UCS and symmetry plane at the center of mass of the part.

Center of bounding box
This allows to us place the UCS and symmetry plane at the center of the bounding box of the part.

CHAPTER 1
The Stress Analysis Environment

Active Planes

Allows too add a symmetry plane in one of the other orthogonal directions.

> **TRY IT!** – Open Shape-generator2.ipt

Shape Generator Settings

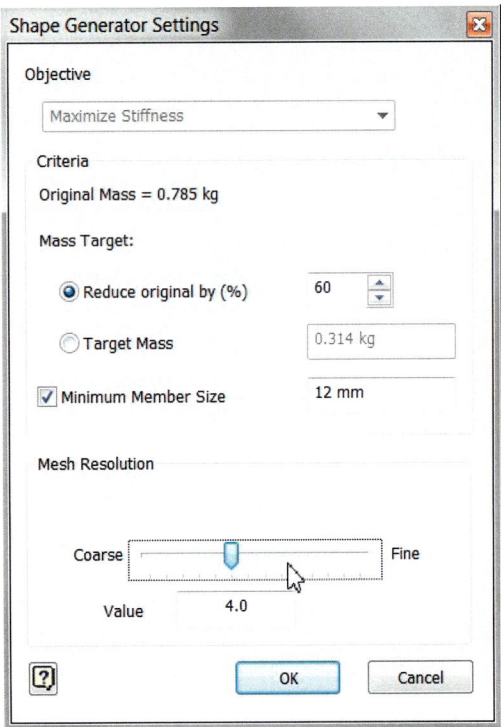

Objective

Will define the criteria for the solver. The solution is currently limited to maximizing stiffness of the structure.

Mass Target

Currently you can define reduced mass target as a percentage or actual value.

Mesh Resolution

This provides a simplified way of deciding the density of the mesh. This is controlled by a scale of 10 (coarse mesh) to 0.5 (fine mesh). You can select Mesh View to visually see the density of the mesh. The values defined are not exact size of the mesh but a ratio. For example if you specify 2 and the largest edge of the bounding box of the component is 100mm. Then the element size will be 20.

$$Size\ of\ mesh\ element\ =\ 100\ x\ 0.2 = 20$$

CHAPTER 1
The Stress Analysis Environment

Minimum Member Size

This allows you to specify the minimum member thickness value which shape generator tries to retain during the simulation. A warning will appear if the thickness is not more than 3 times the average element size. However this does not mean you cannot run a simulation with a member thickness value twice the size of an average element size.

Mesh Settings

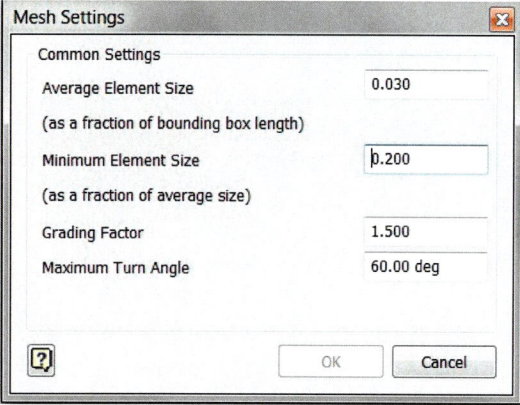

This dialogue box is exactly the same as within Stress Analysis environment. Refer to the mesh section for further details on the above settings.

 Selecting 3, using the slider, for the mesh resolution in the shape generator settings will auto populate the average element size to 0.03 in the mesh settings.

Promote Shape

Allows to save the optimized generated shape as an stl file within the current part or as a new file.

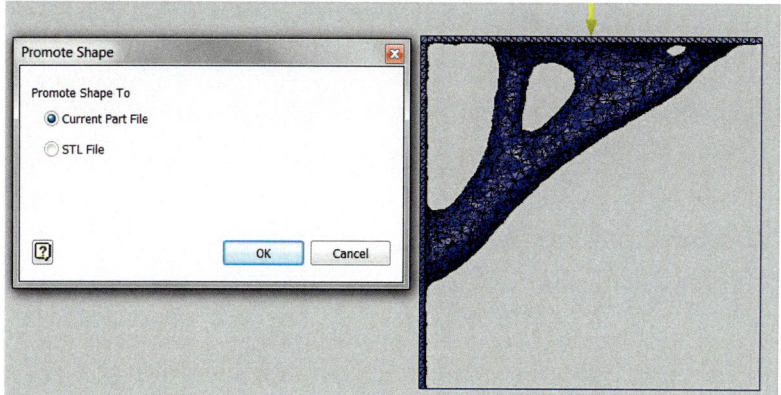

CHAPTER 1
The Stress Analysis Environment

Once saved you can then redesign the original component around the generated shape as shown below.

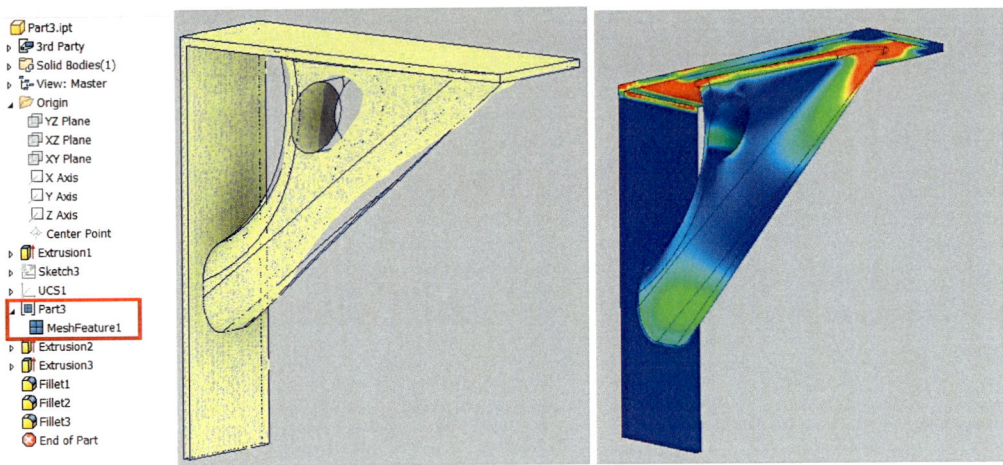

Once the changes have been made the shape generator study can be modified to stress analysis. This way the loads, constraints, materials and mesh data will be populated ready to run stress analysis.

TRY IT! – Open Shape-generator3.ipt

Contacts

If an assembly is being analyzed then you can also define a contact tolerance setting and type of contact to be automatically created.

Tolerance

For solid element mesh a tolerance of 0.1mm will create contacts between all components that have gaps of less than or equal to 0.1mm.

 This setting applies to component faces that have been used to create mid-surfaces (for thin elements) and not the actual mid-surfaces created.

Shell Connector Tolerance

For thin elements a tolerance of 1.750 will create connectors between surfaces that make up the part that have gaps of less than or equal to 1.750 x shell thickness. Let's take the following I Beam example, which has a plate thickness of 2 mm and a radii of 10 mm as shown.

CHAPTER 1
The Stress Analysis Environment

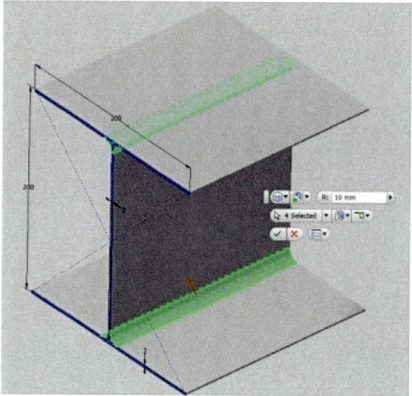

Using the default setting if we select the mid-surface command, in the prepare tab, we get the following mid-surfaces created, for a single component as shown.

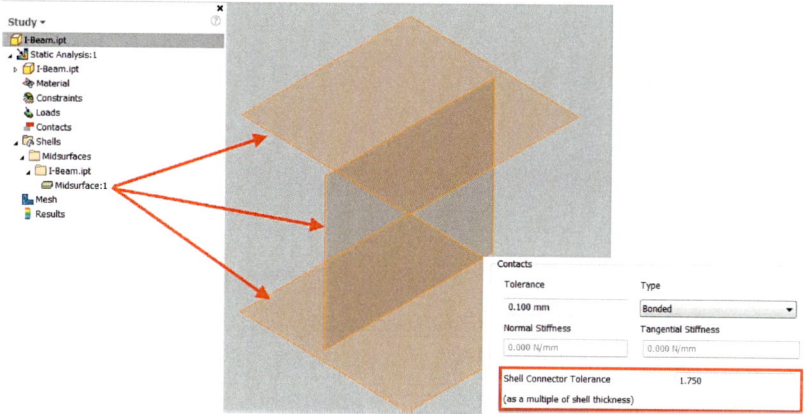

The above image shows only one mid-surface created although it seems like three surfaces. This is a result of having a fillet which develops a variable thickness which cannot be converted to a mid-surface. As it stands these surfaces are not connected and the contact tolerance only works for assemblies. The shell connector tolerance applies to only parts and creates connectors to link mid-surfaces with gaps. The default Shell Connector Tolerance of 3.5 mm (1.750x2) is too small to create connectors as the gap between the edge and surface as shown is 11 mm {10 (fillet) + 1 (half of thickness)}.

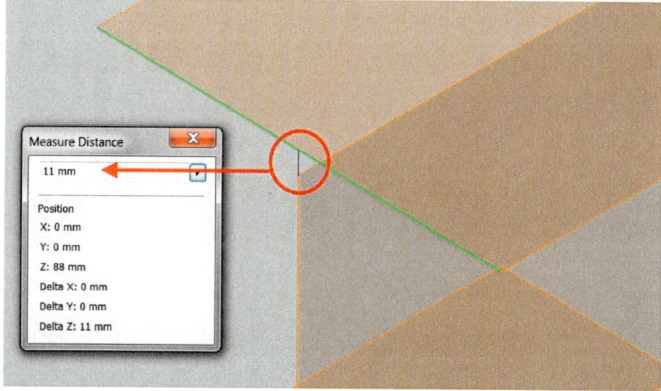

SECTION 1 - Stress Analysis Essentials

CHAPTER 1
The Stress Analysis Environment

In order to create connectors we need to increase the shell connector tolerance to at least 5.5 which will give a tolerance of 11 mm, doing this will create connectors as shown

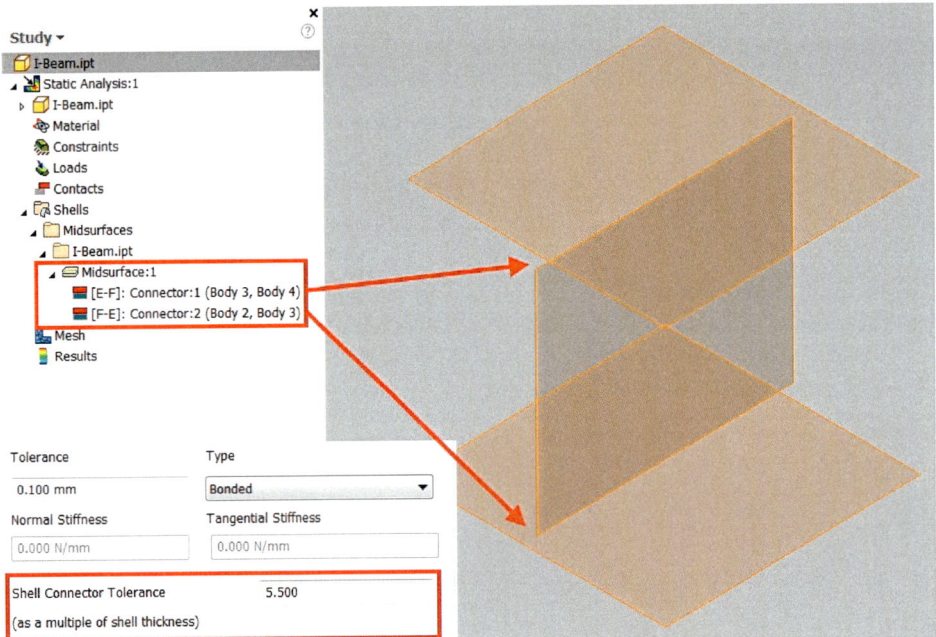

 If possible simplify components by removing fillets/chamfers to avoid creating gaps between surfaces for single components.

Parametric Table

One of the unique and powerful features of inventor stress analysis is the ability to perform parametric optimization studies. Design constraints including mass and others can be accessed and selected by right clicking in the design constraints row.

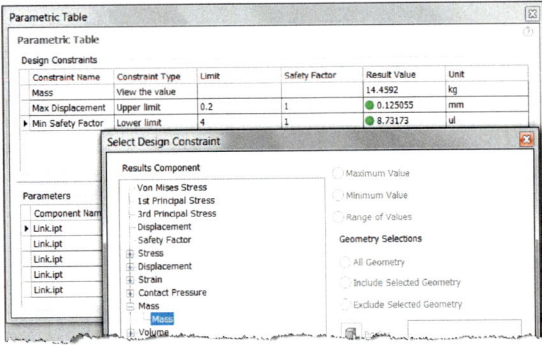

CHAPTER 1
The Stress Analysis Environment

The constraint type values can be set to any of the following.

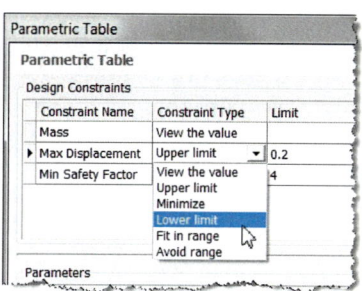

For example, if the criteria was to minimize the mass, we would select minimize and then the optimum design configuration would be selected automatically. By right clicking on any component within the browser, we can select show parameters and then choose any parameters we need to optimize.

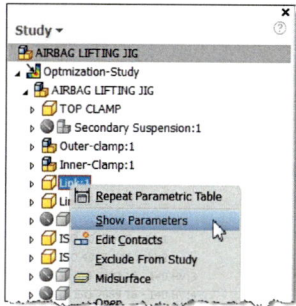

Once the parameters have been selected, the parameter range can be produced by either of the following two methods:

1. If specific values are required, specify the value separated by commas, as illustrated below:

   1,4,6,13   will produce the specified individual values

2. You can specify a range as illustrated below:

   1 – 9: 5 will produce three more values equally spaced between 1 and 9; that is 3,5,7

Parameters

Component Name	Feature Name	Parameter Name	Values	Current Value	Unit
Link		Linkthickness	2,3,6,9,10	10	mm
Link		Slotthickness	10 - 12:2	12	mm
Link		Slotwidth	12,20,30	12	mm
▶ Link		Slotnumbers	1 - 9:5	1	ul

CHAPTER 1
The Stress Analysis Environment

Once the design constraints and parameters are defined, the parameter configurations can be produced by right clicking anywhere in the parameter rows and selecting any of the following.

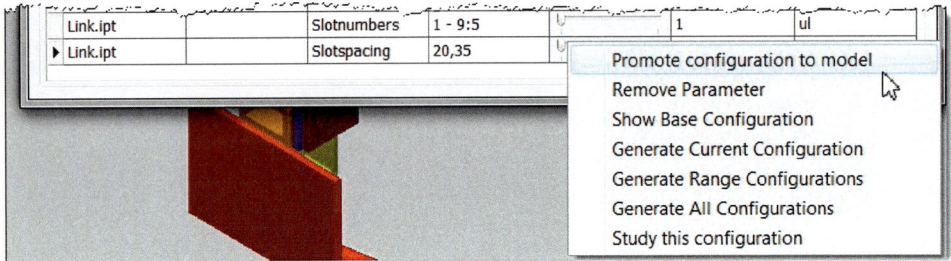

Promote configuration to model – Promotes the value to the part parameter table, over riding the original value.

Remove Parameter – Removes the parameter from the parametric table

Show Base Configuration – Displays the base configuration of the model in the graphics region.

Generate Current Configuration – Generates parameters displayed in the Current Value column.

Generate Range Configurations – Generates all parameters specified in the selected parameter row.

Generate All Configurations – Creates all the possible parameter configurations

 Selecting generate all configurations can take a very long time, especially if there is a large number of parameters.

Study this configuration – Simulates the selected configuration only.

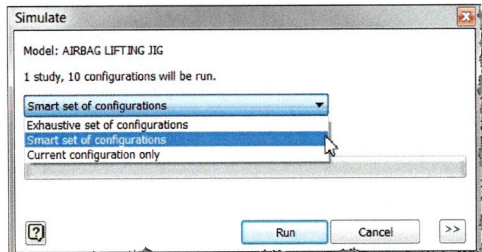

Exhaustive set of configurations – Simulates all the configurations and can take a very long time.

Smart set of configurations – The software will determine and simulate the optimum number of configurations, not necessarily all.

Current configuration only – Simulates the selected configuration only

CHAPTER 1
The Stress Analysis Environment

Material tab

Normally, most components will have their materials assigned within the part environment, thus removing the need to assign materials.

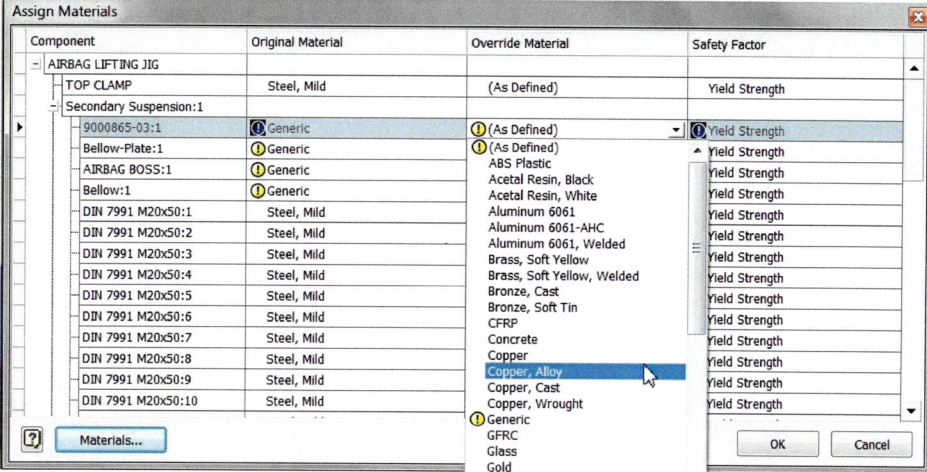

However, the materials can be overridden by selecting other materials from the materials library. New materials can also be created via the materials button.

Further, the safety factor can be calculated from either the yield strength or ultimate strength values.

 Typically any value below a safety factor of 1 will indicate failure. Plus most companies have safety factor values above at least 2.

CHAPTER 1
The Stress Analysis Environment

Inventor stress analysis can only perform linear analysis and cannot perform thermal analysis. Therefore specifying a value of 1 for thermal values will not affect your results. The strength values will also not have an impact on the stress results but will only be used when displaying safety factor results.

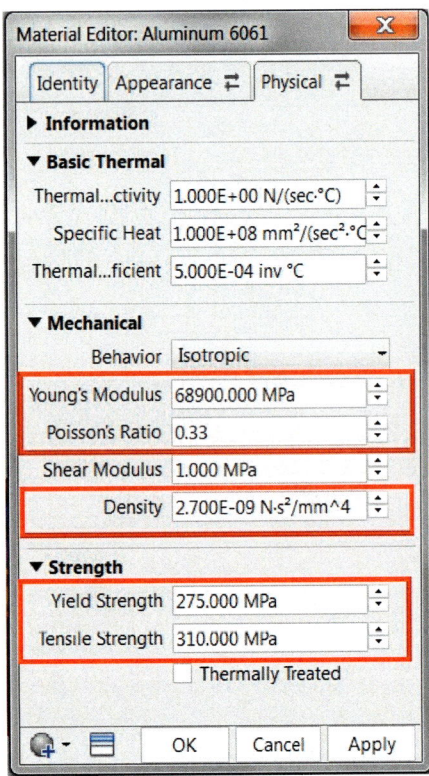

CHAPTER 1
The Stress Analysis Environment

Constraints tab

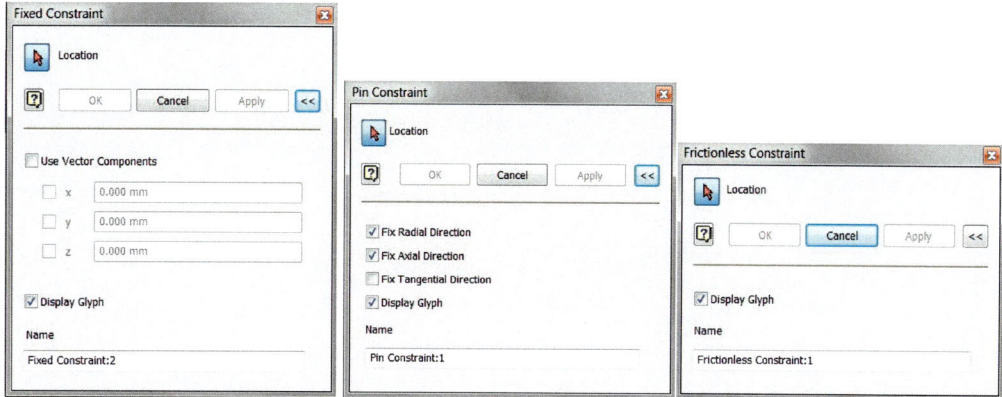

Fixed constraint

The location can be defined by specifying either a point, an edge or a face. A fixed constraint allows you to restrict the translational direction of the component in the x, y, z direction. For example, if a component is fixed or bonded, you will normally fix all three directions.

You can also use fixed constraint to define a predefined displacement on a component, or assembly, as illustrated below.

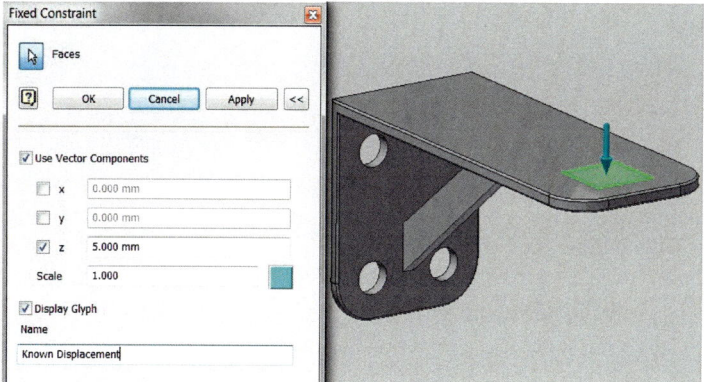

Pin constraint

The location can only be defined by selecting a cylindrical face and this constraint is typically used where holes are supported by bearings or pins. Typically for a pin constraint the tangential surface is free to move about the local cylindrical coordinate systems generated automatically by selecting the cylindrical face.

SECTION 1 -Stress Analysis Essentials

CHAPTER 1
The Stress Analysis Environment

 A pin constraint is the same as a fixed constraint if the tangential direction is also fixed.

Frictionless Constraint

The location can only be defined by a planar face and enables a component to freely slide along a plane and prevent motion normal to the sliding plane or surface.

 Frictional constraints can also be used to model symmetry boundary conditions, for example a quarter or half model.

Loads tab

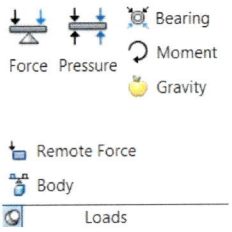

The loads can be generally categorized into

- General loads
- Face loads
- Body loads

General loads

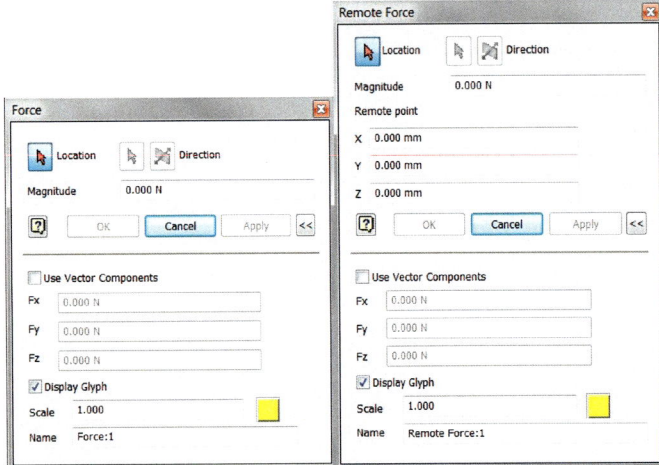

To fully define general loads, a location, direction, and magnitude are all required. Location can be defined by planar face and, in the case of force, can also be defined by an edge or point. Direction can be defined by either a planar face, work plane, edge or work axis.

SECTION 1 - Stress Analysis Essentials

Face loads

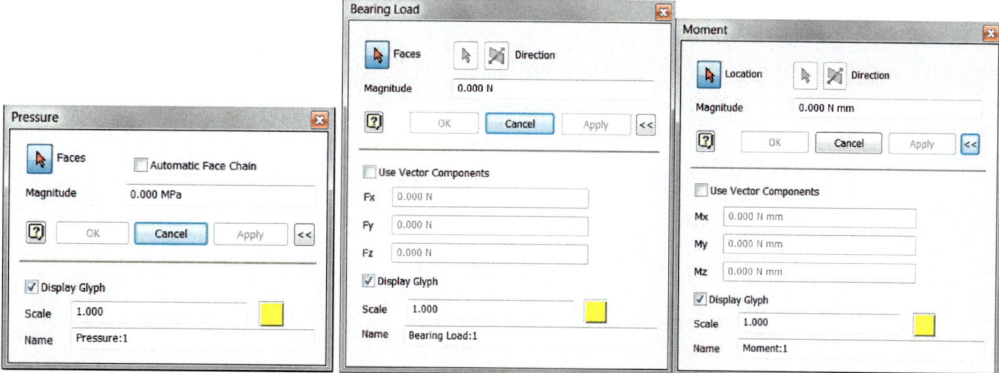

With the exception of pressure, to fully define other face loads, a location, direction, and magnitude are all required. Location can only be defined by a planar face for pressure and moment and, in the case of bearing load, the face needs to be cylindrical. With the exception of pressure, direction can be defined by a planar face, work plane, an edge or work axis. The direction of the pressure is always normal to the face. Also new in 2017 you have the automatic face chain selection to automatically select all adjoining tangential faces after the 1st selected face.

 Pressure is related to area, so, if a component is being parametrically optimized, take care as pressure can also change if the area changes.

Body loads

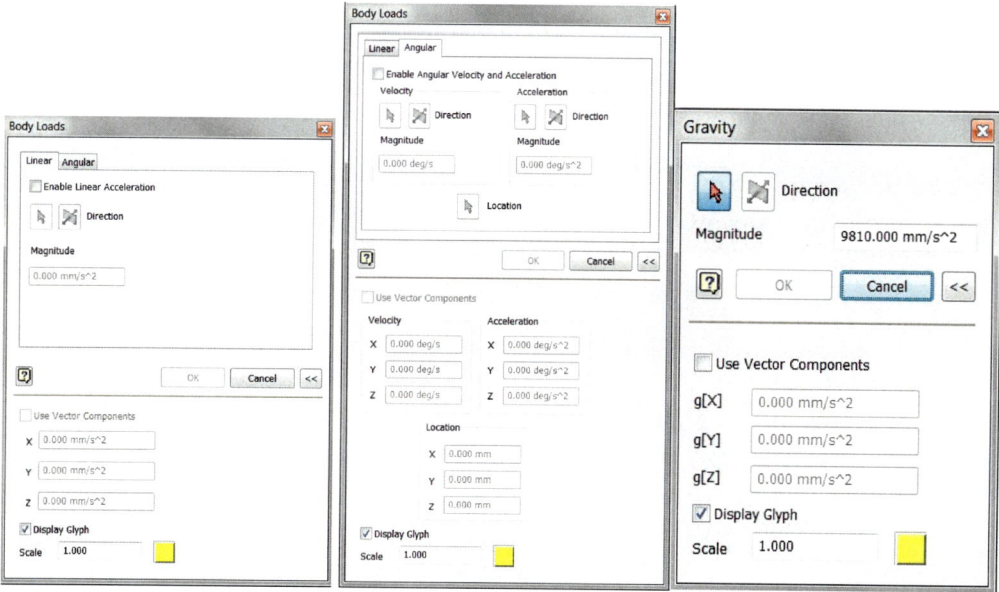

To fully define body loads, a direction and a magnitude are required. Direction can be defined by either a planar face, work plane, edge or work axis.

CHAPTER 1
The Stress Analysis Environment

For all loads, magnitude can be specified by entering an absolute value or a mathematical expression. An example of a mathematical expression could be 100 x sin (45 deg).

With the exception of pressure, the direction and magnitude for loads can be alternatively specified by using vector components

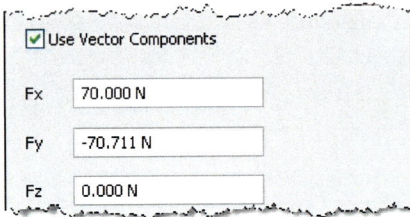

With the exception of body loads and gravity, the display glyph color and scale can be altered in addition to the name.

 When applying loads, it is advisable not to apply loads at points or small edges as this can produce very high localized stresses.

Contacts tab

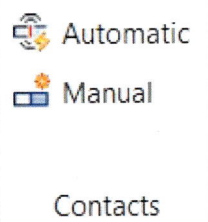

There are seven types of contacts in inventor stress analysis.

Types of contacts

1. **Bonded** – Bonds contact faces to each other, for example, in fabricated structures.

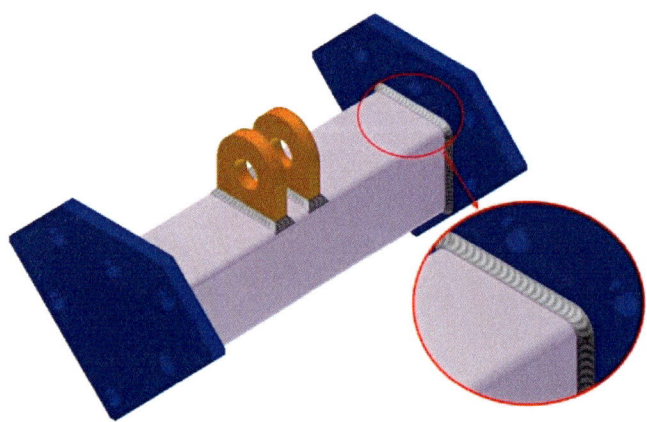

CHAPTER 1
The Stress Analysis Environment

2. **Separation** – Allows adjacent contact faces to separate and slide under deformation; for example, loose bolt hole connections.

3. **Sliding/No Separation** – Maintains contact between adjacent faces and allows sliding when under deformation; for example, hole pin connections.

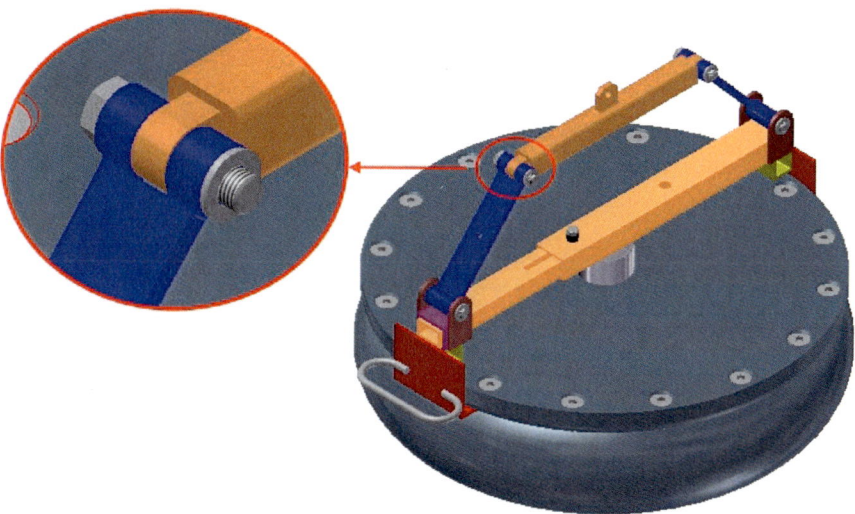

4. **Separation / No Sliding** – Separates contact faces partially or fully without sliding.

5. **Shrink Fit / Sliding** – Similar to **Separation** contact, with the addition of allowing for initial overlaps between components, creating prestress conditions.

6. **Shrink Fit/No Sliding** - Similar to **Separation/No sliding** contact, with the addition of allowing for initial overlaps between components, creating prestress conditions; for example, in seal and pipe/clamp connections.

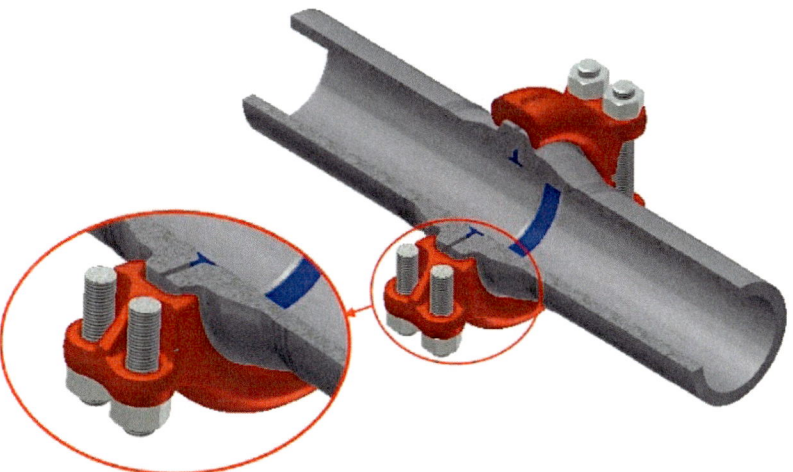

7. **Spring** - Creates spring conditions between two components by applying stiffness properties.

CHAPTER 1
The Stress Analysis Environment

The process of creating contacts

Contacts have to be initially created automatically using the default tolerance settings. Unwanted contacts can then be suppressed.

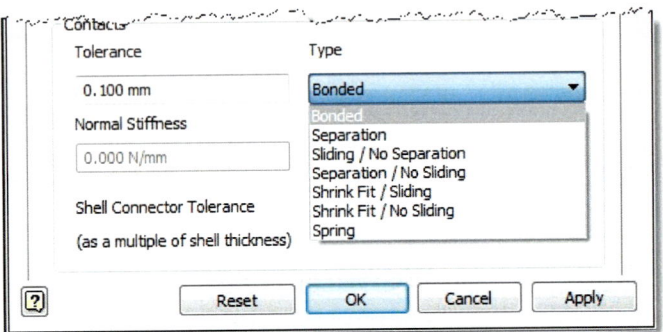

 Contacts created automatically cannot be deleted.

Once automatic contacts have been created you can start to create contacts manually. A typical scenario is when a contact pair has not been created due to gap between parts being higher than the initial tolerance setting.

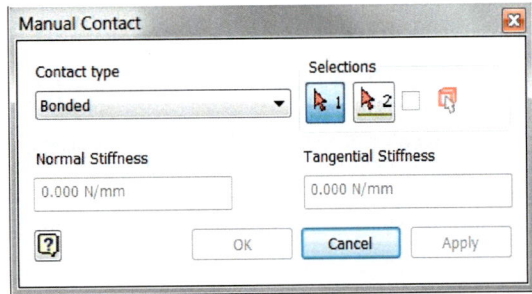

 You can increase the contact tolerance to create contacts between parts that have gaps higher than the default value of 0.1 mm.

CHAPTER 1
The Stress Analysis Environment

Prepare tab

Find Thin Bodies

This tool when selected will automatically determine components to be converted to surfaces, using the mid-surface option. Generally components with a cross section to length ratio greater than 1:250 will be automatically selected as shown below

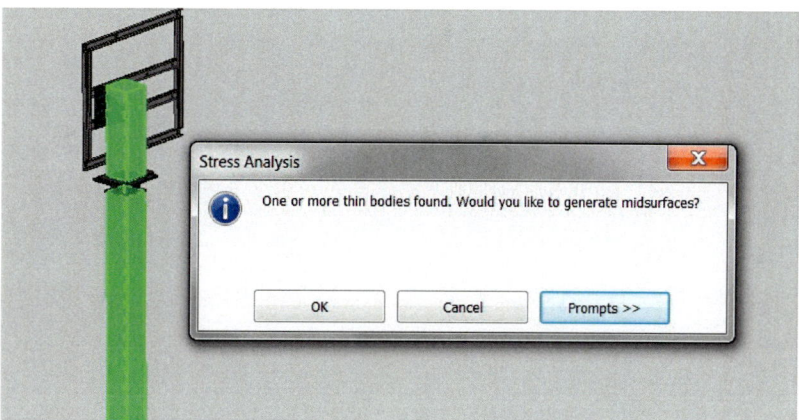

The actual ratio value is calculated using the equation below

Given that:
vol = volume of a body
area = surface area of the body

ratio = $(36 \times \pi \times vol^2)/(area^3)^{1/6}$

> If a ratio is over 250 a warning dialogue will appear indicating that the component should be meshed using thin elements.

CHAPTER 1
The Stress Analysis Environment

Midsurface

This command is used to select any component for which a mid-surface is required that was not automatically detected using the find thin bodies tool. Selecting any face on the component will automatically select all faces of the component to be converted to a midsurface.

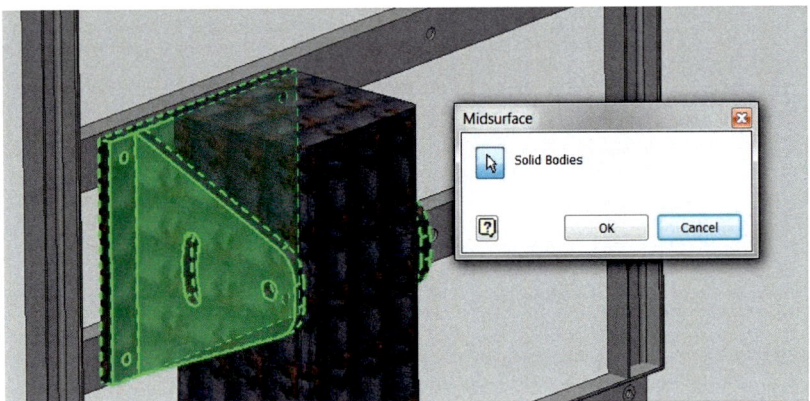

📝 Creating midsurfaces will create gaps between components (surfaces), so take care in manipulating results as in reality there will be no gaps. See Example 1 - Thin Elements

💡 If components are made from the same material then I suggest creating a shrinkwrap before creating a midsurface.

Offset

This command unlike the midsurface gives the user control on what feature/face of the component is to be used to create a midsurface by unselecting **Automatic Face Chain** and specifying the thickness of the component, as illustrated below.

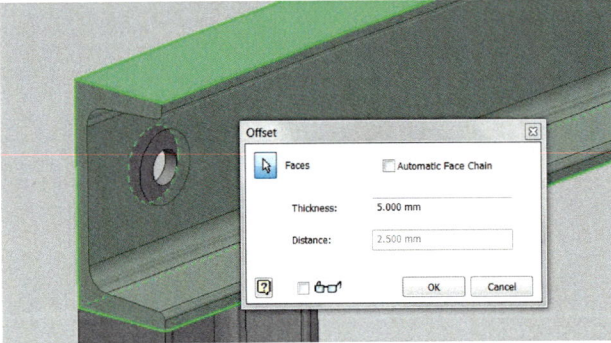

💡 This can be ideally used to simplify the components for the purposes of analysis and meshing, as an alternative to exclude from simulation.

💡 Use this command if you have split faces as this command will not merge the surfaces into one.

CHAPTER 1
The Stress Analysis Environment

Example 1 – Thin Elements

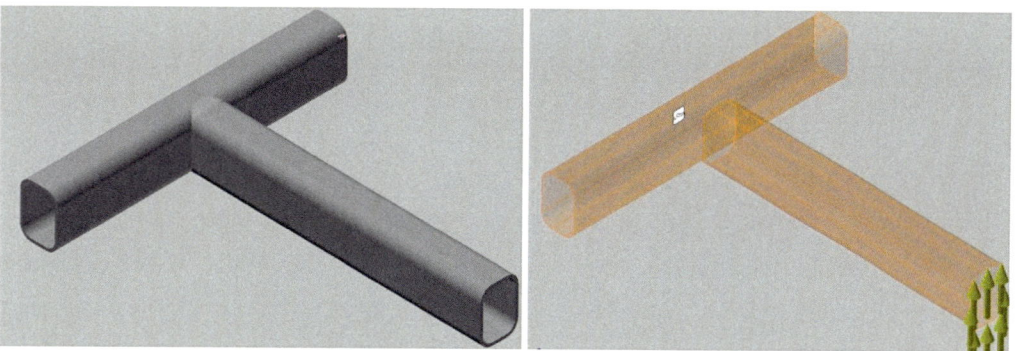

Here I am going to illustrate the potential difference in results at connections as a result of surface creation, using different tools, for thin structures. The key feature to note is the radii of the box sections which if removed can result in providing extra stiffness in the model. The box section is fixed on the far face and a load of 200N is applied on the edges of the other box section as shown above.

Let's first have a look at the results of the model with each box section as a separate components. The first thing you will note is the gap as a result of creating midsurfaces for each box section as shown below.

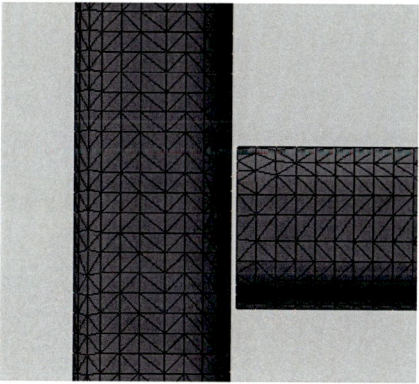

First let's look at the von-mises stress. We can clearly see hot spot as result of the gap and the contact created between the radii as shown below.

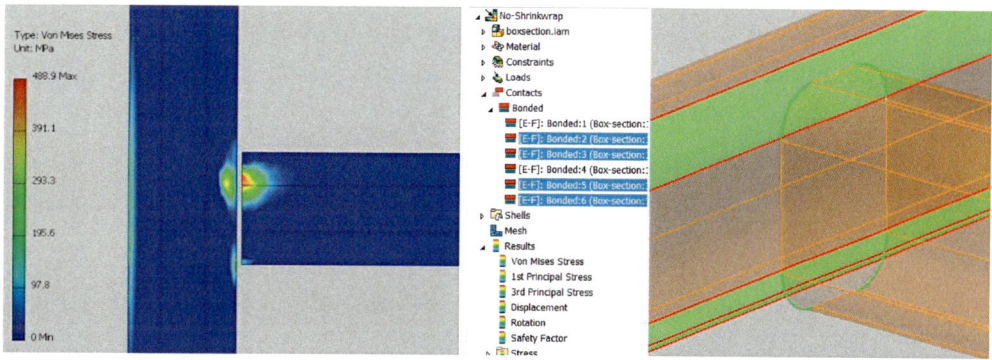

SECTION 1 -Stress Analysis Essentials

CHAPTER 1
The Stress Analysis Environment

Now we will suppress the four contacts as shown in the previous illustrations and see the difference in the results, if any. We can see by removing the contacts on the radii the stress is more uniformly spread across.

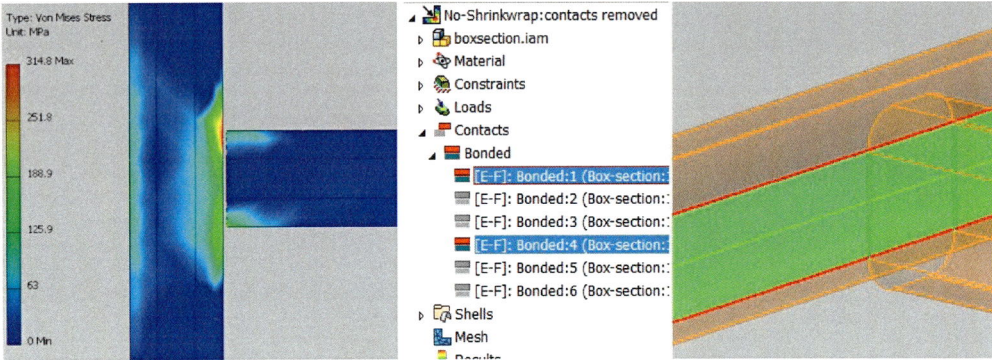

Now we are going to use offset surfaces to create a more connected surface to include the welds as well, leaving no gap between box section. We can clearly see this gives most uniform spread of load across both box sections with minimal hotspots.

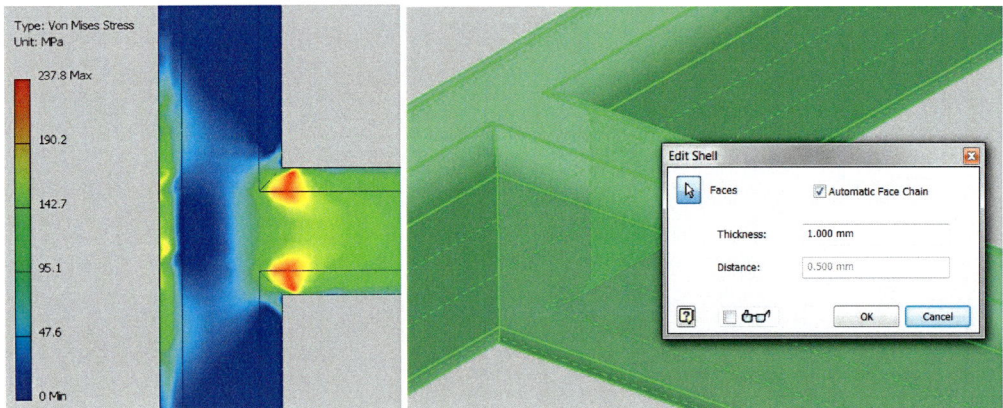

So take care when analyzing results in the areas of the gaps created as a result of using thin elements.

TRY IT! – Open boxsection.iam

CHAPTER 1
The Stress Analysis Environment

Mesh tab

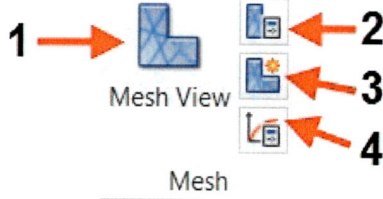

1. Generate and preview mesh
2. Mesh setting
3. Local mesh control
4. Convergence settings

These tools can be further categorized into the following:

1. Manual mesh refinement (or manual convergence)
2. Automatic mesh refinement (or automatic convergence)

Manual mesh refinement

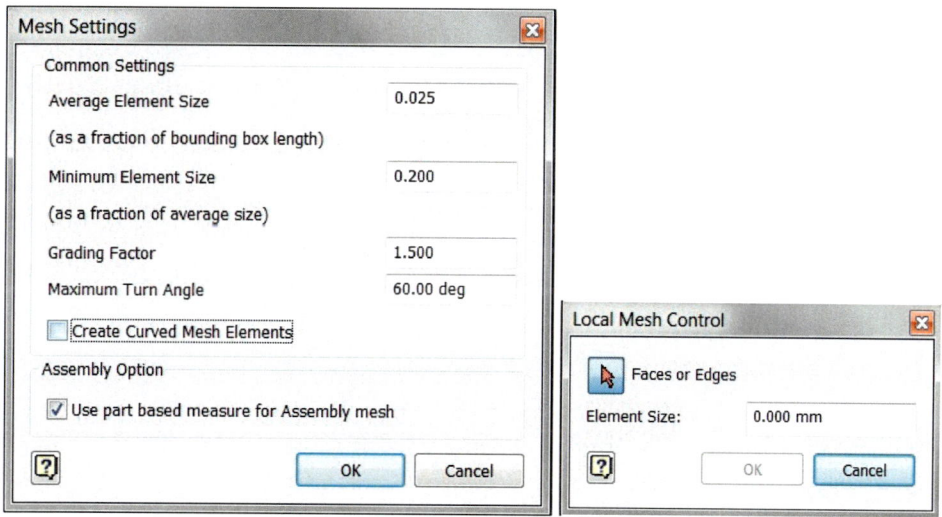

There are two average element size values that can be specified one for solid elements and one for thin elements. This gives the ability to specify different elements sizes for both solid and thin elements. The other settings apply to solid or thin elements in a similar manner. In the following examples solid elements will be used to demonstrate the effect of the mesh settings.

SECTION 1 -Stress Analysis Essentials

CHAPTER 1
The Stress Analysis Environment

Here, an example will be used to explain the manual mesh refinement tools.

Example 2 – Mesh Settings

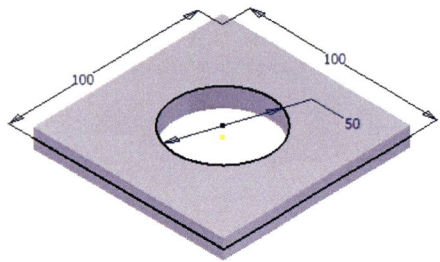

Where the thickness of the component is 10 mm

Average Element Size – Initially, we will check the effect of altering the **Average Element Size**.

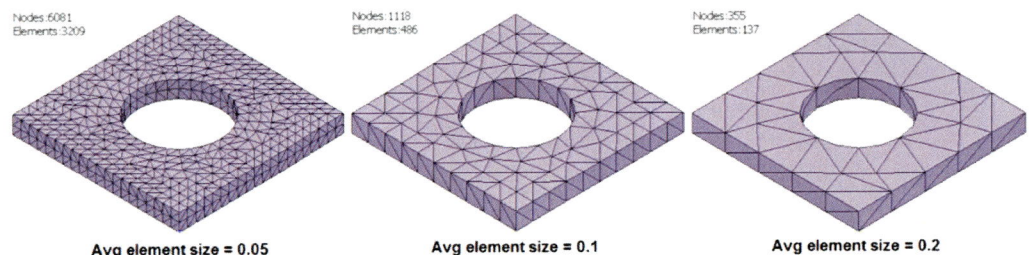

Using a smaller number will produce a denser mesh, as illustrated above.

As a guide, to determine the size of an element, the following can be used:

$$Size\ of\ mesh\ element\ =\ Longest\ parameter\ of\ object\ \times Average\ element\ size$$

So, for an average element size of 0.2 the mesh size would be

$$Size\ of\ mesh\ element\ =\ 100\ x\ 0.2 = 20$$

The maximum **Average Element Size** that can be specified is 1.

A denser mesh will take a longer time to analyze.

Minimum Element Size – Controls the size of the smallest element using value greater than the default value of 0.2 will help in reducing the number of elements. If the value needs changing, use any number in the following range.

$$0.2 \leq minimum\ element\ size\ \leq 0.5$$

CHAPTER 1
The Stress Analysis Environment

Grading Factor – Controls the maximum length of the adjacent element edges for transitioning between coarse and fine regions. A smaller grading factor produces a more uniform mesh.

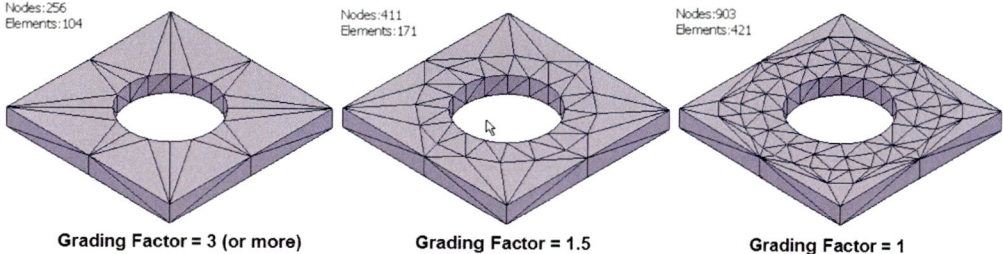

Using a smaller number will produce a denser mesh, as illustrated above.

The value for the grading factor can be specified between 1 and 10. The recommended range is:

$$1.1 \leq Grading\ Factor \leq 1.5$$

Maximum Turn Angle - Allows you to control the number of elements along a 90° arc. Specifying 60° will at least create two or more elements to fill a 90° arc, whereas a maximum turn angle of 30° will create at least three or more elements to fill a 90° arc.

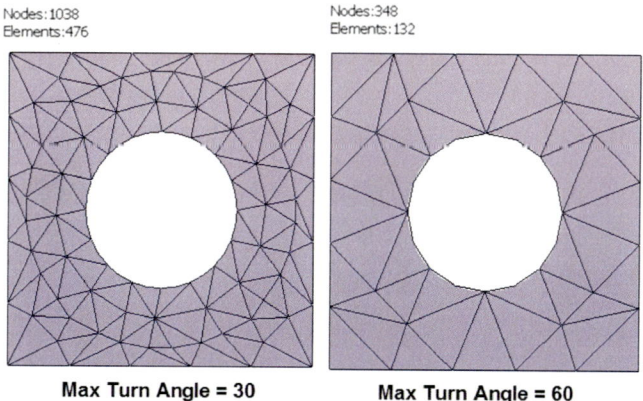

A small angle value of 15, for example, can produce a very dense mesh, especially when the model contains holes and radii. The recommended range is:

$$30 \leq Max\ Turn\ Angle \leq 60$$

💡 It is advisable to suppress small features to avoid creating significantly more elements.

CHAPTER 1
The Stress Analysis Environment

Create Curved Mesh Elements - Represents models with circular features more accurately than straight elements.

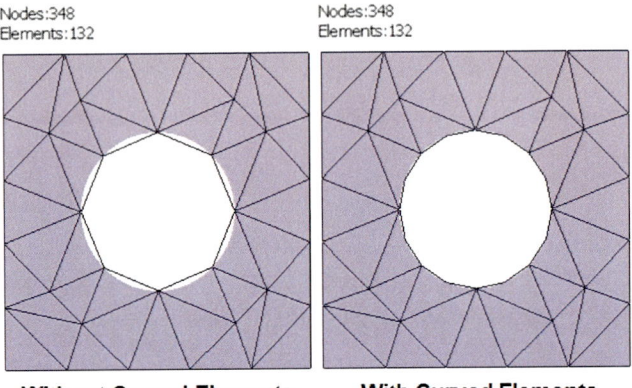

 Curved elements may help to produce more accurate results.

Local Mesh Control – Is used to further refine the model by specifying an absolute value on faces or edges.

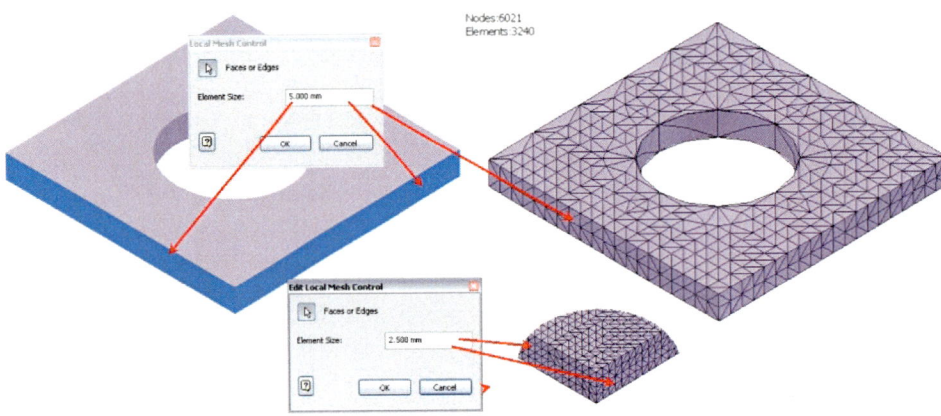

Specifying a value of 5mm will create two elements on the vertical side faces, as the height of the base is 10mm. A local mesh size of 2.5mm will create four elements on the vertical side faces.

TRY IT! – Open plate.ipt

CHAPTER 1
The Stress Analysis Environment

Automatic mesh refinement (or automatic convergence)

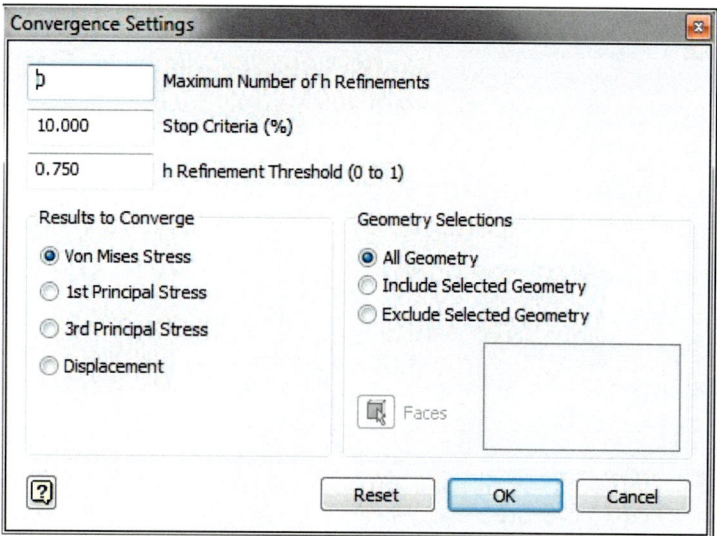

Maximum Number of h Refinements – Here, you specify the maximum number of mesh refinements based around maximum stresses. Values higher than 5 can take a long time to analyse, especially in the case when stress singularities are present in the model.

Stop Criteria (%) – Is used for convergence between two consecutive refinements. If the difference between the two refinements is less than 10%, the convergence process will stop.

H Refinement Threshold (0 to 1) – A value of 0 will include all elements in the model as candidates for refinement, whereas a value 1 will exclude all elements from the H-refinement process. The default value is 0.75 means 25% of the elements around the high stress area will be likely candidates for refinement.

 Use exclude selected geometry where models have stress singularities.

 Use a lower value if the model has multiple stress singularity areas.

Automatic convergence may not necessarily result in convergence of results, especially where models have sharp and small edges, including pointed corners. The solution goes through H-P adaptive refinements process as mentioned earlier.

SECTION 1 -Stress Analysis Essentials

CHAPTER 1
The Stress Analysis Environment

Here an example will be used to explain the convergence settings required to automatically refine the mesh to obtain convergence in results.

Example 3 – Automatic Convergence

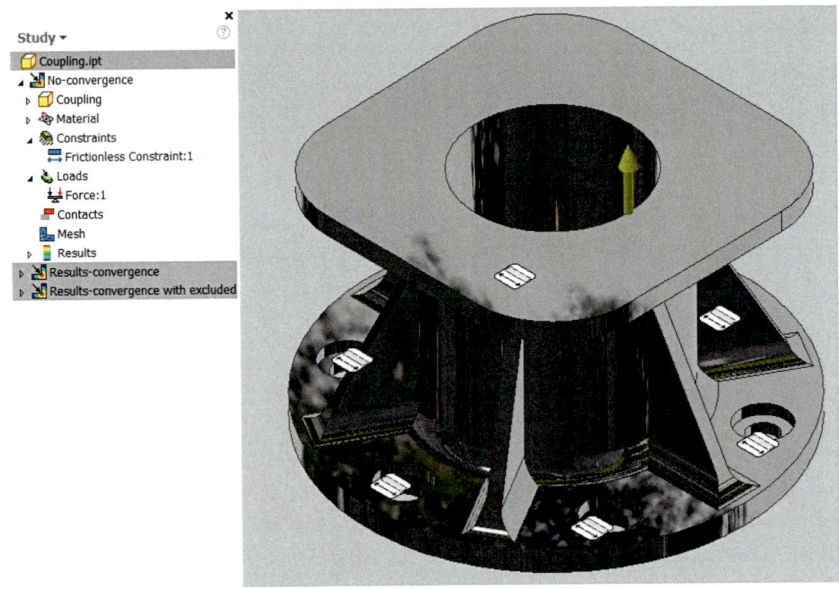

In this example we need to determine whether the component can withstand a load of 1000N, which is fixed at each of the bolt holes, using frictional constraints, as shown above. Secondly, we need to determine the maximum stress, which is required, for example, to determine fatigue life.

Using a mesh setting of average element size of 0.05, the example is analysed yielding peak stresses around all the bolt holes and fillets. The convergence plot shows that the results have not converged with the initial P-refinement (with H -refinement set to 0).

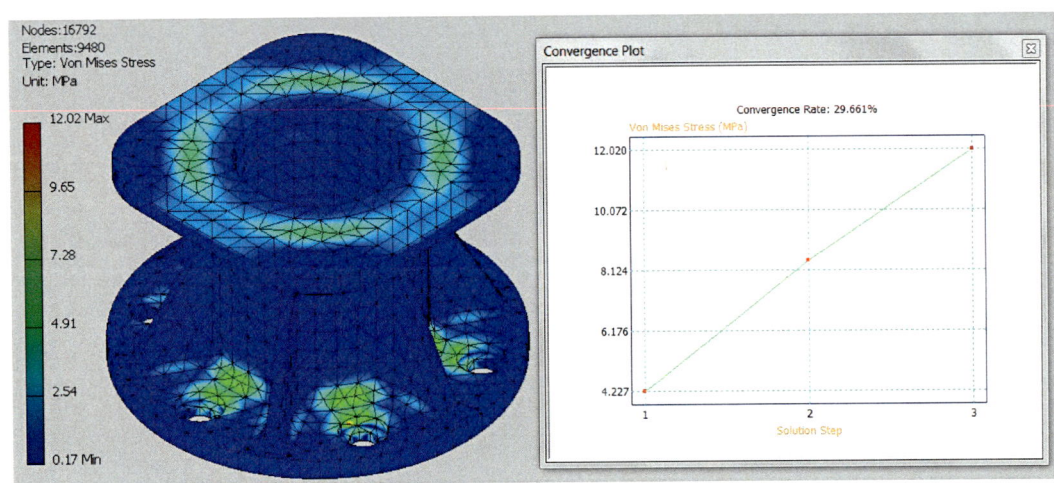

CHAPTER 1
The Stress Analysis Environment

To obtain convergence we will rerun the analysis again, this time with maximum number of h refinements set to **2** and the stop criteria (%) set to 10. The H-refinement threshold will be reduced to **0.5**, as we have multiple areas of high stress. This value will refine at least 50% of the model mesh around peak stress regions.

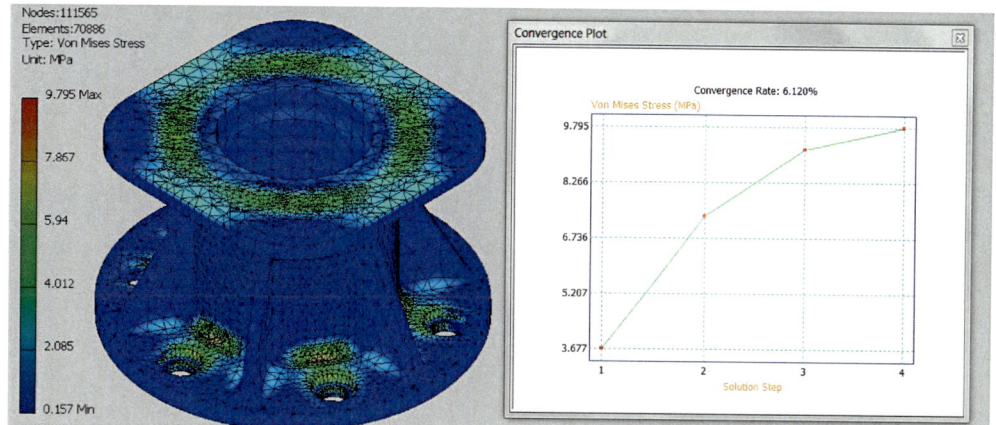

From the results we can see that the stress have converged at the first iteration of H-P Refinement Process (point 4) and therefore does not need to go to second iteration of H-P Refinement Process (point 5). Further, it is important to note that the mesh has been refined around the bolt holes, and other areas of the model, where there was high stress.

In cases where the model has stress singularities, you can still use automatic convergence with excluded selected geometry option selected to obtain automatic convergence of results in key areas of interest, as illustrated below.

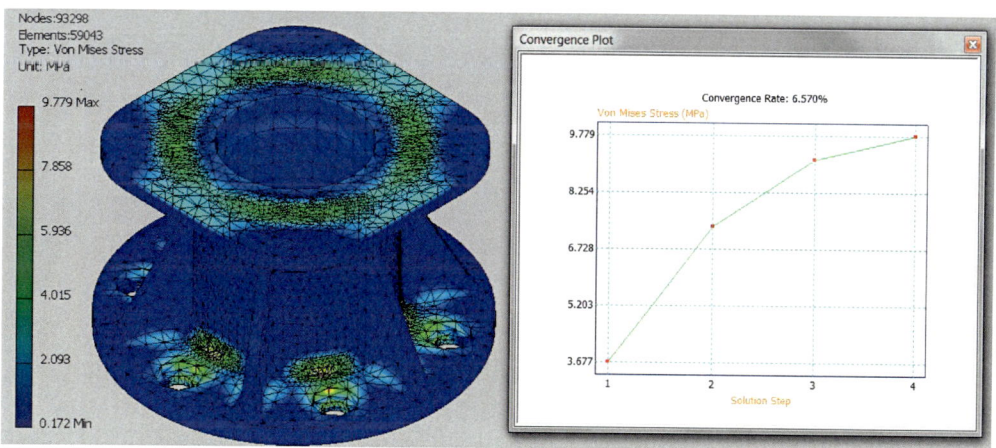

The mesh is not refined around areas of excluded geometry (the top faces of the bolt hole).

TRY IT! – Open Coupling.ipt

CHAPTER 1
The Stress Analysis Environment

An alternative process to using the automatic convergence where models have stress singularities is to use manual convergence.

Example 4 – Manual Convergence

1. Run analysis with **Average Element Size** of 0.1
2. Rerun analysis with **Average Element Size** of 0.05
3. Rerun analysis with **Average Element Size** 0.025

If the difference between the first and last analysis is within 10%, you can assume that your results have converged. Use the color bar to modify legend values to help visualize results better by isolating the stress singularity results.

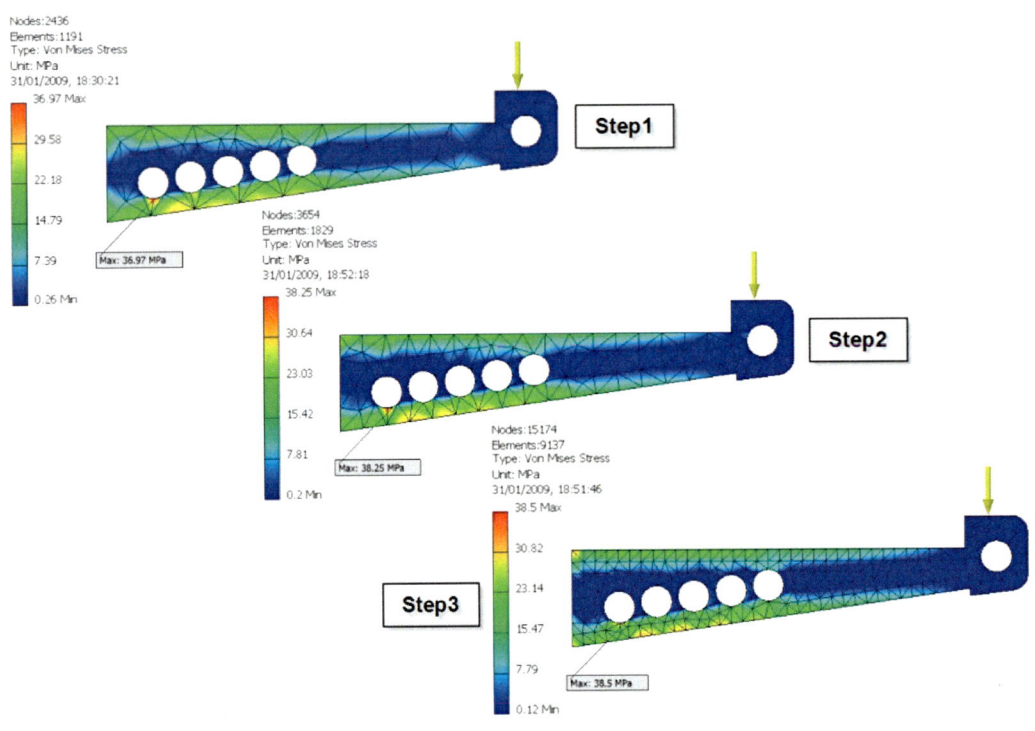

TRY IT! – Open Snap-fit.ipt

CHAPTER 1
The Stress Analysis Environment

Results tab

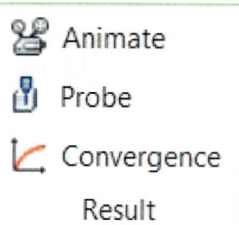

Inventor Stress analysis offers many more result displays, including planar (XX, YY, ZZ) and shear stresses (XY, XZ, YZ).

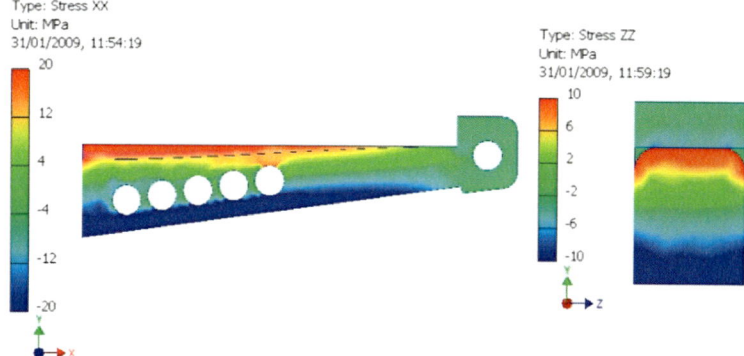

The complete list of result displays available are shown below.

In this version of stress analysis you can now have a look at the results log file providing information including run times. Log file can be accessed by right clicking results node in the browser and selecting study log.

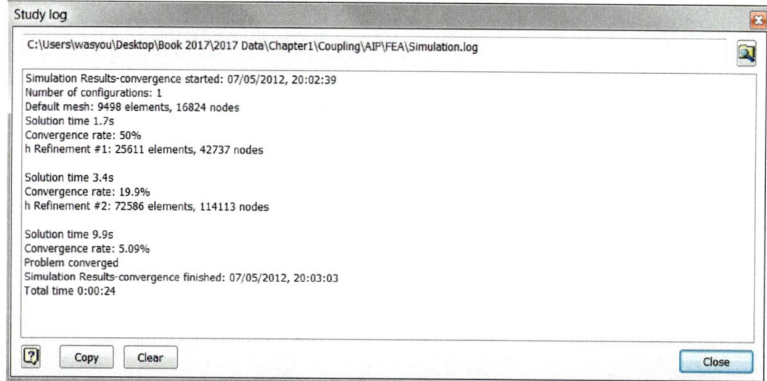

SECTION 1 -Stress Analysis Essentials

CHAPTER 1
The Stress Analysis Environment

Animate
Creates a video file of the animation

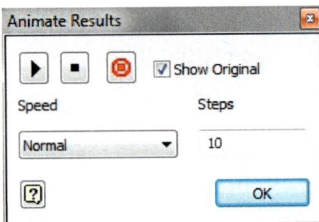

 For a smoother display, increase the number of steps.

 The valid range of steps is 3 ≤ **Steps** ≤ 30.

Probe
Probe helps to pinpoint the key areas of interest in the model, especially when the model has maximum results distorted, due to stress singularities.

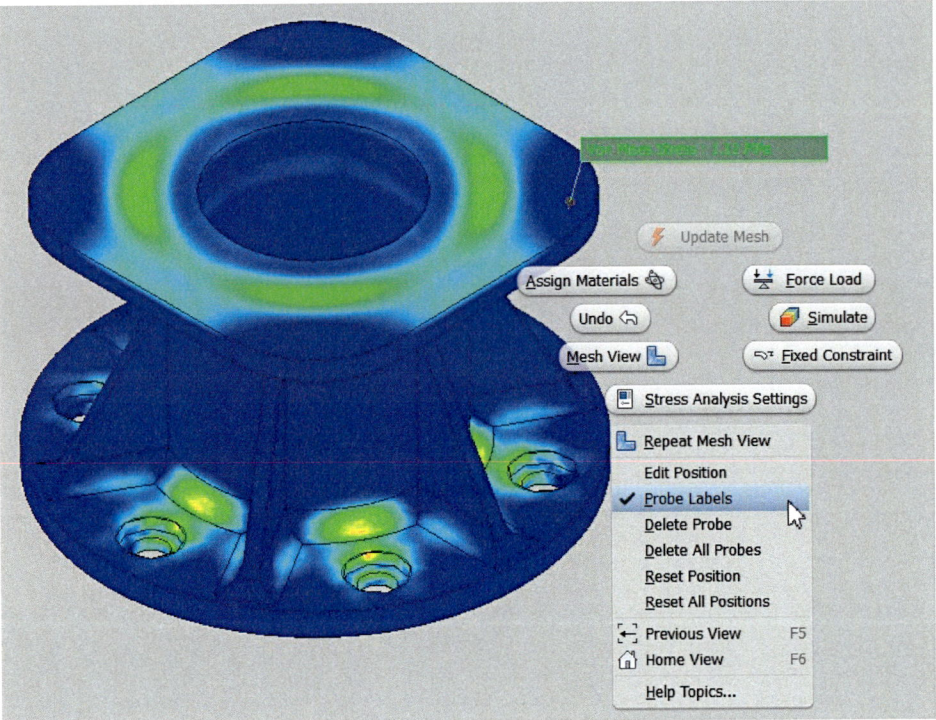

CHAPTER 1
The Stress Analysis Environment

Convergence plot

This helps us to gain confidence by illustrating that the results in the area of interest have converged, as illustrated below.

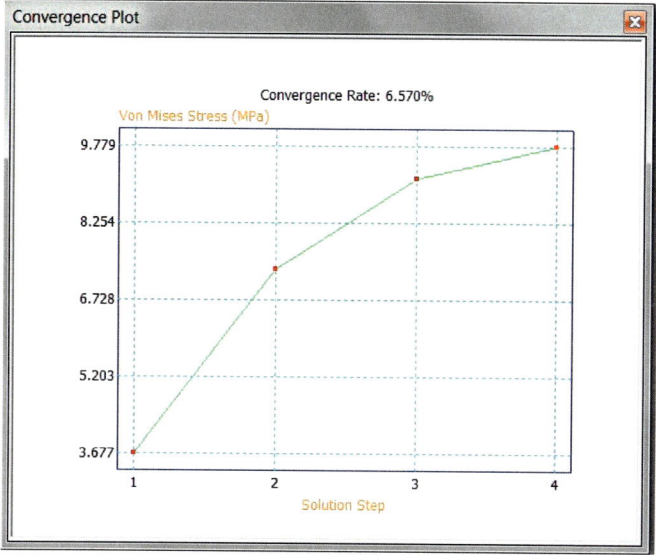

Every analysis goes through an automatic P-refinement. If the results have not converged, then H-refinement can be activated. The above example shows that the results have converged within four iterations - the first three being of P-refinement and the fourth being of H-refinement (for example, H-refinement set to 1). If the results do not converge then the H-refinement value can be further increased to 2, 3 or 4.

For parts, the first three convergence plot points are related to P-refinement.

For assemblies, the first two convergence plot points are related to P-refinement

Display tab

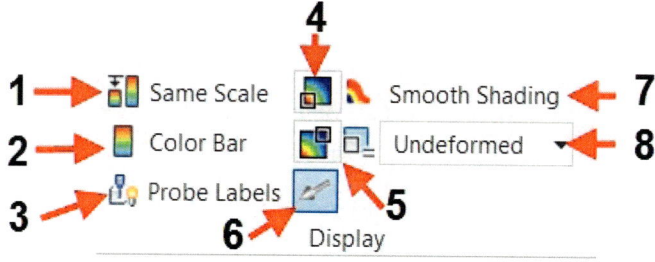

1. Apply Uniform Scale
2. Color Bar
3. Show Probe Labels
4. Show Maximum Value
5. Show Minimum Value
6. Show Boundary Conditions

SECTION 1 - Stress Analysis Essentials

CHAPTER 1
The Stress Analysis Environment

7. Display Results
8. Adjust Displacement Scale

Apply uniform scale

This is switched off by default and can be useful when carrying out a parametric optimization study. When activated, the color bar scale remains the same when viewing different configurations and thus allows you to compare results visually.

 The color bar is scaled based on the maximum and minimum values within the results.

 Use **Apply Uniform Scale** when viewing an isolated component within an assembly to see results in context of the whole assembly.

Color Bar

The color bar is probably the most important tool within the display panel and when effectively used can help you to understand the results with ease. It can be displayed in various locations in the graphic window using the position setting. The maximum and minimum threshold values can be altered by unchecking the maximum and minimum values.

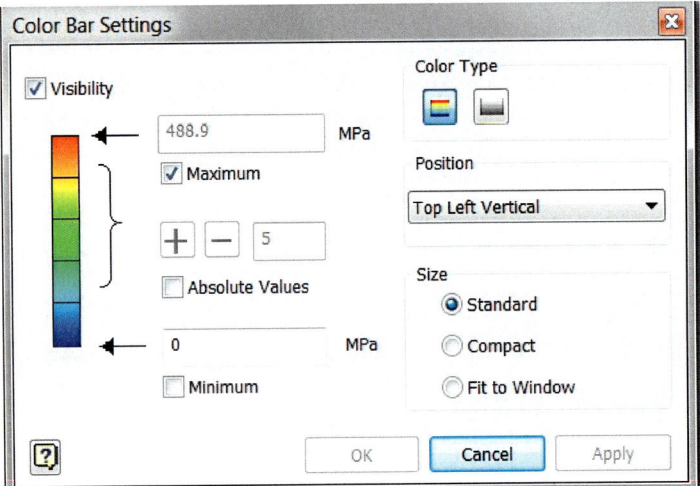

 The numbers of color legends can only be changed when contour shading is selected. Smooth shading by default will use the maximum number of color legends.

Alter maximum and minimum values to help isolate stress singularities.

Show probe labels
Displays all the probe labels created by the user.

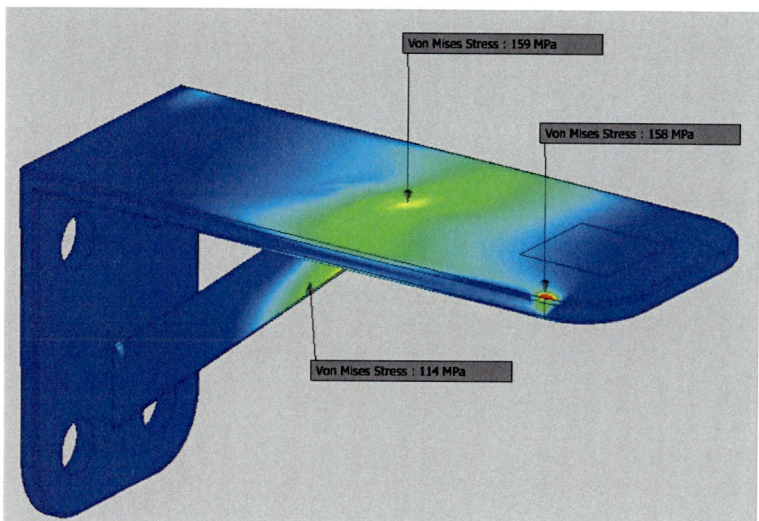

The position of the probe can be altered by right clicking the label and selecting edit position. This will help to identify whether the value has increased or decreased around the original selection area. Individual probes can be deleted by right clicking the probe and selecting delete probe.

Show Maximum and Minimum values
Displays the maximum and minimum values and their locations on the model as illustrated below.

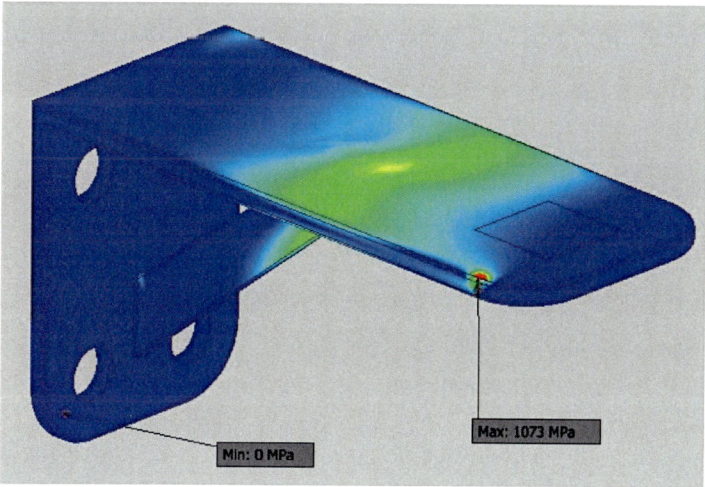

CHAPTER 1
The Stress Analysis Environment

Show boundary conditions
Displays all the boundary conditions, including the loads and constraints applied on the model.

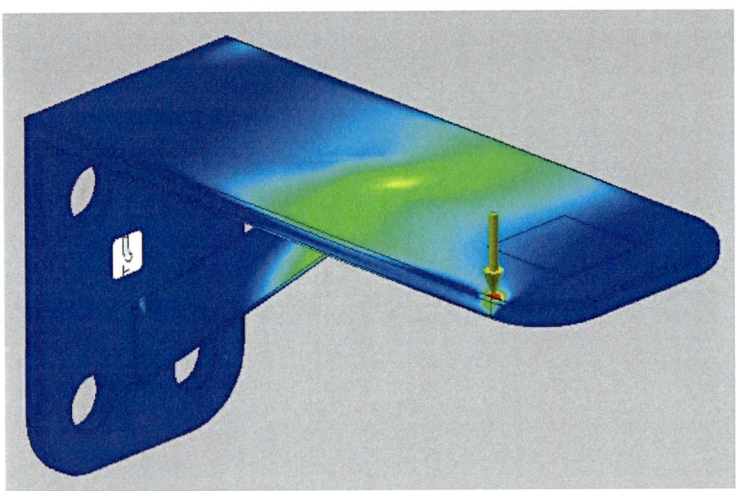

Display results
Here, you can decide whether you want **Smooth**, **Contour** and **No Shading** display.

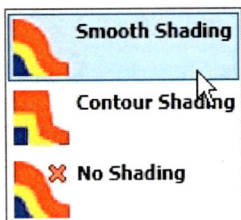

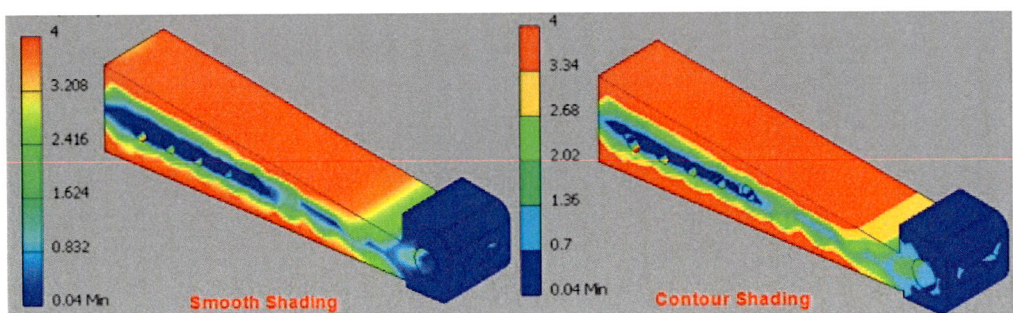

CHAPTER 1
The Stress Analysis Environment

Adjust displacement display

You can adjust the scale of the results to obtain a better indication of whether boundary conditions applied are correct.

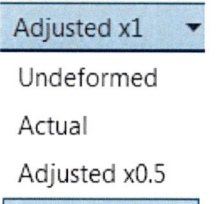

 Adjust the scale so that the deformation is visible before selecting animate results, as animations without visible deformation can be less visual.

Report tab

Report

Autodesk inventor stress analysis– in addition to standard html format – lets you create reports in mhtml (single web page) and rich text formats (Microsoft Word documents), making it very easy to customize the reports to specific requirements.

 Microsoft Word is required to generate the RTF file.

In addition to the ability to customize settings from the general, properties and simulation tabs from with the report generator dialogue box, there are now additional settings within the format tab.

Use dynamic content - Select to include size buttons for image width and buttons that you can click to collapse or expand the associated sections.

 Not available for the RTF format

CHAPTER 1
The Stress Analysis Environment

Create OLE Link - Select to create an OLE link from the model browser to the report. The report icon displays under the third party folder in the model browser. To edit the report, double click the icon or right-click and select edit.

 Not available for the HTML format

Stress Analysis Report

Analyzed File:	Coupling.ipt
Autodesk Inventor Version:	2017 (Build 210142000, 142)
Creation Date:	06/08/2016, 12:50
Study Author:	wasyou
Summary:	

⊞ **Project Info (iProperties)**

⊞ **No-convergence**

⊟ **Results-convergence**

General objective and settings:

Design Objective	Single Point
Study Type	Static Analysis
Last Modification Date	06/08/2016, 12:50
Detect and Eliminate Rigid Body Modes	Yes

Mesh settings:

Avg. Element Size (fraction of model diameter)	0.05
Min. Element Size (fraction of avg. size)	0.2
Grading Factor	1.5
Max. Turn Angle	60 deg
Create Curved Mesh Elements	No

⊞ **Material(s)**

⊞ **Operating conditions**

⊟ **Results**

⊞ Reaction Force and Moment on Constraints

⊞ Result Summary

⊟ **Figures**

⊟ Von Mises Stress

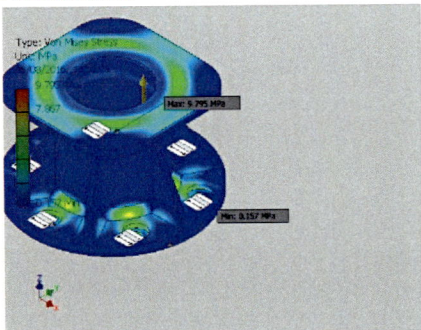

SECTION 1 - Stress Analysis Essentials

CHAPTER 1
The Stress Analysis Environment

Guide tab

The Guide is a useful tool for novice and intermediate users who want advice on certain aspects of study. The Guide tool is accessible from the analysis panel and by right-clicking loads, constraints, contacts and results guide.

Below is an example: the Constraints Guide

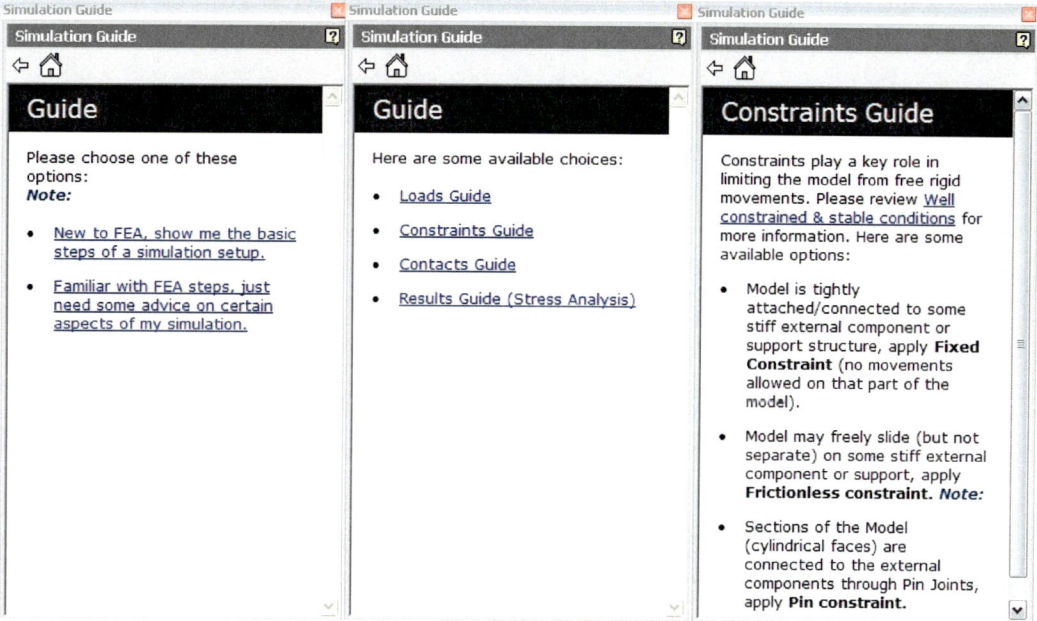

SECTION 1 - Stress Analysis Essentials

Settings tab

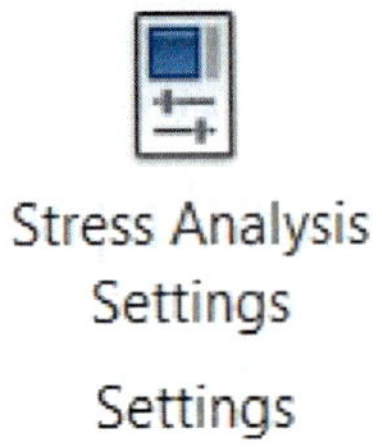

Stress Analysis Settings

Settings

Allows you to predefine settings for current and preceding analyses. Refer to the specific sections for a detailed explanation of the individual settings.

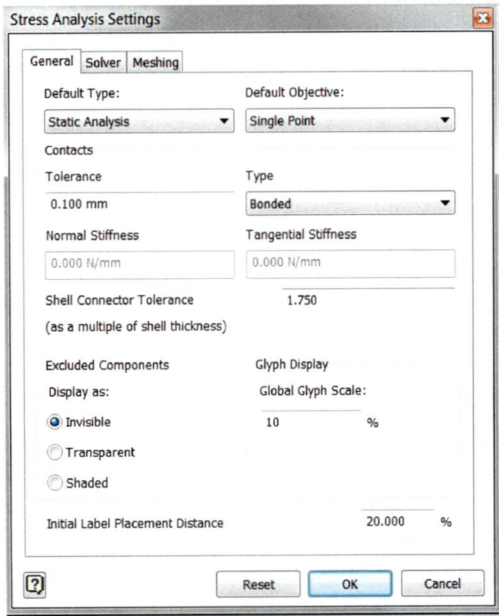

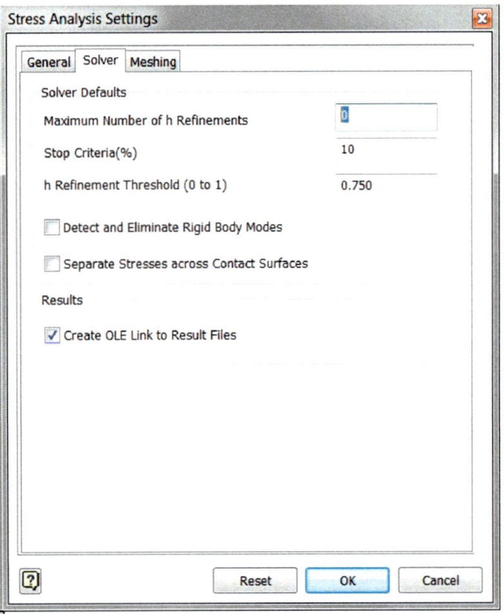

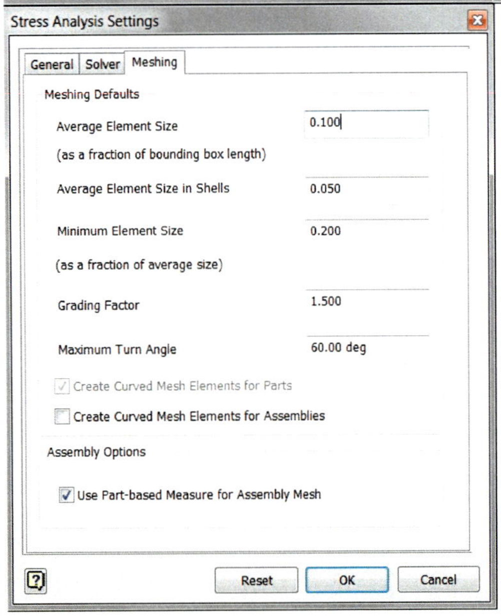

Section 2 - STRESS ANALYSIS
Design Problems
using SOLID ELEMENTS

DP1 – Cyclic Symmetry Analysis

Design of Industrial Centrifugal Fan Blades
(Design problem courtesy of Halifax Fan Ltd)

Key features and workflows introduced in this design problem

	Key Features/Workflows
1	Cyclic symmetry
2	Manual convergence of results

Introduction

Halifax Fan Ltd is one of the world's foremost manufacturers of industrial fans. They design and manufacture a full range of centrifugal fans from a wide range of materials, including mild and stainless steel, from their manufacturing operations in the UK and China. They supply a wide range of industrial customers, including power, pharmaceutical, chemical, nuclear, and marine markets all over the world.

Halifax Fan is fully BSI certified to BS EN ISO9001 – 2000 and manufactures fans to many industrial standards including API 673, API 560, Shell DEP, and ATEX. Many of these designs are engineered to meet the customer's exact requirements and, thus, the company offers a wide range of services on and off site, including stress relief laser shaft alignment, site performance testing, vibration analysis, consultation, problem solving, repairs, and energy testing. As a consequence of offering

CHAPTER 2
DP1 – Cyclic Symmetry Analysis

special bespoke solutions, Halifax is regularly asked by its customers to validate their designs prior to delivery.

Some of the typical requirements include determining the following:
- The maximum stress and deflection of the fan blade.
- The factor of safety of the new design.

In addition to the above requirements, the design criteria to be used for this design problem are as follows;
- Material to be used is either mild Steel or high strength low alloy *
- Factor of Safety required is 1.5
- Maximum deflection to be less than 0.5mm.
- Maximum blade thickness not to exceed 5mm.

* Halifax Fan actually use Carbon Steel to BS EN 10025 grade S275JR for their fans

Workflow of Design Problem 1

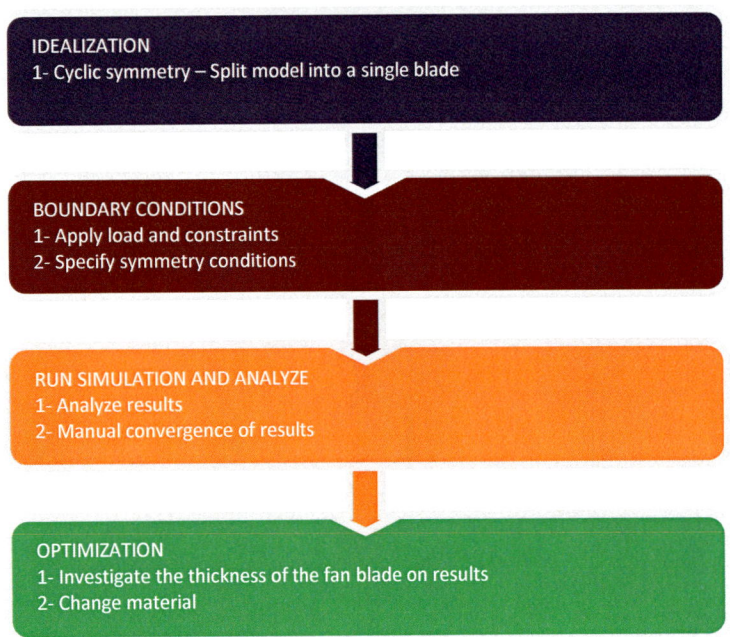

Idealization

Halifax Fans can range from simple small fans to large detailed fans. In the cases of large detailed fans, the size of the mesh can become very large and the time taken to analyze the results can become very lengthy.

Most fans comprise a number of similar blades and, when in operation, the deflection and stress induced in the blades are identical and for this reason it is only necessary to analyze one blade of the fan. This simplification approach is also referred to as cyclic symmetry and it's significantly reduces the model size, giving more scope to refine and analyze the results efficiently. Therefore, in the following steps, the fan model is split such that only one blade remains.

CHAPTER 2
DP1 – Cyclic Symmetry Analysis

Cyclic symmetry – Split model into a single blade

1. Open Fan.ipt

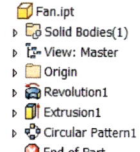
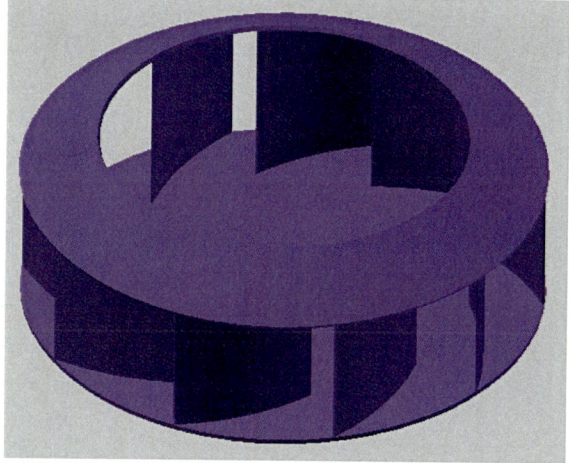

2. Create a new sketch on the YZ plane to the following dimensions

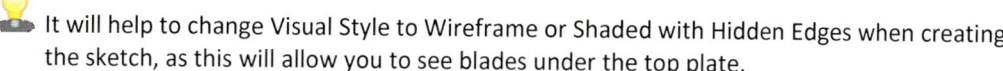

It will help to change Visual Style to Wireframe or Shaded with Hidden Edges when creating the sketch, as this will allow you to see blades under the top plate.

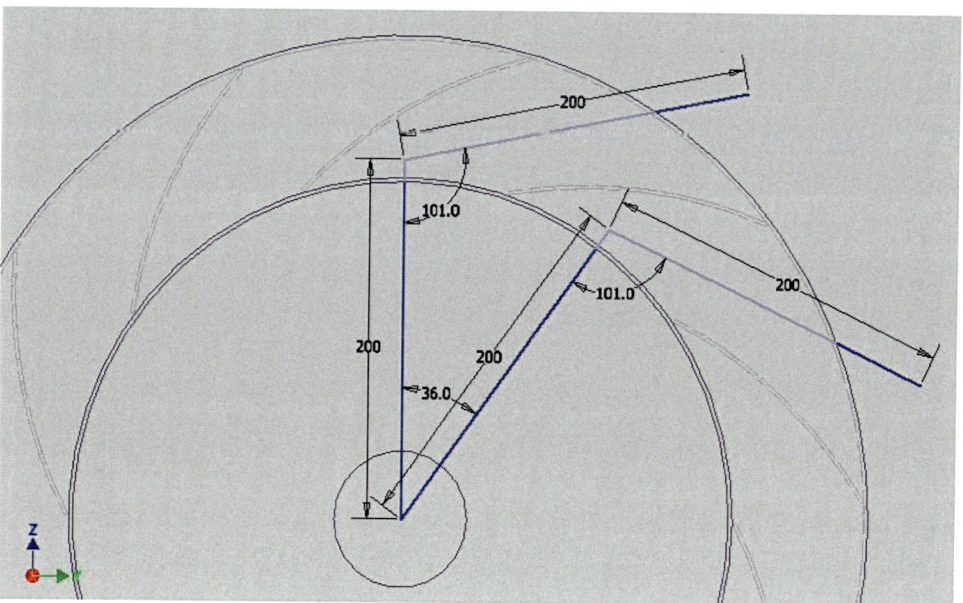

SECTION 2 - Stress Analysis Design Problems using Solid Elements

CHAPTER 2

DP1 – Cyclic Symmetry Analysis

As there are 10 blades, we need to the split the model by 36° angles.

$$\text{Angle of Split to create single blade } = \frac{360}{\text{Number of Blades}} = \frac{360}{10} = 36°$$

3. Select **Finish Sketch** > Select **Shaded** for visual style

4. Select **Split** from the Modify panel > Select **Sketch** created for split tool > Select the **Trim Solid** option > Change the side to **Remove** as shown below

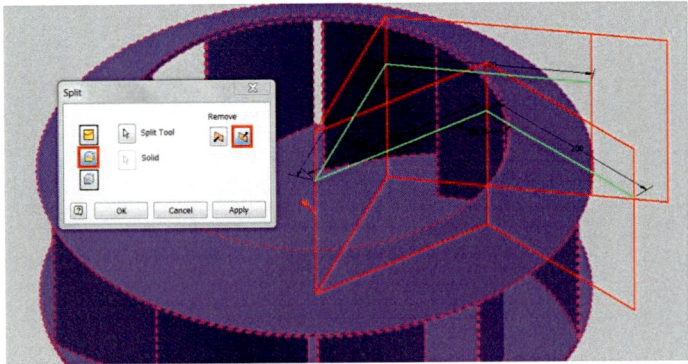

5. Click **OK**.

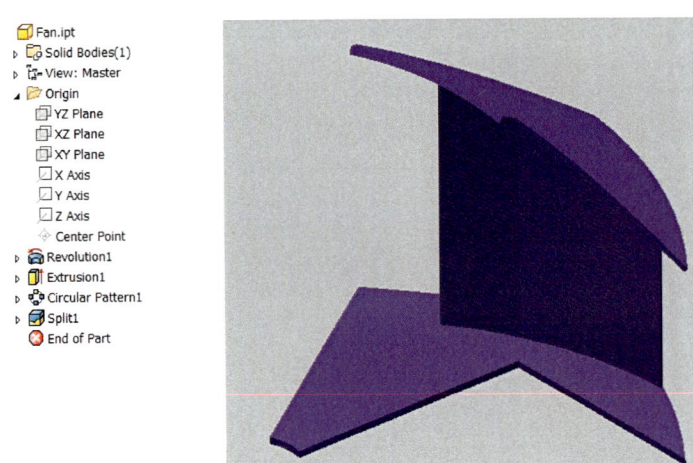

Now, in the next section, the boundary conditions will be applied to the single fan blade.

Boundary conditions

6. Select **Environments** tab > Select **Stress Analysis**

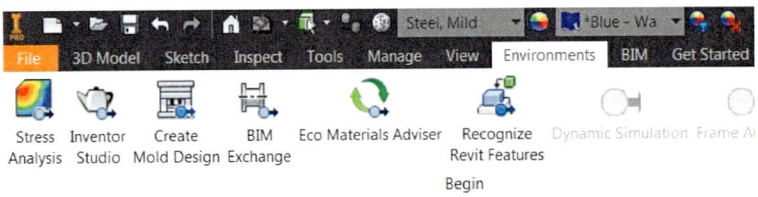

SECTION 2 - Stress Analysis Design Problems using Solid Elements

CHAPTER 2
DP1 – Cyclic Symmetry Analysis

Apply load and constraints

7. Select **Create Study** > Specify **Single-Blade** for Name > Click **OK**.

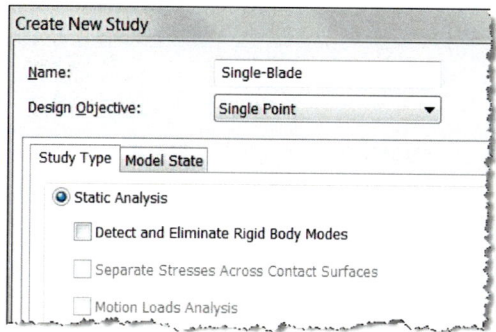

8. Select **Fixed Constraints** > Select the face as shown > Click **OK**

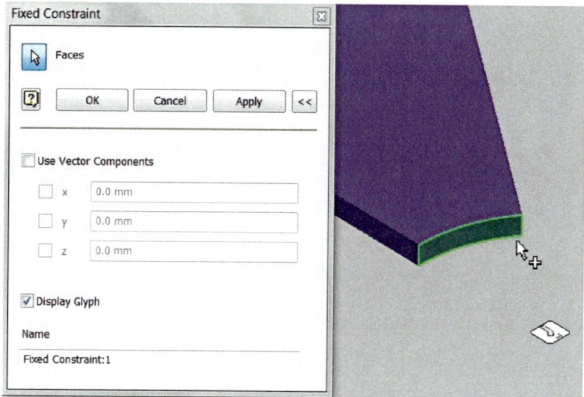

9. Select **Body Loads** > Select **Angular** tab > Select **Enable Angular Velocity and Acceleration** > Select the same face, as before, to specify the location of the fan speed > Specify **2000rpm** > Click **OK**

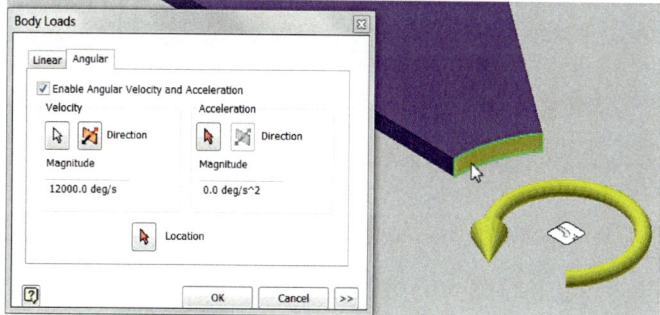

💡 Specifying rpm after the value will convert the value into the default degrees/s.

If the complete Fan was analyzed, the boundary condition specified in step 8 and 9 would suffice. However, as we are only modeling a single blade, we need to specify extra boundary conditions to the single blade to make it behave like a complete fan model. This can be achieved by applying frictional constraints on all faces that are created as a result of the split feature.

SECTION 2 - Stress Analysis Design Problems using Solid Elements

CHAPTER 2
DP1 – Cyclic Symmetry Analysis

Specify symmetry conditions

10. Select **Frictionless Constraints** > Select all eight faces as shown > Specify **Cyclic Symmetry** for Name > Click **OK**

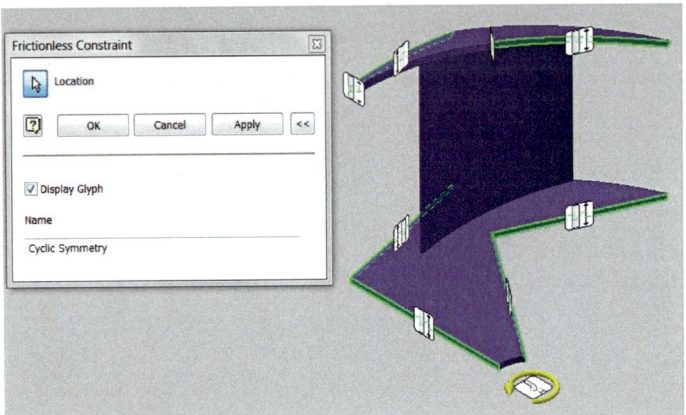

11. Select **Mesh View** > Deselect **Boundary Conditions**

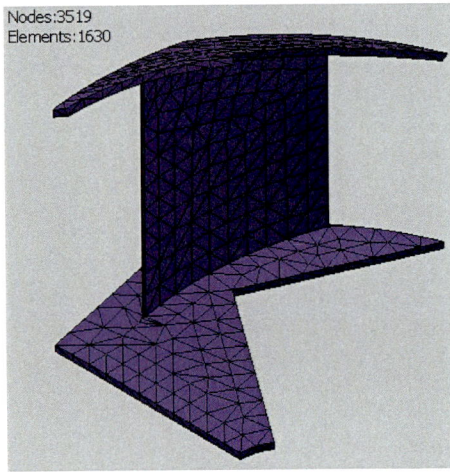

📝 A complete model would create many more elements, as illustrated below;

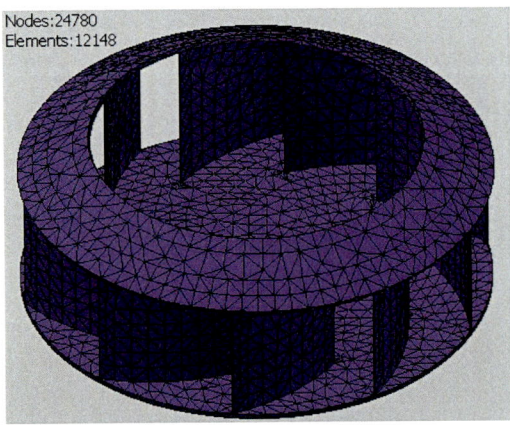

CHAPTER 2
DP1 – Cyclic Symmetry Analysis

Run simulation and analyze

12. Select **Simulate** > Select **Run**

13. Select **Undeformed** from Adjust Displacement Display > Deselect **Mesh View** > Select **Maximum Value** (248.3 MPa)

📝 Stress singularities will appear at the blade and plate interface due to sudden geometrical discontinuities and will be ignored as the area of interest is in the middle of the blades.

📝 Stress singularites may also occur in the area of the split faces and can be ignored as they would have not appeared if the complete fan would have been analyzed.

14. Select **Color Bar** > Unselect **Maximum** > Specify **200** MPa > Click **OK**

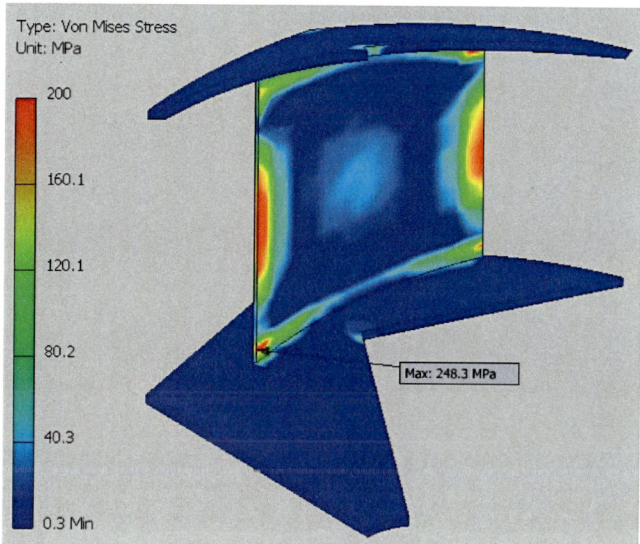

💡 Use Color bar to visually enhance the stress display in the area of interest

As we are interested in the middle of the blade, we can use Probe to display stresses in the area of interest to us.

💡 Zoom into the area of interest before selecting the area of in the Probe

> **IMPORTANT** – The exact stress value of Probe is dependent on the location clicked; hence, the value may slightly differ

CHAPTER 2
DP1 – Cyclic Symmetry Analysis

15. Select **Probe** > Select in the middle of the blade at the front and rear > Deselect **Probe** to end Probe command

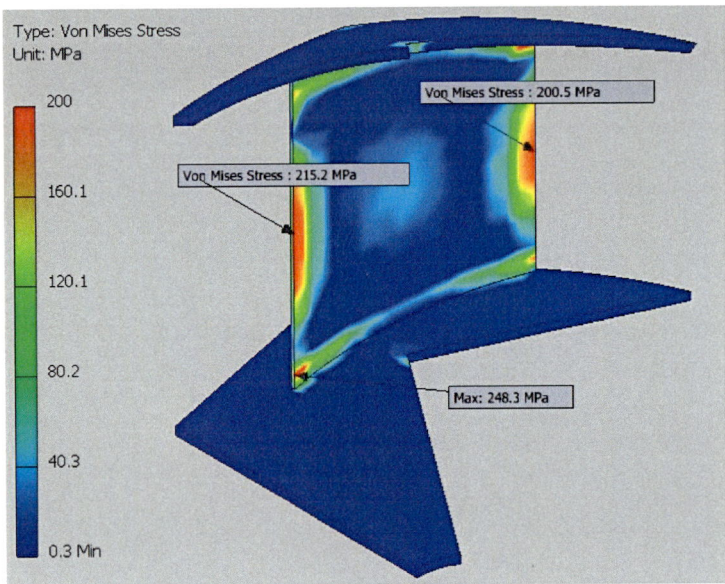

Below is stress plot of a complete model, illustrating similar stresses in all the blades of the fan

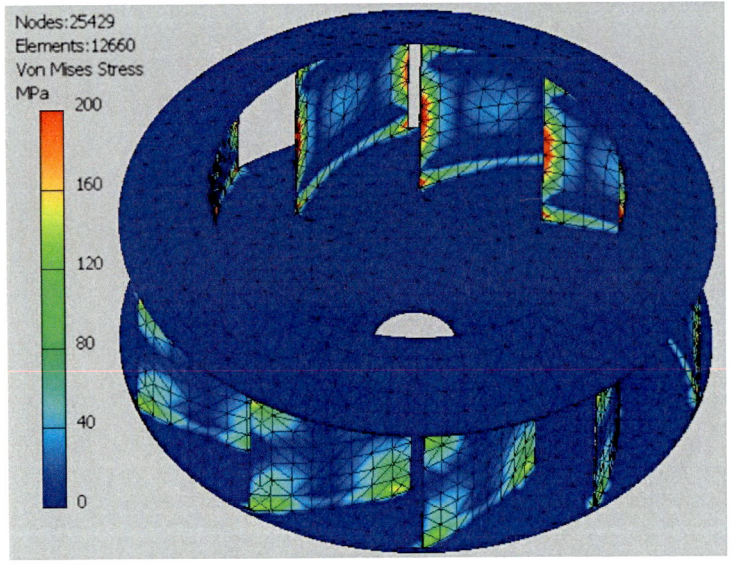

Manual convergence of results

Now, we will increase the mesh to see whether the stress results changes in the middle of the blades.

16. Select **Mesh Settings** > Change Average Element Size to **0.05** > Click **OK**

17. Right click **Mesh** > Select **Update Mesh** > Select **Mesh View**

CHAPTER 2
DP1 – Cyclic Symmetry Analysis

📝 Reducing the average element size can have a significant impact on the size of the model and also will take longer run.

📝 Your element count values may slightly differ as we are using an average element size value across the model.

Reducing the average element size from 0.1 to 0.05 has increased the number of elements to 6592. This has increased the original mesh by 401%. So be careful when deciding to reduce the average element size by half as this will not necessarily increase the number of elements by the same ratio.

18. Rerun **Simulation** > Deselect **Mesh View**

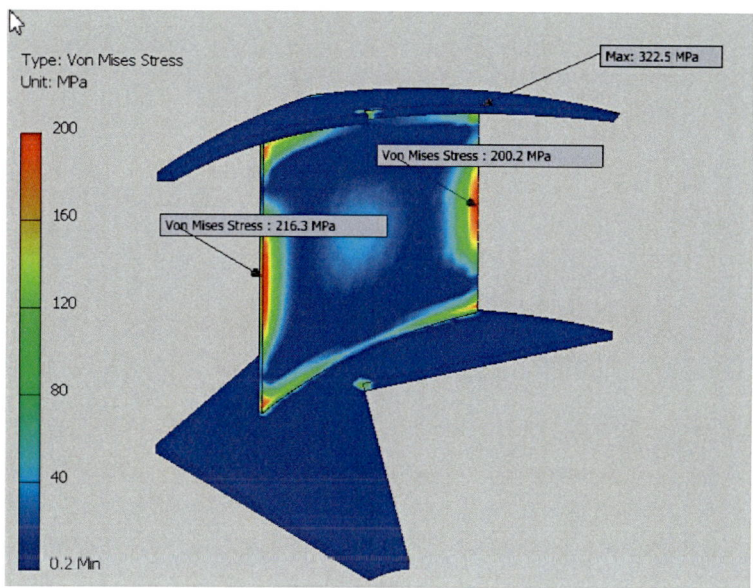

Although the maximum stress has increased to 322.5 MPa, the stress in the middle of the blades, front and back, has hardly changed, less than 1%.

📝 Use your **Probe** values for comparison.

To confirm whether this stress in the middle of the blade has converged, we will rerun one more analysis with a smaller element size.

19. Select **Mesh Settings** > Change average Element Size to **0.025** > Click **OK**

20. Right click **Mesh** > Select **Update Mesh** > Select **Mesh View**

Reducing the average element size from 0.1 to 0.025 has increased the number of element to 36513. This is an increase by 2125% from the default mesh size.

CHAPTER 2
DP1 – Cyclic Symmetry Analysis

A full model with a similar mesh size of 0.025 will create 184,704 elements as illustrated.

21. Run **Simulation** > Deselect **Mesh View**

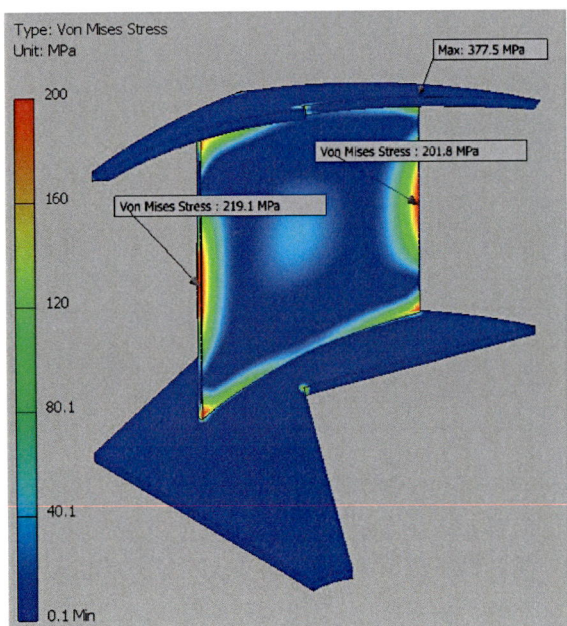

📝 Ignore the maximum stress as it is occurring on the top plate and blade interface due to geometrical discontinuities leading to stress singularities.

The maximum value in the middle of the blade has slightly increased. Since this increase is less than 2% we can confidently say that the results have converged in the area of interest.

CHAPTER 2
DP1 – Cyclic Symmetry Analysis

22. Deselect **Probe Labels** > Double click **Displacement** from the **Stress Analysis** browser

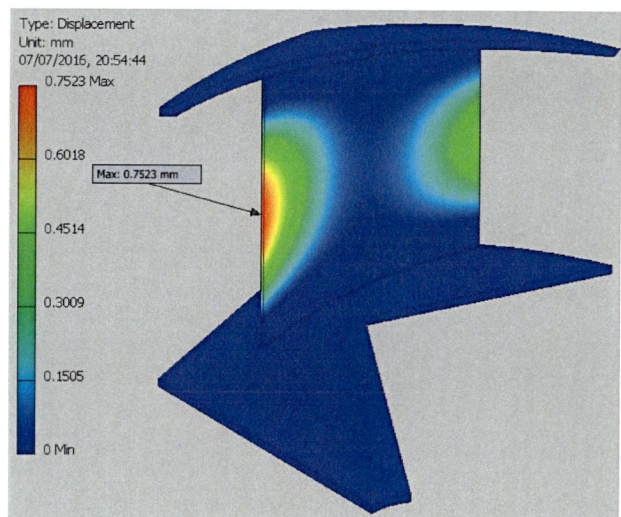

The maximum displacements plots for mesh settings of 0.1 and 0.05 are 0.7370 and 0.7434 respectively. The difference in value between 0.7523 and 0.7370 is less than 2% meaning we can also treat displacement results as being converged.

23. Double Click **Safety Factor** > Select **Probe Labels** > Deselect **Maximum Value**

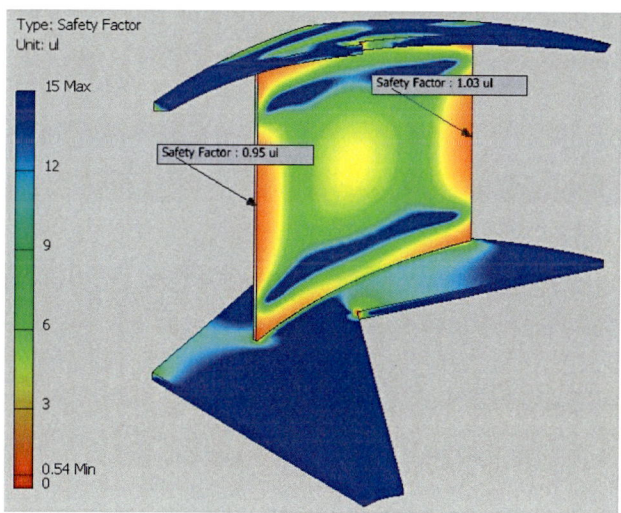

Based on the stress in the middle of the blade (219.1MPa), we have a safety factor below 1, which suggests that the design has failed as the design limit is 1.5.

$$\textbf{Factor of Safety} = \frac{Yield\ Limit}{Calculated\ Stress} = \frac{207}{219.1} = 0.945$$

In the next section, we will perform an optimization study to meet the design limits.

SECTION 2 - Stress Analysis Design Problems using Solid Elements

CHAPTER 2
DP1 – Cyclic Symmetry Analysis

Optimization

In this section, we will alter blade thickness from 2 to 5mm using the parametric study and manually alter the material from mild steel to high strength steel.

24. Right Click **Single-Blade** > Select **Copy Study**

25. Right Click copied **Single-Blade:1** > Select **Edit Study Properties**

26. Specify **Blade-Optimization** for **Name** > Select **Parametric Dimension** for Design Objective > Click **OK**

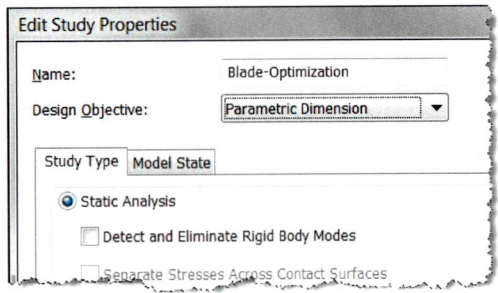

This will, now, allow us to carry out a parametric study

Investigate the effect of the thickness of the fan blade

27. Right Click **Fan.ipt** in the browser > Select **Show Parameters**

28. Select the **bladethickness** user parameter > Click **OK**

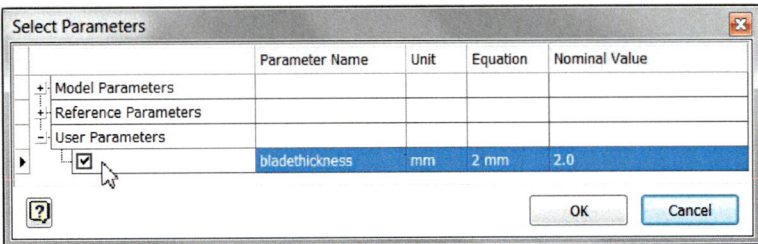

29. Select **Parametric Table** > Double Click to the left or right side of the table to undock it

30. Right Click in the Design Constraints row > Select **Add Design Constraint**

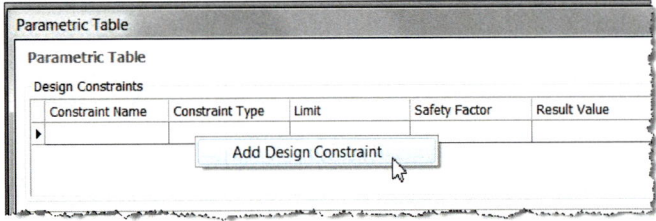

CHAPTER 2
DP1 – Cyclic Symmetry Analysis

31. Select **Von Mises Stress** from the Results Component list > Click **OK**

32. Repeat step 30 to add **Displacement** design constraints

33. Change the Constraint Type for **Max Von Mises Stress** to **Upper Limit** > Specify limit as **207**

📝 The yield limit of Mild Steel used in this design problem is 207 MPa

34. Change the Constraint Type for **Max Displacement** to **Upper Limit** > Specify limit as **0.5**

35. Specify **2-5:4** in the bladethickness Values field

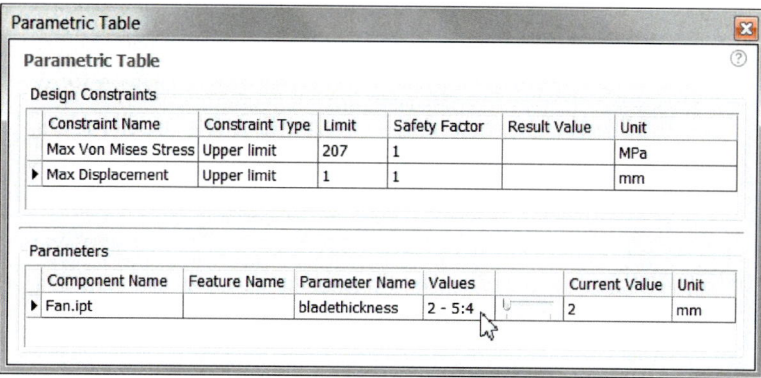

📝 This will generate values 3, 4, 5 in addition to the base value of 2

36. Right Click anywhere in the parameter row and select **Generate Range Configurations**

37. Move slider to see the blade changing its thickness > Specify **2** for **Current Value** > Click **Close**

38. Select **Mesh Settings** > Specify **0.05** for Average Element Size > Click **OK**

39. Select **Mesh View**

40. Select **Simulate** > Run **Simulation**

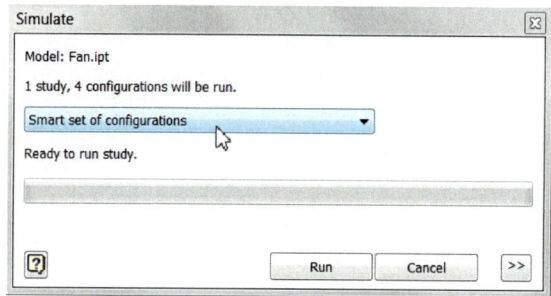

📝 This will run four analyzes for blade thickness values of 2, 3, 4 and 5

SECTION 2 - Stress Analysis Design Problems using Solid Elements

CHAPTER 2
DP1 – Cyclic Symmetry Analysis

41. Select **Undeformed** from Adjust Displacement Display > Deselect **Mesh View** > Select **Contour Shading**

42. Select **Parametric Table**

The red icon indicates unacceptable parameters based on the constraint limits. The Max Von Mises Stress value is also misleading as this value represents stress singularities in the model. To synchronize the stress limit with the model, change the color bar range between 0 and 259. This will provide us a value of 207 MPa on the legend scale. Meaning any value over 207 MPa will be displayed as red.

43. Select **Color Bar** > Specify **259** for **Maximum** value > Select **5** for number of value on legend scale > Click **OK**

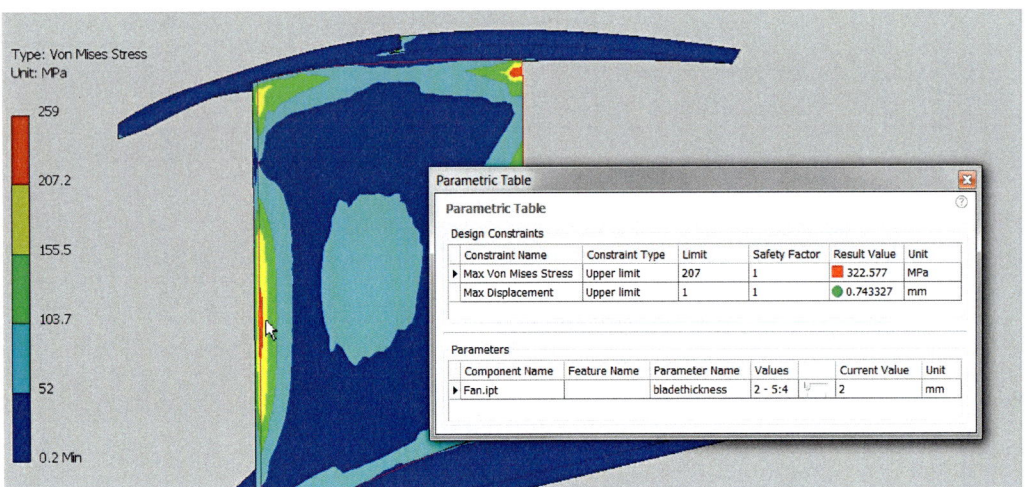

Now compare the color plots as you move the slider between 2 and 5. From the color plots, blade thickness values 3, 4 and 5 do not show any red color in the blades, indicating low stress, with thickness 5 showing the least stress.

44. Move the slider to read a value of **5** > Select **Close**

We will now use the probe to determine the exact value of stress in the middle of blade

45. Select **Probe** and select the position on the blade showing the highest stress location > **Deselect** Probe

46. Double click **Safety Factor**

CHAPTER 2
DP1 – Cyclic Symmetry Analysis

81

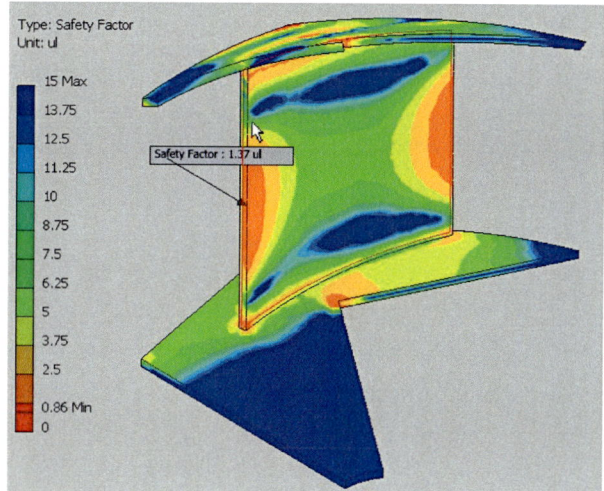

The safety factor value of 1.37 is still below the design limit of 1.5, so we will now assign a new material.

Change material

47. Select **Assign Material**

48. Select **Steel, High Strength Low Alloy** from the **Override Material** list > Click **OK**

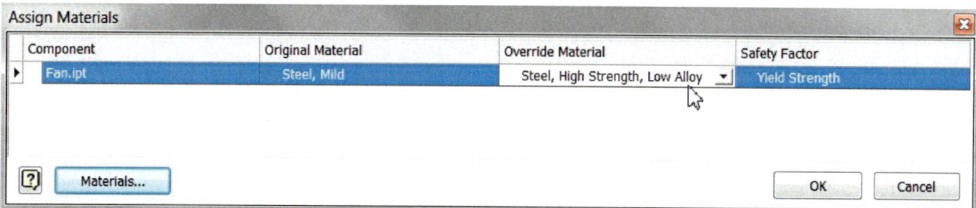

49. Select **Parametric Table** > Move the slider to read **Current Value** of **5**

50. Select **Simulate** > Change study to **Current configuration only** > Select **Run**

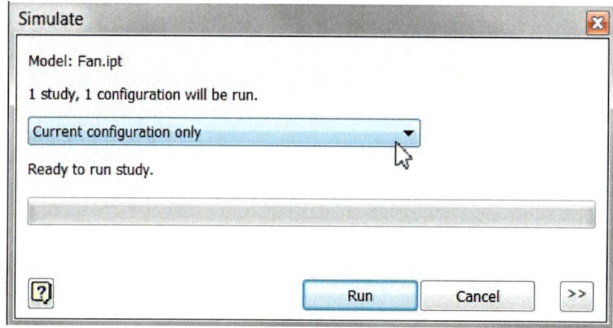

SECTION 2 - Stress Analysis Design Problems using Solid Elements

CHAPTER 2
DP1 – Cyclic Symmetry Analysis

51. Double Click **Safety Factor**

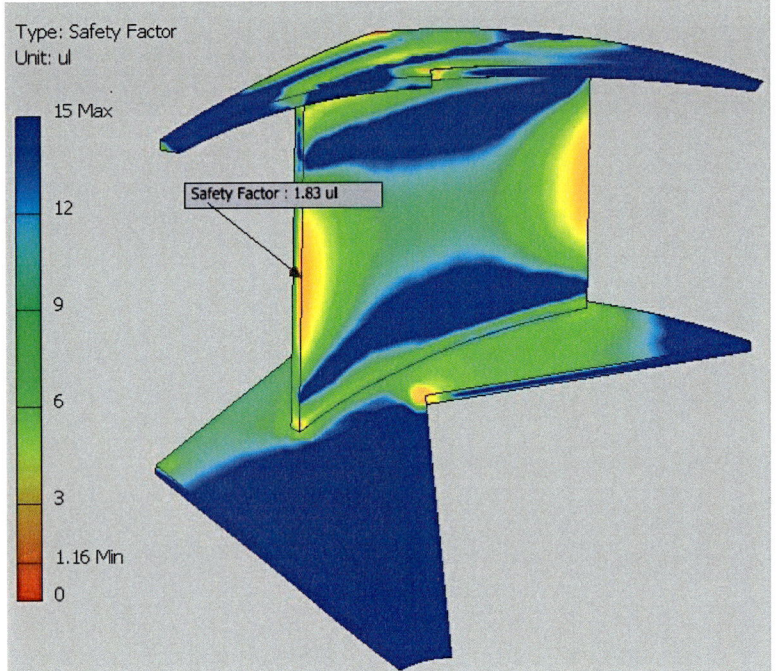

Now, by changing the material, we have reached our goal of having a safety factor of 1.83 which is above 1.5 and a max displacement below 0.5 mm.

Ignore maximum stress as it is occurring on the top plate; in reality, this does not exist. Refer to the stress display of the complete fan shown earlier.

52. Close the file

DP2 – Assembly Optimization

Structural Optimization of a Lifting Mechanism
(Design Problem courtesy of Unipart Rail Ltd)

Key features and workflows introduced in this design problem

	Key Features/Workflows
1	Assembly contacts - Manual and Automatic
2	Local mesh refinement
3	Planar X,Y,Z stress plots
4	Parametric optimization

Introduction

Unipart Rail is part of Unipart Group, one of Europe's leading independent logistic companies, employing more than 9,000 people worldwide with annual turnover of more than £1.1 billion.

Unipart Rail combines extensive engineering, logistic, and manufacturing experience with industry-leading supply chain & lean expertise.

Bogie Secondary Suspension System

CHAPTER 3
DP2 – Assembly Optimization

Autodesk Inventor is used within the design & development division of Unipart Rail to produce, validate and document complete digital prototypes. In addition, the stress analysis is used extensively, making it possible to optimize, validate, and predict how designs will work under real-world conditions, before the product or part is even built.

Within Unipart Rail's bogie overhaul facility at Doncaster, UK, there is a requirement for the design of innovative jigs and fixtures in order to facilitate lean processes. One such requirement identified is the need for a lifting devise to handle the secondary suspension units fitted to the rail vehicle bogies as illustrated below. There are two secondary suspension units per bogie, each weighing 78Kg.

In this design problem, we need to determine the structural integrity of the lifting mechanism in addition to the following:

1. The maximum working stress in the key components.
2. The maximum deflection.
3. How to reduce the overall weight.

- Material to be used is mild steel
- Factor of Safety to be at least 4

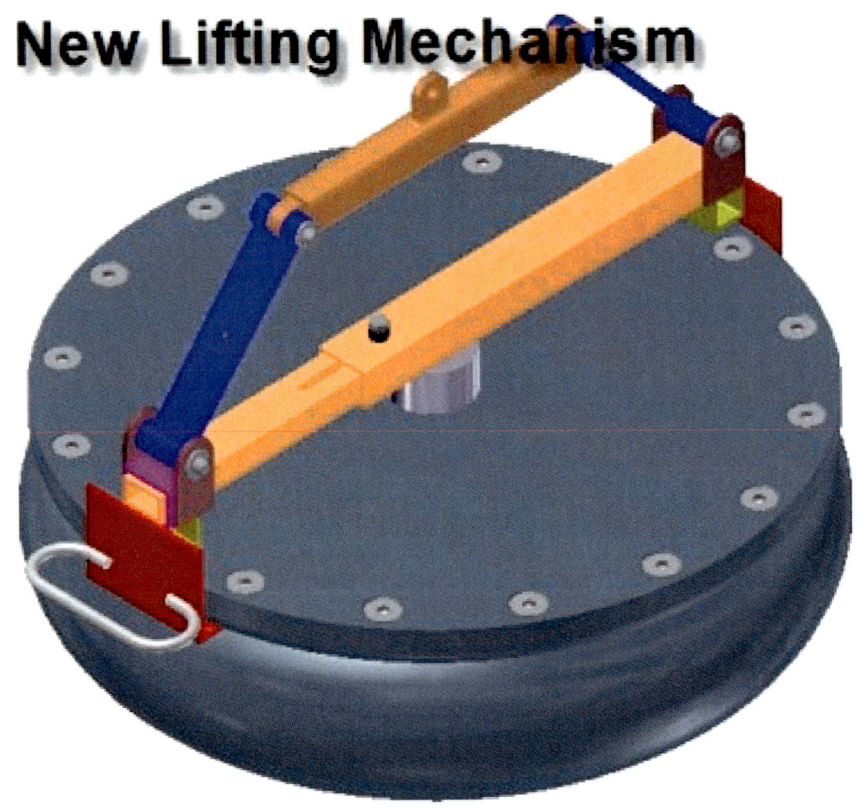

CHAPTER 3
DP2 – Assembly Optimization

Workflow of Design Problem 2

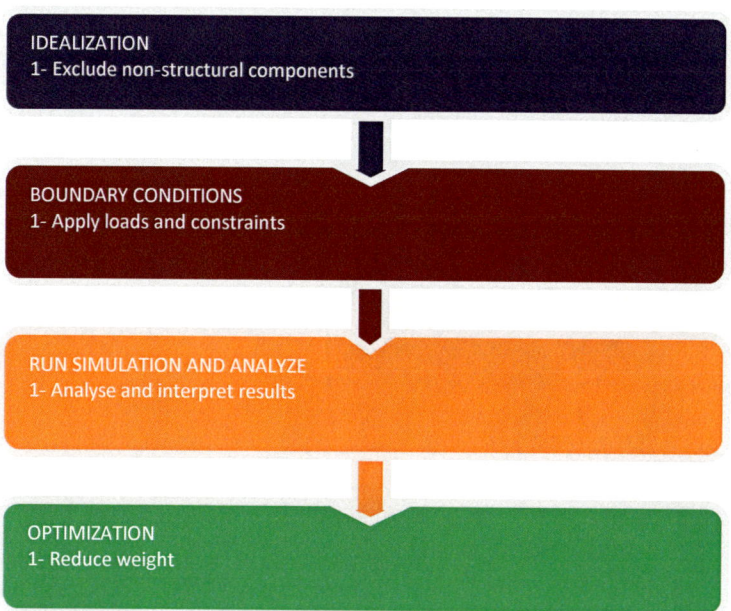

Idealization

In this stage of the FEA workflow, the components and assemblies need to be simplified in terms of having nonstructural features, including holes and fillets to be suppressed. In this design problem, most of the non-critical features have already been suppressed.

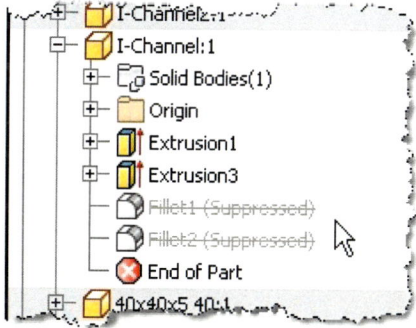

Further, nonstructural components will not be suppressed but instead will be excluded from the simulation within the Stress Analysis environment.

CHAPTER 3
DP2 – Assembly Optimization

1. Open Airbag lifting jig.iam

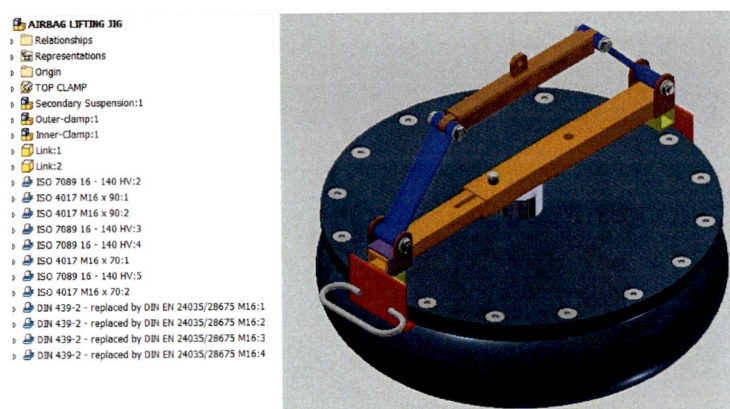

2. Select **Environments** tab > Select **Stress Analysis**

3. Select **Create Study** > Specify **Optimization-Study** for Name > Select **Parametric Dimension** for Design Objective > Specify **0.3mm** for Tolerance > Click **OK**

📝 Changing Tolerance to 0.3mm will create contacts between faces of adjacent components that have gaps of 0.3mm or less.

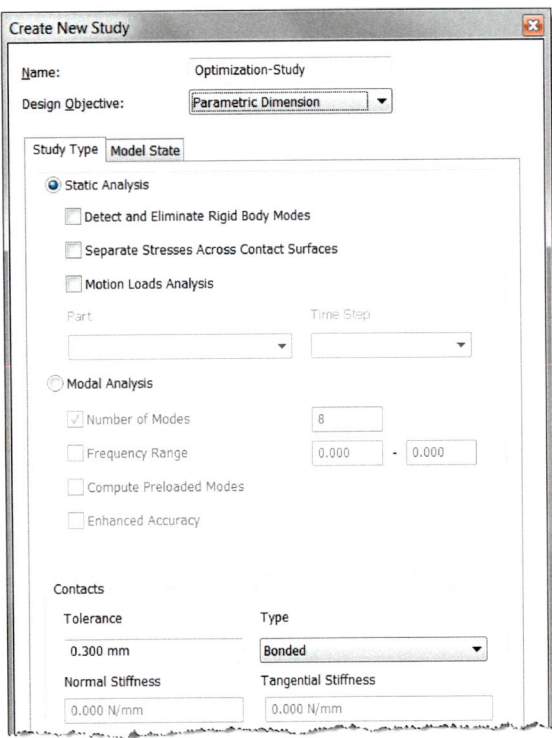

💡 Excluding non-structural components can further simplify the model, including reducing the number of contacts created.

CHAPTER 3
DP2 – Assembly Optimization

4. Select the following components > Right Click > Select **Exclude from Study**

- Secondary Suspension
- BOSS (Within the Outer-clamp subassembly)
- ISO 4018 M12 x 30 (Within the Outer-clamp subassembly)
- Handle (Within the Inner-Clamp subassembly)
- ISO 7089 16 -140 HV:2
- ISO 7089 16 -140 HV:3
- ISO 7089 16 -140 HV:4
- ISO 7089 16 -140 HV:5
- DIN 439-2 – replaced by DIN EN 24035/28675 M16:1
- DIN 439-2 – replaced by DIN EN 24035/28675 M16:2
- DIN 439-2 – replaced by DIN EN 24035/28675 M16:3
- DIN 439-2 – replaced by DIN EN 24035/28675 M16:4

The excluded components will now become transparent. At this stage, we can make the components invisible by altering the **Stress Analysis Settings**.

5. Select **Stress Analysis Settings** > Select **Invisible** for Excluded Components > Click **OK**

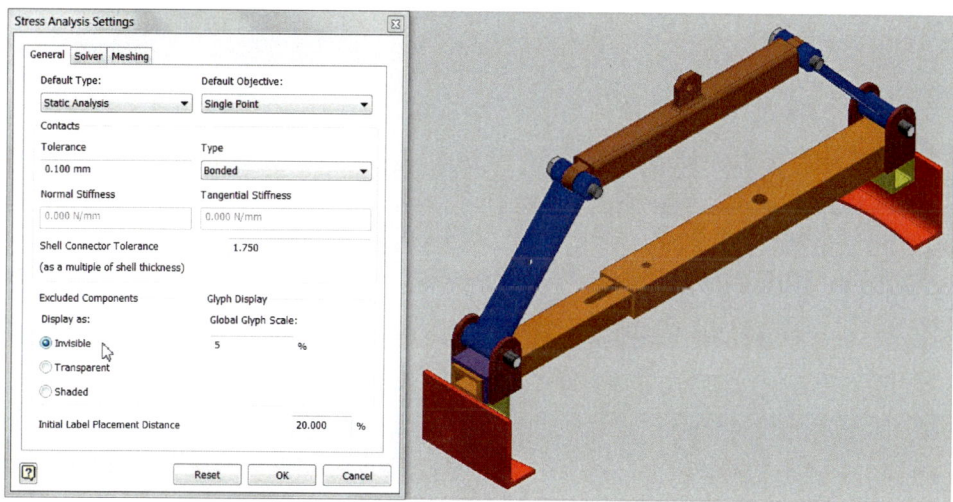

The next stage is to apply boundary conditions including loads, restraints and materials.

Boundary Conditions

The primary goal of this design problem is to determine the structural integrity of the new design to lift the secondary suspension. We will apply its mass as a force on the new design as it is excluded from the simulation. The following will be used to convert mass to force:

$$Force = Mass \times Acceleration$$

Were; Mass of unit is 78Kg & Acceleration (Gravity) = 10m/s² (Actual value is 9.81m/s²)

Therefore, $Force = 78 \times 10 = 780N$

CHAPTER 3
DP2 – Assembly Optimization

6. Select **Force** > Select faces as shown > Specify **780** for Magnitude > Click **OK**

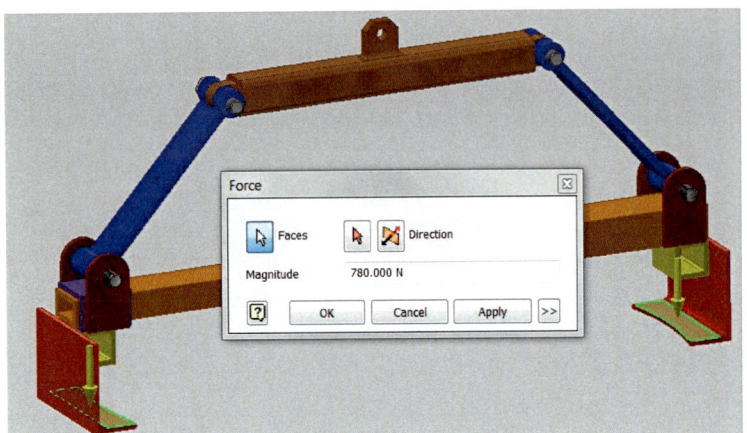

Selecting both separate faces, using the same force command, will split the force equally to 390N on each face. Plus in reality, the weight of the suspension unit will be equally distributed through the new lifting mechanism design.

7. Select **Fixed constraints** > Select the internal hole of top clamp, as shown > Click **OK**

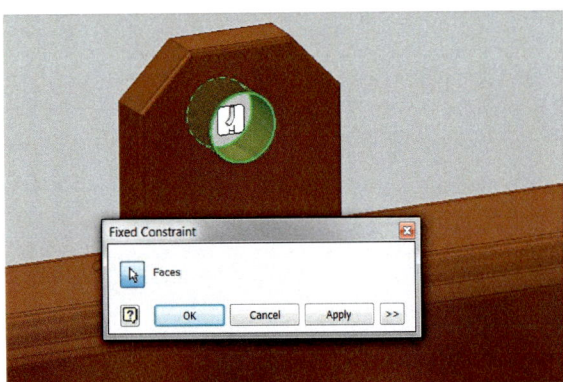

8. Select **Automatic** from the Contacts panel. This will create 32 contacts in total

 To easily identify contacts created between components, it is best to expand the components and subassemblies within the browser as shown below.

From further analyzing the contacts we can see there is a contact between the bolt head and the adjoining plate or link arm, for all bolts. We need to suppress these as in reality these bolts will not be fixed to the plate or link arm. In addition the loading is vertical and suppressing these contacts

CHAPTER 3
DP2 – Assembly Optimization

will transfer all load to the bolt shanks, worst case. In addition to these bolt contacts there are additional contacts which need to be suppressed.

 You cannot delete automatic contacts.

9. Right Click Bonded contacts 1 and 2 for the top two bolts > Select Suppress

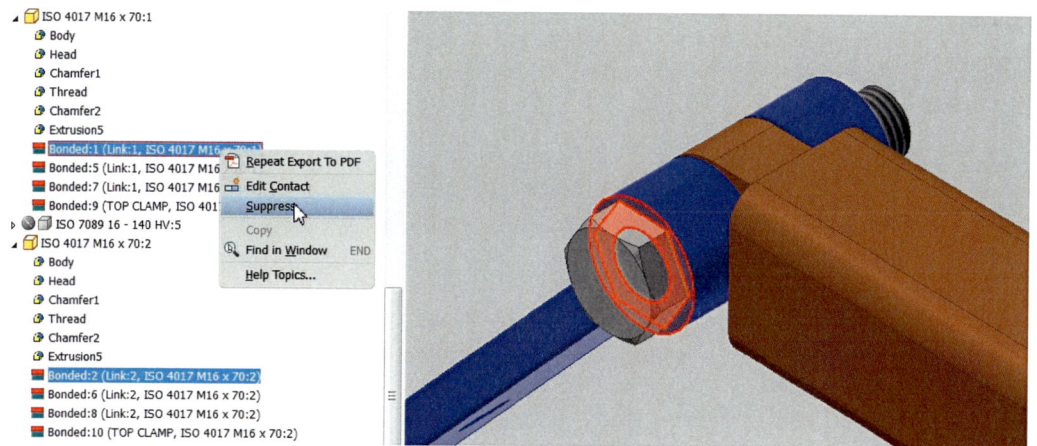

10. Right Click Bonded contacts 23 and 24 for the bottom two bolts > Select Suppress

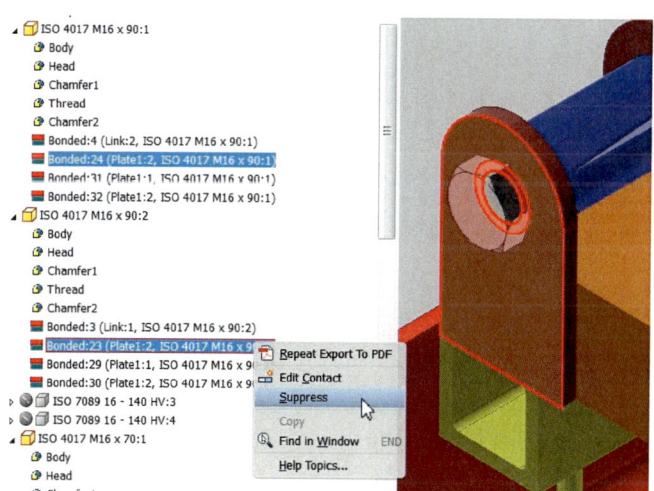

SECTION 2 - Stress Analysis Design Problems using Solid Elements

CHAPTER 3
DP2 – Assembly Optimization

11. Expand Outer-clamp:1 > Expand the 40x40x5 40:1 component > Right Click Bonded contacts 25 & 26 contacts > Select **Suppress**.

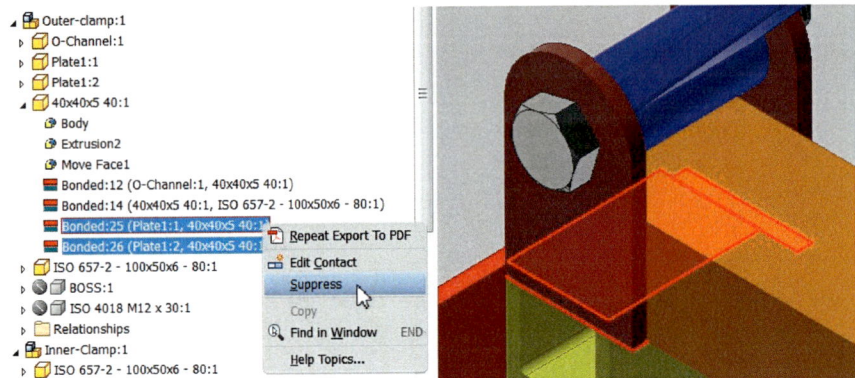

Repeat step 11 for the clamp on the other side.

12. Expand Inner-clamp:1 > Expand the 40x40x5 40:1 component > Right Click Bonded contacts 27 & 28 > Select **Suppress**.

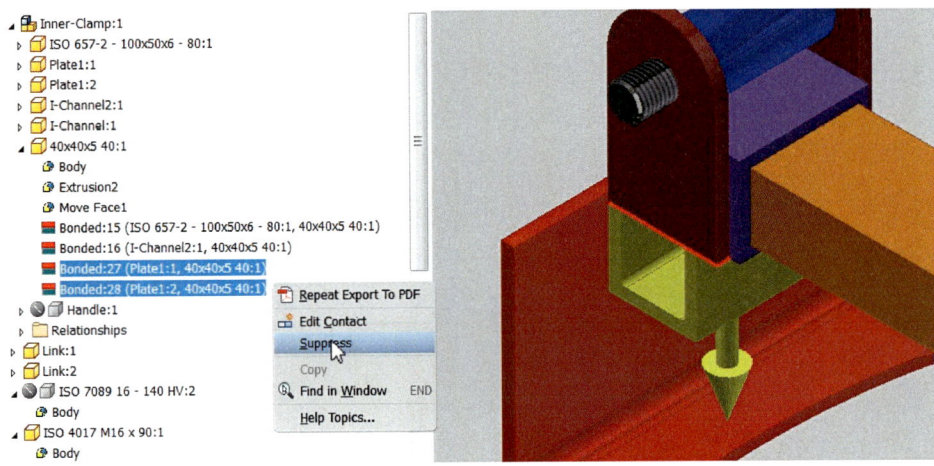

In the following steps, all bonded contacts associated with the four bolts will be changed to sliding no separation contact. This will simulate the behavior of bolts correctly.

13. Right click all contacts associated with the 4 bolts, 12 in total > Select **Edit Contacts** > Select **Sliding/No separation** for contact type > Click **OK**

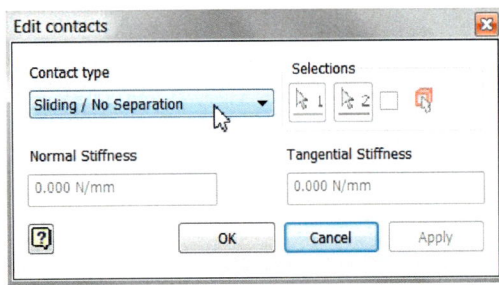

CHAPTER 3
DP2 – Assembly Optimization

The following contacts should now be created in.

- **Bonded**
  - Bonded:1 (Link:1, ISO 4017 M16 x 70:1)
  - Bonded:2 (Link:2, ISO 4017 M16 x 70:2)
  - Bonded:11 (O-Channel:1, Plate1:2)
  - Bonded:12 (O-Channel:1, 40x40x5 40:1)
  - Bonded:13 (O-Channel:1, Plate1:1)
  - Bonded:14 (40x40x5 40:1, ISO 657-2 - 100x50x6 - 80:1)
  - Bonded:15 (ISO 657-2 - 100x50x6 - 80:1, 40x40x5 40:1)
  - Bonded:16 (I-Channel2:1, 40x40x5 40:1)
  - Bonded:17 (I-Channel2:1, I-Channel:1)
  - Bonded:18 (I-Channel2:1, I-Channel:1)
  - Bonded:19 (I-Channel2:1, I-Channel:1)
  - Bonded:20 (I-Channel2:1, I-Channel:1)
  - Bonded:21 (Plate1:2, I-Channel2:1)
  - Bonded:22 (Plate1:1, I-Channel2:1)
  - Bonded:23 (Plate1:2, ISO 4017 M16 x 90:2)
  - Bonded:24 (Plate1:2, ISO 4017 M16 x 90:1)
  - Bonded:25 (Plate1:1, 40x40x5 40:1)
  - Bonded:26 (Plate1:2, 40x40x5 40:1)
  - Bonded:27 (Plate1:1, 40x40x5 40:1)
  - Bonded:28 (Plate1:2, 40x40x5 40:1)
- **Sliding / No Separation**
  - Sliding / No Separation:1 (Link:1, ISO 4017 M16 x 90:2)
  - Sliding / No Separation:2 (Link:2, ISO 4017 M16 x 90:1)
  - Sliding / No Separation:3 (Link:1, ISO 4017 M16 x 70:1)
  - Sliding / No Separation:4 (Link:2, ISO 4017 M16 x 70:2)
  - Sliding / No Separation:5 (Link:1, ISO 4017 M16 x 70:1)
  - Sliding / No Separation:6 (Link:2, ISO 4017 M16 x 70:2)
  - Sliding / No Separation:7 (TOP CLAMP, ISO 4017 M16 x 70:1)
  - Sliding / No Separation:8 (TOP CLAMP, ISO 4017 M16 x 70:2)
  - Sliding / No Separation:9 (Plate1:1, ISO 4017 M16 x 90:2)
  - Sliding / No Separation:10 (Plate1:2, ISO 4017 M16 x 90:2)
  - Sliding / No Separation:11 (Plate1:1, ISO 4017 M16 x 90:1)
  - Sliding / No Separation:12 (Plate1:2, ISO 4017 M16 x 90:1)

We now need to create a bonded contacts between I-Channel:1 and O-Channel:1 components, as no contacts have been created between these components. This is because the gap between them is 1 mm, which is higher than the default 0.3 mm contact setting. At this stage, we can edit the study properties and change the contact tolerance to 1mm, which will create additional contacts between I-Channel:1 and O-Channel:1.

Alternatively we can create the contacts manually and for the following steps the contact will be created manually.

CHAPTER 3
DP2 – Assembly Optimization

14. Select **Manual Contact** > Select faces of I-Channel and O-Channel as shown > Click **OK**

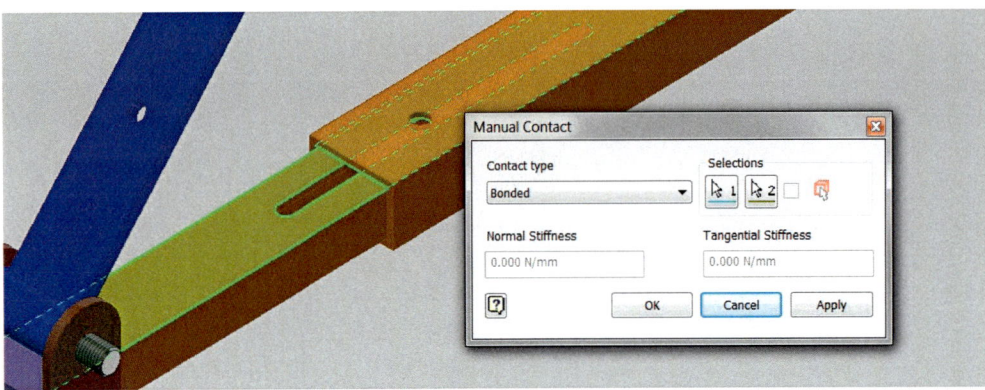

A single manual contact will be created within the bonded contact node group.

15. Select **Mesh View** > Deselect **Boundary Conditions**

This will generate mesh and thus enable us to view the mesh so that we can further refine it if required. In this instance, the default mesh seems reasonable.

Run simulation and analyze

16. Select **Simulate** > Run **Simulation** > Deselect **Mesh View** > Select **Actual** for Adjust Displacement Display

 Ignore the warnings as they relate to sliding/no separation contacts, meaning that the components can slide away from one another. Hence, the software adds a soft spring to stop them sliding away. In this case the soft spring is attached to the bolts.

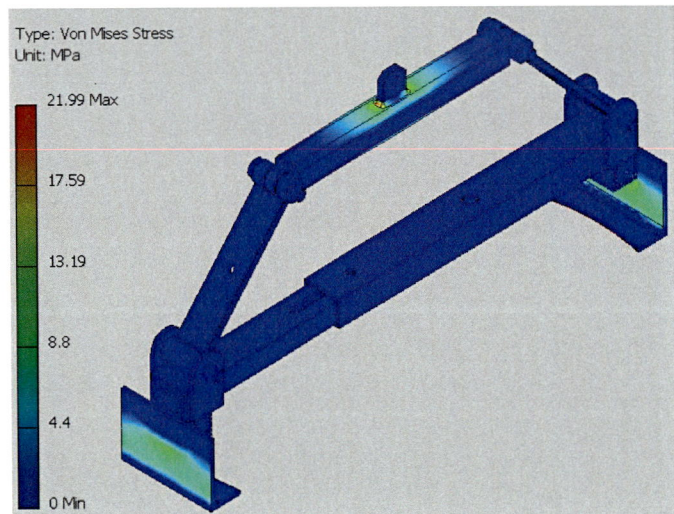

The maximum Von Mises Stress calculated is 21.99 MPa. To obtain a better understanding of the stresses in the top clamp and plates, were the suspension unit is held, the planar stress results will be used.

17. Double click **Stress YY** to display compressive and tensile stresses on top clamp > Select **Color Bar** > Change color bar maximum and minimum values to **8** and **-8** > Click **OK** > Select **Maximum Value**

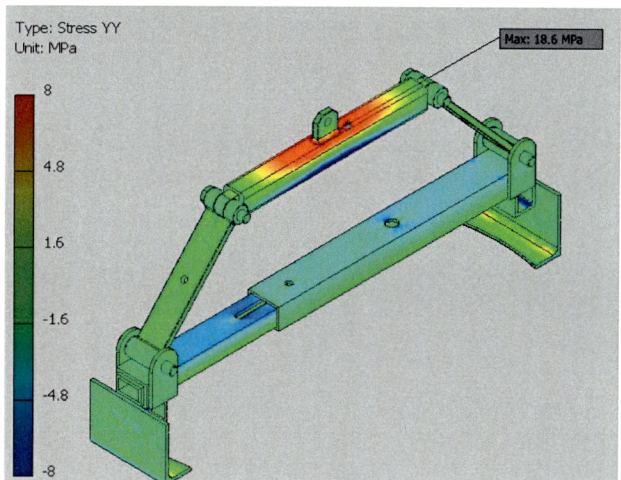

The peak stress is 18.6 MPa which is concentrated around the lug. The tensile stress on the beam is in the region of 10 – 13 MPa and the maximum compressive stress is 9.66 MPa.

18. Now double click **Stress ZZ** to display compressive and tensile stress on the clamp plates were the suspension unit is held

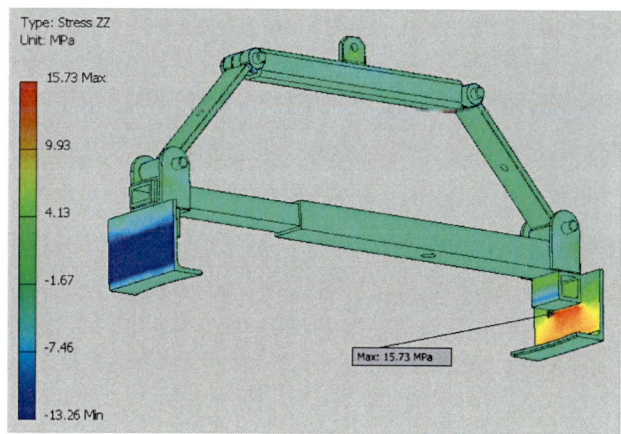

The maximum tensile stress is 15.73 MPa and the maximum compressive stress is 13.26 MPa

19. Now double click **Stress XX** to view the third and final planar stress

The stresses in the X plane are small when compared to the Y and Z planar stresses. As the maximum stress is at the top face of the top clamp, we will refine the mesh using a local mesh control and then compare the maximum stresses again.

20. Right Click **Stress XX** results > Deselect **Activate**

CHAPTER 3
DP2 – Assembly Optimization

21. Select **Local Mesh Control** > Select the top face and fillet faces around lug > Specify **5**mm for element size > Click **OK**

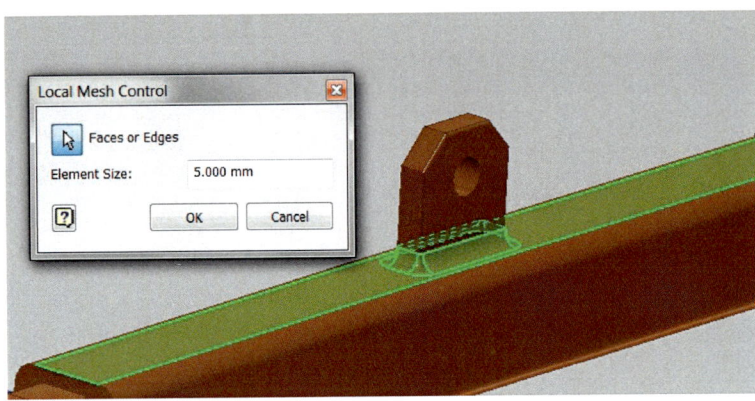

22. Right click **Mesh** > Select **Update Mesh** > Select **Mesh View** > Select **Simulate** > Run **Simulation**

23. Double click **Stress YY**

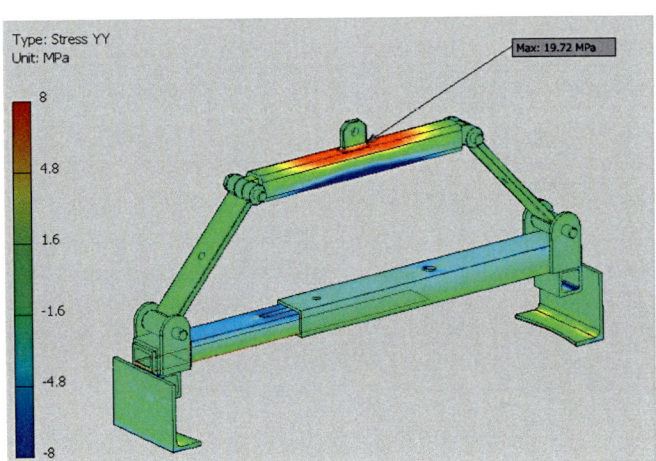

In the top clamp, the stress is significantly higher around the lug in comparison to the stress along the top clamp mount. This localized peak stress is mainly due to the geometrical discontinuity between the lug and top face of the clamp, also referred to as a stress raiser. Further mesh refinement will potentially further increase the stress due to stress singularities, due to geometrical discontinuities. In this case, as the top clamp geometry is simple and pin jointed, at either end we can treat the top clamp as a simply supported beam and therefore will use the classical bending equation to calculate bending stress in the beam.

$$\sigma = Mx\frac{y}{I}$$

Load is applied centrally on the beam, therefore to find the maximum bending moment, we can use:

M = P x L / 4   y = Distance to neutral axis
  = 780N * 390mm / 4   = Section height / 2
  = 76050 Nmm   = 40mm / 2 = 20 mm

I = 2nd Moment of Area (for box section)
  = Outer 2nd Moment of Area - Inner 2nd Moment of Area
  = (BD^3 / 12) - (bd^3 / 12)
  = (40 x 40^3 / 12) - (30 x 30^3 / 12)
  = 2560000 - 675000
  = 145833 mm^4

Therefore, Max Tensile or Compressive Stress due to bending is:
σ = 76050 x 20 / 145833
  = 10.43 N/mm^2 = 10.43 x 10^6 N/m^2 = **10.43 MPa**

This stress calculation is based on the assumption that the maximum stress is occurring evenly in the centre of the beam. In reality, when we examine the model, we can see that the lifting lug acts as a stiffener on the beam section. Although maximum moment occurs in the centre the maximum stress will be redistributed to either side of the lug, on the upper surface of the beam.

We can see below that the section to the side of the lug marked Z-Z exhibits a maximum tensile stress on the upper face in the region of 10MPa. This is where we would expect to see the redistributed maximum tensile stress within the beam.

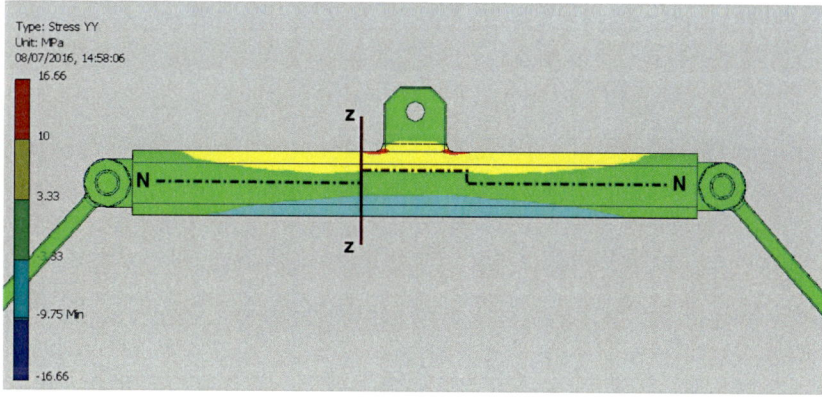

Further, as the top portion of the beam is stiffened by the lug, the neutral axis (zero stress) moves upwards, causing a greater internal moment on the underside of the beam. We would expect this to act as a stress raiser on the bottom face of the beam. On the lower face, maximum compressive stress is still in the middle but does increase in comparison to the upper tensile stress, as expected.

These stress redistributions show good correlation between the FEA and the simple approximated hand calculation, giving us a high degree of confidence in the overall integrity of the FEA solution.

24. Double click **Displacement** (Max displacement is 0.1251 mm)

CHAPTER 3
DP2 – Assembly Optimization

25. Double click **Safety Factor**

Use the color bar to enhance clarity of display. The minimum safety factor is around the lug at the top of the top clamp, as illustrated below (the position of maximum stress). Change the minimum value of the color bar to obtain a better display of the safety factor results.

This suggests that the design can be further optimized, as the calculated safety factor of 8.73 is more than twice the design limit of 4.

Optimization

Here, we will use the parameters from the Component and Assembly environment and alter them to determine the best configuration that satisfies the design constraints.

26. Select **Parametric Table**

27. Right Click in the **Design Constraints** row > Select **Add Design Constraint**

28. Select **Mass** from the list. This will be used to determine the best design/parametric configuration for minimum weight.

29. Repeat step 27 to add **Displacement** and **Safety Factor** design Constraints

30. Change the Constraint Type for Max Displacement to **Upper Limit** > Specify limit to be **0.2**

31. Change the Constraint Type for Min Safety Factor to **Lower Limit** > Specify limit to be 4

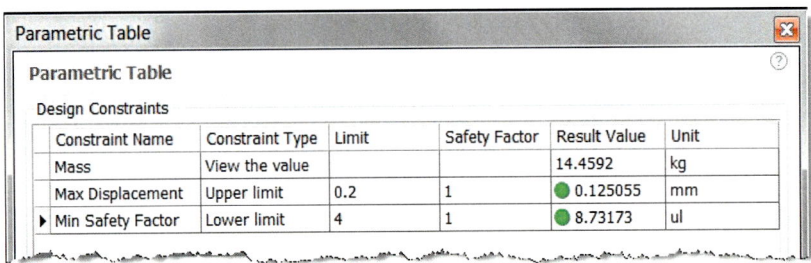

CHAPTER 3
DP2 – Assembly Optimization

32. Right Click **Link:1** > Select **Show Parameters** > Select all of the 5 **User Parameters** > Click **OK**

The Linkthickness parameter will allow us see the effect of changing the thickness of the link arms. The Slotthickness and Slotwidth parameters together allow us to control the shape of the cutouts in the link arms. The shape of the cutout can be either a slot or circle. The Slotnumbers parameter will allow us to control the number of weight-saving cutouts in the Link arms. The Slotspacing parameter will allow us to control the spacing between weight-saving cutouts in the Link arms.

33. Select **Parametric Table**, if not already selected.

All selected parameters now appear in addition to the design constraints, both of which can be used for the optimization study.

34. Specify the following values to complete the parametric table

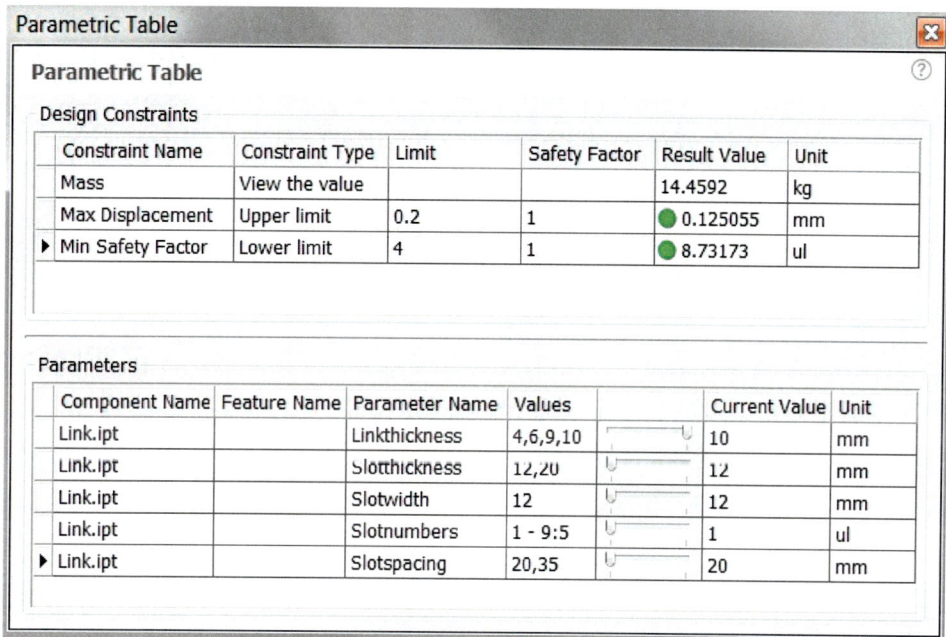

 1-9:5 will produce three more parameters, equally spaced between 1 and 9. Here, the additional parameters created are 3, 5 and 7.

 Choosing too many parameters and values can result in taking a long time to generate and produce results.

35. Now move the sliders for each parameter to the following values

Parameters						
Component Name	Feature Name	Parameter Name	Values		Current Value	Unit
Link.ipt		Linkthickness	4,6,9,10		4	mm
Link.ipt		Slotthickness	12,20		20	mm
Link.ipt		Slotwidth	12		12	mm
Link.ipt		Slotnumbers	1 - 9:5		5	ul
▶ Link.ipt		Slotspacing	20,35		35	mm

CHAPTER 3
DP2 – Assembly Optimization

36. Select **Simulate** > Change study to **Current configuration only** > Select **Run**. This will generate visual results, to take account of the selected parameter values.

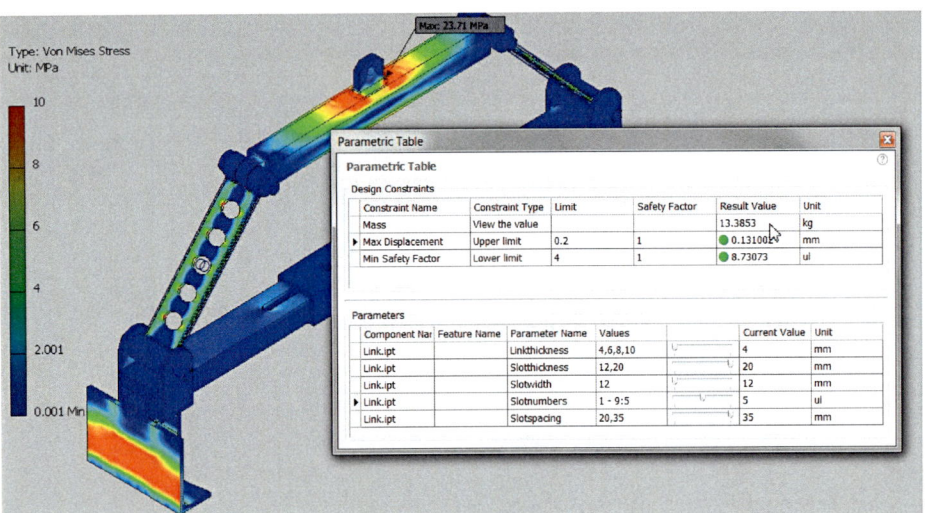

Notice total mass has dropped to 13.38 Kg from original mass of 14.4592 Kg. Here you can further add more parameters, change design constraint limits, etc., to further optimize the design.
The number of design configurations is unlimited and the above configuration can be further enhanced by adding more holes and reducing the thickness of the other channels of the lifting mechanism. Another possible configuration is illustrated below. However, it is important to note that selection of the design is dependent on various criteria including manufacturability, company/designer preferences, best practices etc.

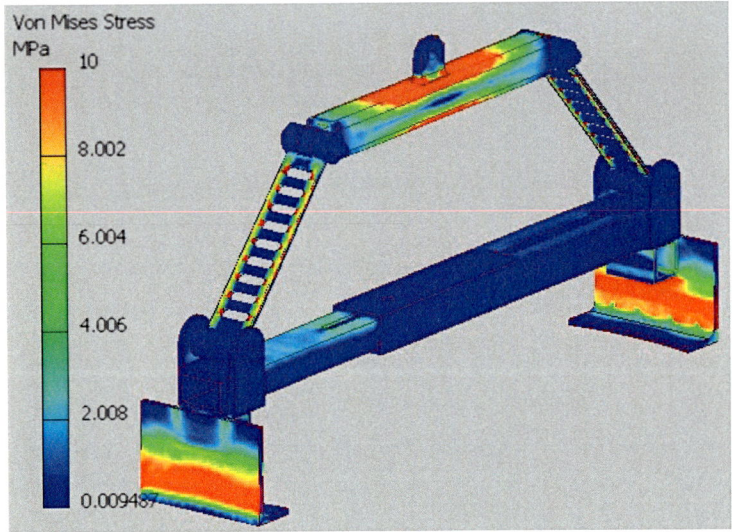

💡 If you have a powerful machine you can run all possible configurations, rather than just one.

37. Close File

CHAPTER 4
DP3 – Bolted Connection

Pre-Stressing a Bolted Clamp Assembly
(Design Problem Courtesy of Destec Engineering Ltd)

Key features and workflows introduced in this design problem

	Key Features/Workflows
1	Symmetry conditions
2	Simulating bolt preloads
3	Non-linear contacts
4	Local mesh refinement
5	Displaying symmetrical results using ground plane and reflections

Introduction

Destec Engineering Ltd was formed in 1969 and for the past 40 years has been developing both products and services to industry, particularly where design and supply is concerned, with 'High Pressure Containment' and 'On-Site Machining' being the specialist lines.

SECTION 2 - Stress Analysis Design Problems using Solid Elements

CHAPTER 4
DP3 – Bolted Connection

One of the products designed by Destec Engineering Ltd is the G-Range clamp connector, as used in the previous picture, which provides an ideal solution to piping installations, used extensively in production manifold, flow line and valve installations.

One of the key benefits of the G-Range product is it offers up to 75% weight saving over an ANSI flange. Only four bolts per joint, makes this product an easy and cost effective assembly. It is the recognized standard for clamp connectors by the Oil & Gas industry.

The main requirements of this design problem are to determine:

1. Maximum stress in the clamp assembly, for a given allowable bolt stress of 172.4 MPa
2. Determine whether contact is made between seal and pipe
3. Friction will not be taken into account

Workflow of Design Problem 3

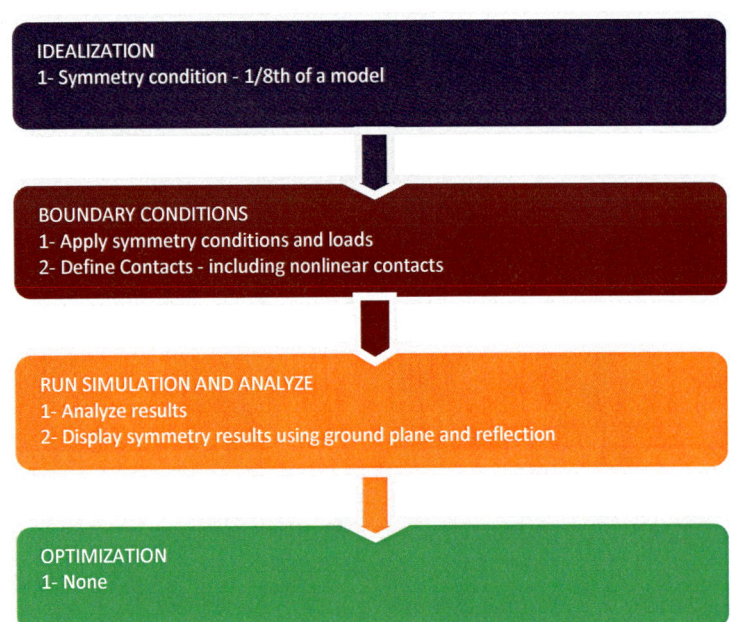

CHAPTER 4
DP3 – Bolted Connection

Idealization

In this example all the bolts have the same torque applied meaning the stress in all the bolts will be the same. As a result of this we can take advantage of symmetry conditions which will also help to run the simulation faster.

However in inventor stress analysis we cannot apply a bolt torque/preload to stress up the bolt, for this reason we will split the bolt and apply a load at the split force to simulate preload.

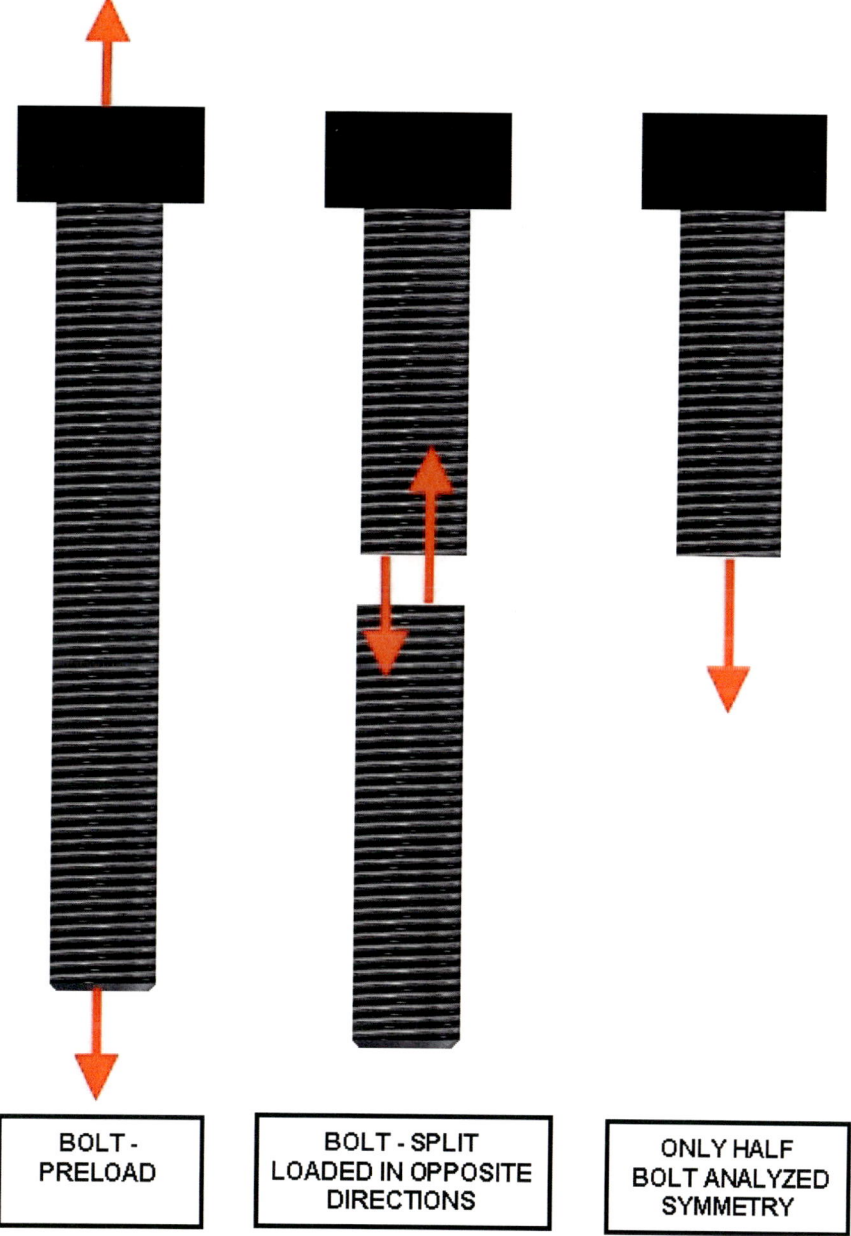

BOLT - PRELOAD

BOLT - SPLIT LOADED IN OPPOSITE DIRECTIONS

ONLY HALF BOLT ANALYZED SYMMETRY

SECTION 2 - Stress Analysis Design Problems using Solid Elements

CHAPTER 4

DP3 – Bolted Connection

The following equation and information will be used to determine the load to stress the bolt to a given specified value based on its diameter. This method agrees with the method given by the **American Petroleum Institute Standard API 6A**.

Bolt Size :- 1.1/8"-8UN

Nominal Bolt Size	$NB = 1.125 \text{in}$	
Pitch of Thread	$P = 0.125 \text{in}$	
Bolt Stress Area	$A_b = \dfrac{\pi}{4} \cdot (NB - 1.3 \cdot P)^2$	
	$A_b = 0.728 \cdot \text{in}^2$	$(A_b = 469.4 \cdot \text{mm}^2)$
Assembly Bolt Stress	$\sigma_b = 25000 \text{psi}$	$(\sigma_b = 172.4 \cdot \text{MPa})$
(Load on Bolt stress Area $\sigma_b \cdot A_b =$ **80912.9 N**)		

The following information is used to calculate the bolt torque required to stress the bolt to the allowable stress.

Nominal Thread Effective Diameter	$D = 1.0438 \text{in}$
Half Thread Angle	$\alpha = 30 \text{deg}$
Coefficient of Friction	$\mu = 0.12$
Inside Radius of Nut Contact Face	$R_1 = \dfrac{1.25}{2} \text{in}$
Outside Radius of Nut Contact Face	$R_2 = \dfrac{1.813}{2} \text{in}$
Friction Torque at Thread	$A = \dfrac{\mu \cdot A_b \cdot \sigma_b \cdot D}{2 \cdot \cos(\alpha)}$
Friction Torque between Nut Face and Clamp/Cover	$C = \left(2 \cdot \mu \cdot A_b \cdot \dfrac{\sigma_b}{3}\right) \cdot \dfrac{R_2^3 - R_1^3}{R_2^2 - R_1^2}$
Torque Required to Stretch Bolt Without Friction	$B = \dfrac{A_b \cdot \sigma_b \cdot P}{2 \cdot \pi}$
Total Torque Required	$T = (A + B + C)$
	$T = 280.6 \cdot \text{lbfft}$ $(T = 380.5 \cdot \text{N} \cdot \text{m})$

CHAPTER 4
DP3 – Bolted Connection

1. Open Bolted-Connection.iam

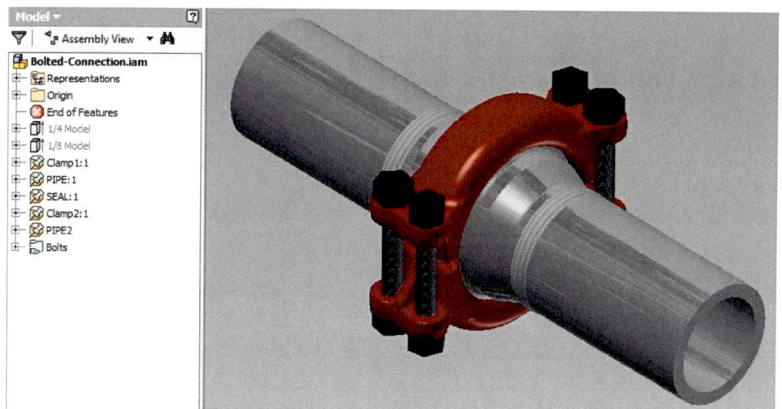

2. Activate **FEA-Symmetry** Level of Detail

3. Move **End of Features** below **1/8 Model**

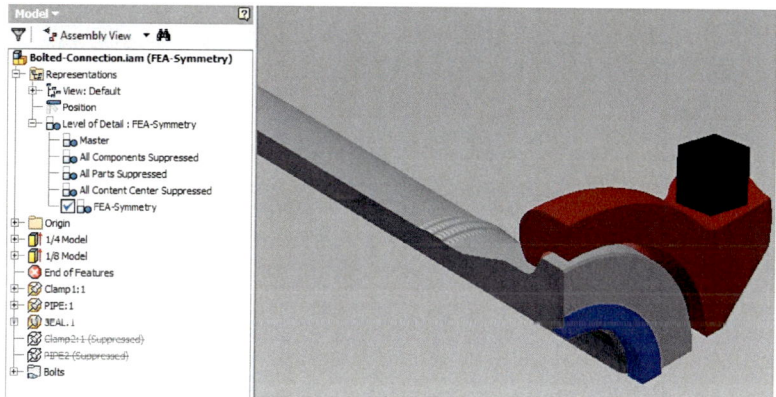

This will create 1/8th of the original model which will be used for analysis. Now, we can begin the second stage of the analysis by applying boundary conditions.

Boundary conditions

4. Select **Environments** tab > Select **Stress Analysis**

5. Select **Create Study** > Specify **Bolt-Preload** for Name > Click **OK**

   Initially we are going to apply symmetry conditions on all the split faces, except the bolt, using frictional constraint

CHAPTER 4
DP3 – Bolted Connection

6. Select **Frictionless Constraint** > Select three faces as shown > Specify **Y Symmetry** for Name > Click **Apply**

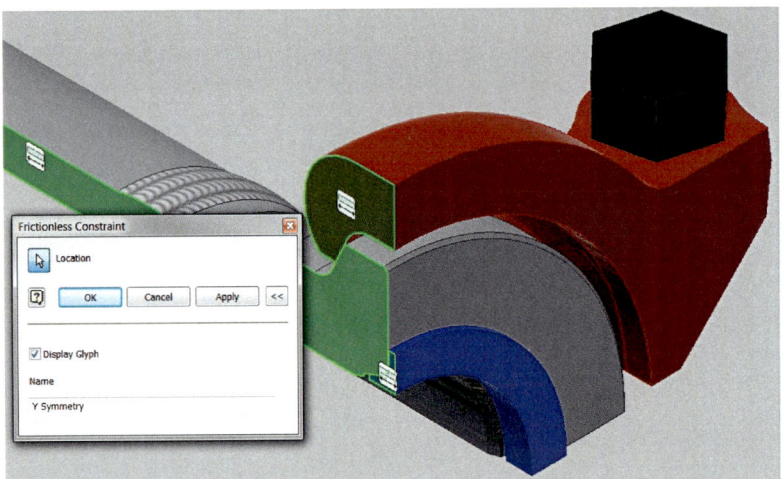

7. Now select two faces as shown > Specify **X Symmetry** for Name > Click **Apply**

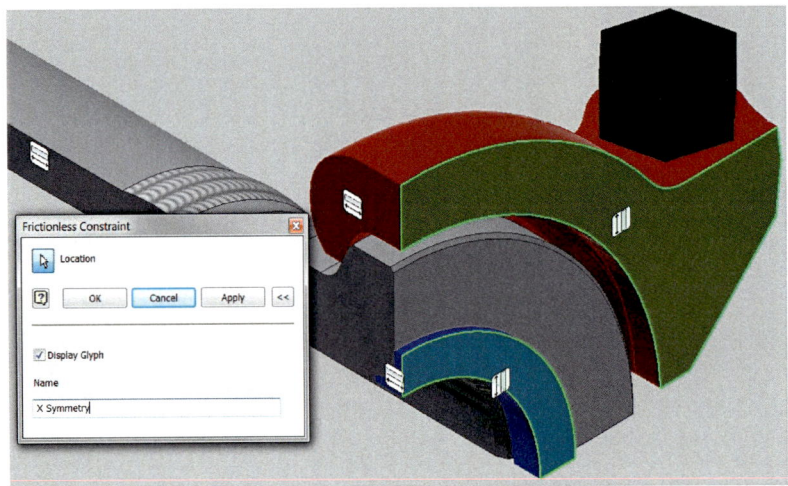

8. Finally select two faces as shown > Specify **Z Symmetry** for Name > Click **OK**

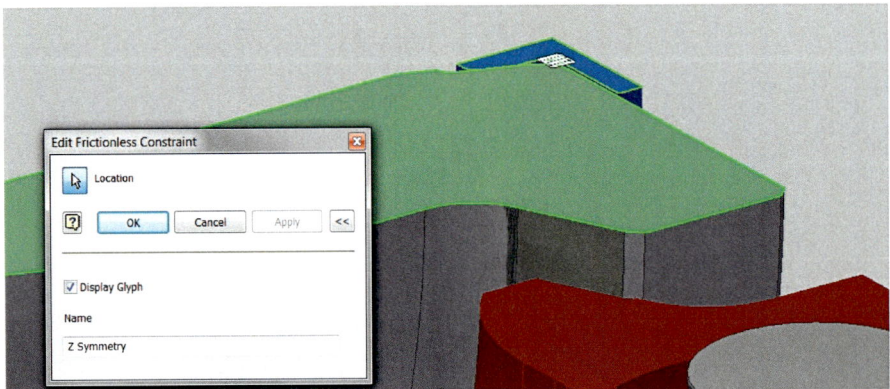

CHAPTER 4
DP3 – Bolted Connection

9. Select **Pressure** and specify **39.6MPa** > Select all internal exposed faces of pipe and seal > Specify **Internal Pressure** for Name > Specify **0.2** for Scale > Click **OK**

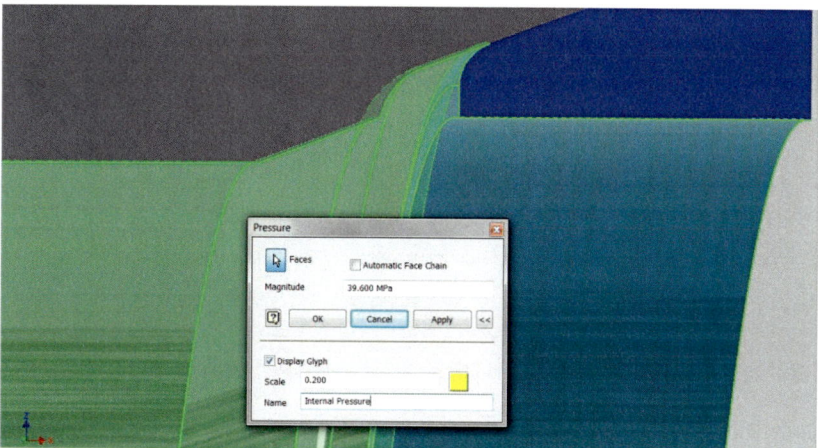

10. Select **Force** and specify **80,912.9 N** > Select the bottom of the bolt split face > Flip the direction of Load > Specify **Bolt preload** for Name > Change color of load to **red** > Click **OK** twice

11. **Deselect** Boundary Conditions > Select **Automatic Contacts**

12. Right Click **Separation:1 (Clamp1:1,Bolt:2)** contact > Select **Edit Contact** > Select **Sliding / No Separation** for Contact type > Click **OK**

13. Right Click **Separation:2 (Clamp1:1,PIPE:1)** contact > Select **Edit Contact** > Select **Sliding / No Separation** for Contact type > Click **OK**

> Having a lot of separation contacts in the analysis can result in long analysis runs, as these contacts are nonlinear and go through an iterative process to obtain convergence in results.

CHAPTER 4
DP3 – Bolted Connection

14. Select **Manual Contact** > Select faces of Pipe and Seal as shown > Select **Separation** for Contact type > Click **OK**

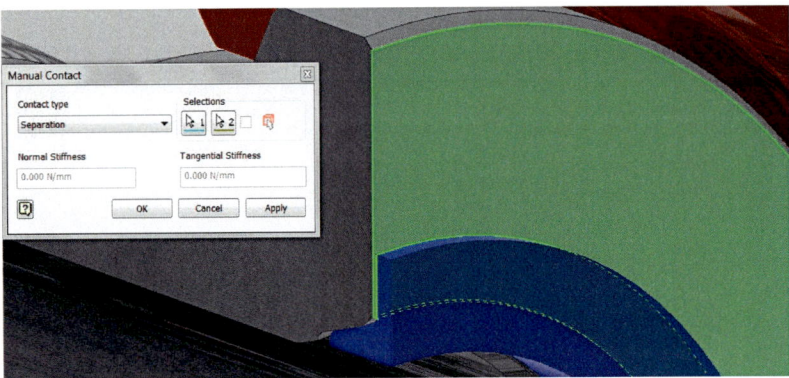

This is the contact between the seal and the pipe. As the contact tolerance, defined in the simulation settings, was less than this gap the contact was not automatically created

In total 5 contacts will be created as follows

If the contact between components is never going to separate once contact is made then use sliding/no separation instead of separation contact, as this will result in faster analysis times.

Now we will set the mesh settings including local refinement around the seal.

Unselect **Use part based measure for Assembly mesh**, if already preselected, before clicking OK below. As this can result in excessive mesh elements.

15. Select **Mesh Settings** > Specify **0.02** for Average Element Size > Unselect **Create Curved Mesh Elements,** if already selected > Click **OK**

CHAPTER 4
DP3 – Bolted Connection

16. Select **Local Mesh Control** > Specify **1.5 mm** for Element Size > Select the following faces which are in contact between the seal and pipe (two for pipe and three for seal) > Click **OK**

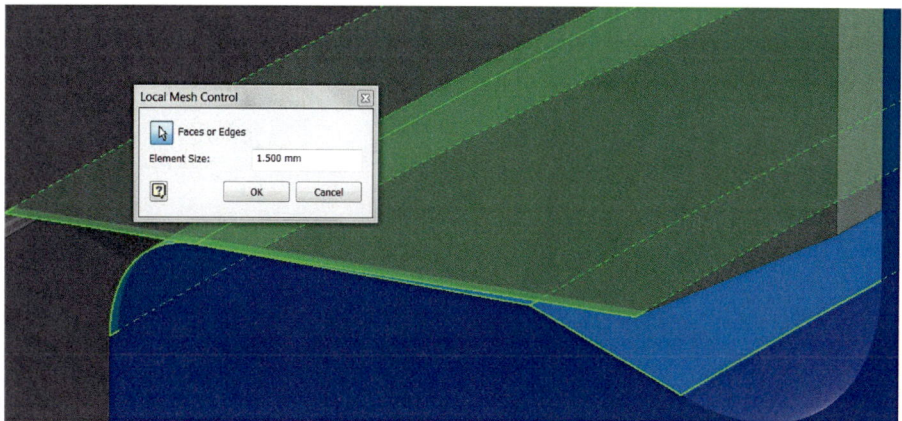

17. Select **Local Mesh Control** again > Specify **4 mm** for Element Size > Select the following face on the seal > Click **OK**

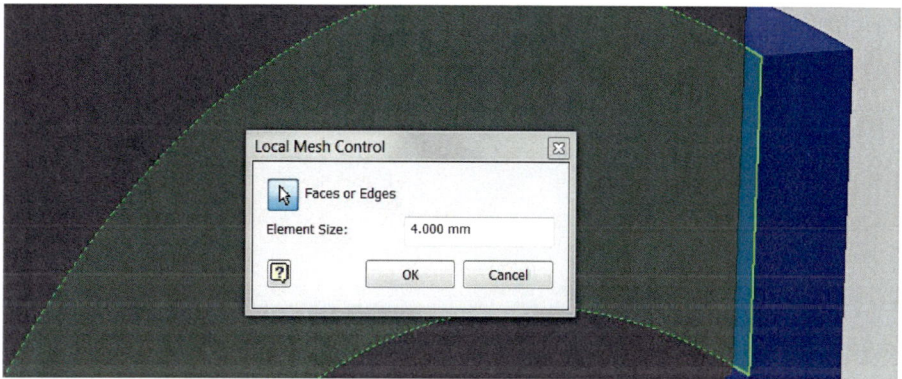

18. Select **Mesh View**

A total of 40819 elements will be created.

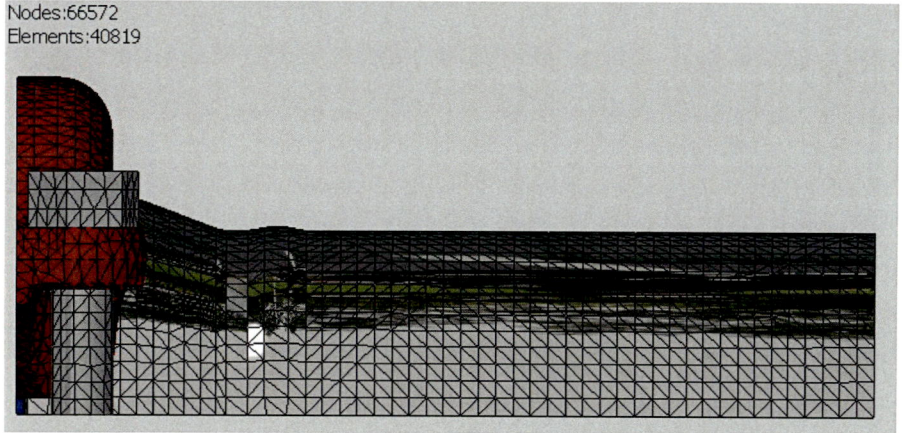

SECTION 2 - Stress Analysis Design Problems using Solid Elements

CHAPTER 4
DP3 – Bolted Connection

Run simulation and analyze

19. Select **Simulate** > Run **Simulation**

20. Select **Actual** from Adjust Displacement Display > Select **Contour Shading** > Select **Maximum Value** > Deselect **Mesh View**

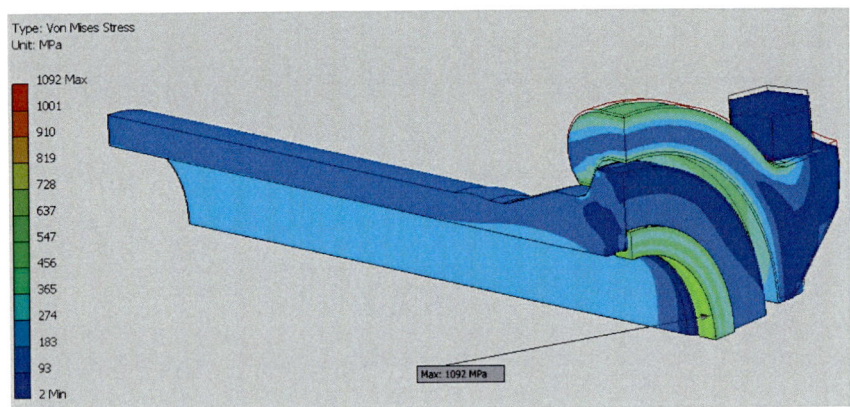

21. Select **Animate** > Select **Play** to see if seal comes in contact with pipe > Click **OK** once finished with animation

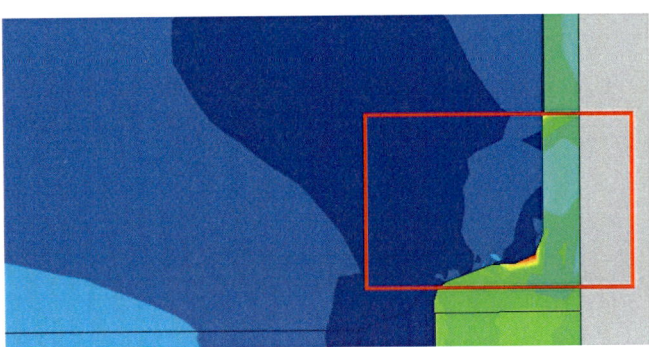

22. Select **SEAL:1** in graphics window > Right Click and select **Isolate** > Select **Color Bar** > Unselect **Maximum** > Specify **900** maximum value > Click **OK**

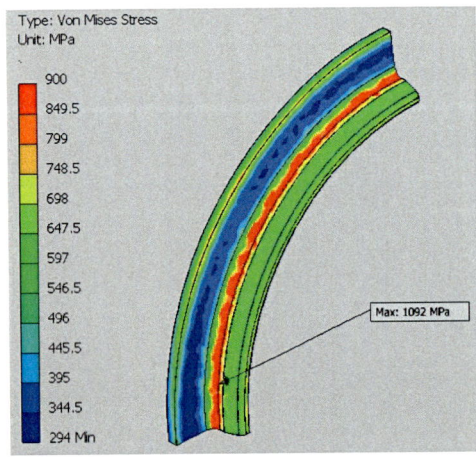

SECTION 2 - Stress Analysis Design Problems using Solid Elements

CHAPTER 4
DP3 – Bolted Connection

The maximum stress is way higher than the yield limit and in reality these seals are permanently deformed locally around the radii when loaded for the first time. For this reason the high stress is not an issue for the seal. What is more important, is to see whether a contact between the seal and pipe is made, as this is crucial in operation as non-contact will cause leakage.

23. Now select **SEAL:1** in graphics window > Right Click and select **Undo Isolate**

24. Select **Bolt:2** in graphics window > Right Click and select **Isolate** > Select **Color Bar** > Select **Maximum Value** > Click **OK**

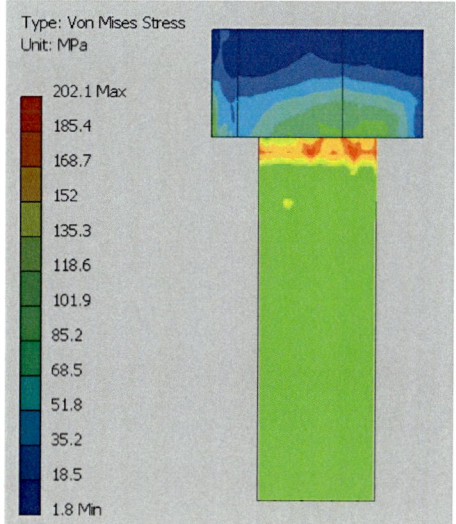

The maximum stresses in the bolt is below yield limit but its value is different to the allowable stress of 172.4 MPa. This may be down to several reasons of one which maybe down to stress singularities as the stress is very close to the edge between bolt shank and bolt head.

25. Select **Safety Factor**

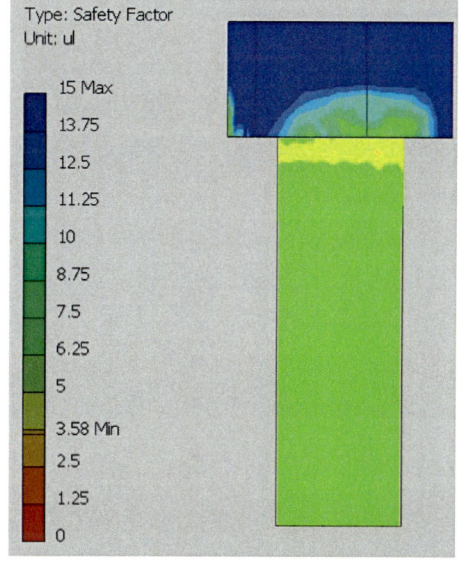

CHAPTER 4
DP3 – Bolted Connection

The important point to note is that a minimum value of 3.58, proves the bolt is strong enough to withstand the bolt pre torque. In the case of trying to achieve a higher safety factor the results need to be carefully interpreted.

In the following step we will use ground planes to display symmetry results.

26. Select **bolt:2** in graphics window > Right Click and select **Undo Isolate**

27. Select **Von Mises Stress** results > > Select **Color Bar** > Unselect **Maximum** > Specify **300** maximum value > Click **OK**

28. Select **Undeformed** from Adjust Displacement Display

29. Change the view of the model using cube as shown below

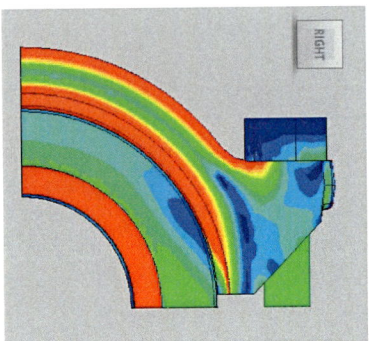

30. Right Click cube > Select **Set Current View** as **Front** > Display **Ground Plane**

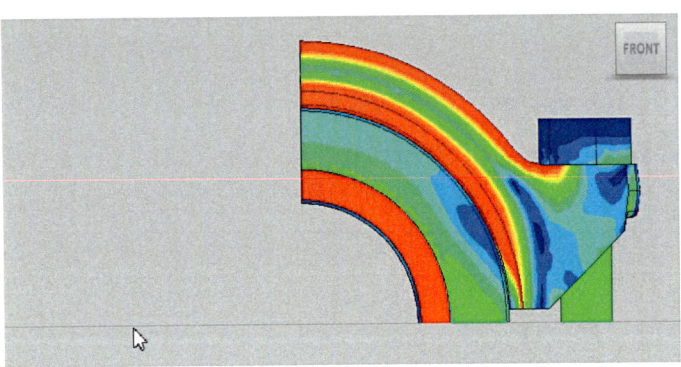

31. Select Reflections > Select Ground Plane Settings

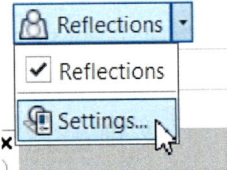

32. Change the Ground Plane Settings as shown below

CHAPTER 4
DP3 – Bolted Connection

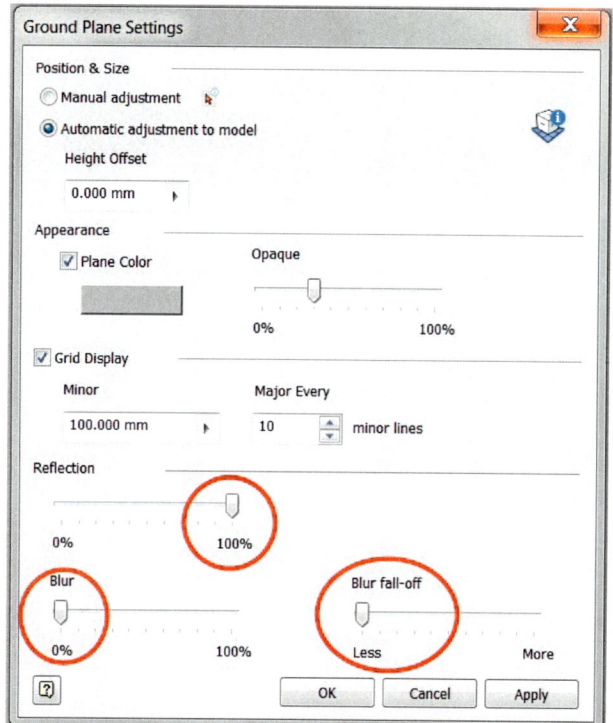

33. Deselect **Ground Plane** > Move the model slightly until you see the reflection.

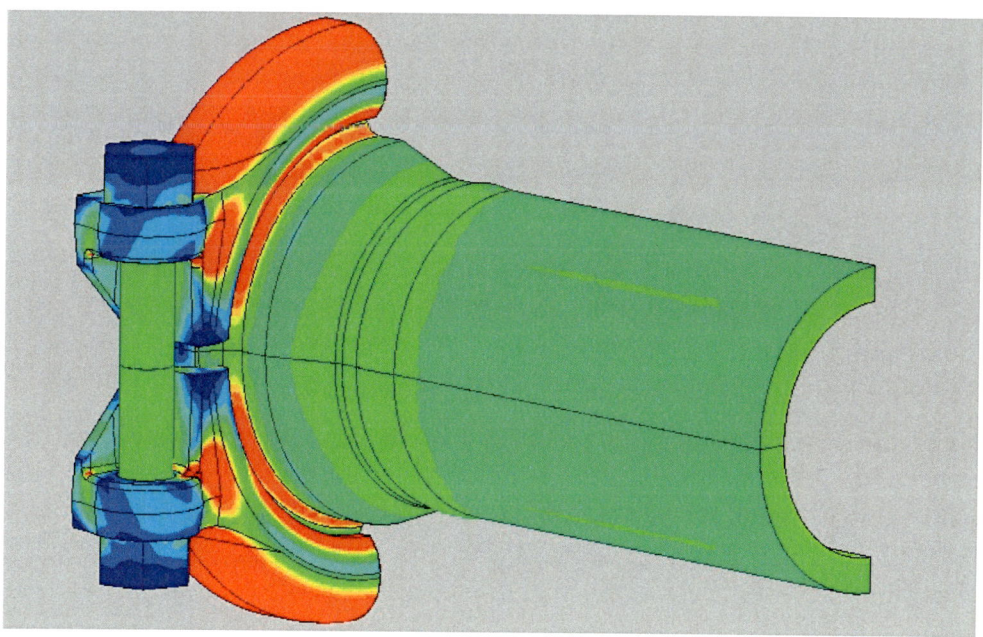

34. Close File, after viewing and analyzing results

CHAPTER 4
DP3 – Bolted Connection

CHAPTER 5
DP4 – Propshaft

DP4 – Propshaft

Analysis of a propshaft yoke
(Design Problem Courtesy of GKN Land Systems Ltd)

Key features and workflows introduced in this design problem

	Key Features/Workflows
1	Moment Load
2	Section View to view internal results.
3	Dummy component to transfer load

Introduction

GKN Land Systems is a leading supplier of engineered power management products, systems and services. They design, manufacture and supply products and services for the agricultural, construction, mining and utility markets and key industrial segments, offering integrated powertrain solutions. GKN Land Systems also provides a global aftermarket distribution and through-life support service.

A sub-sector of GKN Land Systems is GKN Motorsport, providing driveshafts, propshafts and CV joints for applications such as World Rally Cars and Touring cars, as well as driveline components and assemblies for high performance road cars. Motorsport parts are often highly stressed, however weight is also an important aspect, and parts must be lightweight, without compromising performance.

The example used in the exercise is a high strength yoke used on a WRC propshaft.

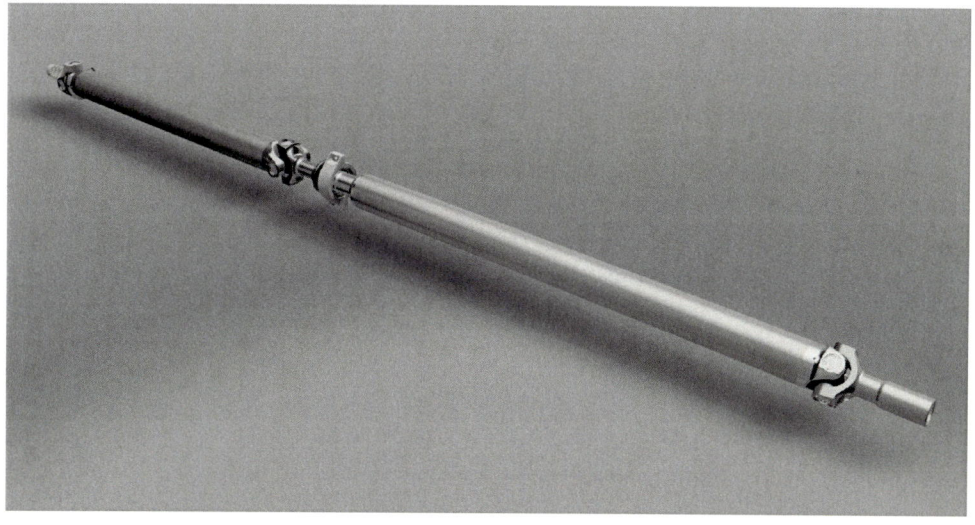

SECTION 2 - Stress Analysis Design Problems using Solid Elements

CHAPTER 5
DP4 – Propshaft

The main requirements of this design problem are to determine:

1. Maximum stress in the yoke.
2. Safety factor – needs to be above 1.

Workflow of Design Problem 4

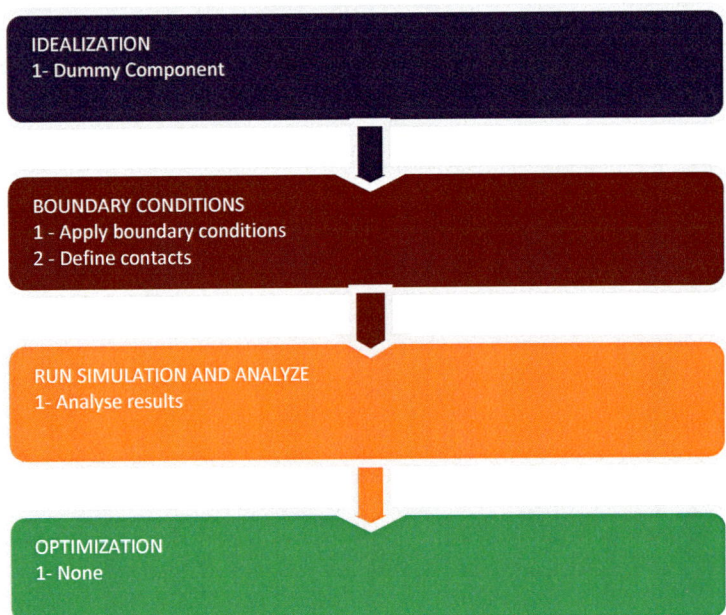

Idealization

The following dummy part was created to transfer moment load to yoke being analyzed, as it's not possible to directly apply moment load to yoke correctly.

CHAPTER 5
DP4 – Propshaft

1. Open Yoke.iam

Boundary conditions

2. Select **Environments** tab > Select **Stress Analysis**

3. Select **Create Study** > Specify **Yoke** for Name > Click **OK**

4. Select **Automatic Contacts**

5. Select **Bonded:2 (Female Rear yoke:1, slave cross pin:1)** and **Bonded:4 (Female Rear yoke:1, slave cross pin:1)** > Right Click > Select **Suppress**

CHAPTER 5
DP4 – Propshaft

6. Select **Moment** load > Specify **3000 N m** for magnitude > Select face on dummy part as shown > Click **OK**

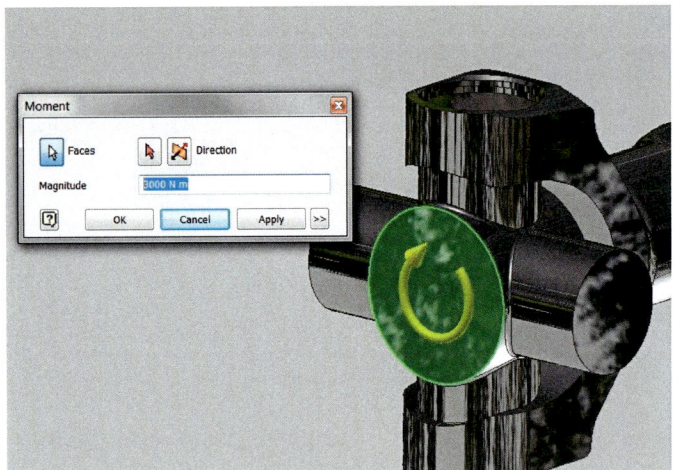

7. Select **Fixed Constraint** > Select one side of all the teeth's of the yoke as shown > Click **OK**

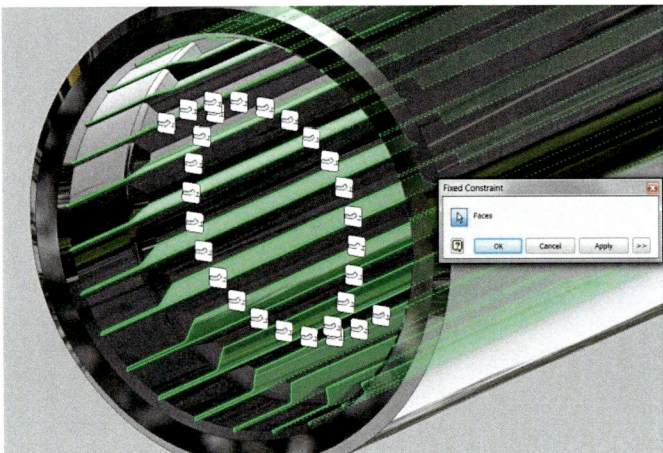

8. Select **Mesh Settings** > Unselect **Use part based measure for Assembly mesh** > Select **Create Curve Mesh Elements** > Specify **0.02** for Average Element Size > Click **OK**

9. Select **Mesh View** > Deselect **Boundary Conditions**

A total of 73294 elements will be created.

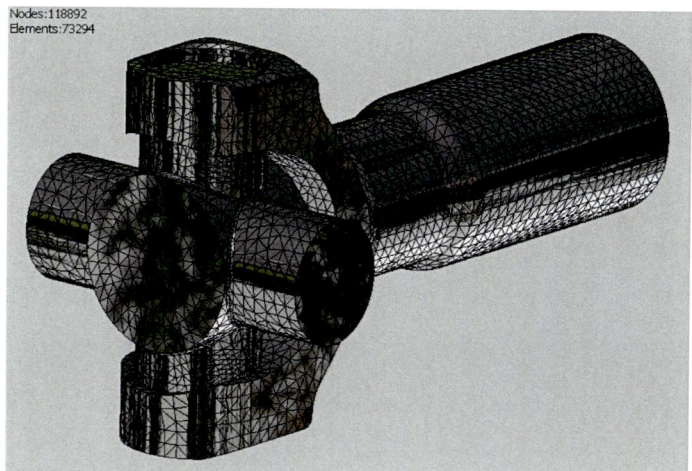

Run simulation and analyze

10. Select **Simulate** > Select **Run**

11. Select **Undeformed** from Adjust Displacement Display > Select **Contour Shading** > Select **Maximum Value** > Deselect **Mesh View** > Right Click **Yoke** in graphics window > Select **Isolate**

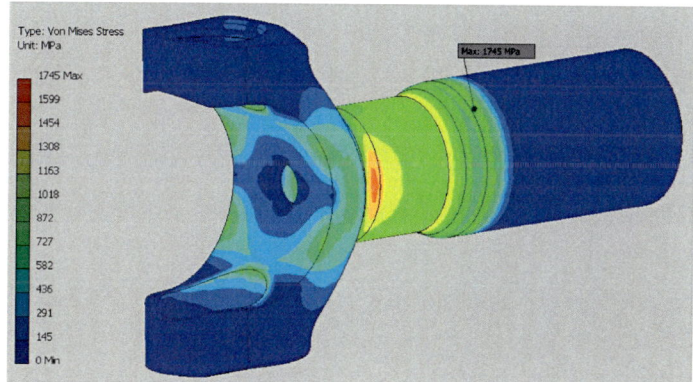

The maximum value of 1745 MPa is higher than the yield limit of 1550 MPa suggesting a possible safety factor below 1. So we need to now look into the high stress a little closer. As the stress is located inside the component and is difficult to see the where the actual stress we are going to make use of Inventor's section views.

12. Select **Finish Analysis** > Make **XY Plane** visible

13. Select **Environments** tab > Select **Stress Analysis**

CHAPTER 5
DP4 – Propshaft

14. Select **View** tab > Select **Object Visibility** > Select **Origin Planes**

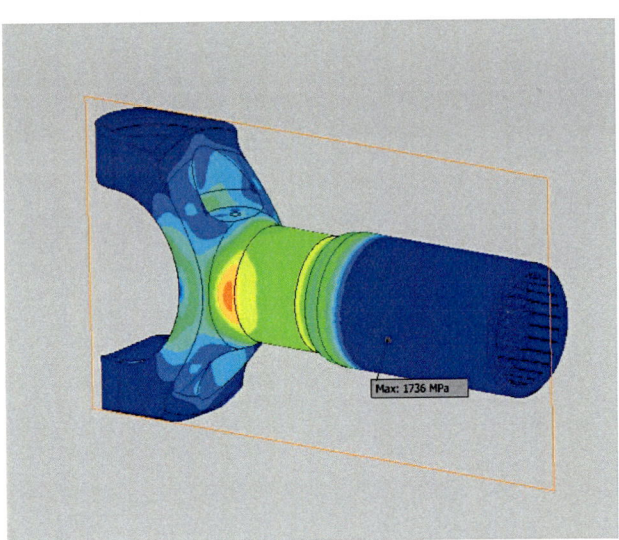

📝 Make sure the maximum stress value is behind the plane. Because once you create half section you will not be able to see location of maximum stress if it's in front of plane.

15. Select **Half Section View** > Select **XY Plane** > Click **OK**

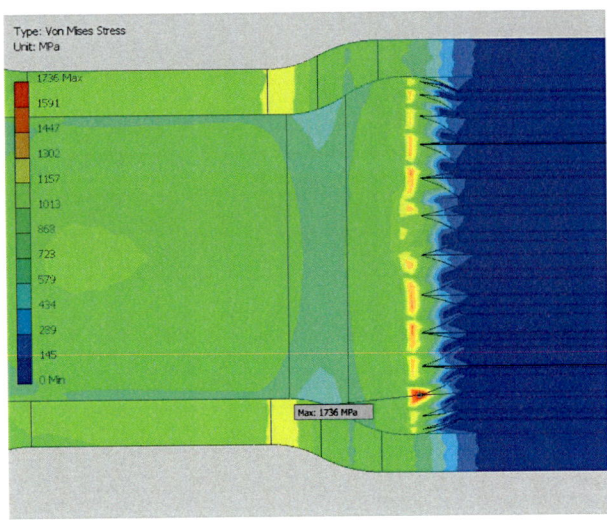

The stress looks like a hotspot as the stress values at the edge of other teeth are not so high. We will change the color bar to get a better understanding of the stress around the teeth

📝 The results across geometry thickness look hollow once you create a section view. This is because inventor does not create volume mesh. This does not mean the results are wrong. The results are just numerically extrapolated for calculation purposes.

36. Select **Color Bar** > Unselect **Maximum** > Specify **1550** for maximum value > Click **OK**

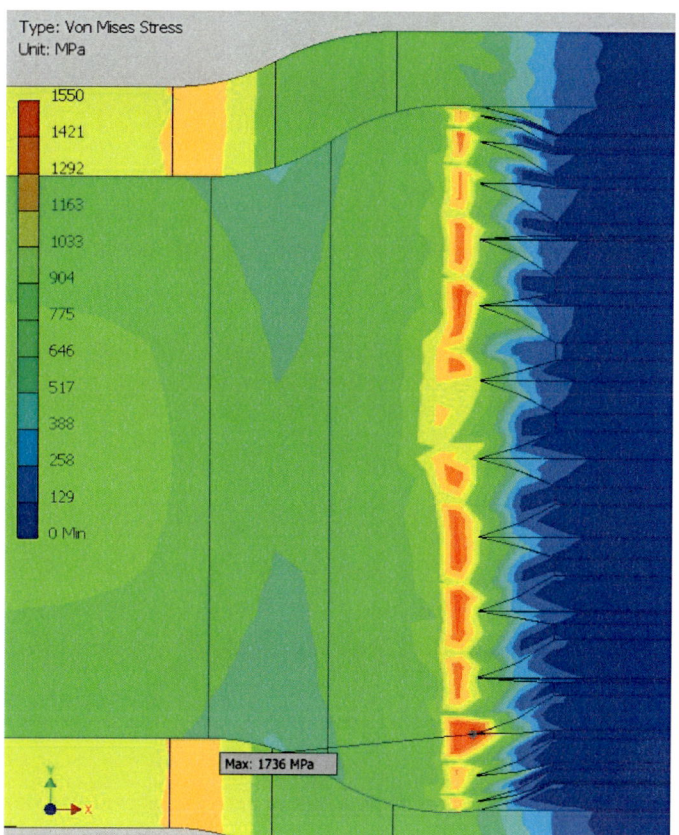

1550 MPa is the yield limit of the material.

We can see the stress around the tip of the most teeth's are starting to appear above 1292 MPa and the spread of stress above 1421 MPa (red region) is very little. This indicates stress around the teeth are below the yield limit.

16. Select **View** > Select **End Section View**

17. Deselect **Maximum Value** > Select **Probe**

CHAPTER 5
DP4 – Propshaft

18. Select at the following location

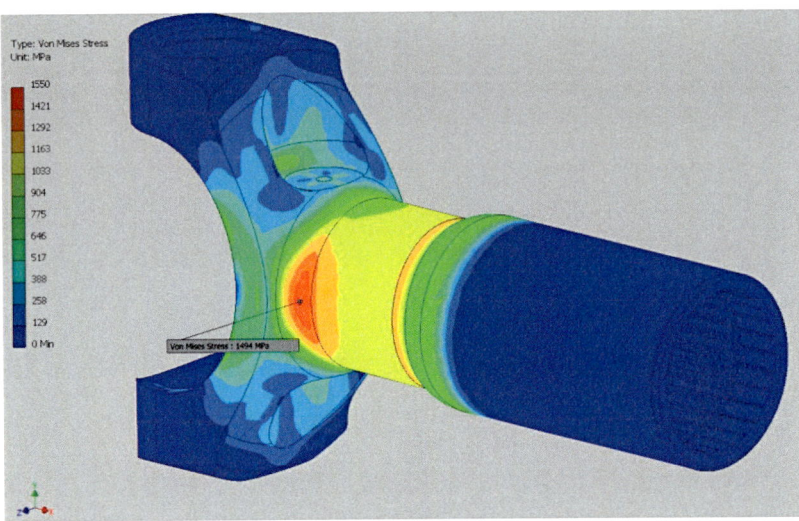

Again the stress value of 1494 MPa is below the yield limit. So based on this value we have a safety factor of

$$Factor\ of\ Safety = \frac{1550}{1494} = 1.04$$

19. Close File

DP5 – Weldment Analysis

Structural Design of Moving Bridge

(Design Problem Courtesy of British Waterways Ltd)

Key features and workflows introduced in this design problem

	Key Features/Workflows
1	Weld Calculator
2	Interpreting results with and without welds

Introduction

In this design problem British Waterways team where involved in designing a new Jack mechanism to open the canal bridge. The Jack force of **30,000 N** was determined, using Dynamic Simulation, which will be used to validate the structural integrity of the new structure, which is to be incorporated into the existing structure beneath the bridge.

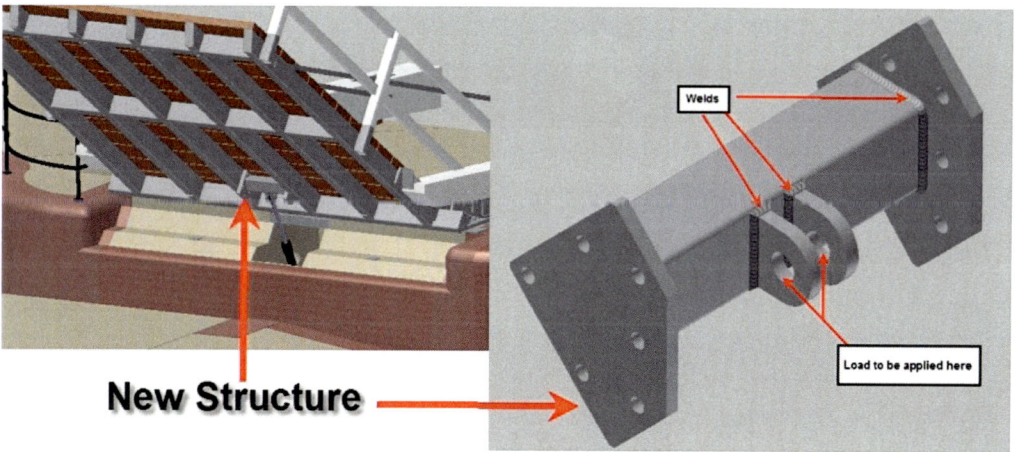

As this new structure is designed with welds incorporated as a weldment assembly we will use the weld calculator to size the welds. We will then further investigate results around the vicinity of weld regions with and without welds.

The main requirements of this design problem are to determine:

- The maximum stress in the structure whilst the bridge is being opened.
- The maximum deflection in the structure.
- The factor of safety of the new design - from which the fatigue life could be predicted.

CHAPTER 6

DP5 – Weldment Analysis

In addition to the main requirements the design criteria to be used for this design problem are;

- Material to be used is mild steel
- Minimum Factor of Safety required is 2

Workflow of Design Problem 5

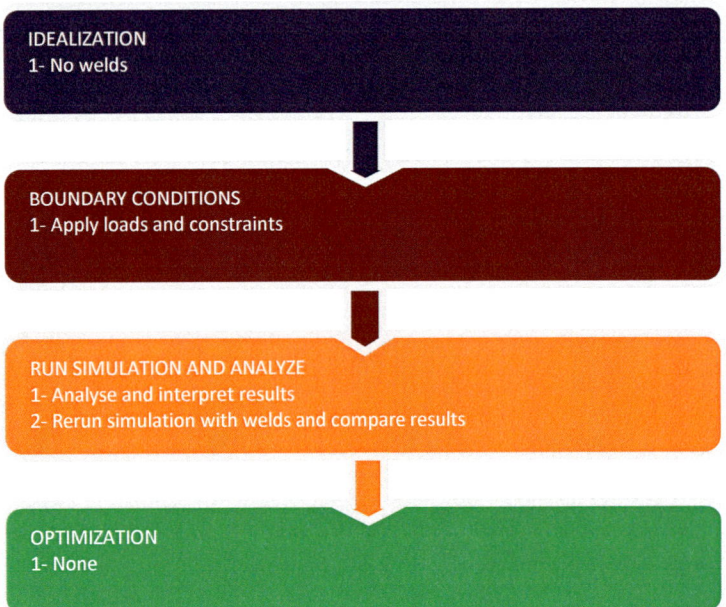

Idealization

Welds are not modelled.

1. Open Cylinder reaction beam.iam

Initially we will analyze the structure without welds.

Boundary conditions

2. Select **Environments** tab > Select **Stress Analysis**

CHAPTER 6
DP5 – Weldment Analysis

3. Select **Create Study** > Specify **Without Welds** for Name > Click **OK**

4. Select **Fixed constraints** > Select the faces on both sides of the structure as shown > Specify **Bolted-Plates** for Name > Click **OK**

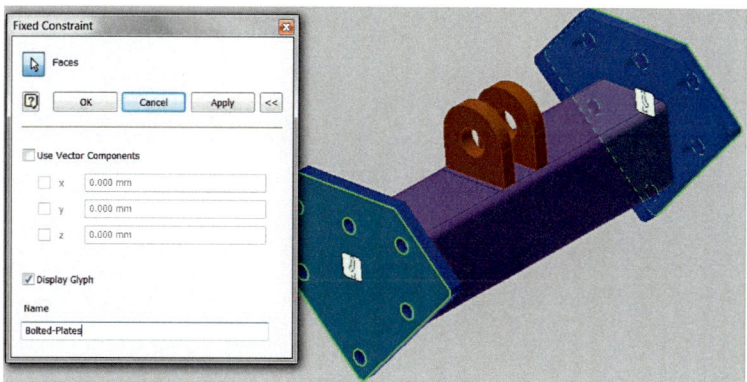

5. Select **Bearing Loads** > Select the internal circular face of both lugs to specify the location > For **Direction**, select the top face of the channel > Change direction of load > Specify **30000 N** for Magnitude

   The force will be split for the bearing loads when both faces are selected together using the same bearing load command.

6. Specify **0.5** to reduce the force display size > Change color to **Red** > Specify **Jack Reaction Load** for Name > Click **OK**

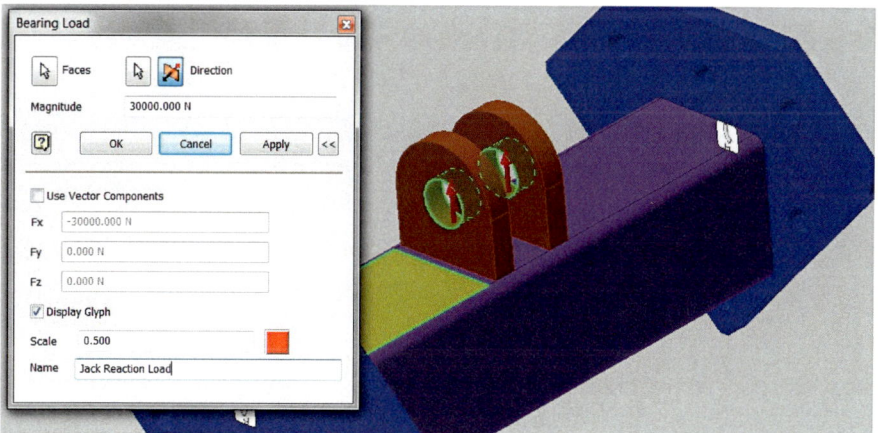

CHAPTER 6
DP5 – Weldment Analysis

7. Select Mesh Settings > Change **Average Element size** to **0.02** > Change **Maximum Turn Angle** to **45** > Select **Create Curved Mesh Elements** > Deselect **Use part based measure for Assembly mesh** > Click **OK**

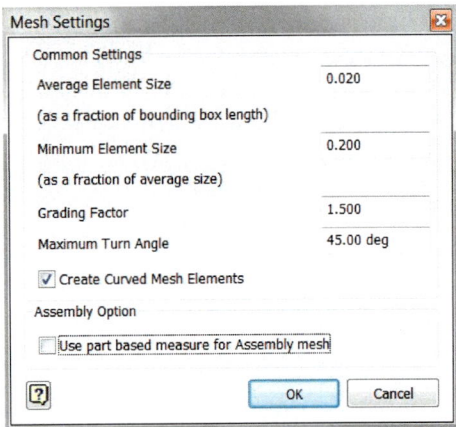

8. Select **Simulate** > Select **Run**

9. Select the left view as shown > Select **Undeformed** for Adjust Displacement Display > Select **Maximum Value** > Deselect **Mesh View** > Select **Contour Shading**

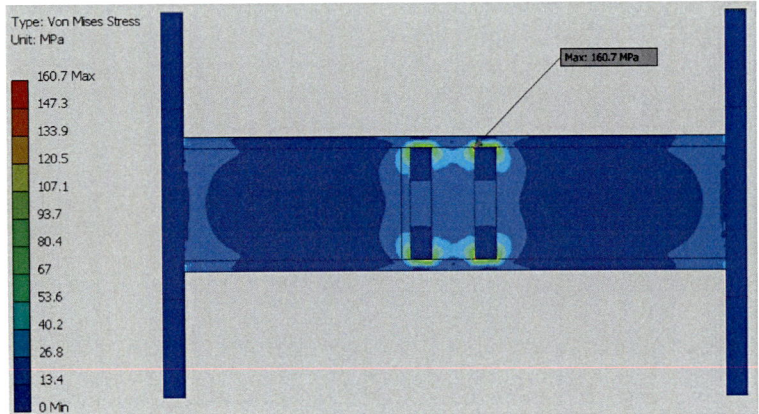

The Max Value is at the position which would normally be covered by a weld. This value is a stress singularity meaning further refinement of the mesh will further increase the stress above the yield limit of 207 MPa in this case. In these scenarios the best practices is to look at the stress further away from the weld position (or stress singularity position). A suggested value would be to look at stresses at a distance of 2x weld size as we will do in the following steps.

10. Select **Color Bar** > Deselect **Maximum Value** > Specify **100** MPa > Click **OK**

11. Select **Probe** > Select at locations shown below

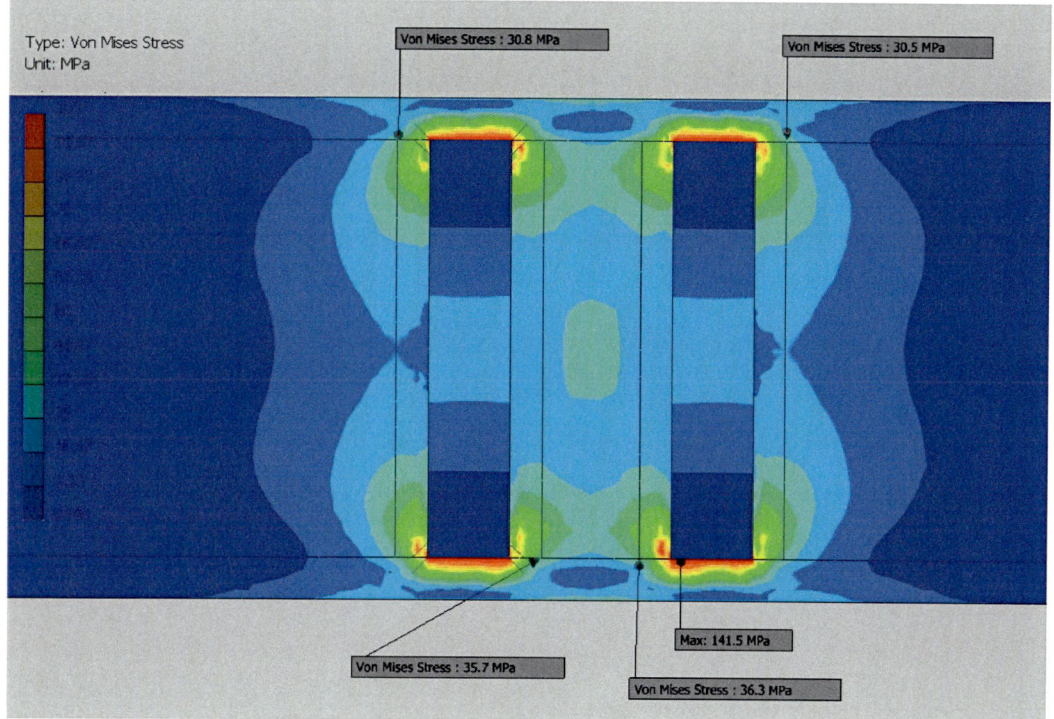

The edges parallel to the lugs are at a distance of 8 mm (twice the size of the potential weld size). These were created so that we can position the probes at the same locations again to compare the stress values in the copied study. We need to check what the impact of the welds will have on our stress values around the region of the lug. At the moment the stress values range between 30 MPa and 36 MPa.

Rerun simulation as assembly and compare results

12. Right Click **Without Welds** > Select **Copy Study**

13. Right click **Without Welds:1** > Select **Edit Study Properties**

14. Specify **Weldment-Analysis** for Name > Click **OK**.

As we do not have welds in this example we will make use of the weld calculator to size the welds around the lugs.

15. Select **Finish Analysis**

CHAPTER 6
DP5 – Weldment Analysis

16. Select **Fillet Weld Calculator (Spatial)** from **Weld Calculator** within the Weld panel

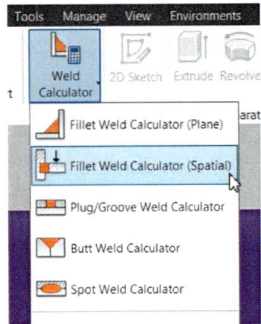

17. Select the following **Weld Form** and **Weld Load**

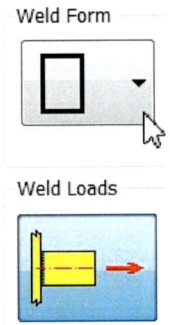

18. Specify the following values in the Fillet Weld Calculator dialogue box

Axial Force	15000 N	Yield Strength	207 MPa
Weld Height	4 mm	UTS	345 MPa
Beam Height	100 mm	Safety Factor	2
Beam Width	20 mm		

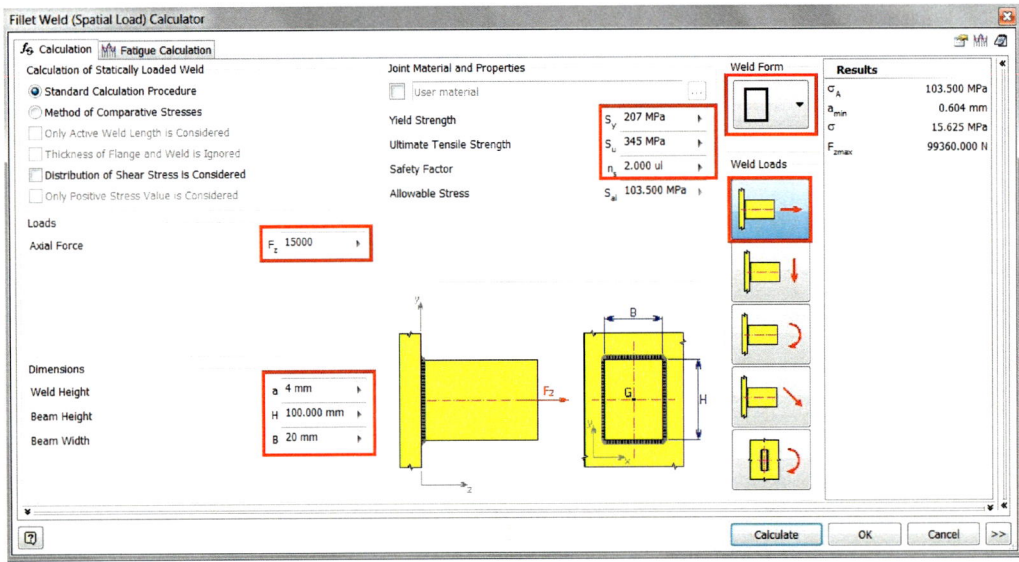

SECTION 2 - Stress Analysis Design Problems using Solid Elements

CHAPTER 6
DP5 – Weldment Analysis

19. Click **Calculate**

Based on the dimensions of the lug 100mm x 20mm and a weld height of 4mm the following minimum weld size is calculated. This was dependent on the load of 15000 N on each lug and specified material data.

Allowable Stress (σA)	103.5 MPa
Minimum Weld Height (amin)	0.604 mm
Weld Normal Stress (σ)	15.625 MPa
Max Axial Force (Fzmax)	99,360 N

Next we are going to size the welds between the box section and welded plates as shown here

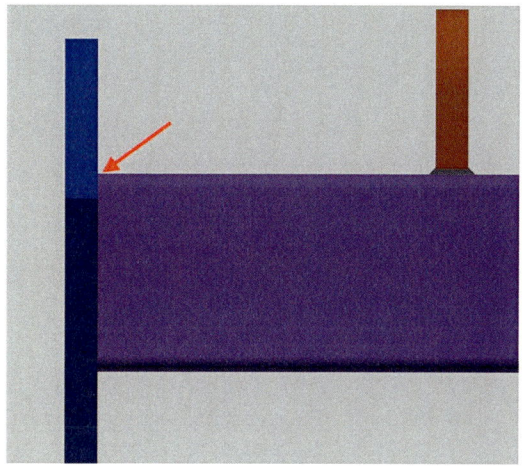

20. Change Weld Loads to **Bending force parallel with the weld plane**

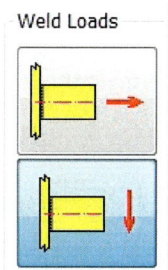

21. Specify the following values in the Fillet Weld Calculator dialogue box

Bending Force	15000 N	Yield Strength	207 MPa
Force Arm	210 mm	UTS	345 MPa
Weld Height	4 mm	Safety Factor	2
Beam Height	120 mm		
Beam Width	120 mm		

CHAPTER 6
DP5 – Weldment Analysis

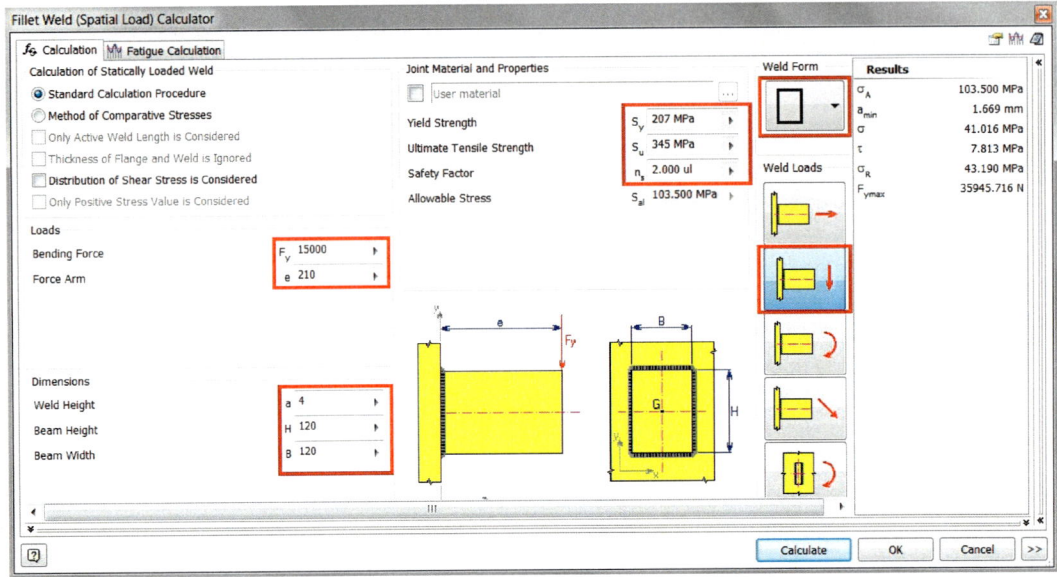

22. Click **Calculate**

Based on the dimensions of the box section 120mm x 120mm and a weld height of 4mm the following minimum weld size is calculated.

Allowable Stress (σA)	103.5 MPa
Minimum Weld Height (amin)	1.669 mm
Weld Normal Stress (σ)	41 MPa
Weld Shear Stress	7.8 MPa
Resulting Reduced Stress	43 MPa
Max Bending Force	35,945 N

So based on these calculations we can safely specify a weld size of 4mm on the whole structure. Here we create a weld on one of the lugs only so we can compare stress distribution around the lug without the weld.

23. Select **Welds** > Select **Fillet Weld** > Specify **4** for leg1 and leg2 of weld > Select the following **3 faces** for selection **1**

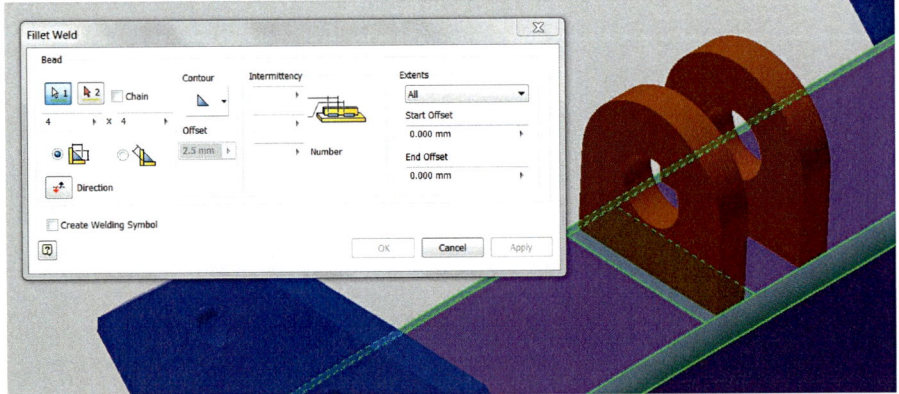

SECTION 2 - Stress Analysis Design Problems using Solid Elements

CHAPTER 6
DP5 – Weldment Analysis

24. Now select the **4 faces** of the lug as shown for selection **2**

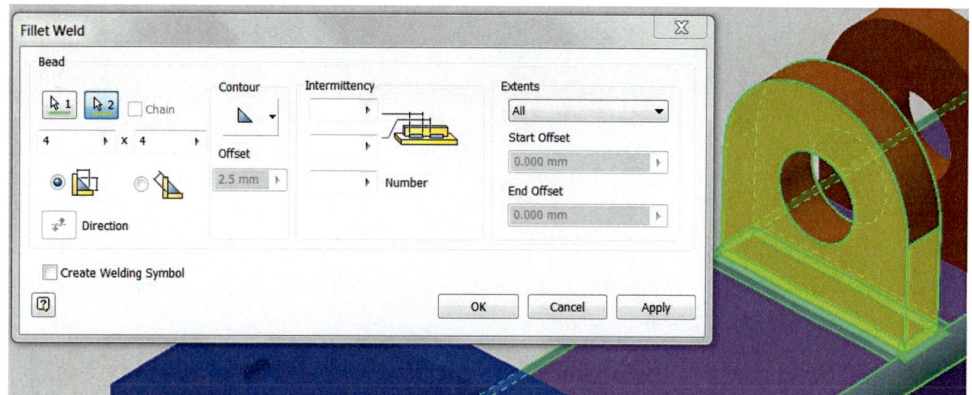

25. Click **OK** > Select **Return**

26. Select **Environments** tab > Select **Stress Analysis** > Right click **Contacts** > Select **Update Automatic Contacts**

A total of 12 contacts will be created within the Weldment Assembly.

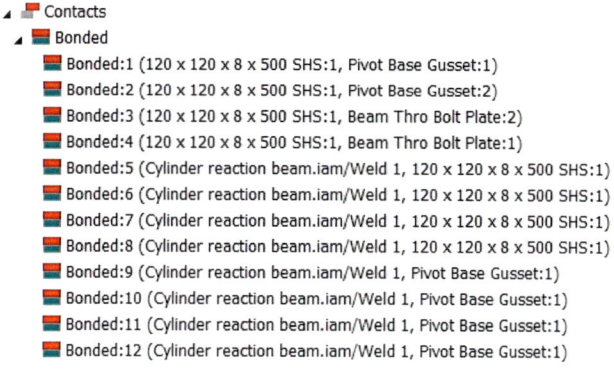

Using fillets and welds will increase the number of contacts produced.

As we have created welds on one of the lugs we will suppress the contact between the lug and box section. So the load is only transferred through the welds

SECTION 2 - Stress Analysis Design Problems using Solid Elements

CHAPTER 6
DP5 – Weldment Analysis

27. Right click **Bonded: 1** contact > Select **Suppress**

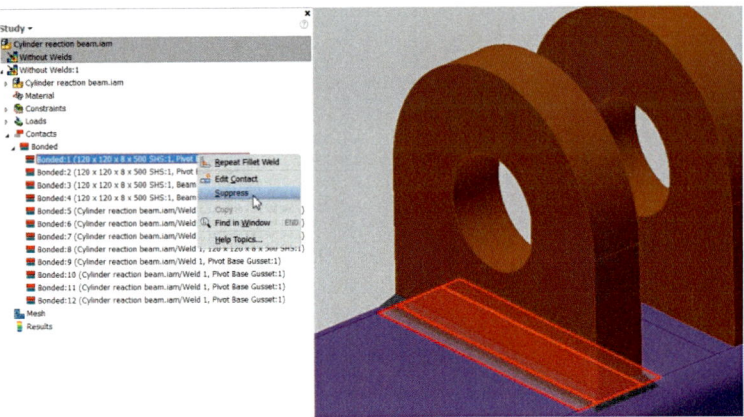

📝 Make sure you suppress the contact where the weld is defined (Bonded:1 or Bonded:2)

28. Select **Local Mesh Control** > Specify **2 mm** for element size > Select all faces of the new weld created as shown

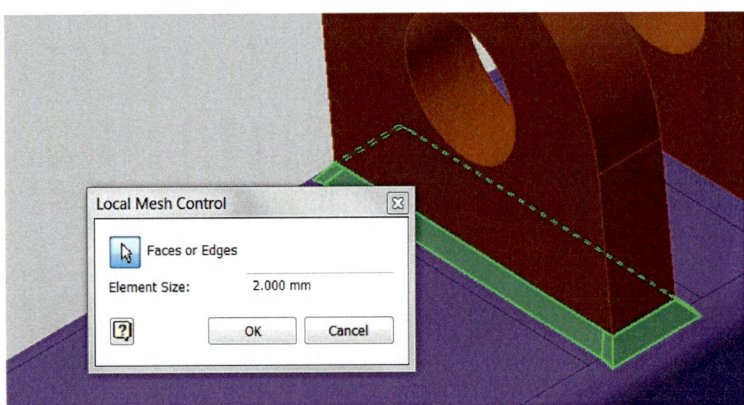

29. Click **OK** > Select **Mesh View**

Run simulation and analyze

30. Select **Simulate** > Select **Run**

Although the maximum stress has increased we will look at the stress area as before at a distance of 2x the weld size before.

31. Select **Color Bar** > Deselect **Maximum Value** > Specify **100** MPa > Click **OK**

CHAPTER 6
DP5 – Weldment Analysis

32. Deselect **Mesh View** > Select **Probe** > Select at locations shown below

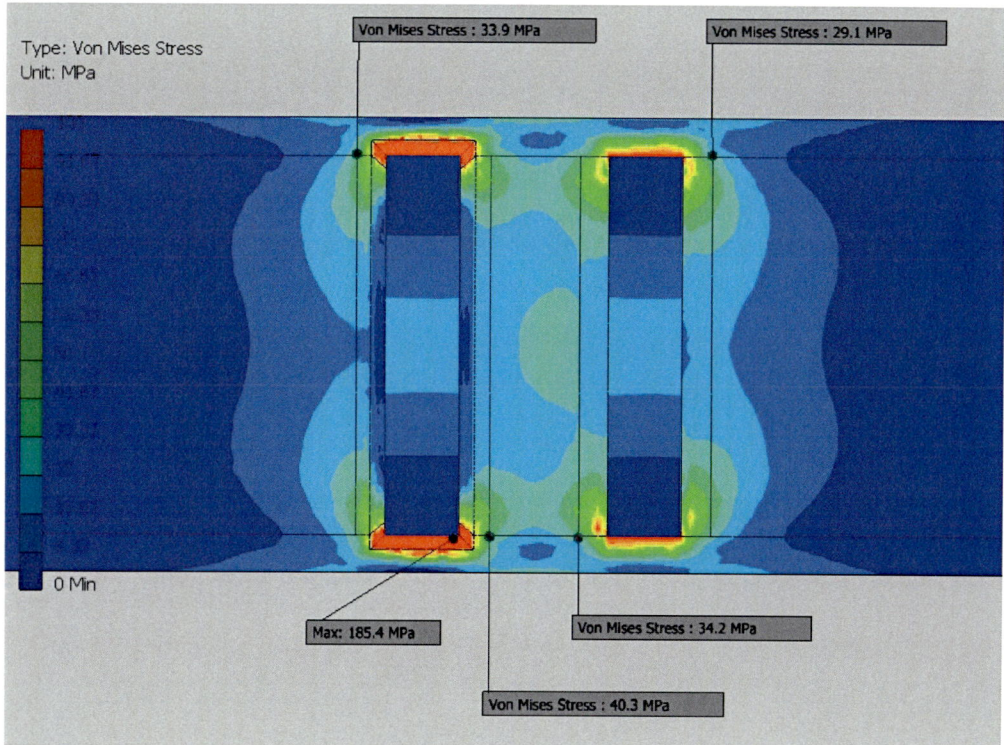

Comparing the stress locations we can see the stress values are between 10% with the exception of where the high stress area increasing the difference to above 10%. So is there a benefit to include welds within our analysis or not?

First of all let's take a look at our weld geometry as shown below.

Does this weld geometry represent reality? Are the welds meant to be sharp at the corners?

CHAPTER 6
DP5 – Weldment Analysis

Below is a typical geometry of weld in practice. Plus there is an image detailing the regions of an actual weld including heat affected zones.

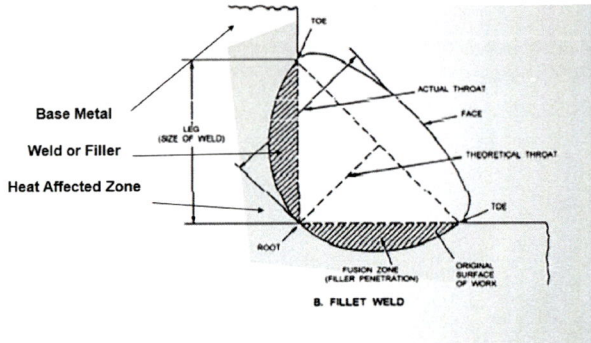

Although the geometry may not exactly measure physical attributes of the real weld there are other areas of the weld which are difficult to take account of within Inventor Stress Analysis including,

- Weld Geometry: Penetration, Convexity, Continuity, Grinding
- Chemistry: Carbon, Manganese, Hydrogen
- Temperature: Weld, Preheat, Cooling
- Base Material: Porosity, Composition
- Heat Affected Zone: Uniformity, Property Degradation (Ductility)
- Microcracking at perimeter of Weld
- Residual Stress after cooling
- Part Geometry: Surface Finish, Alignment, Warpage

For these reason its best practice to size welds using standards whether it being hand calculations or something similar to the inventor weld calculator. In addition even though it was reasonably easy to add welds in this example, in large fabrications it becomes tedious and impractical to add welds from both a CAD and FEA perspective.

In some cases it might help to add welds (preferably modelled as fillets) to help distribute the loads more uniformly.

CHAPTER 6
DP5 – Weldment Analysis

In summary.

Weld Size – Based on the weld calculator the weld size of 4 mm is more than sufficient.

Box Section – Using the best practice approach of investigating stresses at a distance of around 2 x weld size and at least 2 elements away we can see the stress values in the region of 35-37 MPa are well below the yield limit of the material.

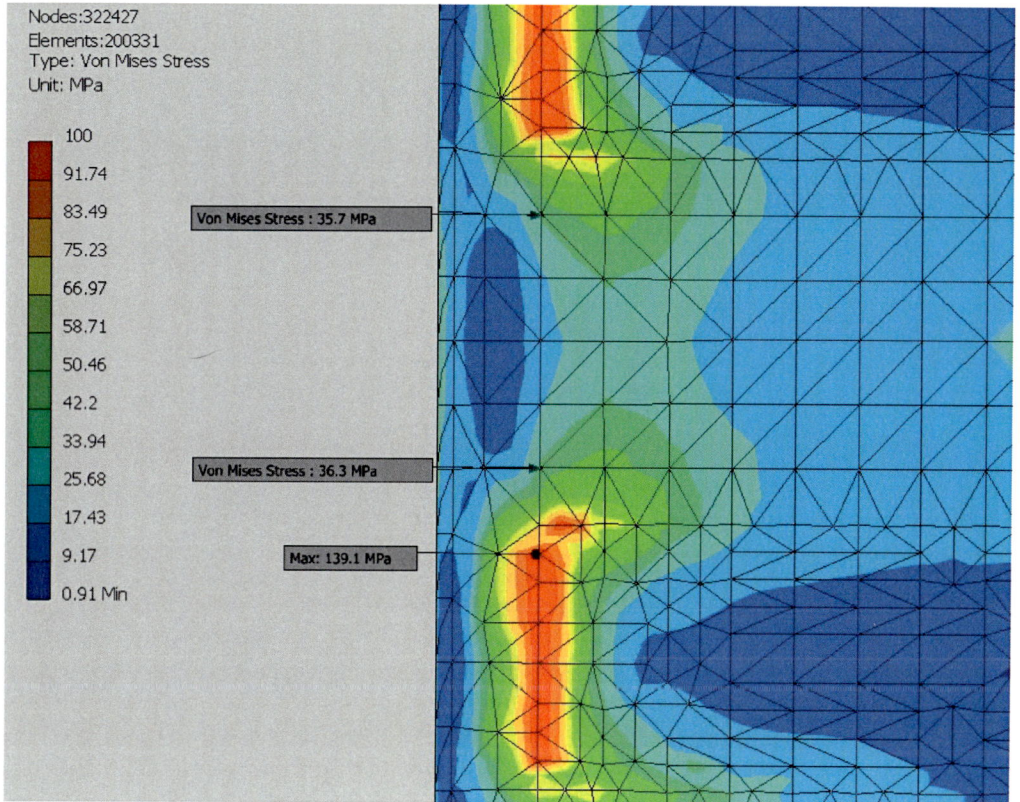

So based on 36 MPa (average value of the two above)

$$Factor\ of\ Safety = \frac{207}{36} = 5.75$$

CHAPTER 6
DP5 – Weldment Analysis

Lugs – Using a similar approach for the lugs

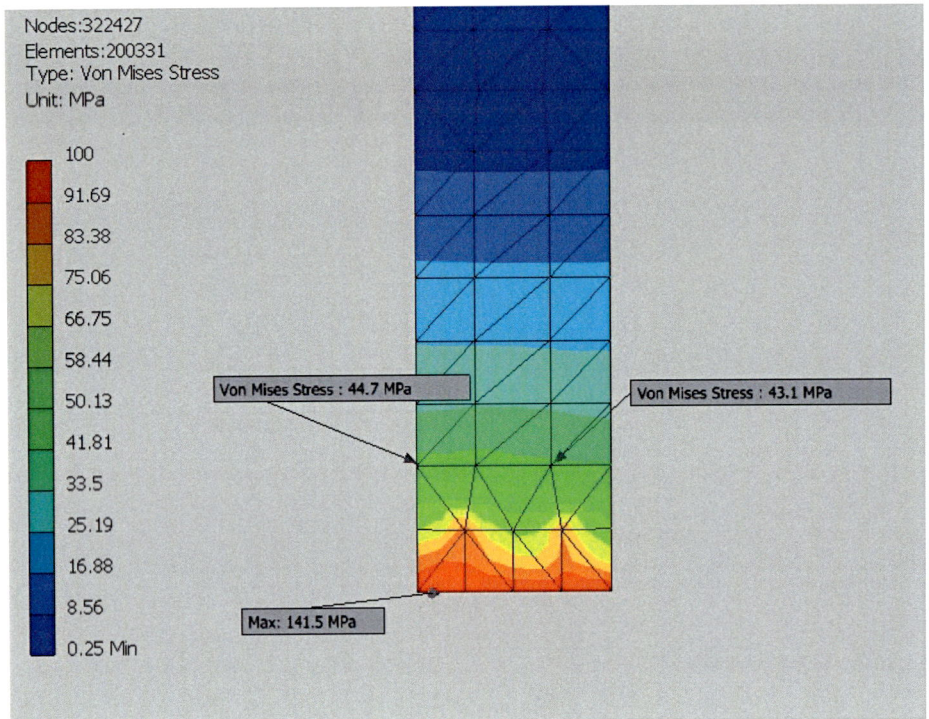

$$\textbf{\textit{Factor of Safety}} = \frac{207}{44} = 4.7$$

Interpretation of results require careful consideration based on experience, best practices and industry standards.

33. Close File

DP6 – Assembly Analysis with built-in welds

Structural Validation of Trailer Chassis

(Design Problem courtesy of Wright Resolutions Ltd)

Key features and workflows introduced in this design problem

	Key Features/Workflows
1	Automatic bonded contacts - Welded fabricated structure analysis
2	Multiple-loads
3	Interpretation of results with stress singularities present

Introduction

Wright Resolutions Ltd is a design consultancy specializing in agricultural cultivation and crop establishment machinery. Current clients include a number of well-known UK and European agricultural machinery manufacturers.

As part of a project to design a new concept for a trailer chassis, it was necessary to determine the loadings on and strength/deflections of a conventionally manufactured trailer chassis, as can be seen in the following picture. Such chassis are generally manufactured from hollow section steel together with flame-cut steel plates and flat bar parts.

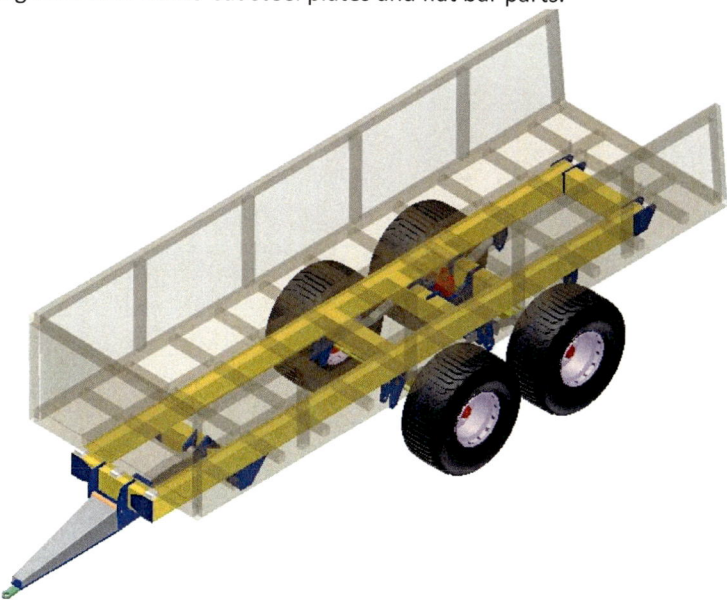

CHAPTER 7

DP6 - Assembly Analysis with built-in welds

Initially, the trailer was modeled in Dynamic Simulation to determine the loads at all critical areas including the drawbar, axle spring mountings, tipping cylinder, and rear hinges to the body. Maximum load situations during tipping were then taken and applied via FEA to determine the parameters listed below. One such situation, simplified, is used for this design problem.

The requirements of this design problem are to determine:

1. The maximum compressive and tensile stresses in the chassis.
2. The maximum deflection of the chassis under load.
3. The factor of safety.
4. The key stress zones for potential reinforcement when designing an alternative chassis.

In addition to the above requirements, the design criteria to be used for this design problem are as follows.

1. Material to be used is EN 50D / S355J2G3 steel.
2. Factor of safety required is 1.5.

Workflow of Design Problem 6

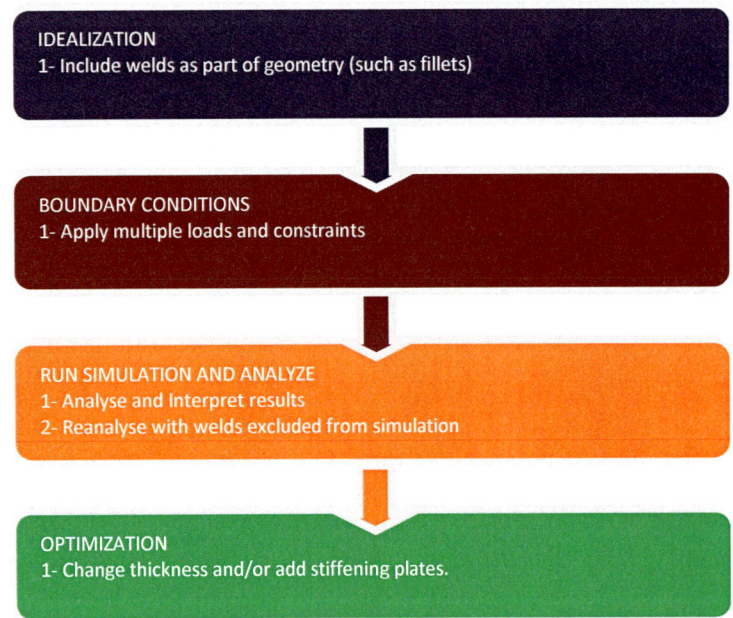

CHAPTER 7
DP6 - Assembly Analysis with built-in welds

Part 1-Chassis design with Welds and RHS Channel Radii

Idealization

To simplify the analysis of the fabricated chassis, the welds have been modeled as fillets within the components, which will greatly help to reduce the number of contacts produced.

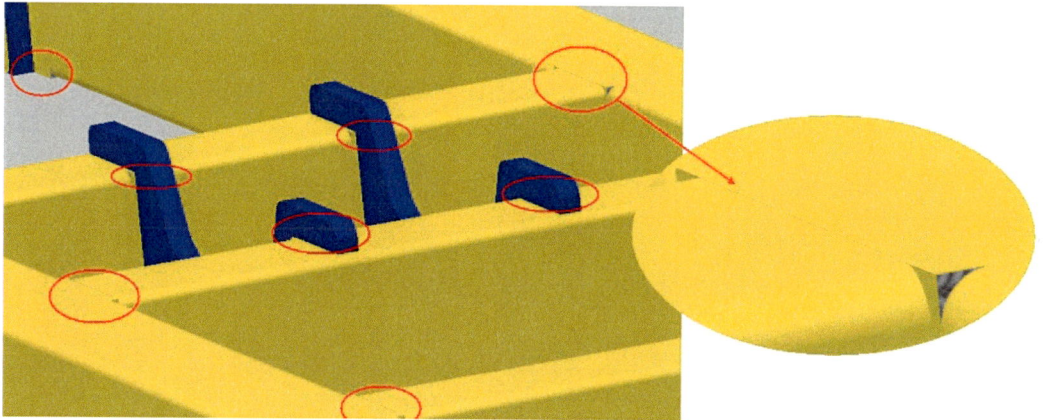

As the strength and characteristics of RHS are dependent on the corner radii, it is important to include these for more meaningful results. If welds are modeled separately to the RHS, the joints created in FEA are often complex and can be based on very thin slivers (highly distorted mesh elements) at the limits of the corner radii. Stress singularities produced can be very high. In practice, provided that the welds are correct and homogenous to the sections to which they are applied, such slivers are not present. Extruding the weld as part of the original section can represent nearer to a realistic situation. *It is important to simulate welds in a manner that represents reality, as close as possible, for the results to be meaningful.* The use of filler materials to bridge over the joints, or partial V butt welds, for example, would alter the strength and integrity of the structure in practice and lead to different results from those simulated.

1. Open Chassis.iam

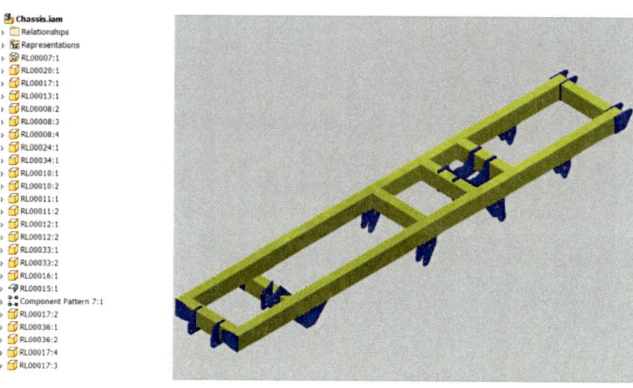

2. Select **Environments** tab > Select **Stress Analysis**

3. Select **Create Study** > Specify **Chassis-Analysis** for Name > Click **OK.**

SECTION 2 - Stress Analysis Design Problems using Solid Elements

CHAPTER 7
DP6 - Assembly Analysis with built-in welds

Boundary conditions

4. Select **Automatic** contacts to detect adjacent faces between components and welds

A total of 100 contacts will be created within the weldment assembly.

 Many more contacts would have been created if the welds had been modeled separately as a weldment assembly.

The chassis is attached to the tractor via a drawbar arm, which is secured to the chassis via locking pins. Therefore, we will apply pin constraints to secure the chassis

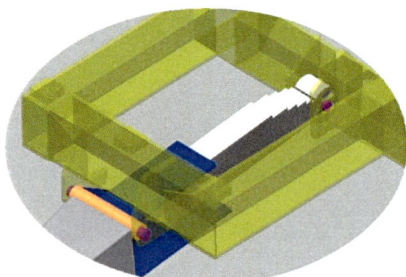

5. Select **Pin Constraint** > Select the faces of both holes as shown > Click Apply

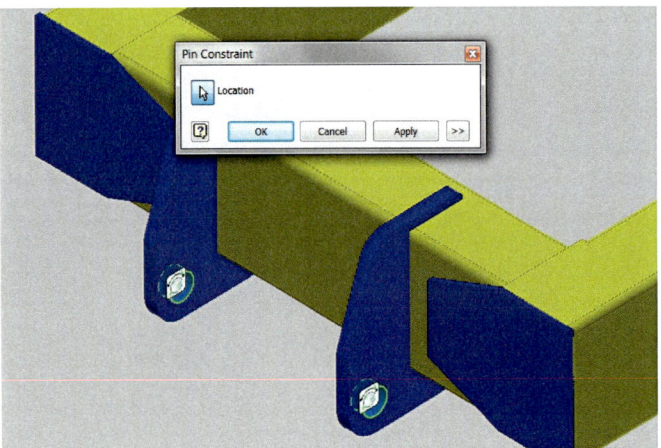

6. Now select the back faces of the two middle slots as shown > Click **OK**

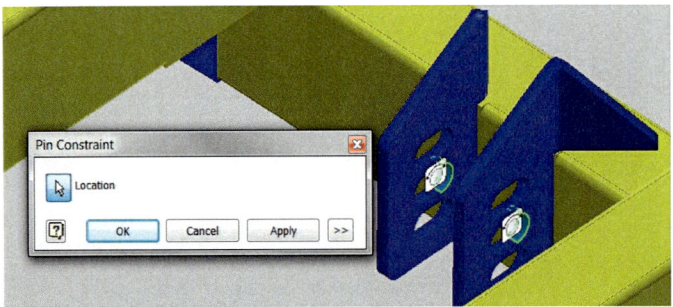

CHAPTER 7

DP6 - Assembly Analysis with built-in welds

With the aid of Dynamic Simulation, the trailer is used to simulate tipping to determine the maximum reaction forces on the chassis.

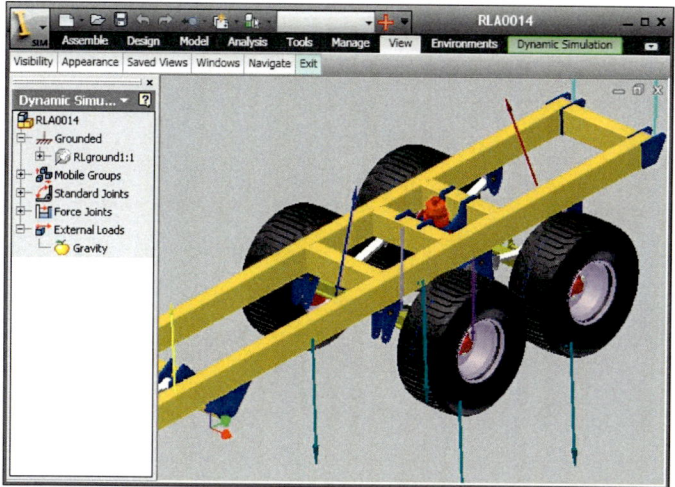

As the loads cannot be exported automatically, because this function only supports single parts, we will specify these bearing loads manually. First, we will apply the forces generated by the load and weight of chassis.

7. Select **Gravity** > Select **Use Vector Components** > Specify **-9810** in the Z direction > Click **OK**

As there are many bearing loads to be applied, we will select multiple bearing load faces, lying on the same axis, to help speed up the creation of loads. As the bearing loads are split equally by the number of faces selected, we will simply multiply the actual loads by the number of faces selected. Alternatively, you can create a load on each individual face.

8. Select **Bearing Load** > Select two internal circular faces as shown below > Specify top face of plate to specify the **Direction** of the force as shown > Specify **280,000** for Magnitude

9. Specify **0.5** for scale to reduce size of the force display > Specify **Jack Main Load** for Name > Click **Apply**

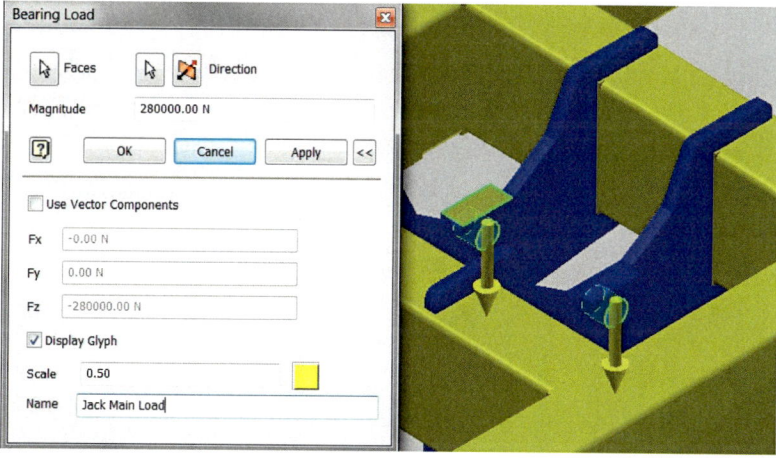

SECTION 2 - Stress Analysis Design Problems using Solid Elements

CHAPTER 7
DP6 - Assembly Analysis with built-in welds

10. Now select the two internal circular faces of the bushings as shown > Specify top face of plate to specify the **Direction** of the force as shown > Specify **50,000** for Magnitude

11. Specify **Reaction-load-1** for Name > Click **Apply**

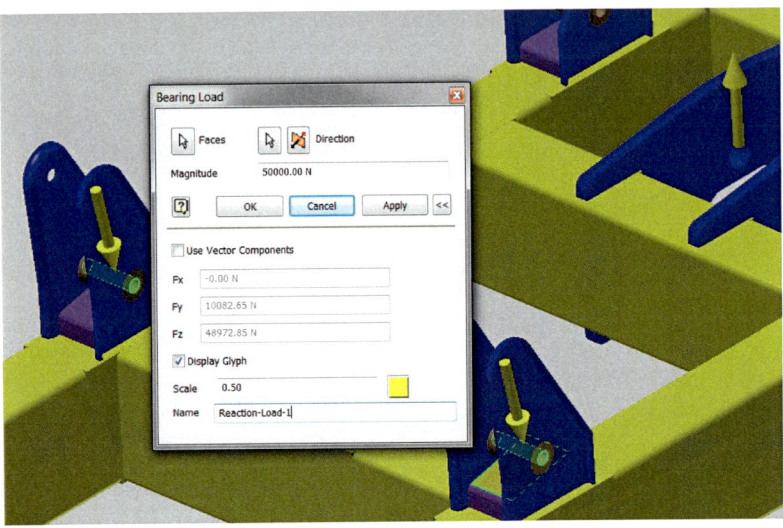

12. Now select the two internal circular faces of the bushings as shown > Specify the top face of plate to specify the **Direction** of force, as shown > Specify **82000** for Magnitude

13. Specify **Reaction-load-2** for Name > Click **Apply**

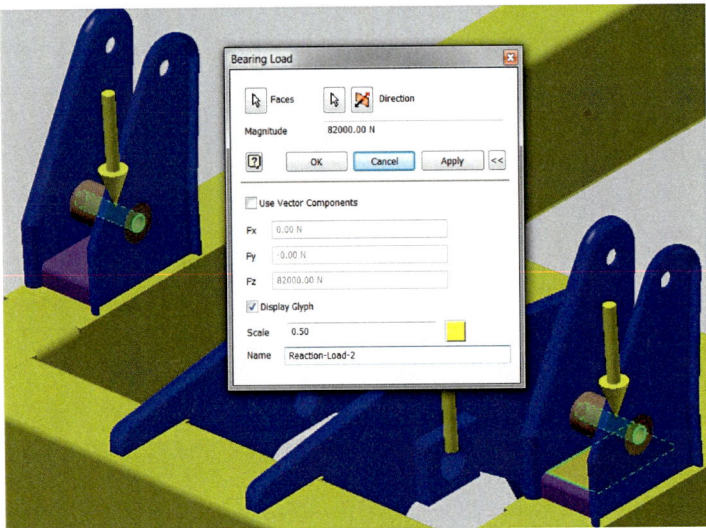

CHAPTER 7
DP6 - Assembly Analysis with built-in welds

14. Now select the two internal circular faces of the bushings as shown > Specify the top face of the plate to specify the **Direction** of force as shown > Specify **58000** for Magnitude

15. Specify **Reaction-load-3** for Name > Click **Apply**

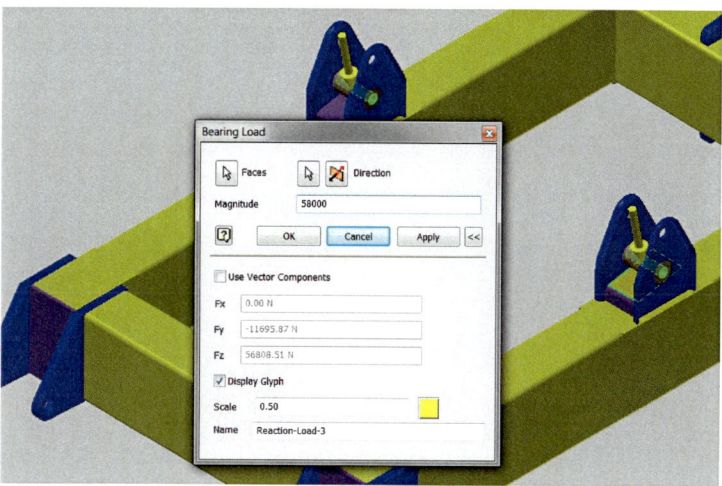

16. Now select the four internal circular faces of the bushings as shown below > Specify the top face of the chassis to specify the **Direction** of force, as shown > Specify **84000** for Magnitude

17. Specify **Reaction-load-4** for Name > Click **OK**

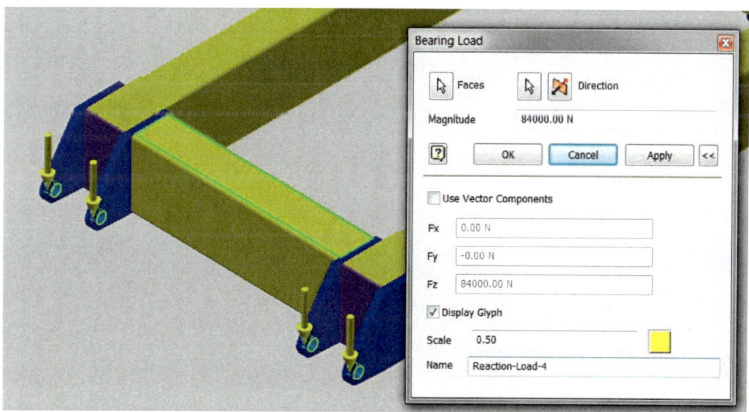

18. Select **Mesh Setting** > Specify **0.025** for Average Element Size > Unselect **Use part based measure for Assembly mesh** > Select **Create Curved Mesh Elements** > Click **OK**

19. Select **Mesh View**

152,624 elements are generated. Leaving Use part based measure for Assembly mesh selected would have created more elements.

CHAPTER 7
DP6 - Assembly Analysis with built-in welds

Run simulation and analyze

20. Select **Simulate** > Select **Run**

21. Deselect **Mesh View** > Deselect **Boundary Conditions** > Select **Undeformed** from Adjust Displacement Display > Select **Maximum Value**

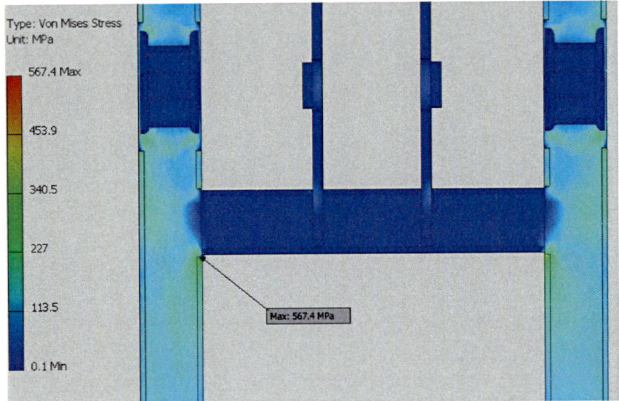

The maximum stress value of 567.4 MPa is around a small area of the weld and is largely due to stress singularities as a result of discontinuity in the geometrical shape. In these high stress regions localized yielding can occur under initial loading. The permanent deformation is normally so localized that it will have negligible impact on the structural integrity of the structure. The only exception being cyclic loading which can lead to fatigue failure, this is not the case in this design problem.

Refining the mesh around these areas will not necessarily reduce stresses and in most cases will further increase the stresses. As the result stands, the safety factor value of 0.63 relating to the maximum stress indicates failure.

In these situations, we can make use of the color bar to better understand the results, as suggested in the following steps:

22. Select **Von Mises Stress** > Select **Color Bar** > Unselect **Maximum** > Specify **355** MPa (this is yield limit of material) > Click **OK** > Select **Contour Shading**

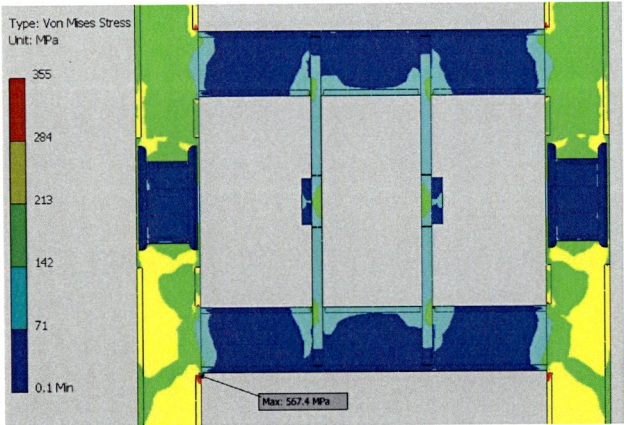

SECTION 2 - Stress Analysis Design Problems using Solid Elements

CHAPTER 7
DP6 - Assembly Analysis with built-in welds

The concentration of red stress plot, above a value of 284 MPa, is extremely low. As stress reversals are unlikely in this design we can assume the safety factor for this design is:

$$Factor\ of\ Safety = \frac{355}{284} = 1.25$$

We can further manipulate the color bar to get a better estimate of the actual safety factor of the design we start from the 284 MPa.

23. Select **Color Bar** > Specify **284 MPa** for maximum Value

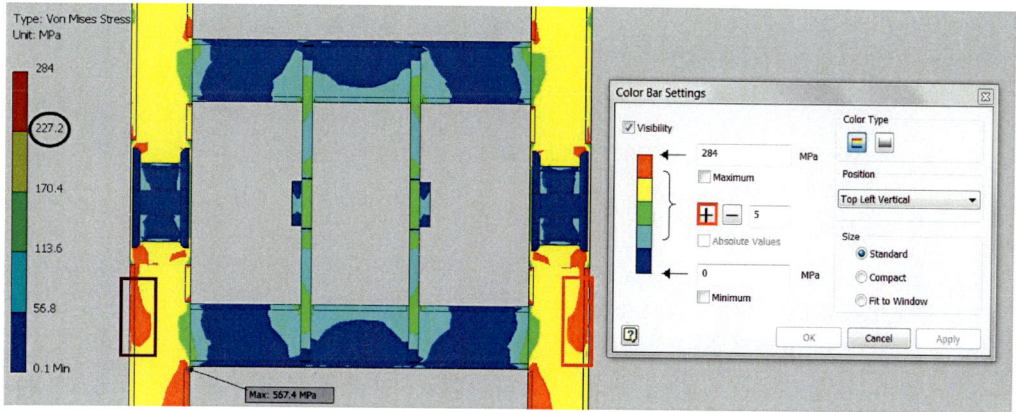

We can now see red stress plot on the other side of the channel, away from the welds. In the following steps we are going to increase the legend number (6) until we start to see small amount of red stress away from the welds.

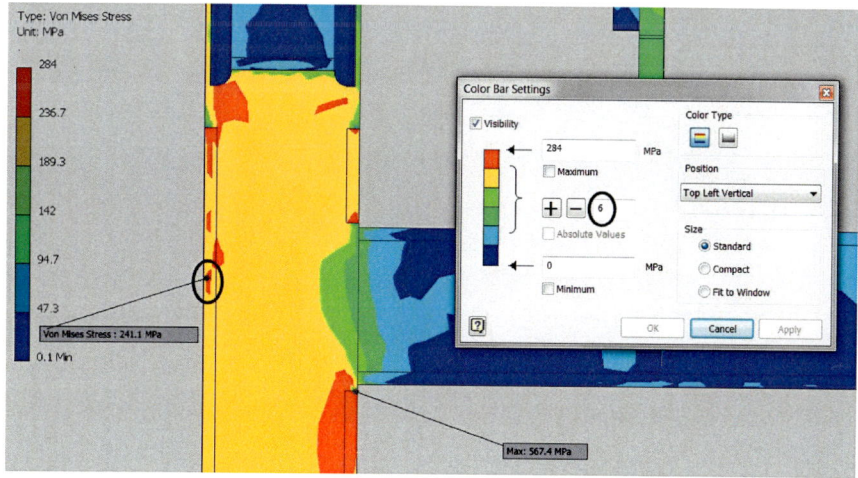

We can now see that stress above 236.7 MPa appears on the other side and with further investigating with a probe we find the stress is around 241 MPa. So now we have:

$$Factor\ of\ Safety = \frac{355}{241} = 1.47$$

CHAPTER 7
DP6 - Assembly Analysis with built-in welds

📝 As a rule of thumb, if such singularities result from static loading and are concentrated in small localized areas, then they can be ignored for the purposes of calculating the overall safety factor, for example. _Experience of the effect of such high stress points is needed to ensure that the correct interpretation is made of FEA results_. For example, dynamically loaded situations can have stress reversals; where these occur at welded joints, there is a high chance of fatigue failure occurring.

As the value is close to the design limit of 1.5, we need to look at optimizing the design.

Optimization

Based on the previous analyzes of the chassis, the results indicate that the design does not meet the design criteria. To meet the design criteria, we have two options.

1. Increase the thickness of the RHS members; however, this approach is not cost-effective when compared to option 2 or if the component has already been manufactured.

2. Place a plate (suggested thickness ≥ 10mm) between the mounts and the RHS members as illustrated below.

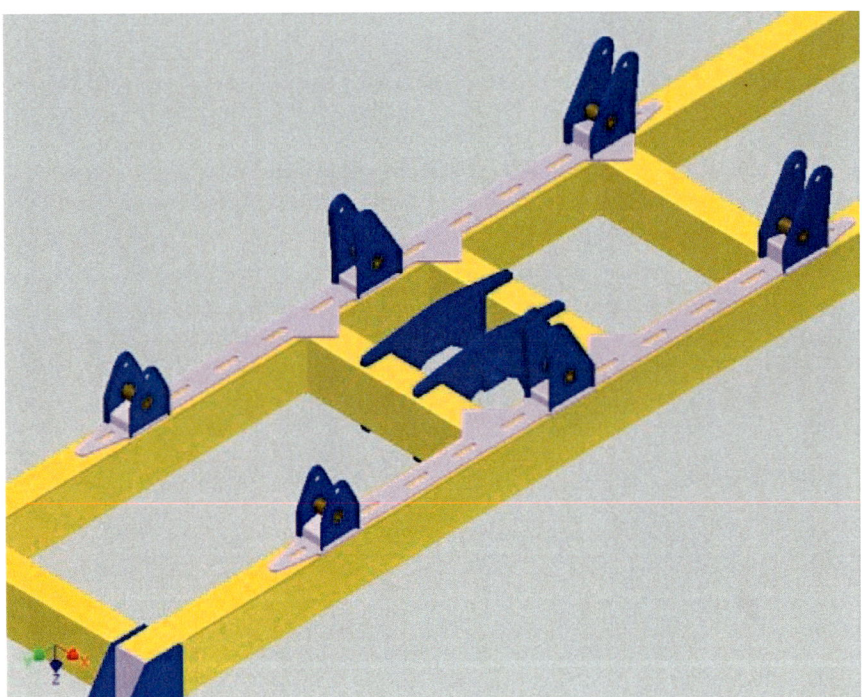

If the chassis design is not built, a combination of option 1 and 2 can be used to manufacture a more rigid chassis.

In practice, additional loading scenarios are analyzed; for example, when the chassis has a torsional load applied down its length. In this case, stress reversals are often present that need to be taken into account when determining the final design of reinforcements to be made.

Section 3 - STRESS ANALYSIS *Design Problems* using THIN and SOLID ELEMENTS

DP7 – Wind Load analysis

Structural Integrity of Traffic Sign Posts
(Design Problem Courtesy of VMS Ltd)

Key features and workflows introduced in this design problem

	Key Features/Workflows
1	Effective use of multi-bodies with respect to different mid surface thicknesses
2	Creating surfaces using midsurface command
3	Mixed solid and shell elements analysis
4	Wind speed load converted to force

Introduction

Variable Message Signs Limited (VMS) has been a market leader for a quarter of a century and supplied thousands of messaging signs and traffic management systems. VMS products fall into two main categories: Road - with a product range covering applications in the highways, urban, and traffic management equipment sectors, and Rail, where their new super lightweight range of rail LED trackside signals and LED long-distance signals are breaking the mold in this sector.

CHAPTER 8

DP7 - Wind Load Analysis

The main requirements of this design problem are to determine:

1. Maximum stress in the structure.
2. Maximum displacement of the structure
3. Minimum safety factor.

In addition to the above requirements, the design criteria to be used for this design problem are:

- The material to be used is mild steel.
- Wind speeds to be taken as 25 mph and 50 mph
- Weight of Display panel is 60 Kg.

Workflow of Design Problem 7

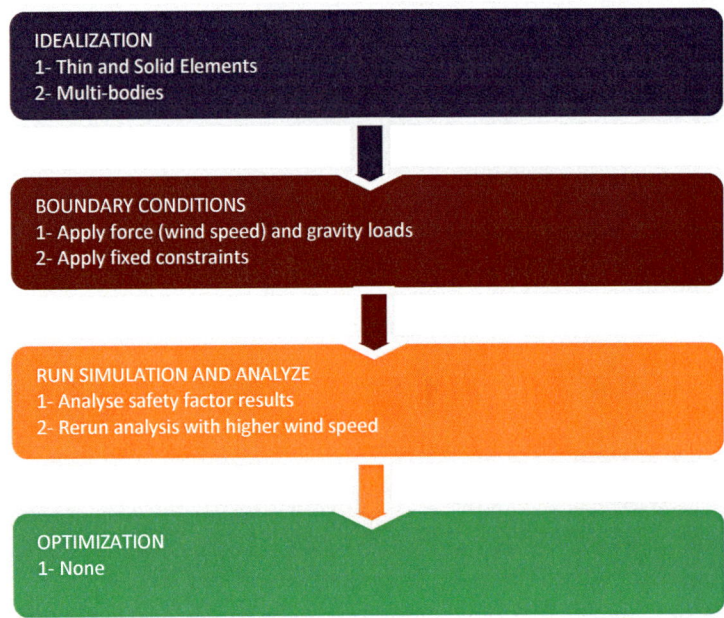

CHAPTER 8
DP7 - Wind Load Analysis

Idealization

As Inventor Simulation only creates midsurfaces for a single thickness component, we are going to make use of multibodies, with different thicknesses, as illustrated below. This way Inventor Stress Analysis will select all features, modelled as individual solids, as separate midsurfaces. To further simplify the analysis process for this design; the display, fixtures and the concrete base, will be excluded from the simulation. This simplification and idealization are saved as a different level of detail within the assembly environment.

1. Open SignPost.iam

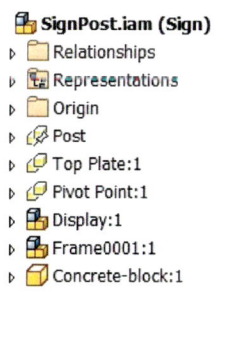
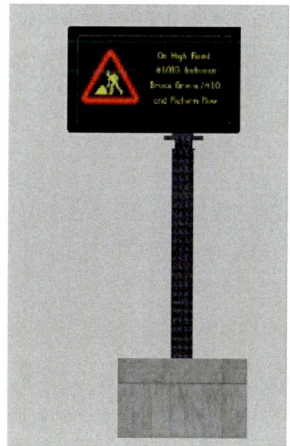

2. Activate **FEA-Analysis** Level of Detail

This will suppress the sign and concrete block for the purposes of this analysis

3. Select **Environments** tab > Select **Stress Analysis**

4. Select **Create Study** > Specify **Signpost** for Name > Click **OK**

SECTION 3 - Stress Analysis Design Problems using Thin Elements

CHAPTER 8
DP7 - Wind Load Analysis

📝 Create midsurfaces before applying constraints and loads as these will be lost if applied on component faces.

5. Select **Find Thin Bodies** > Click **OK** in the prompt dialogue box

6. Select other components, except frame behind panel > Expand **Prompts** button > Select **Do not show this message again this session** > Click **OK** > Continue selecting the rest of the component > Click **OK,** once selected all.

💡 If you miss a component just select the midsurface button and continue selecting rest of components

As the post is made up of different thicknesses we have made use of multibodies as this results in different midsurface thicknesses as illustrated below. The alternative would have been to create the post as an assembly comprised of different component thicknesses.

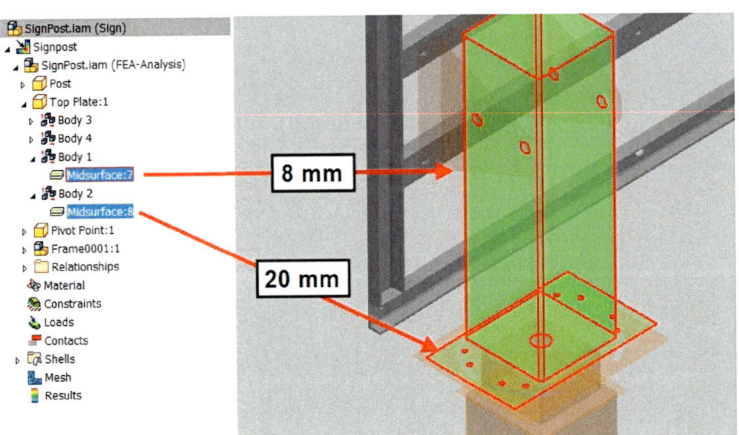

📝 Inventor Stress Analysis will create a single midsurface with average thickness for a part with multiple thicknesses if used without multibodies.

CHAPTER 8
DP7 - Wind Load Analysis

The frames supporting the LED panel comprise of tapered structures, meaning that the structures will result in multiple disconnected surfaces as shown below

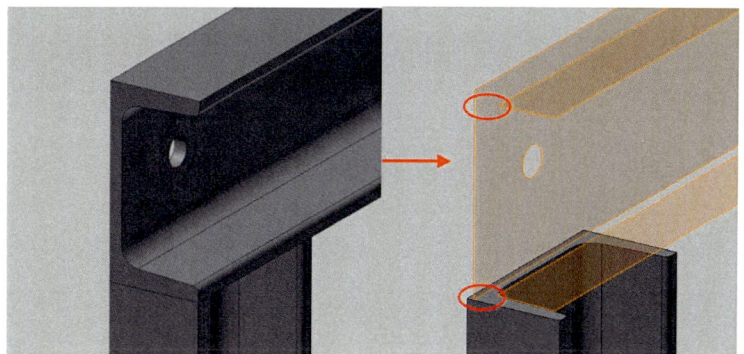

This can be avoided by using offset surfaces command as illustrated below

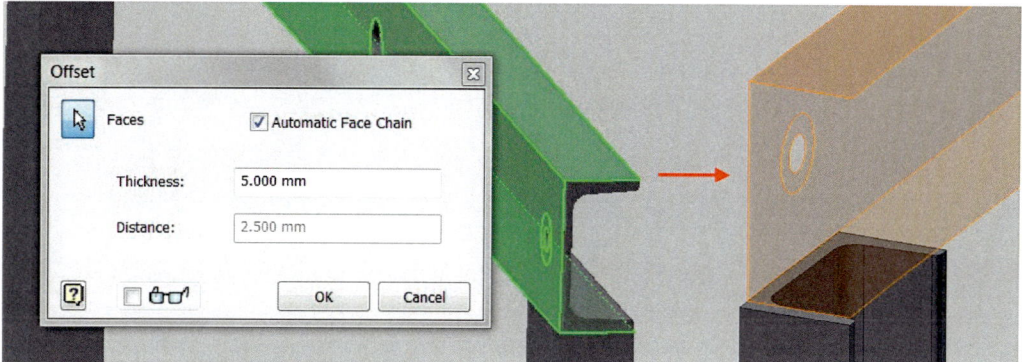

The thickness parameter is an estimate of the channel as the thicknesses varies from 5 to 8mm. The value chosen illustrates worst case scenario. The benefit of this method is that all surfaces are connected. In the following steps this frame will be meshed using solid elements.

 Inventor Simulation generally picks up components with a length to thickness ratio of 200 to 1 respectively, and above, as potential candidates for midsurfaces when using find thin bodies.

It is up to you the designer if you wish to treat any components that have a length to thickness ratio of less than 200 to 1 respectively, as surfaces for thin elements. The tapered beams in this example supporting the sign panel have a length: thickness ratio less than 200, taking the thickest section of the channel. In this exercise we will analyze the beams supporting the panel using solid elements.

CHAPTER 8
DP7 - Wind Load Analysis

Boundary conditions

In the following steps we will apply constraints and loads.

7. Select **Fixed Constraint** > Select the four faces as shown > Click **OK**

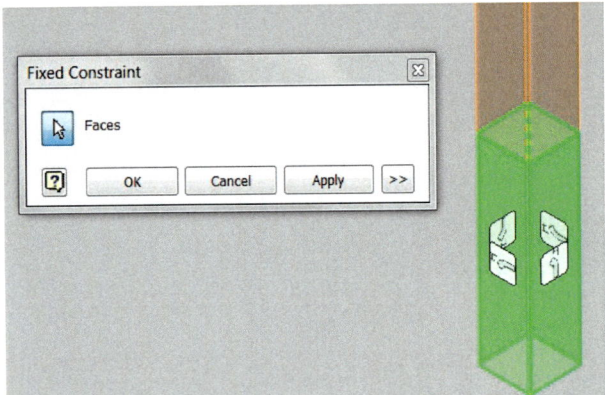

📝 The faces have already been split in the part environment. These faces are normally restrained by the concrete base, excluded from this analysis.

In the next steps we need to apply wind speed exerted directly on to the LED display panel. Here we have two overcome two issues first too convert wind speed into force as we cannot apply wind speed in Inventor Stress Analysis. Secondly we need to apply this force on the panel attached via bushings to the channels, both of which are excluded from simulation. In this situation we will equally spread the load by applying on the four split faces representing the location of the bushings. So first for the purposes of calculating force from a given wind speed we will use the following generic formula (googled on the World Wide Web)

$$Force\ F = A\ x\ P\ x\ Cd\ and\ P = 0.12257\ x\ V^2$$

Where:

F is force in Newton's (N)

A is the cross section of the LED display panel in Meters (approx 2m²)

P is the pressure in Pascal's (N/m)

V is the wind speed in (Mph)

Cd is the drag coefficient (2 to be used for rectangular flat areas)

For a wind speed of 25mph we get the total force to be

$$P = 0.12257\ x\ 25^2 = 76.6$$

$$Force\ F = 2\ x\ 76.6\ x\ 2 = 306\ N$$

CHAPTER 8

DP7 - Wind Load Analysis

8. Select **Force** and specify **306** N > Select the circular face as shown below

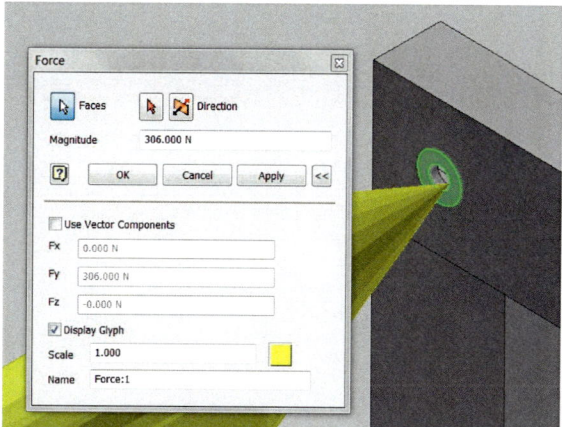

9. Select the other three circular faces > Specify **25** mph for Name > Click **Apply**

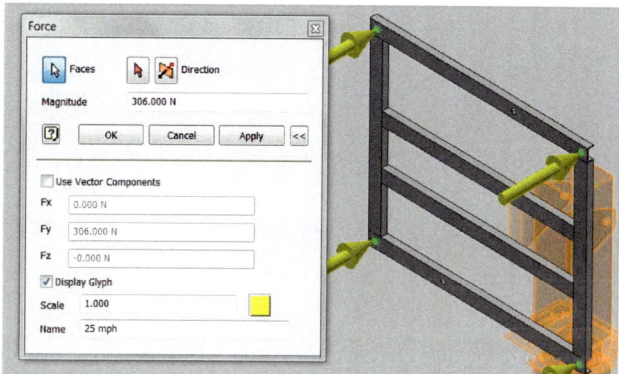

Now we are going to account for the 60 Kg weight of the display panel. This converted to force will be approximately 600 N

10. Specify **600** N > Select the same circular hole faces again > Specify **Weight of panel** for Name > Select face of top frame for **Direction** of load > Change color of Load to **red** > Click **OK** twice

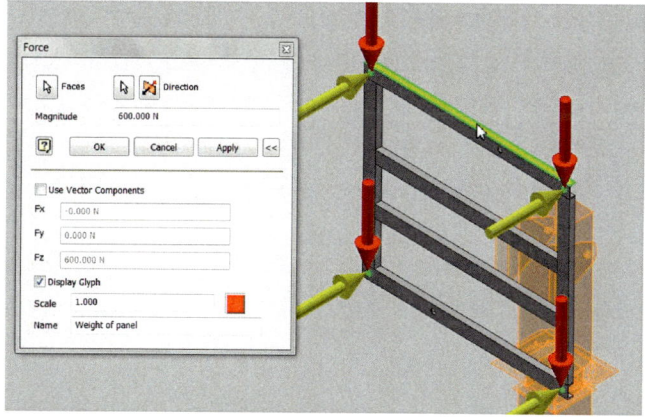

11. Select **Automatic Contacts**

SECTION 3 - Stress Analysis Design Problems using Thin Elements

CHAPTER 8
DP7 - Wind Load Analysis

12. Select **Mesh Settings** > Specify **0.01** for **Average Element Size** > Specify **0.03** for **Average Element Size in Shells** > Unselect **Use part based measure for Assembly mesh** > Select **Create Curved Mesh Elements** > Click **OK**

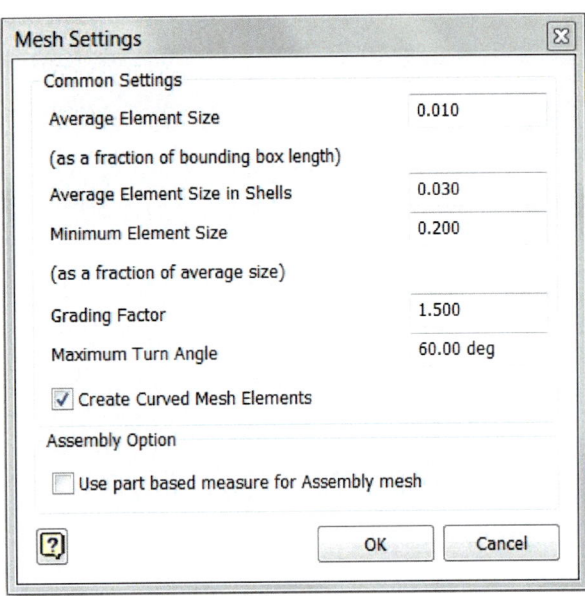

13. Select **Mesh View**

A total of 56,043 elements will be created, value may differ slightly.

Run simulation and analyze

14. Select **Simulate** > Select **Run**

15. Select **Undeformed** for Adjust Displacement Display > Deselect **Boundary Conditions** > Deselect **Mesh View** > Select **Maximum Value**

16. Select **1st Principal Stress** > Select **Contour Shading** > Select **Bottom** view using cube

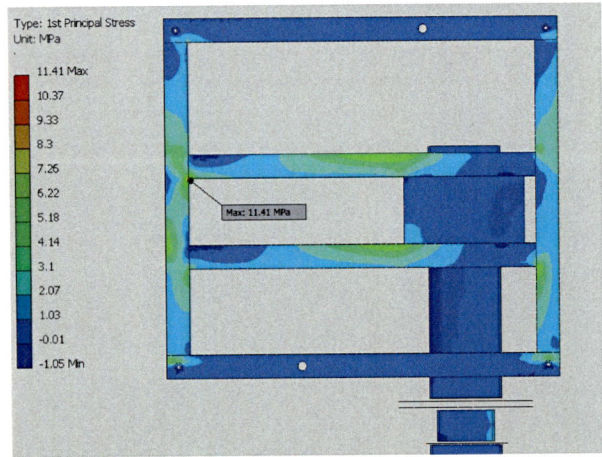

The maximum value of 11.41 MPa is stress hot spot (stress singularity due geometry discontinuity). Meaning further refinement of the mesh will increase this stress further. One of the options to reduce this hot spot is to include weld geometry whether as a separate part or as a feature within a part. Simplification of the channels may also help to reduce hot spots, features like holes and fillets are prime candidates.

17. Select **Displacement**

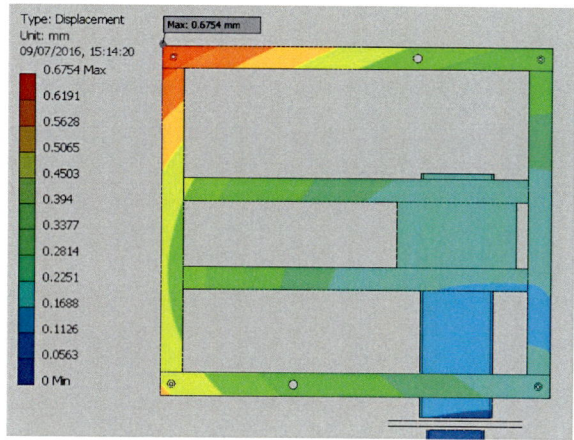

Maximum value is 0.6754 mm. Now we are going to copy the simulation and reanalyze structure for a wind speed of 50mph.

18. Right Click **Signpost** > Select **Copy Study**

19. Right Click 25 mph Load > Select **Edit Force Load** > Specify **1225.7** N > Specify **50** mph for **Name** > Click **OK**

$$P = 0.12257 \times 50^2 = 306.425$$

$$Force\ F = 2 \times 306.425 \times 2 = 1225.7\ N$$

20. Select **Simulate** > Select **Run**

21. Select **1st Principal Stress** > Select **Contour Shading** > Select **Bottom** view using cube

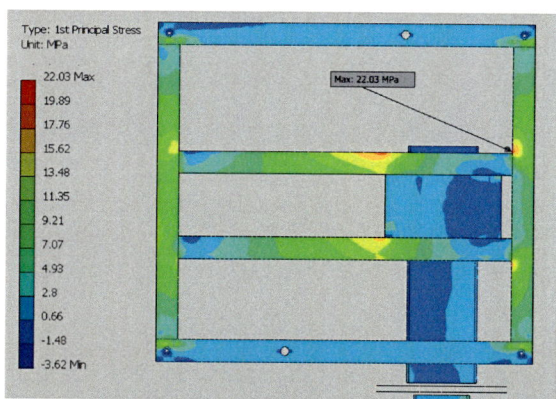

CHAPTER 8
DP7 - Wind Load Analysis

Although the maximum value has increased to 22.03 MPa, again it looks like a hot spot. Below are results plot of both scenarios using same legend scale.

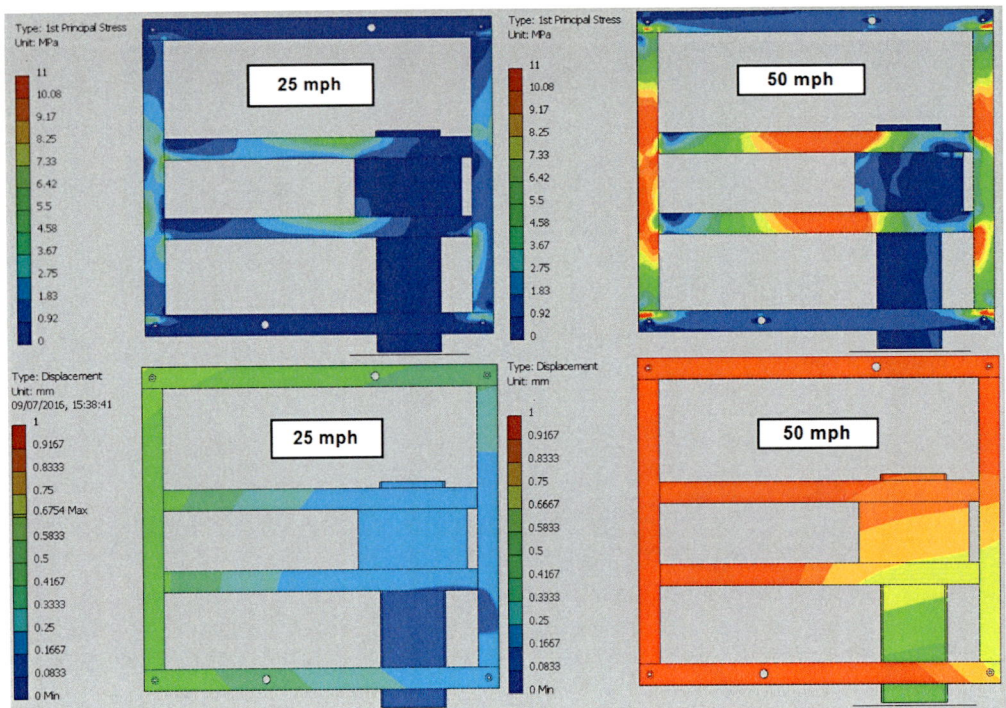

22. Close File

CHAPTER 9
DP8 - Fabrication Analysis

DP8 – Fabrication Analysis

Structural Integrity of Container
(Design Problem Courtesy of Croft Associates Ltd)

Key features and workflows introduced in this design problem

	Key Features/Workflows
1	Creating Surfaces using Midsurface command
2	Creating Surfaces using Offset command
3	Combined thin and solid elements

Introduction

Croft Associates Limited specializes in all aspects of the packaging and transport of radioactive materials. Since establishment in 1980, the company has developed an extensive range of packaging designs for standard products, and for customers' individual requirements.

CHAPTER 9

DP8- Fabrication Analysis

Croft customers are often governmental organizations and private companies in the nuclear materials and waste industries. In addition, research reactors, hospitals and medical equipment suppliers also use the company products to transport radioactive materials for recovery, verification, testing, compliance assurance and medical applications.

The main requirements of this design problem are to determine:

1. Maximum stress within the base structure of the container assembly
2. Maximum displacement under the loads specified under the various regulatory specifications pertaining to hazardous material transport

In addition to the main requirements, the design criteria to be used for this design problem are:

- The material to be used is Steel, High Strength Low Alloy
- The maximum allowable vertical permanent displacement of 6 mm, ie. the floor cannot be allowed to (displace) below the main supporting components (the four corner fittings which interface with corresponding components in, for example, a nine high stack of equivalent containers). The floor may displace further than 6 mm, but must recover to an extent that any permanent set allows sufficient clearance for the container to be stored in a stacking arrangement.
- The maximum operational stress not to exceed 2/3rd of material yield limit.

Workflow of Design Problem 8

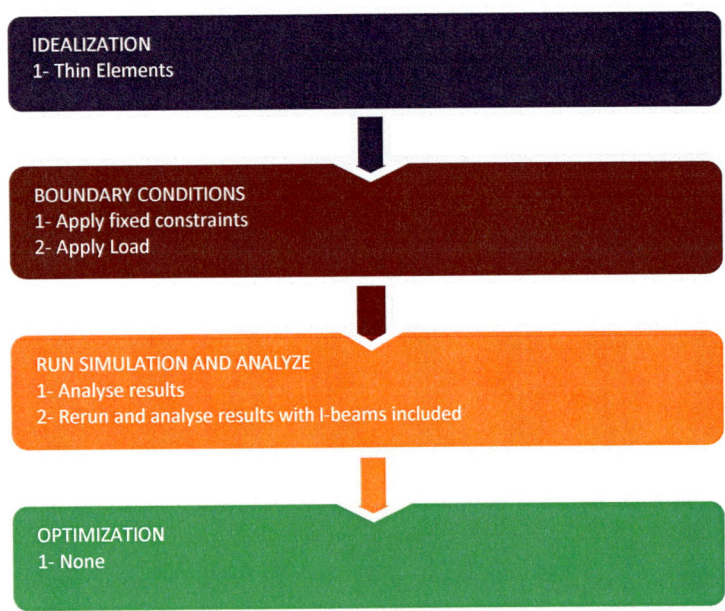

Idealization

In this example we going to only consider the base of the component as the main structural item of the container as this will carry the bulk of the load. Although the rest of the components will provide some structural support it is assumed it will beminimal and will be neglected for the purposes of this design problem. In reality the I-Beams will be actually fixed to the base of the components before container is loaded. In this example we will consider the effect of I-Beams having on the overall structural integrity of the base when loaded. Further, to simplify the modeling process for this example, all welds and the fixture and fittings of the base plate will be excluded from the simulation. This simplification and idealization are saved as different level of details within the assembly environment and will be used in the analysis.

1. Open Container.iam

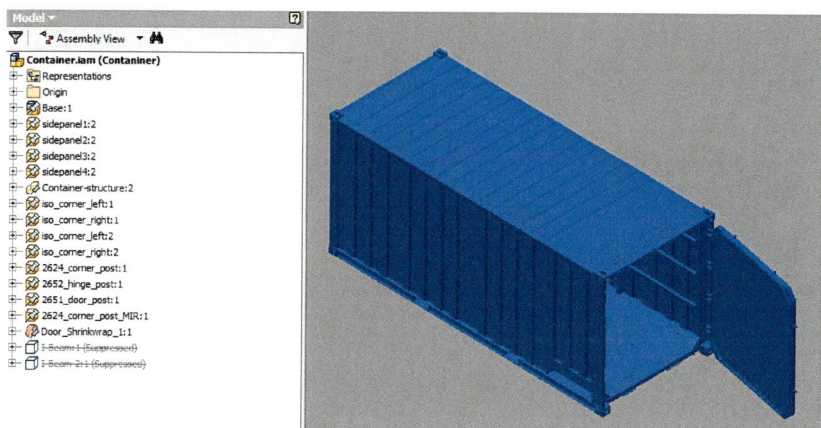

2. Activate **FEA** Level of Detail

This level of detail suppresses the side and top panels, including door and fittings. In additional all fixture and fitting on the base panel are also suppressed.

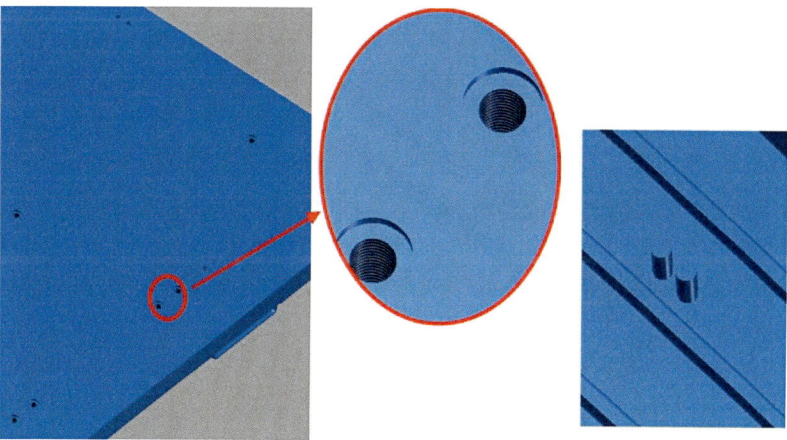

CHAPTER 9
DP8- Fabrication Analysis

To also reduce hotspots in the base panel some of the base panel members have been further simplified by removing the radii's as illustrated below.

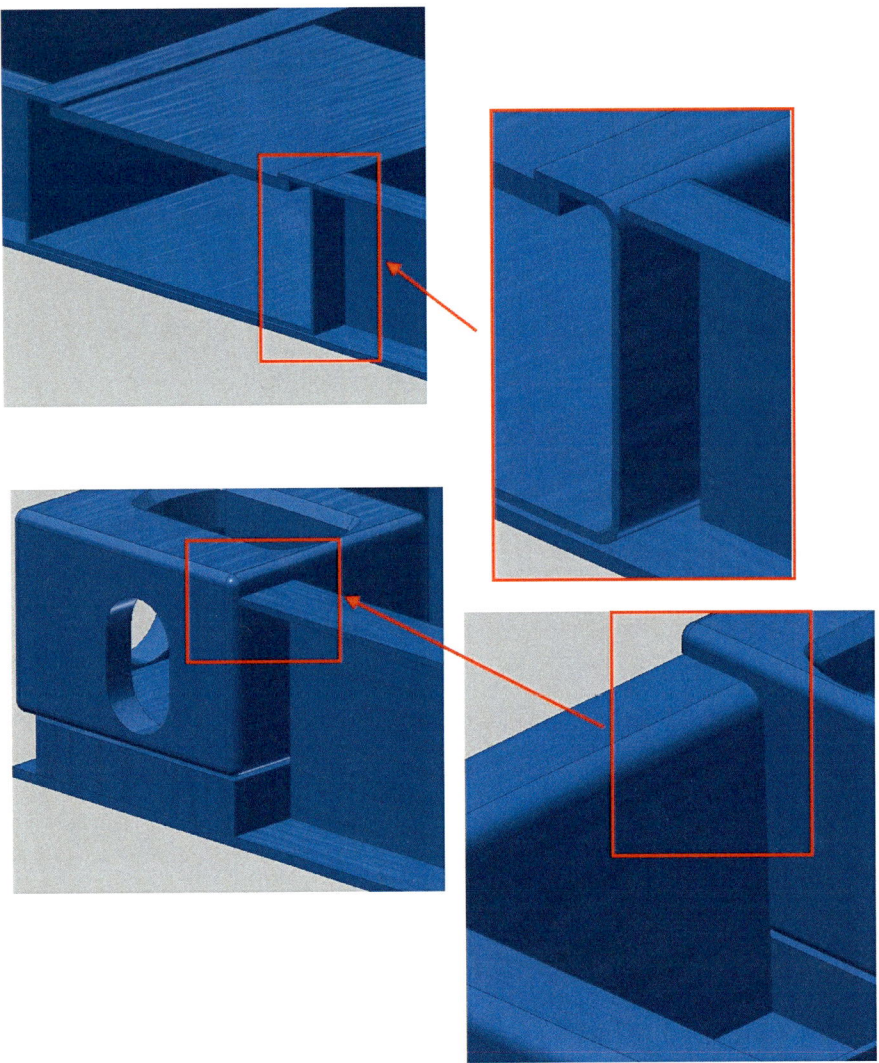

Leaving the radii can result in excessive edge to edge or edge to face contacts resulting in high stresses. So check the contacts carefully in high stress areas. For shells you need to remove or suppress automatic edge to edge contacts and replace with, at least, edge to face contact. As this will help to transfer load between components more uniformly, if available, face to face contact is best option.

Boundary conditions

3. Select **Environments** tab > Select **Stress Analysis**

4. Select **Create Study** > Specify **Base** for Name > Click **OK**

You can further simplify by excluding the holes from the analysis. Remember as theses holes were referenced in some assembly constraints using exclude from simulation feature will not work. One of the workarounds will be to suppress the features within assembly environment and then accept warnings referring to loss of assembly constraints reference. In this example we will not suppress the holes.

5. Select **Fixed Constraint** > Select bottom face of corner component as shown

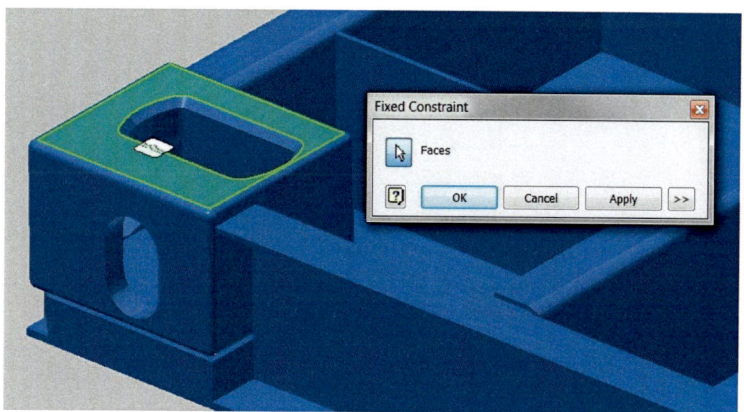

> If you are going to use thin elements then suggest applying constraints after creating midsurfaces as the face selected for constraints (on solid) will be lost. Here we are going to mesh the corners using solid elements.

6. Now select the faces of the other three corners > Click **OK**

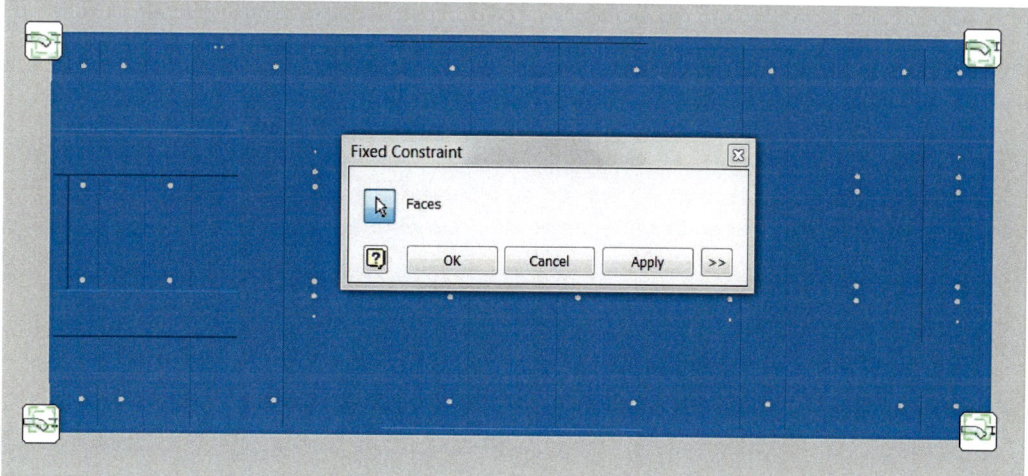

In the next steps we are going to apply loads to the base. In reality there will be a pair of I-beams fixed to base, at the location of the holes. In this example we want to see what impact the I-beams will have on the overall stiffness of the base when loaded. The top face of base plate component has faces already split in the part environment, enabling us to select them to apply loads, otherwise the load will have to be applied on whole face which can produce different results.

CHAPTER 9
DP8- Fabrication Analysis

7. Select **Force** and specify **100,000** N > Select the two split faces > Specify **Total Load** for **Name** > Click **OK**

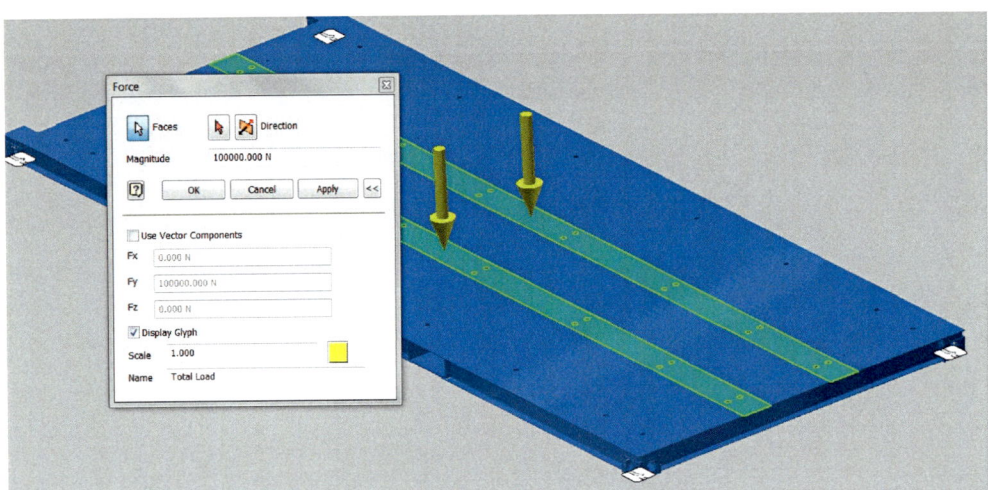

📝 Do not select Automatic Contacts before creating midsurfaces to be used for thin elements, as the contacts produced will be between solid components and not the midsurfaces.

8. Select **Find Thin Bodies** > Click **OK**

As there are a lot of bodies to be converted we will stop and see which ones need converting

💡 None converted components will not be shown as transparent surfaces

9. Click **OK**

As we had applied the loads on the base plate we have lost the load associativity, as the original face does not exist. Also as we have used the midsurface option the split faces have been merged with the rest of the plate faces. The workaround to this is to delete the midsurface created and to use offset command instead. Also worth mentioning, as indicated previously, is to create surfaces first and then apply boundary conditions on the newly created surfaces.

10. Expand **Shells** folder > Then expand **Base:1::3123_floor_panel:1** folder > Right Click Midsurface:22 > Select **Delete**

11. Select **Offset** command from Prepare panel > Specify **6** mm for **Thickness** > Select one of the faces of the base panel component > Click **OK**

SECTION 3 - Stress Analysis Design Problems using Thin Elements

CHAPTER 9
DP8 - Fabrication Analysis

📝 A separate folder will be created for surfaces created by using Offset command

12. Right Click **Total Load** > Select **Edit Force Load** > Select the two split faces again > Click **OK**

13. Select **Midsurface** > Select all the remaining components (except corner block and corner plates) > Click **OK** (to finish command)

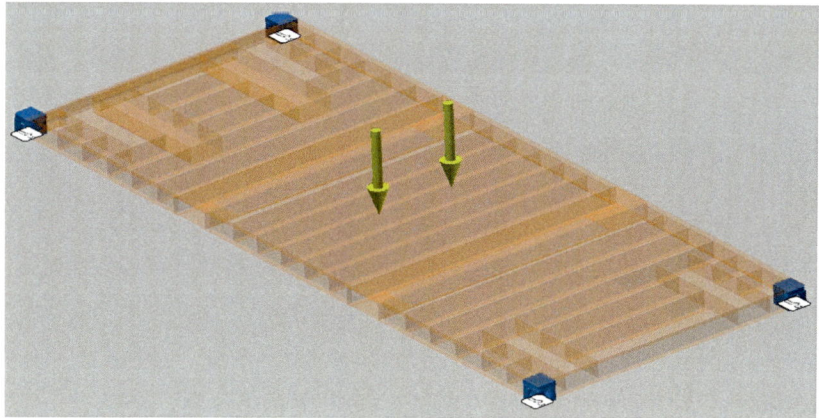

💡 You can press OK anytime and if any components are left over (still blue) you can select the Midsurface command again. Sometimes it's good practice to do this especially when there are too many components to be converted manually to midsurfaces

14. Select **Mesh Settings** > Unselect **Use part based measure for Assembly mesh** > Click **OK**

15. Select **Mesh View**

CHAPTER 9
DP8- Fabrication Analysis

 Contacts will be automatically created once you select mesh view if you forget to select automatic contacts

A total of 35348 elements will be created, value may differ slightly.

Run simulation and analyze

16. Select **Simulate**

A warning will appear saying that materials have not been defined correctly

17. Select **Cancel** > Select **Assign** > Select first row of unassigned material in **Override Material** column > Keeping the **shift key pressed** select the last row > Select **Steel, High Strength Low Alloy** > Click **OK**

18. Select **Simulate** > Select **Run**

19. Select **Undeformed** from Adjust Displacement Display > Select **Contour Shading** > Select **Maximum Value** > Deselect **Mesh View**

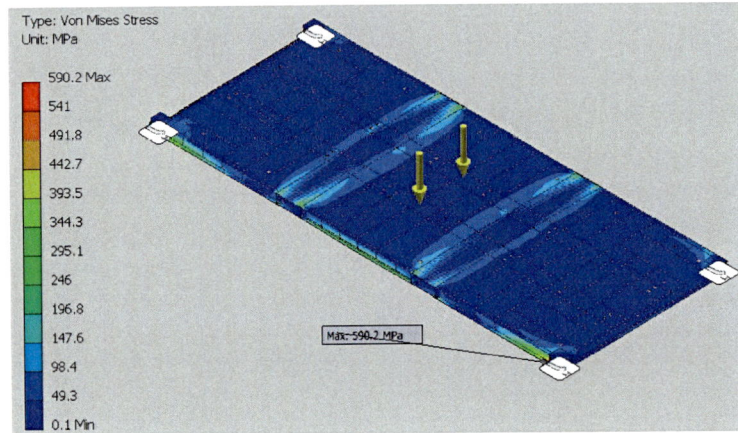

20. Select **Displacement**

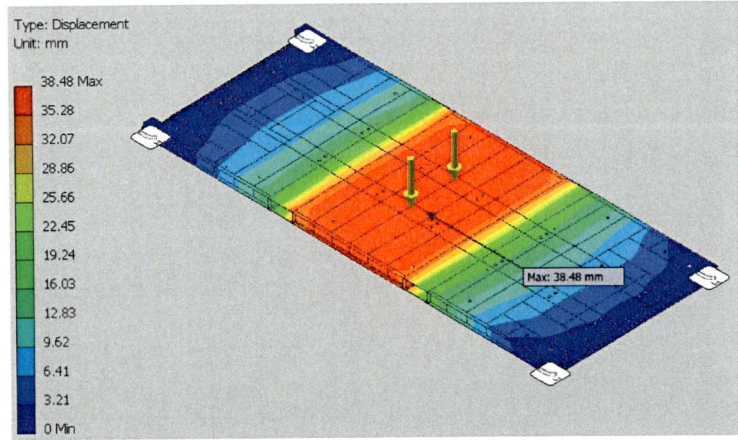

CHAPTER 9
DP8 - Fabrication Analysis

The maximum displacement of 38.48 mm is too high. Due to this high deflection we get high working stresses which are well above the yield limit of the material, which is 275 MPa. Now we will see the effect of adding the two I-Beams on the base.

21. Right Click **Base** > Select **Copy Study**

22. Right Click **Base:1** > Select **Edit Study Properties** > Select **Model State** tab > Change **Level of Detail** from **FEA** to **FEA With I-Beams** > Click **OK**

23. Select **Midsurface** command > Select both I-Beams > Click **OK**

24. Now Right Click **Contacts** > Select **Update Automatic Contacts**

25. Right Click **Total Load** > Select **Edit Force Load** > Keeping the **Shift Key** pressed select the split surfaces used to define the original load (this will deselect the faces) > Select the top surfaces of each I-Beam.

26. Click **OK**

27. Select **Mesh View**

A total of 44176 elements will be created, value may differ slightly

28. Select **Simulate** > Select **Run**

29. Unselect **Mesh View** > Deselect **Boundary Condition**

CHAPTER 9
DP8- Fabrication Analysis

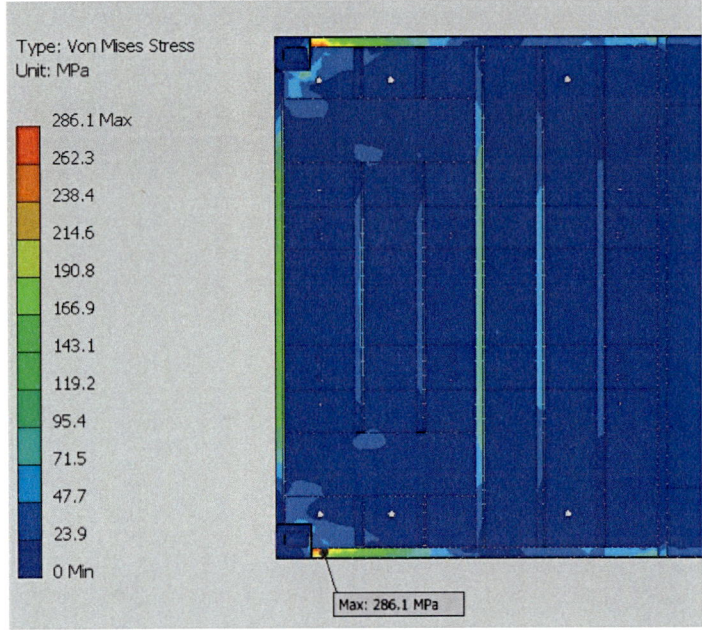

The maximum von mises stress has now reduced to 286.1 MPa which is still higher than 2/3rd of chosen material. So we need to further investigate this stress value, it is possible it may be a high compressive stress value. To confirm we can display 3rd prinicipal stresses.

30. Select **3rd Prinicipal Stress** > Select **Minimum Value** > Deselect **Maximum Value**

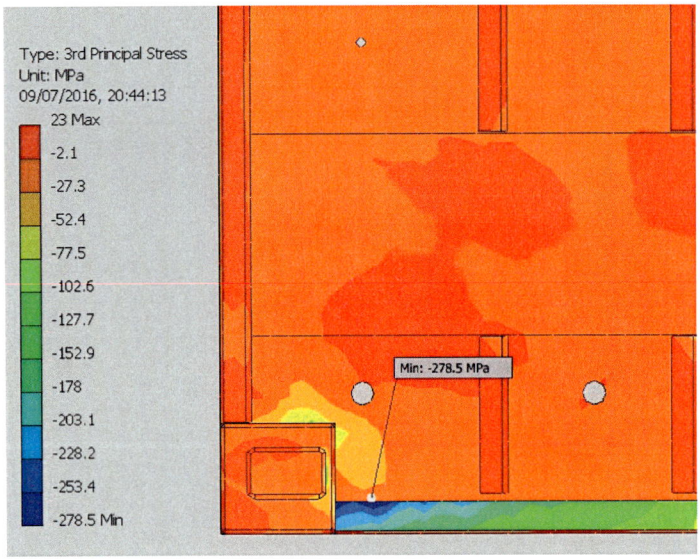

The 3rd Principal Stress plot clearly shows the high von mises is actually a compressive stress. Metals tend to have a very high compressive yield limit and do not tend to fail under compressive loading. Metals tend to commonly fail under tensile loading.

CHAPTER 9
DP8 - Fabrication Analysis

31. Now select **1st Prinicipal Stress** > Deselect **Minimum Value**

The maximum tensile stress although further reduced to 200.8 MPa seems to be stress hot spot (or stress singularity). This stress is on the radii which is due to a contact and more importantly in reality it may not even happen as there will be welds present, which are not included in this exercise. On alternative approach is to remove the radii from the simulation.

32. Right Click **Fillet 1** feature for **iso_corner_left:1** and **iso_corner_left:2** > Select **Exclude from Study**

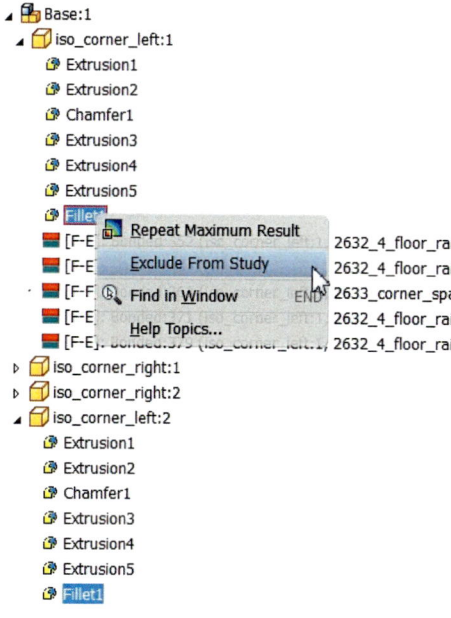

33. Right Click **Contacts** > Select **Update Automatic Contacts** > Right Click **Mesh** > Select **Update Mesh**

34. Select **Simulate** > Select **Run**

SECTION 3 - Stress Analysis Design Problems using Thin Elements

CHAPTER 9
DP8- Fabrication Analysis

35. Select **1st Prinicipal Stress** > Select **Maximum Value** > Deselct **Mesh View**

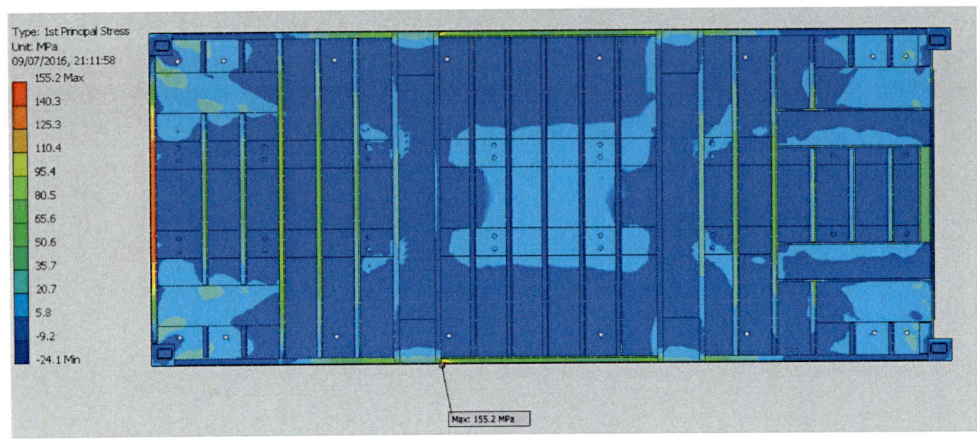

The maximum tensile stress has now reduced to 155.2 MPa near fork lift pockets. So based on 1st Principal Stress we can confidently say the design is okay as the limit of the working stress is 183 MPa (2/3rd of 275 MPa). If the design criteria is to be based on Von Mises stress then a higher yield limit would be recommended.

36. Select **Displacement**

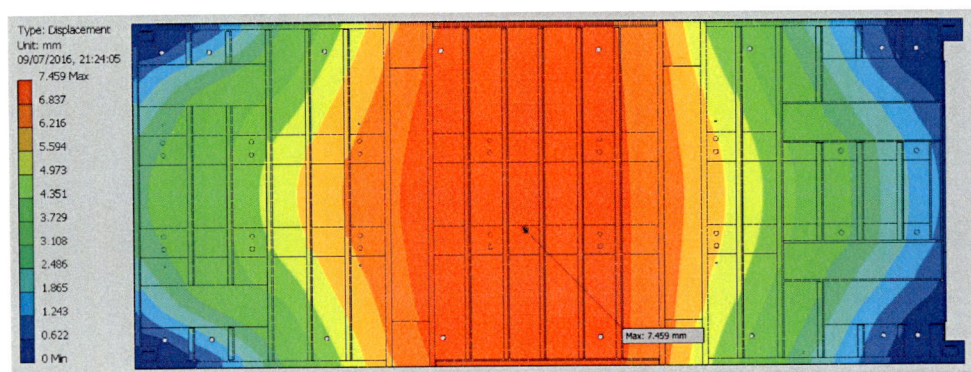

The displacement has significantly reduced from 38.48 mm to 7.459 mm which is acceptable under normal loading conditions.

37. Close File

DP9 – Sheet Metal Analysis

Structural Validation of Hopper
(Design Problem Courtesy of Simba Great Plains Ltd)

Key features and workflows introduced in this design problem

	Key Features/Workflows
1	Symmetry conditions using thin elements
2	Displaying symmetrical results using ground plane and reflections

Introduction

On 30th April 2010, Simba International Limited was acquired by Great Plains Mfg., Inc, based in Salina, Kansas, USA bringing together the product innovation, expertise, experience and knowledge of two of the world's leading brands in tillage equipment. Backed by the vast resources of North America's largest non-tractor, privately owned agricultural implement manufacturing company, the future for Simba, now rebranded Simba Great Plains, looks brighter than ever

Simba Great Plains products mainly cater for the agricultural industry and a typical product is a seed hopper as illustrated in the above image.

CHAPTER 10

DP9 - Sheet Metal Analysis

The main requirements of this design problem are to determine:

1. Whether the seed hopper can withstand a load of 3000 Kg
2. Maximum Stress and Displacement.

In addition to the above requirements, the design criteria to be used for this design problem are:

- The material to be used is mild steel.
- Minimum factor of safety required is 2.

Workflow of Design Problem 9

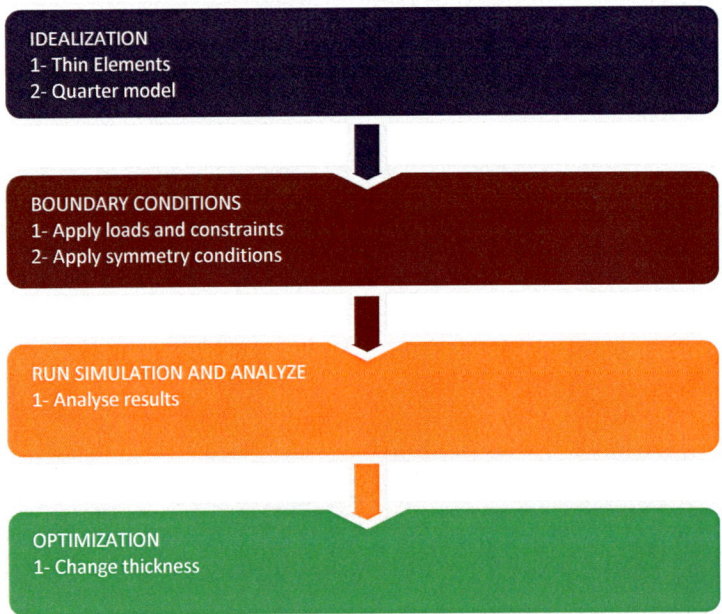

CHAPTER 10
DP9 - Sheet Metal Analysis

Idealization

In this design problem due to the symmetrical loading and geometry of the hopper we are going to analyze a quarter of the model and suppress all the non-structural components including lid and all fasteners. Again all of this information is saved as a level of detail and an extrusion within assembly environment used to split the assembly into a quarter assembly.

1. Open Hopper.iam

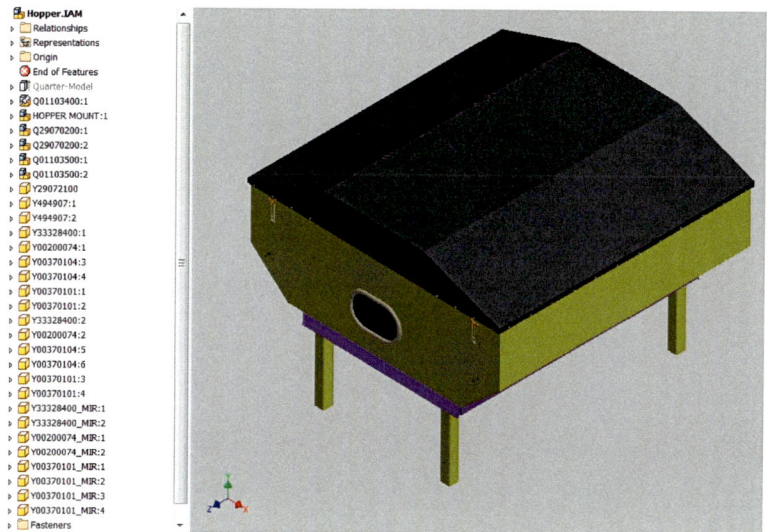

2. Activate **Hopper-Analysis** > Move **End of Features** below **Quarter-Model** feature

CHAPTER 10
DP9 - Sheet Metal Analysis

Boundary conditions

3. Select **Environments** tab > Select **Stress Analysis**

4. Select **Create Study** > Specify **Quarter-Model** for Name

5. Change Contacts Tolerance to **1** mm > Click **OK**

6. Select **Offset** > Select component **Z01103400 SIDE PANEL:2** > Specify **2 mm** for thickness > Click **OK**

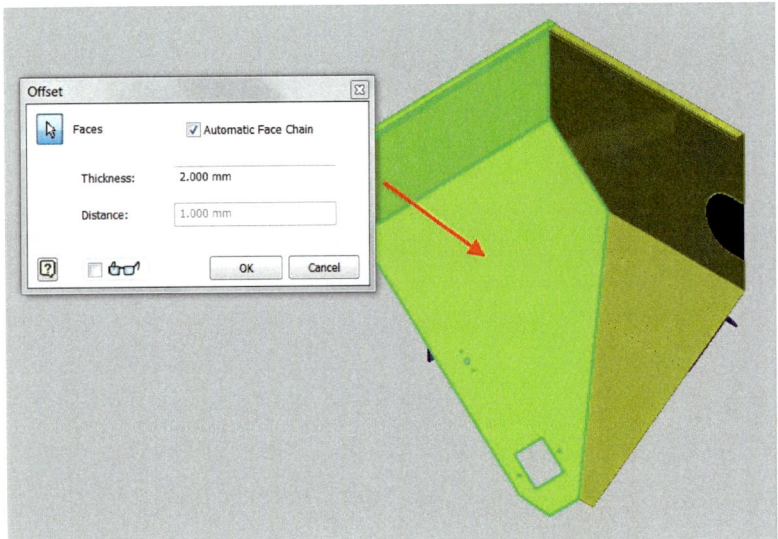

7. Select **Offset** > Select component **Z01103400 END PANEL:2** > Specify **2 mm** for thickness > Click **OK**

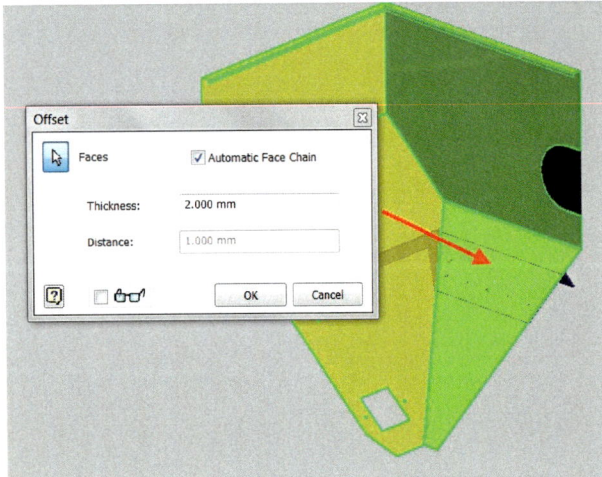

 By using Offset command you can perform different simulations by altering the thickness parameters to see the effect on the structure

SECTION 3 - Stress Analysis Design Problems using Thin Elements

CHAPTER 10
DP9 - Sheet Metal Analysis

8. Select **Offset** > Select component **Y00210111:2** > Specify **2 mm** for thickness > Click **OK**

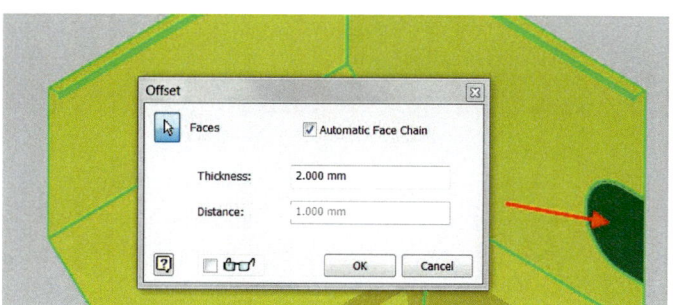

9. Select **Fixed Constraint** > Select bottom face of leg > Click **OK**

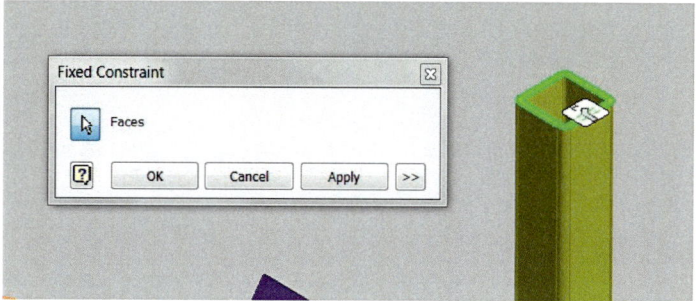

10. Select **Frictionless Constraint** > Select all the edges and faces created as a result of using the split command as shown > Specify **Symmetry** for **Name** > Click **OK**

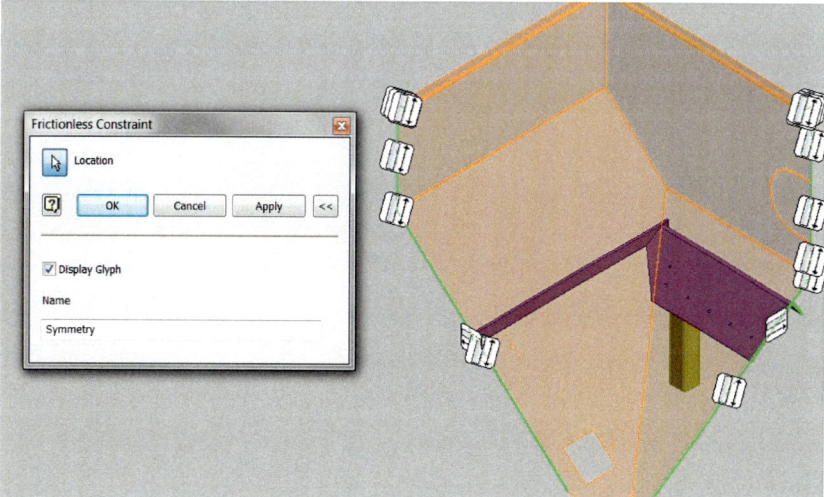

CHAPTER 10
DP9 - Sheet Metal Analysis

11. Select **Force** > Select **Use Vector Components** > Specify **-7500** N for Fy value > Select the two sloping surfaces as shown below > Specify **Weight** for Name > Click **OK**

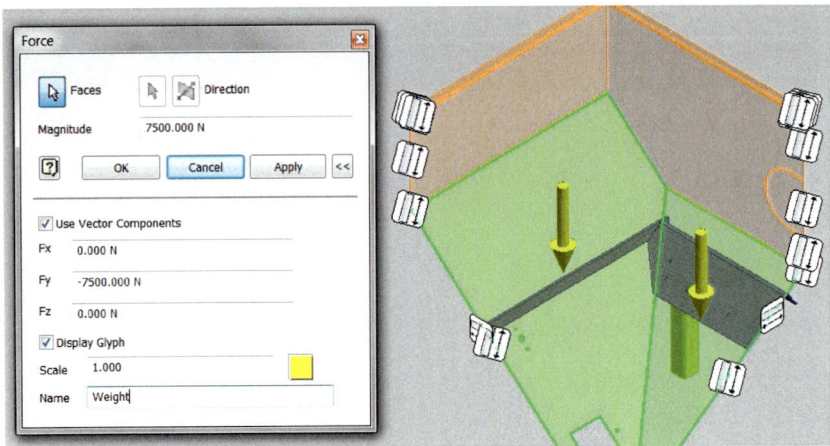

📝 As we are analyzing a quarter model we will divide total load of 3 tonnes (30,000N) by 4 giving 7500N

12. Select **Automatic Contacts**

A total of 27 contacts will be created. We will now create contacts manually for windows and mount frame in the following steps

13. Select **Manual Contact** > Select two edges as shown > Click **Apply**

14. Select the next two edges as shown > Click **Apply**

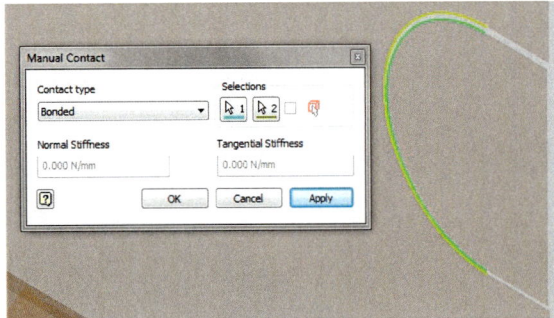

CHAPTER 10
DP9 - Sheet Metal Analysis

15. Select the final two edges as shown > Click **Apply**

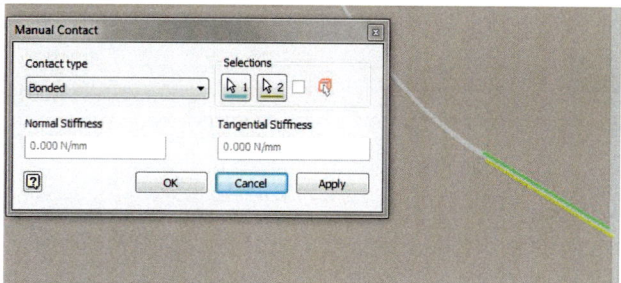

16. Now select the surfaces as shown > Click **OK**

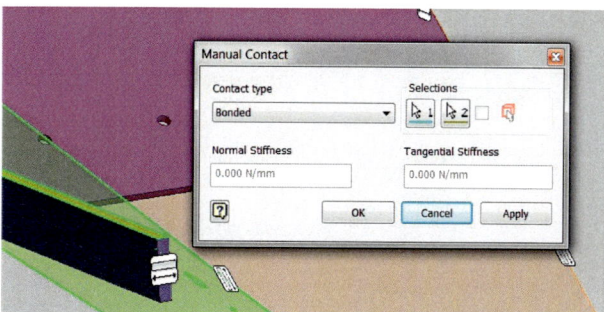

17. Select **Mesh View**

A total of 24054 elements will be created, value may differ slightly.

Run simulation and analyze

18. Select **Simulate** > Select **Run**

19. Deselect **Mesh View** > Select **Undeformed** > Deselect **Boundary Conditions** > Select **Contour Shading** > Select **Maximum Value**

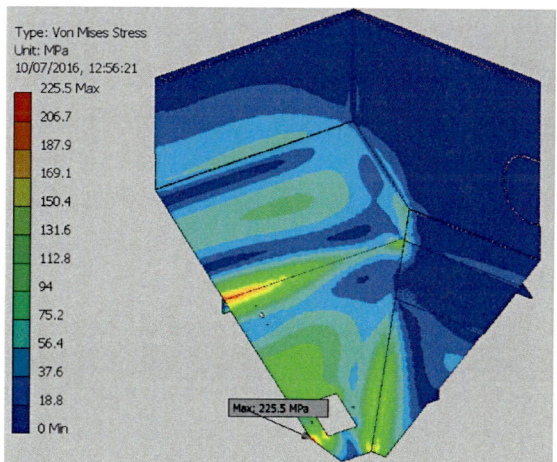

SECTION 3 - Stress Analysis Design Problems using Thin Elements

CHAPTER 10
DP9 - Sheet Metal Analysis

For the following steps we are going to modify the offset values of the hopper main body and see its impact on safety factor. This is a more effective way than parameters especially for sheet metal components. As we are not interested in the mount supports we will make them invisible so we only display main hopper body results.

20. Right Click **HOPPER MOUNT:1** subassembly > Select **Visibility** to hide mounts

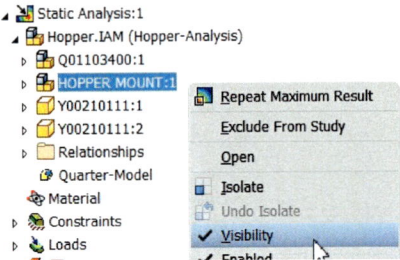

21. Right Click **Offset:1** > Select **Edit Shell** > Specify **3 mm** > Click **Ok**

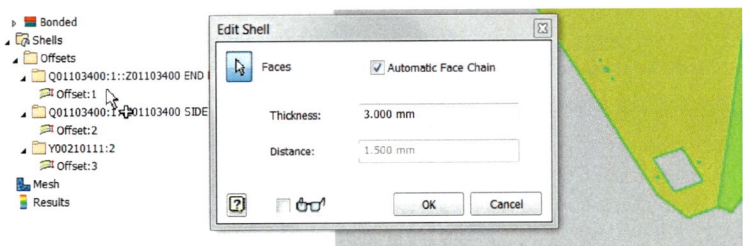

22. Repeat Step 21 for **Offset:2** and **Offset:3**

23. Update **Contacts** and **Mesh** > Select **Simulate** > Select **Run** > Deselect **Mesh View**

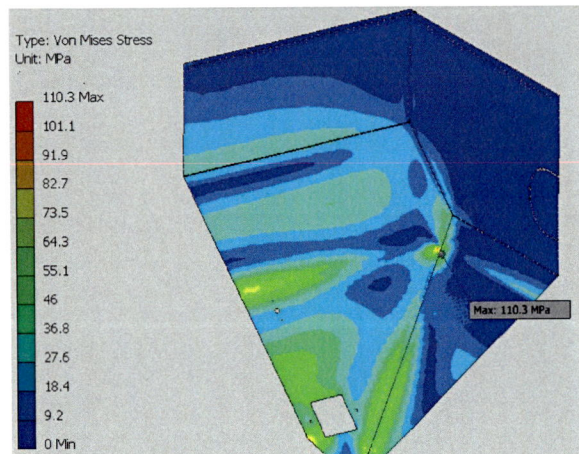

We can see the stress has now reduced from 225.5 MPa to 110.3 MPa. This will increase our safety factor for the hopper body.

CHAPTER 10
DP9 - Sheet Metal Analysis

24. Select **Safety Factor** > Deselect **Maximum Value** > Select **Minimum Value**

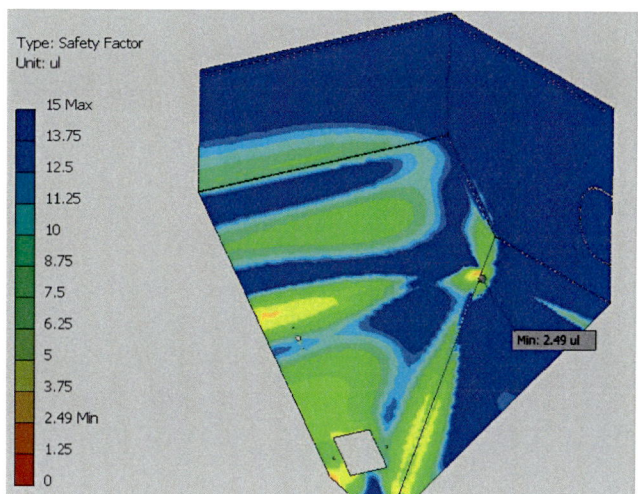

25. Select **Displacement** > Deselect **Minimum Value**

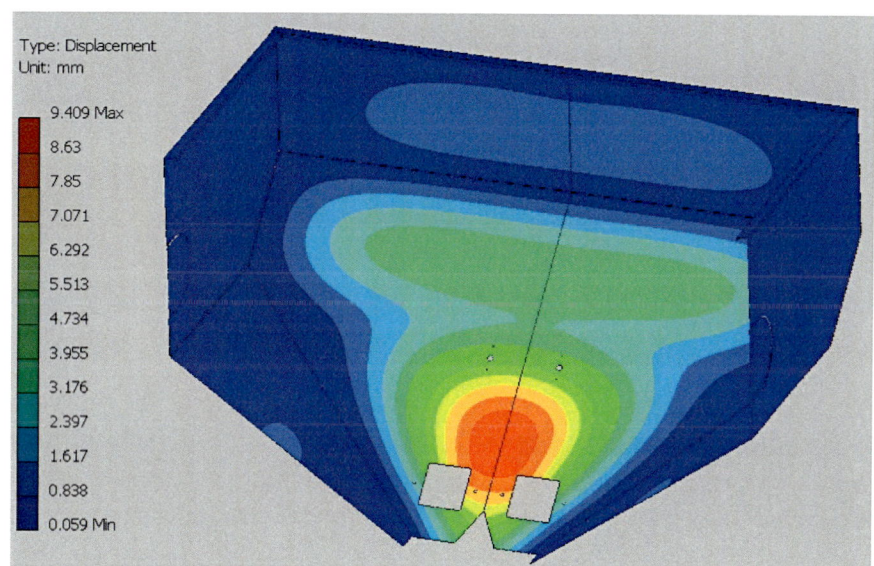

The above displacement result has made use of ground plane and 100% reflection, refer to chapter 4 details of how to do this.

26. Close File

CHAPTER 10
DP9 - Sheet Metal Analysis

CHAPTER 11
DP10 - 20g Acceleration

DP10 – 20g Acceleration
Structural Integrity of Police Van Cell
(Design Problem Courtesy of James Alpe Ltd)

Key features and workflows introduced in this design problem

	Key Features/Workflows
1	Idealization including shrinkwrap with multibodies
2	Manual contacts
3	Acceleration loads

Introduction

James Alpe Vehicle Conversions, based in Clitheroe UK, specialise in bespoke conversions for both the public and private sectors. They have built up a strong reputation as one of the country's leading vehicle conversions specialists carrying out work for many Police Forces, Ambulance Trusts, MOD, Her Majesty's Prison Service, Schools, local councils, and many private sector organisations. From Police cell vans to dog vans from horse boxes to exhibition trailers.

James Alpe Vehicle Conversions offer a comprehensive range of solutions for all commercial and specialist vehicle users. Their in-house team of coachbuilders, fabricators, electricians and technicians can fulfill almost any brief. Whether it is a mass fleet vehicle production or a bespoke one-off specialist conversion we can meet the unique requirements of our broad customer base.

SECTION 3 - Stress Analysis Design Problems using Thin Elements

CHAPTER 11

DP10 - 20g Acceleration

On occasions James Alpe subcontracts out expensive and timely physical tests of their products, in this case a police van cell. The test is basically causing a frontal crash of a police van into a brick wall at 30mph, generating around 20g accelerations. Although the actual test will have a dummy passenger in the cell, in this example we will simulate a police van cell crashing at 30mph without any occupants. The main emphasis of this example will be around preparing the model for simulation as this is a typical example of complex fabrication which is too detailed for analysis. This problem presents a common dilemma of whether to rebuild a model again for analysis purposes or try to simplify the CAD model. In this example the latter approach is taken.

Workflow of Design Problem 10

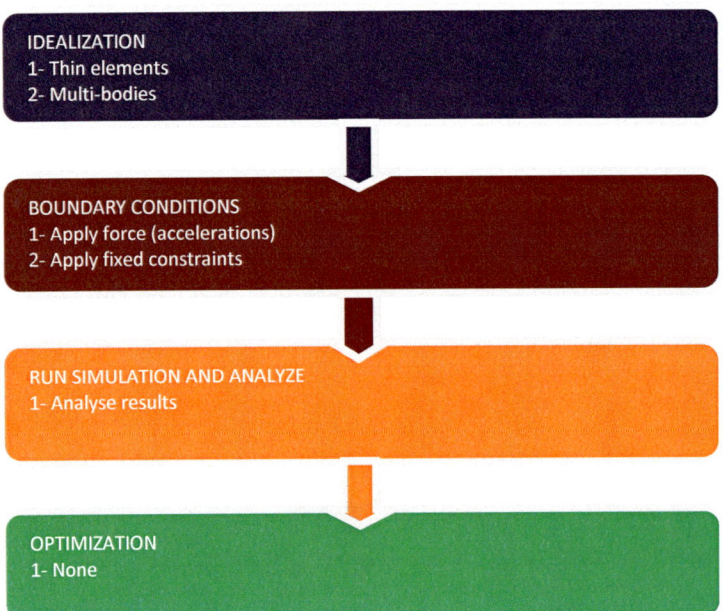

Idealization

The model to be used for this design problem is too detailed for stress analysis environment. The model needs to be significantly simplified. At this stage we have two options either create a new model for analysis purposes or simplify original model, both methods will require time. The benefit of the latter method is the link between design and analysis will be maintained thus making it easier for reanalysis, once a design change has been made. In most cases the designer and analyst will be the same person hence making sense to simplify the model. The designer has various options to simplify including;

1. Level of Details
2. Shrinkwrap Substitute
3. De-featuring
4. Shrinkwrap
5. Direct modelling

I will go through each option explaining the pros and cons.

Level of Details: This is fastest and easiest method to suppress non-structural components. As soon as the non-structural components are suppressed inventor will create a new level of detail. Once

CHAPTER 11

DP10 - 20g Acceleration

this new level of detail is saved the designer can switch between levels of details by simply clicking on the desired level of detail. This method does not work at the feature level.

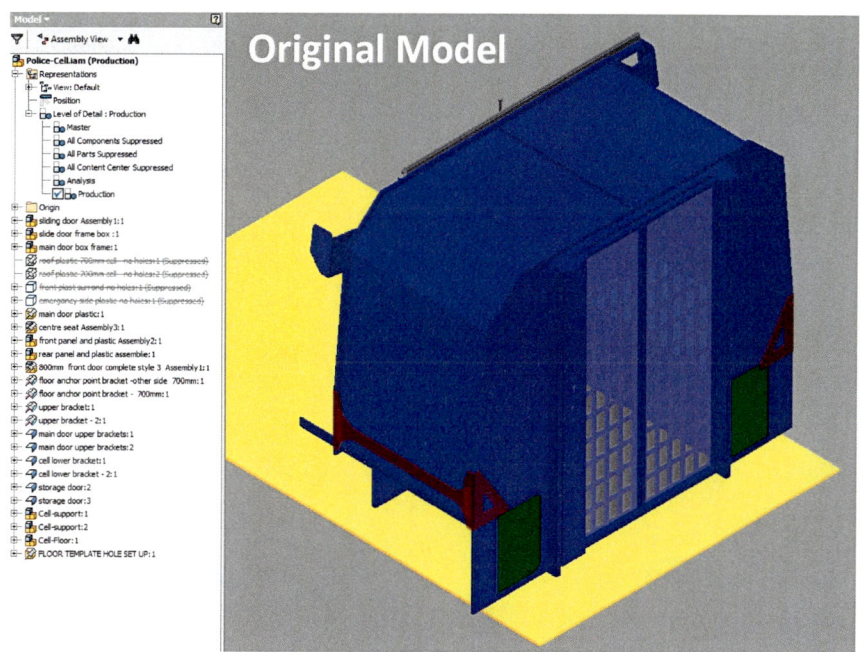

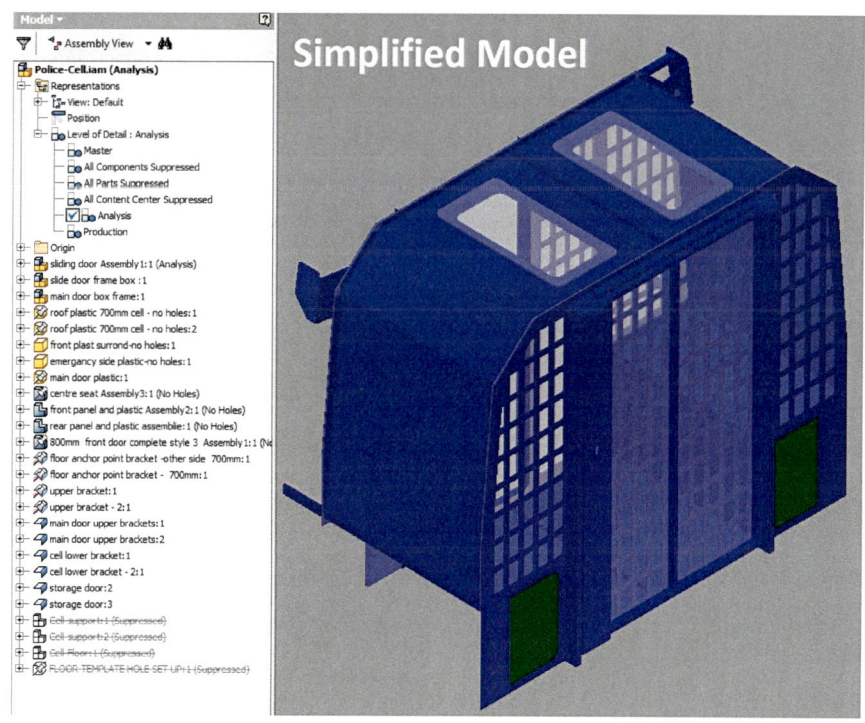

SECTION 3 - Stress Analysis Design Problems using Thin Elements

CHAPTER 11
DP10 - 20g Acceleration

Shrinkwrap Substitute: This method works just like a level of detail with the added benefit of being able to simplify geometry mainly by suppressing unwanted holes.

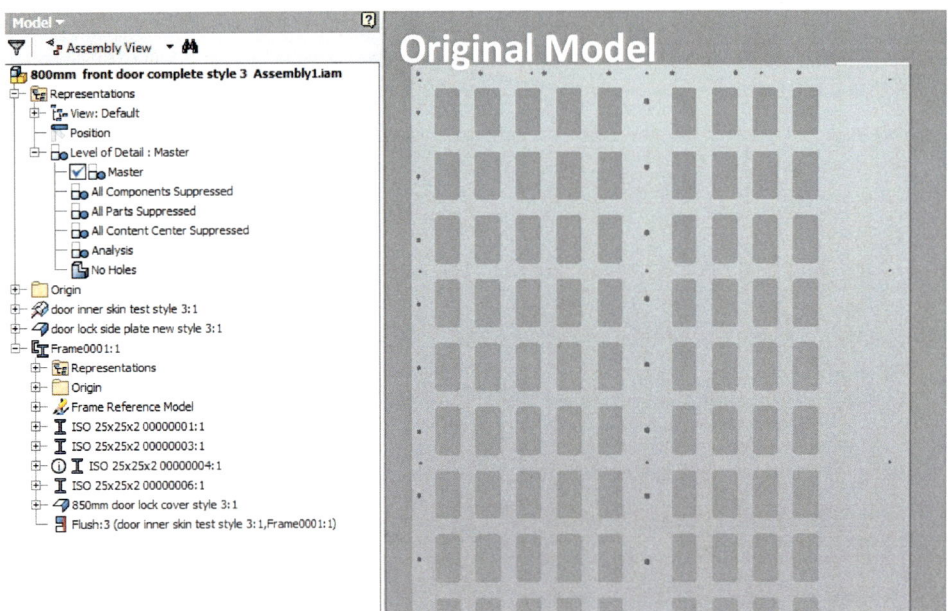

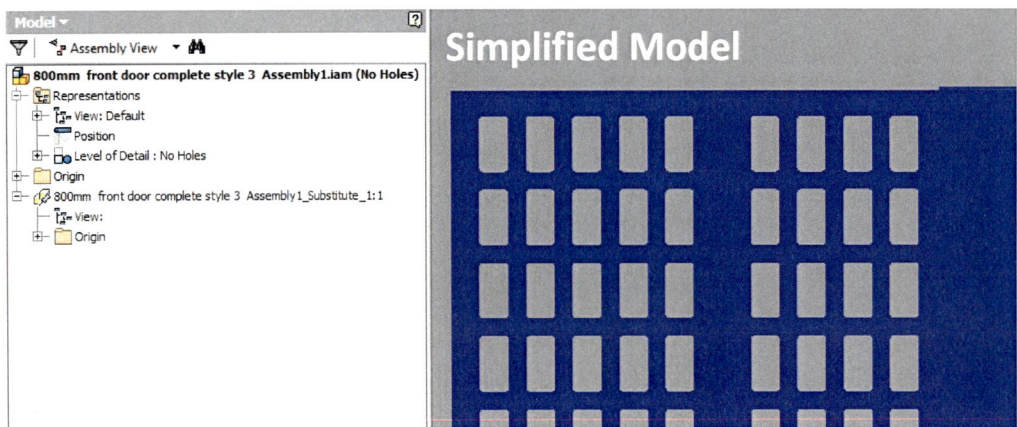

Defeaturing: This method allows to simplify components by suppressing features of parts. The main disadvantage of this method is that it will change the component and taking these changes through to the drawings. This method will only work if you make a copy of the original and then defeature

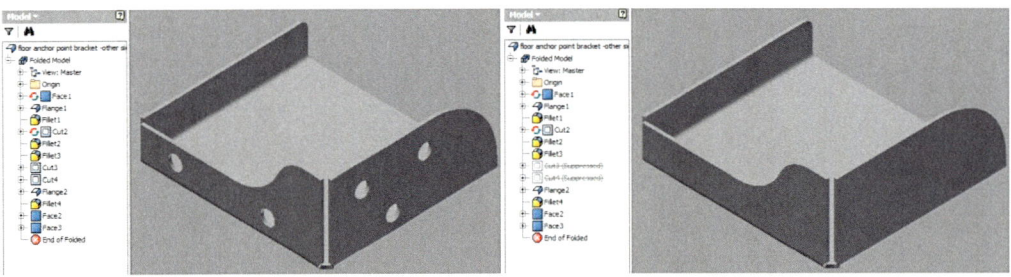

CHAPTER 11
DP10 - 20g Acceleration

Shrinkwrap: This method is similar to Shrinkwrap Substitute with the main difference that the simplified model is saved as a separate file and not as a level of detail. This method in combination with defeaturing will prove to be useful if the model is complex and requires a lot of defeaturing. To maintain the link the simplified model will have to be placed in the original assembly over the original model. Then using level of details suppress and unsuppress the desired component. Yes I know it sounds tedious but the other option is to create a new model, which can be more tedious.

Direct Modelling: This is a clever to way to remove unwanted features within Inventor without the need to understand how the features were initially created. Once the analysis has been completed and finalized you can simply move the end of part above all the direct modelling operations. Typically direct modelling will at the bottom of the feature tree. Alternatively you can copy the original part and then go through direct modelling to simplify the part.

Suggested Idealization Workflow for Detailed Fabrications

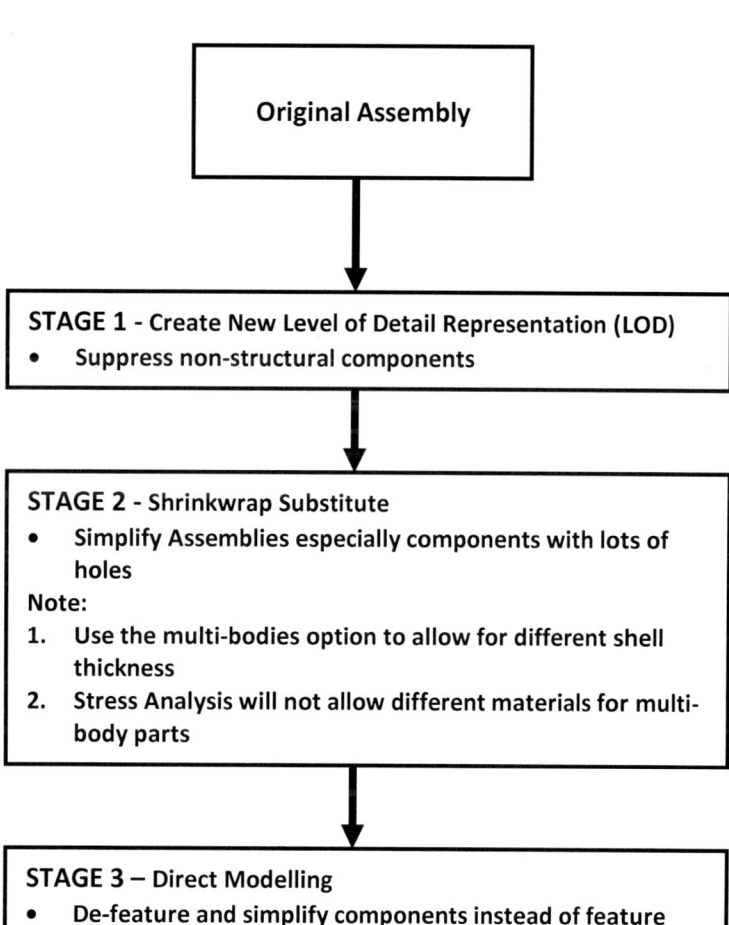

Original Assembly

STAGE 1 - Create New Level of Detail Representation (LOD)
- Suppress non-structural components

STAGE 2 - Shrinkwrap Substitute
- Simplify Assemblies especially components with lots of holes

Note:
1. Use the multi-bodies option to allow for different shell thickness
2. Stress Analysis will not allow different materials for multi-body parts

STAGE 3 – Direct Modelling
- De-feature and simplify components instead of feature suppression

Notes:
1. You will need to place the simplified component in the original assembly. I suggest place over original component and use LOD to manage component suppression
2. If there are too many parts suggest copy the assembly and replace with simplified components

CHAPTER 11
DP10 - 20g Acceleration

1. Open Police-Cell.iam

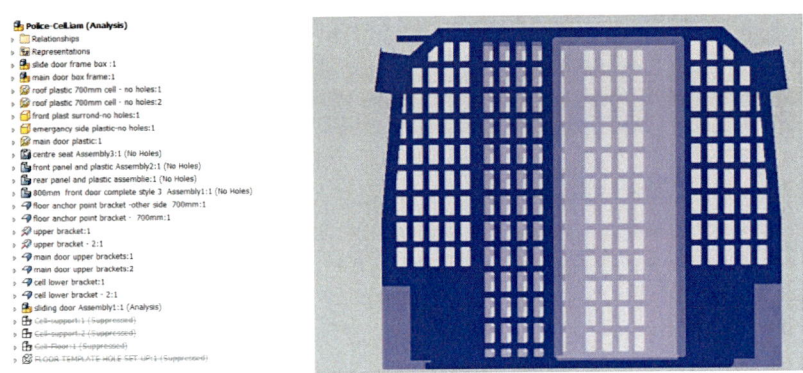

This assembly has already been through the simplification process based on the suggested workflow.

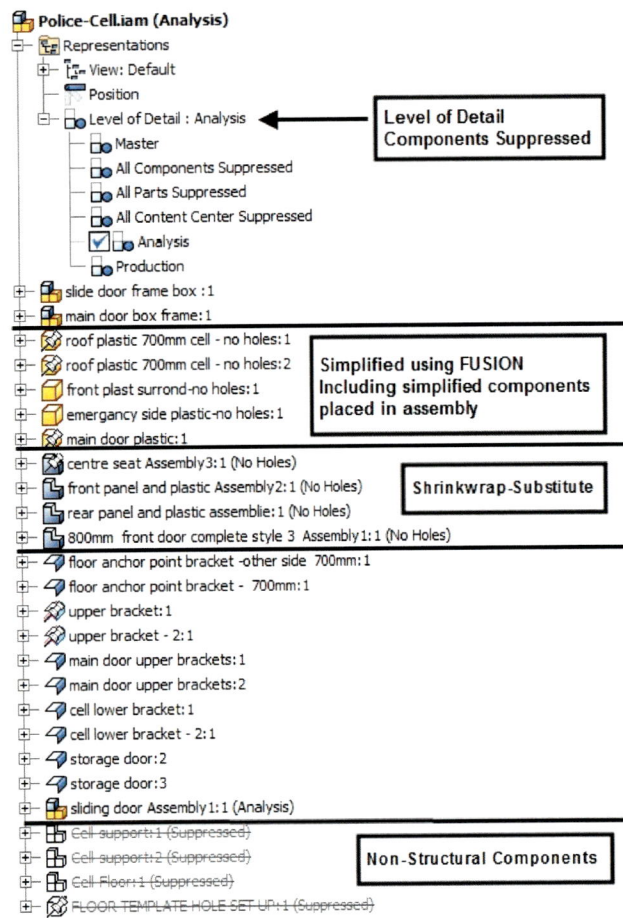

SECTION 3 - Stress Analysis Design Problems using Thin Elements

CHAPTER 11
DP10 - 20g Acceleration

Boundary conditions

2. Select **Environments** tab > Select **Stress Analysis**

3. Select **Create Study** > Specify **20g Acceleration** for Name > Click **OK**

4. Select **Midsurface** > Select **all components**

💡 Suggest you create midsurfaces in stages rather than selecting all.

📝 Find Thin Bodies can take between 20 to 30 minutes to create midsurfaces automatically.

5. Select **Fixed Constraint** > Select the nine faces as shown below > Click **OK**

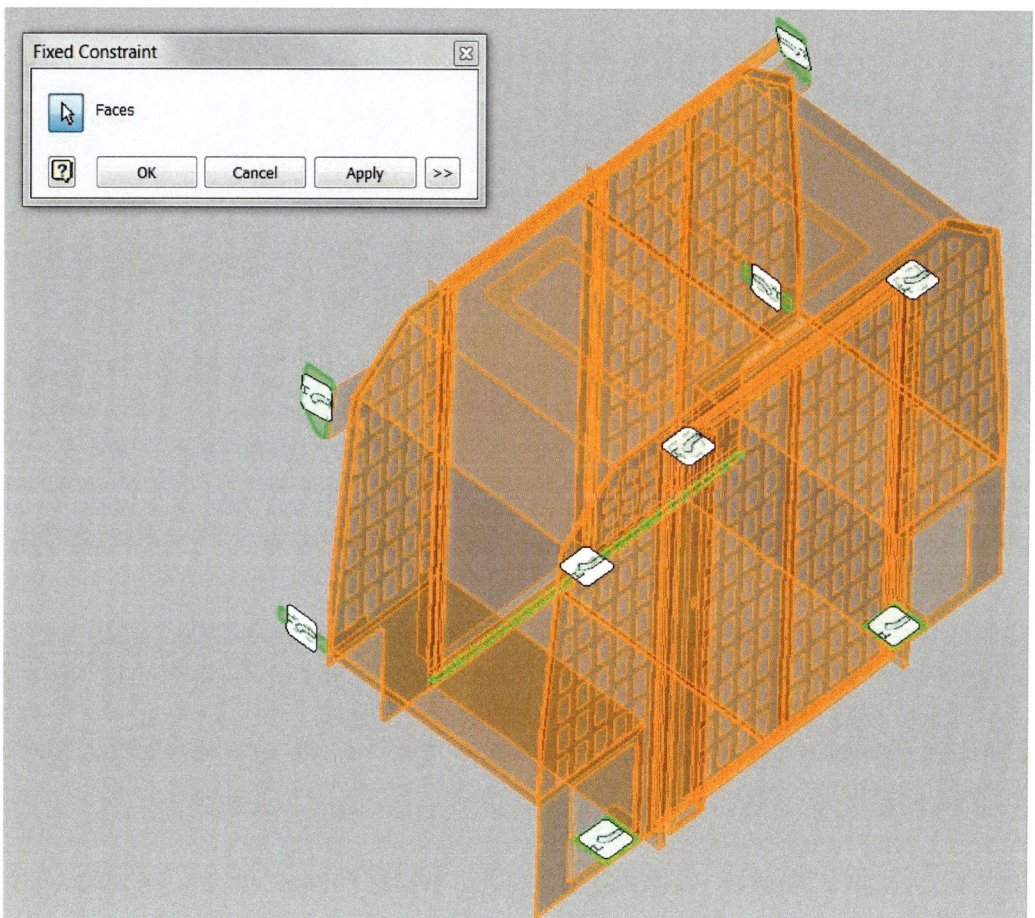

CHAPTER 11
DP10 - 20g Acceleration

6. Select **Body Loads** from the **Load** panel > Activate **Enable Linear Acceleration** > Activate **Use Vector Components** > Specify **9810*20** in the Z Vector Component magnitude field > Click **OK**

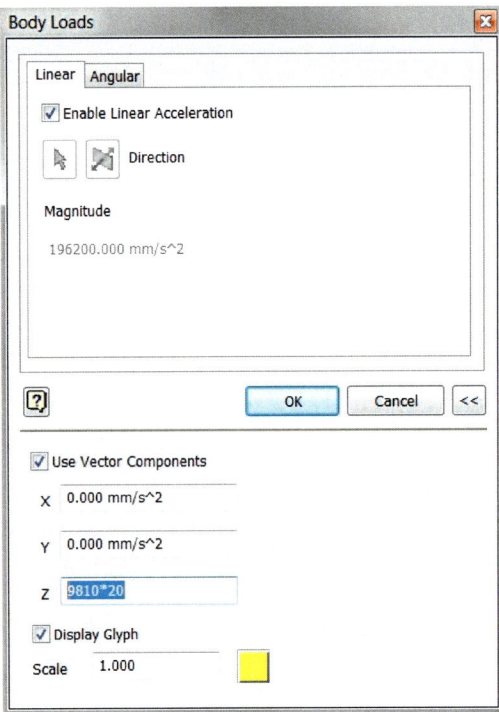

7. Select **Automatic Contacts.**

166 contacts will be created. As there are too many contacts it is tedious to go through all to make sure all surfaces and edges are in contact. I suggest not to examine contacts at this stage but only after you select Simulate as the software will detect any components that are not in contact. It is at this stage you can quickly create contacts between components as specified by the software.

8. Select **Mesh Settings** > Specify **0.1** for **Average Element Size in Shells** > Specify **0.05** for **Minimum Element Size** > Unselect **Use part based measured for Assembly Mesh** > Click **OK**

Specifying a higher value for Minimum Element Size will help to reduce the number of elements generated.

9. Select **Mesh View**

63404 Elements will be created. May differ slightly as we are using average element size.

Run simulation and analyze
10. Select **Simulate**

CHAPTER 11
DP10 - 20g Acceleration

The following error and warning will appear in the Simulate dialogue box as shown > Click **Cancel**

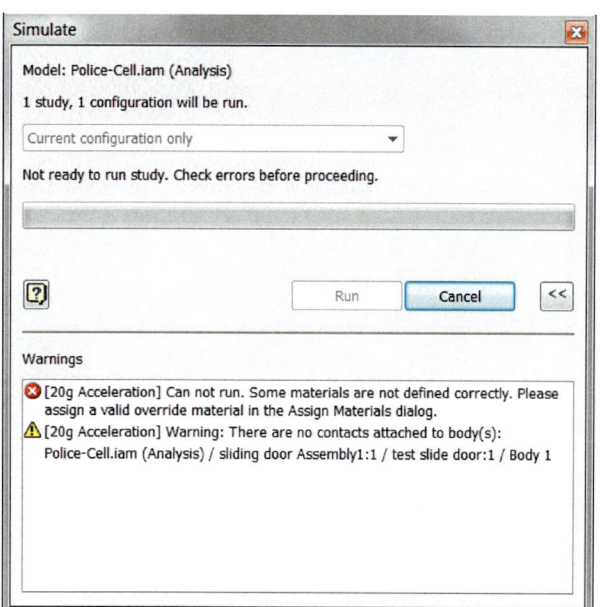

The error is due to the fact the assemblies which were shrink-wrapped were not assigned materials with the assembly environment. Therefore we will assign materials within the Stress Analysis environment. The warning suggests there are no contacts between some components as they have gaps in excess of the specified simulation contact settings. To remove the warning we will create manual contacts.

11. Select **Assign** from the **Materials** panel > Select all four subassemblies as shown using left mouse button and shift key > Select **Steel Mild** from the Override Material column > Click **OK**

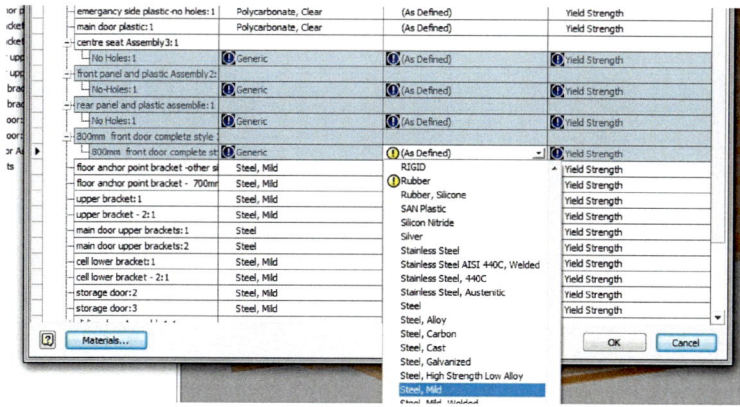

12. Select **Manual Contact** from the **Contacts** manual

SECTION 3 - Stress Analysis Design Problems using Thin Elements

CHAPTER 11
DP10 - 20g Acceleration

13. Select the face of the back door and support as shown > Click **Apply**

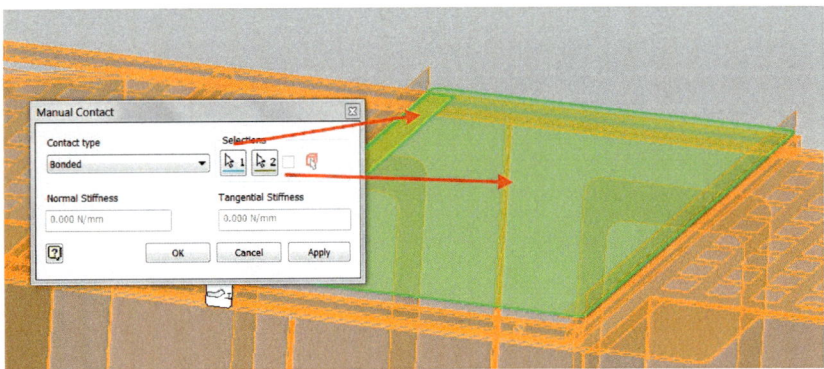

14. Now repeat for the other side of the door > Click **OK**

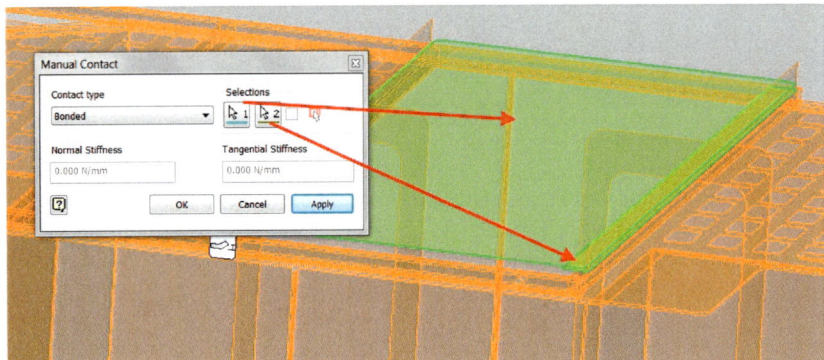

15. Select **Simulate** > Select **Run**

In this example we will just analyze the displacement results, as the mesh defined is to coarse for the purposes of stress analysis. If you would like to analyze stress results the mesh would need to be a lot finer. Care would also need to be taken when analyzing stress results as this type of assembly is prone to high stress singularities or hotspots. The reasons for these high stresses can be due to various factors including coarse mesh, unnecessary contacts, discontinuous geometry etc.

CHAPTER 11
DP10 - 20g Acceleration

16. Select **Displacement** Results

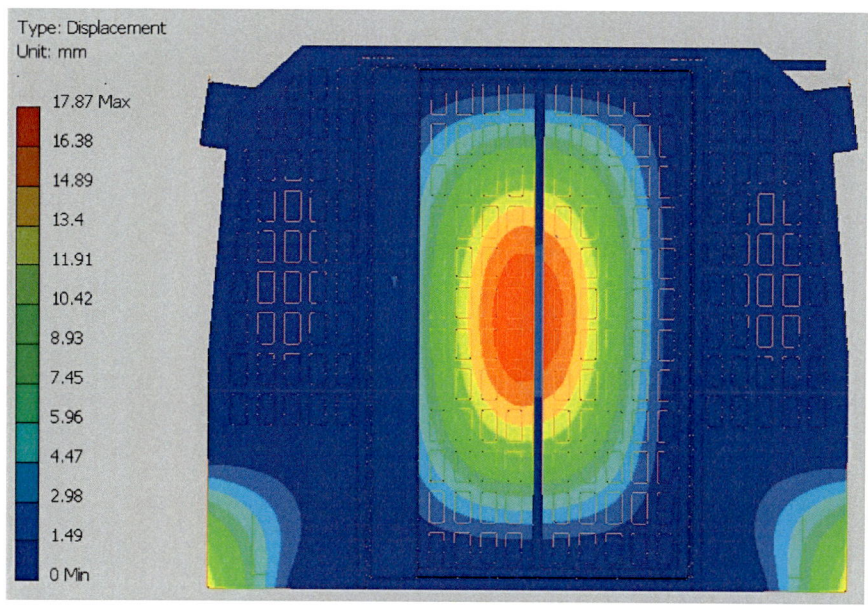

Maximum displacement is 17.87 mm and is located on the main door.

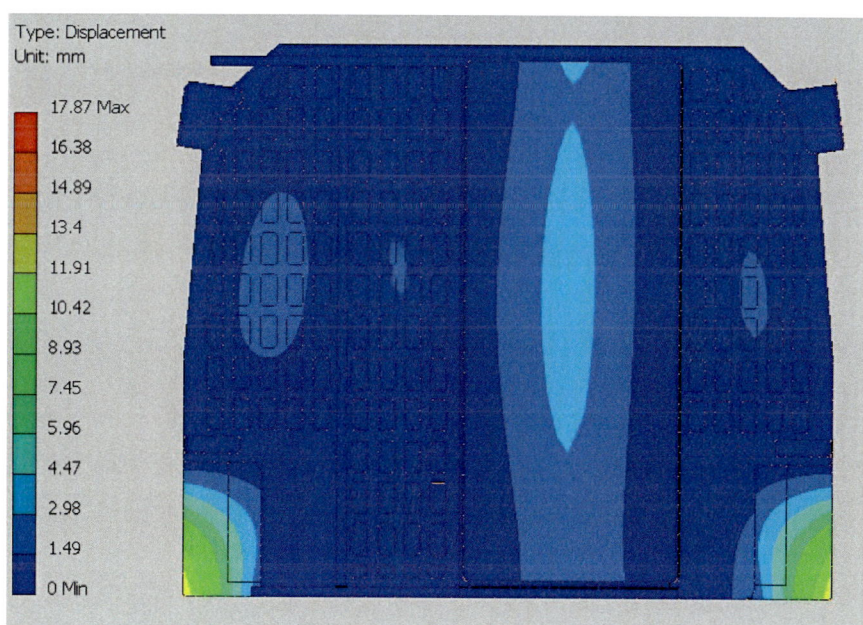

17. Close File

CHAPTER 11
DP10 - 20g Acceleration

Section 4 - STRESS ANALYSIS *Design Problems* using MOTION LOADS from Dynamic Simulation

NB: Dynamic Simulation not covered in this book

DP11 – Motion Load Transfer Analysis

Structural Validation of Mounting Lugs

(Design Problem Courtesy of In-CAD Services Ltd)

Key features and workflows introduced in this design problem

	Key Features/Workflows
1	Motion loads
2	Manipulating constraints - to remove peak stresses
2	Optimization

Introduction

This design problem will look at the effective use of Dynamic Simulation to validate the structural integrity of the mounting lugs. The force will be exported from Dynamic Simulation and will be directly used in the Stress analysis environment removing the need to apply loads and restraints.

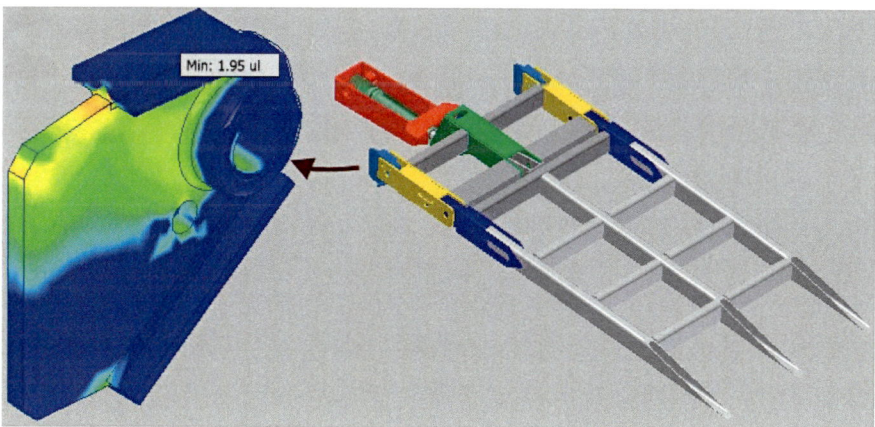

The main requirements of this design problem are to determine:

1. Maximum stress in the mounting lugs when the ramp is fully loaded.
2. Factor of safety.

In addition to the above requirements, the design criteria to be used for this design problem are:

- The material to be used is mild steel.
- The factor of safety required is 2.
- Impact loading will not be taken into account.

SECTION 4 - Stress Analysis Design Problems using Motion Loads from Dynamic Simulation

CHAPTER 12
DP11 – Motion Load Transfer Analysis
Workflow of Design Problem 11

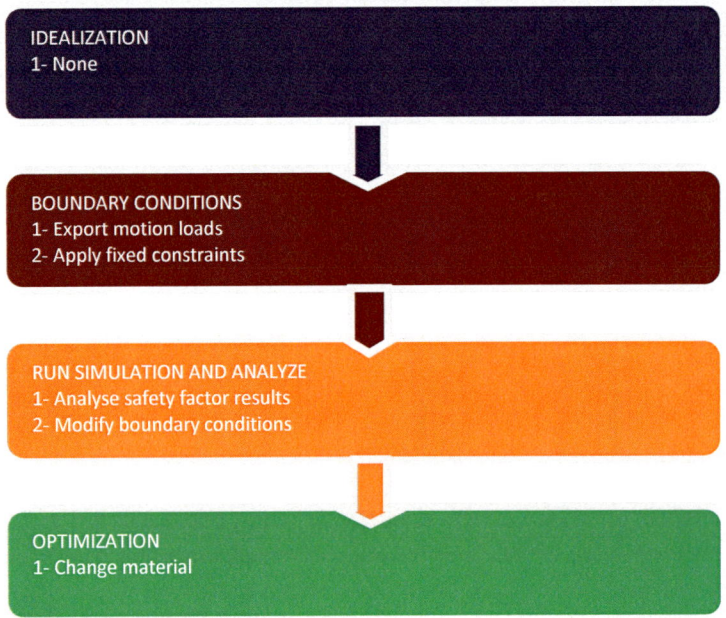

Idealization

The geometry of the model to be analyzed is simple and therefore is no need to further simplify. However, the loads in this example will be transferred from the Dynamic Simulation environment.

1. Open Ramp-Open.iam

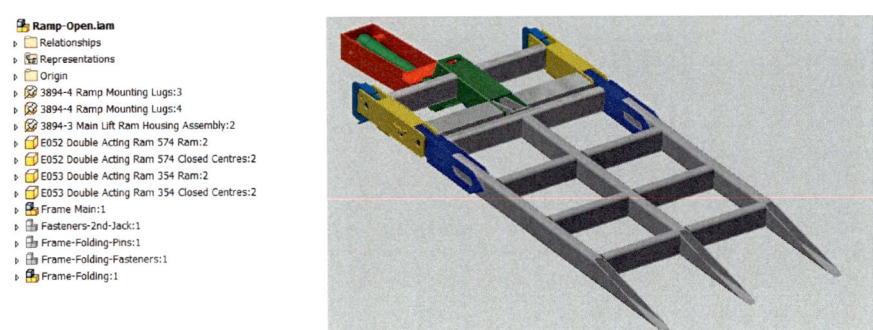

2. Select **Environments** tab > Select **Dynamic Simulation**

Boundary conditions

3. Play **Simulation** > Select **Yes** to accept warning > Select **Output Grapher**

4. Right Click Force (Spherical:3) column > Select **Search Max**

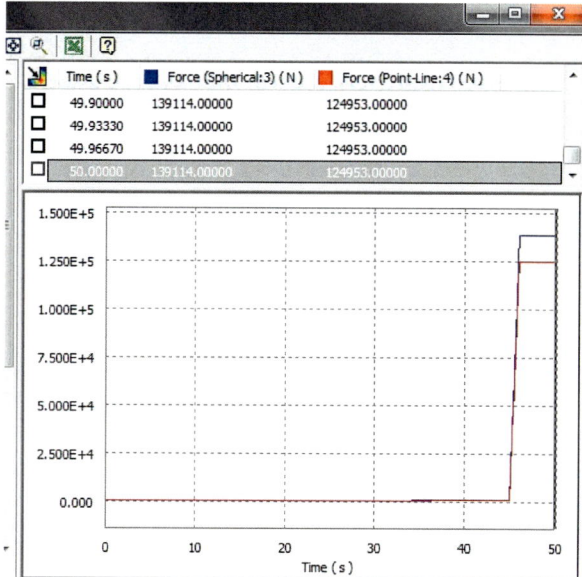

The maximum force for Force (Spherical:3) joint is 139114N and it's the same between 46 and 50 seconds. We will export this force to the Stress Analysis environment.

Export motion loads

5. Tick in the **Export to FEA** column at 50 seconds to export loads at this time frame

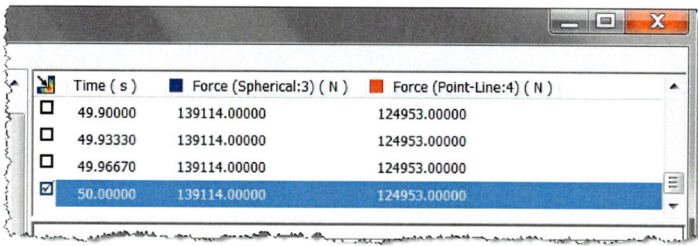

This time step is now added. Note that any time step between 46 and 50 can be used.

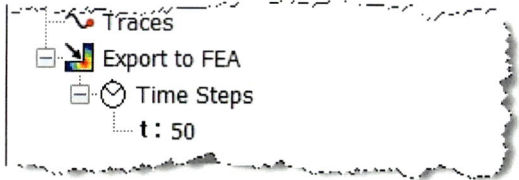

CHAPTER 12
DP11 – Motion Load Transfer Analysis

6. Select **Export to FEA** in the Output Grapher

7. Select Mounting Lugs:3 > Click **OK**

📝 This component has now been added to the Stress Analysis environment.

📝 There is no need to specify bearing load faces as they are already preselected. To see which face has been selected, right click the component 3894-4 Ramp Mounting Lugs:3 and select **Edit Load bearing Faces**.

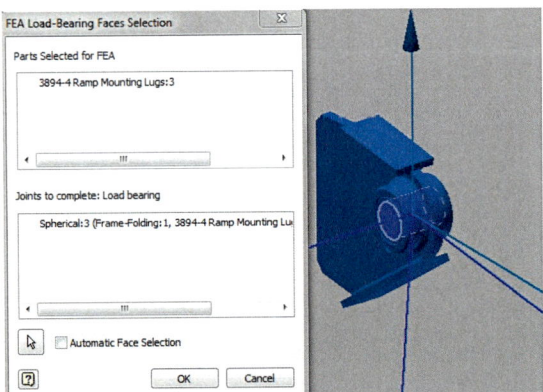

SECTION 4 - Stress Analysis Design Problems using Motion Loads from Dynamic Simulation

CHAPTER 12
DP11 – Motion Load Transfer Analysis

8. Close **Output Grapher** > Select **Finish Dynamic Simulation**

9. Select **Environments** tab > Select **Stress Analysis**

10. Select **Create Study**> Select **Motion Loads Analysis**

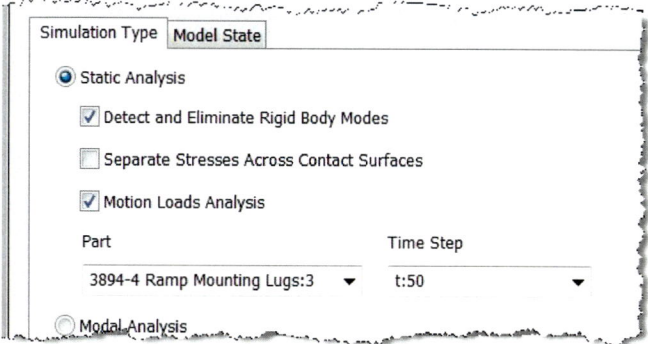

11. Select the **Model State** tab > Select **Mount-Lug** for **Level of Detail** > Click **OK**

12. Click **OK** to **Grounded Part Warning**

📝 This message states the part is grounded in dynamic simulation and therefore also needed to be restrained within the Stress Analysis Environment

Apply fixed constraints

13. Select **Fixed Constraint**

14. Select the 3 faces of Component **3894-4 Ramp Mounting Lugs:3** > Click **OK**

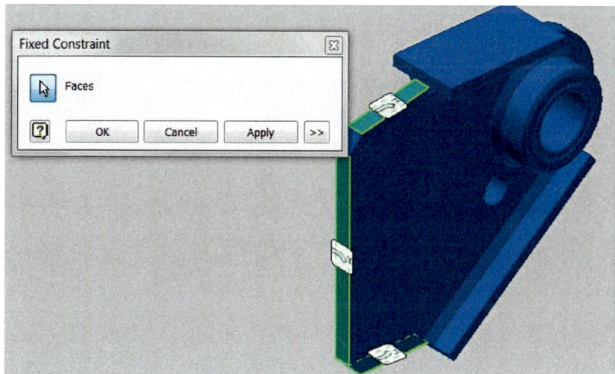

15. Select **Automatic Contacts** > Select **Mesh View**

CHAPTER 12
DP11 – Motion Load Transfer Analysis

Run simulation and analyze

16. Select **Simulate** > Select **Run**

Analyze safety factor results

17. Deselect **Mesh View** > Select **Contour Shading** > Select **Undeformed** from Adjust Displacement Display > Deselect **Boundary Conditions**

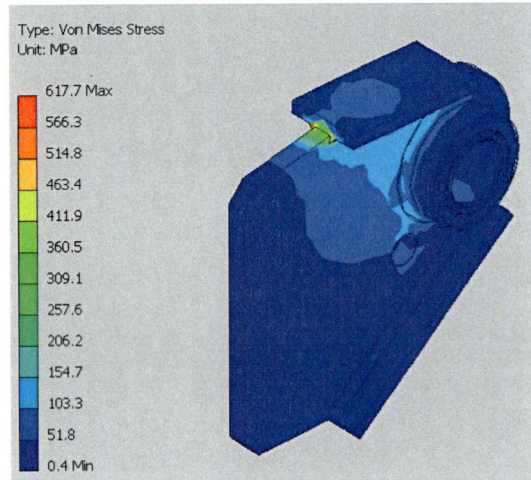

This stress display shows peak stresses around the top face, which was constrained. In reality, this lug is welded to a PFC channel at the fixed faces. Hence, the stresses that we will obtain will be slightly higher, as these faces will have no movement, whereas in reality these faces will transfer some movement into the PFC channel. To remove the peak stress and to allow extra movement in the lug, we will apply frictional constraints at the top and bottom face, instead of fixed constraints.

Modify boundary conditions

18. Double click **Fixed Constraints:1** > Deselect the top and bottom faces > Click **OK**

19. Select **Frictionless Constraint** > Select the top and bottom faces > Click **OK**

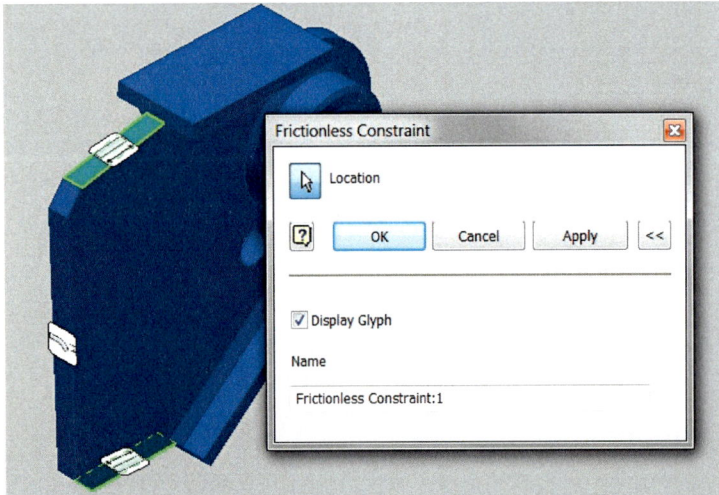

SECTION 4 - Stress Analysis Design Problems using Motion Loads from Dynamic Simulation

CHAPTER 12
DP11 – Motion Load Transfer Analysis

20. Select **Simulate** > Select **Run**

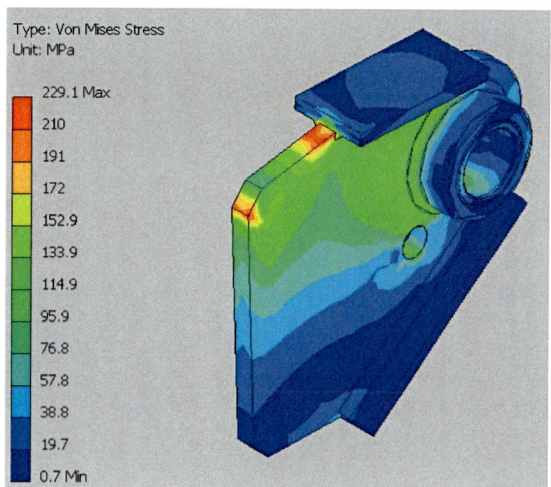

📝 By applying Frictionless constraints we have removed the peak localized stress and introduced some extra movement in the lug. Therefore care should be taken when manipulating boundary conditions in addition to interpreting results.

21. Double Click **Safety Factor**

The minimum value of 0.9 suggests the component has failed. This does not represent reality, as the load is twice as big, as explained in the Dynamic Simulation course. So, we will alter the remote force by half. We do not need to alter the moment and body load as they are zero. Gravity does not need to be altered, either, as it is the same.

22. Right click Remote Force:1 > Select **Edit Remote Force Load**

23. Select **Use Vector Components**, and specify half the value of Fx and Fy vector components > Click **OK**

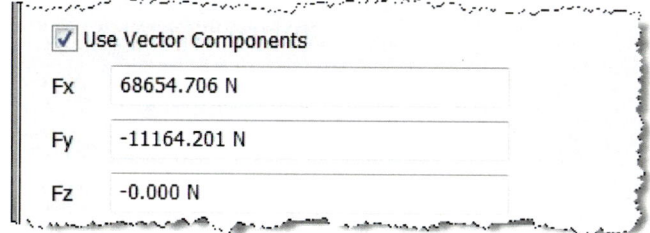

📝 There is no need to edit remote point values

24. Select **Simulate** > Select **Run** > Select **Safety Factor** results

CHAPTER 12
DP11 – Motion Load Transfer Analysis

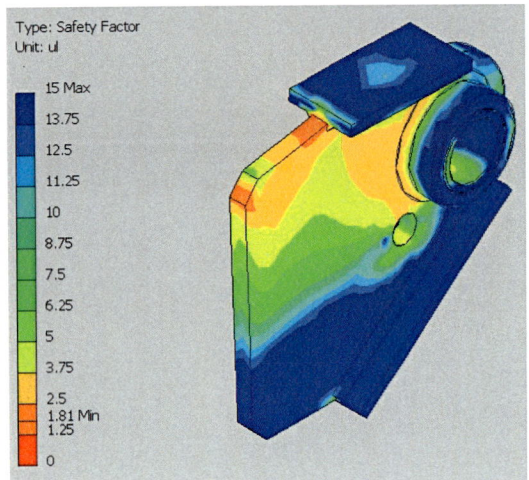

The safety factor has increased to 1.81. The safety factor is still lower than the limit and needs to be increased. One option is to use a higher strength material.

Optimization

25. Select **Assign Materials** > Change the material to **Steel, High Strength Low Alloy** in the **Override Material** column > Click **OK**

26. Select **Simulate** > Select **Run** > Select **Safety Factor**

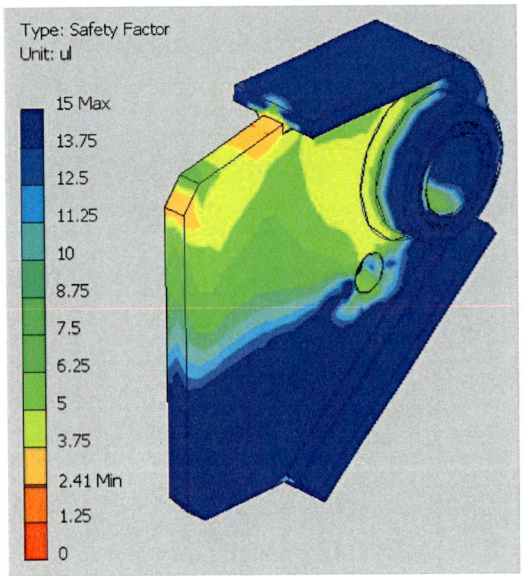

The safety factor has now increased to 2.41, which means that the component is strong enough to withstand the full load.

27. Close File

DP12 – Multiple Motion Load Transfer

Structural Validation of Connecting Rod
(Design Problem Courtesy of 888 Racing Ltd)

Key features and workflows introduced in this design problem

	Key Features/Workflows
1	Motion loads – Multiple time steps
2	Modify joint position
3	Automatic convergence of results

Introduction

This design problem will look at the effective use of Dynamic Simulation to validate the structural integrity of the connecting rod. The force will be exported from the simulation study and will be directly used in the Stress Analysis environment, removing the need to apply loads and restraints.

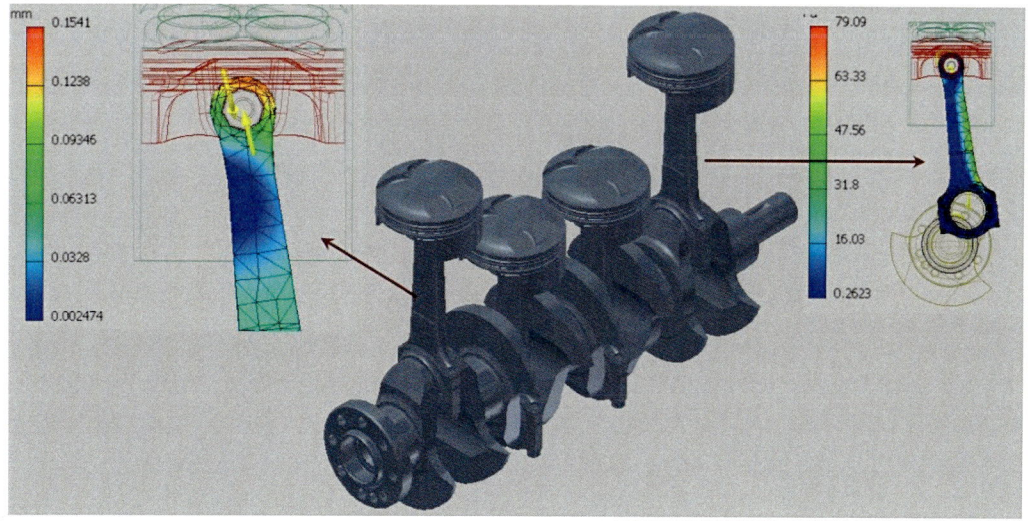

The main requirements of this design problem are to determine:

- Maximum stress in the connecting rod whilst in operation.
- Maximum deflection in the connecting rod.
- Factor of safety.

CHAPTER 13

DP12 – Multiple Motion Load Transfer

In addition to the main requirements, the design criteria to be used for this design problem are the following:

- The material to be used is mild steel *
- Piston: minimum weight is 350g
- Conrod: minimum weight is 500g (including all bolts and bearings)
- Crank-shaft: minimum weight is 11.0kg

*Triple Eight Racing will actually use a higher strength grade of steel

Workflow of Design Problem 12

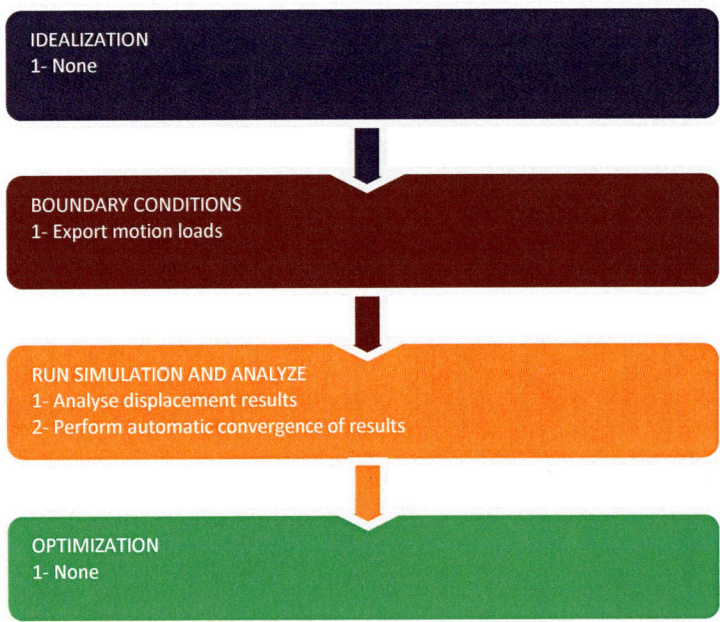

CHAPTER 13
DP12 – Multiple Motion Load Transfer

Idealization

The connecting rod has already been derived into a single part and hence no further simplification is required. In this design problem, the loads will be transferred from the Dynamic Simulation environment.

1. Open completed.iam

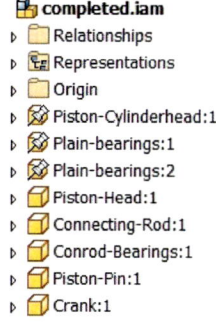
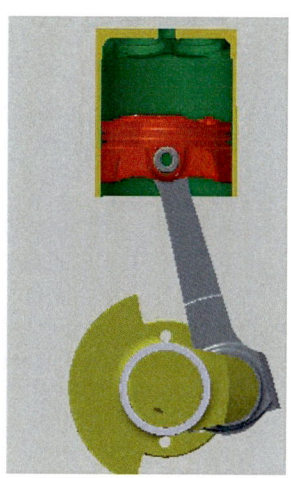

2. Select **Environments** tab > Select **Dynamic Simulation**

Boundary conditions

3. Play **Simulation** > Select **Output Grapher**

4. Right Click the Time data column > Select **Unselect all Curves**

5. Select Force for Revolutions:3 and Point-Line:4 joints

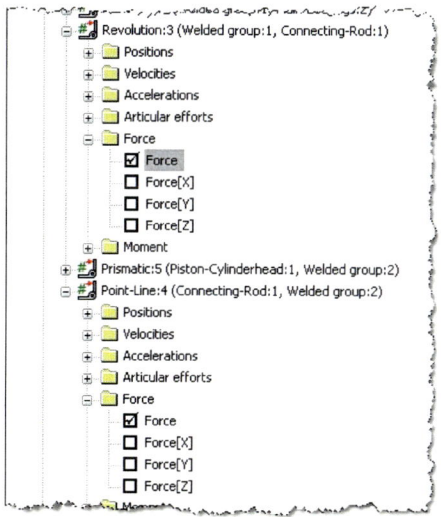

SECTION 4 - Stress Analysis Design Problems using Motion Loads from Dynamic Simulation

CHAPTER 13
DP12 – Multiple Motion Load Transfer

6. Right Click Force (Revolution:3) column > Select **Search Max**

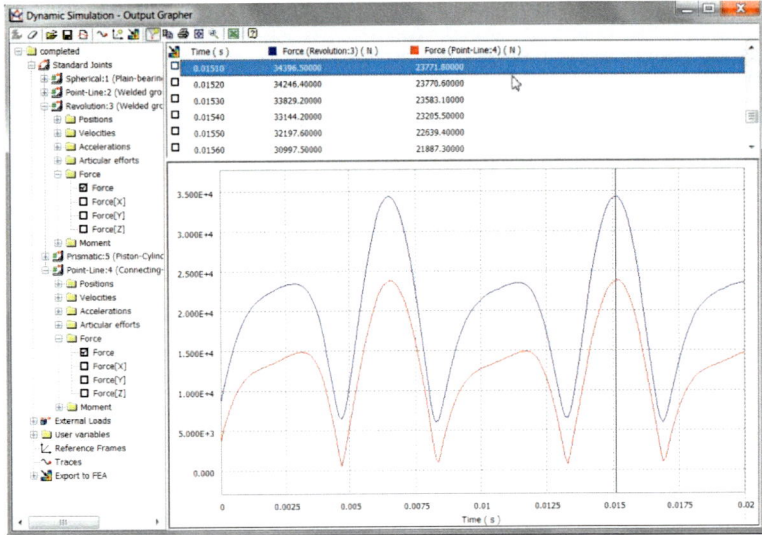

The maximum force for the Force (Revolution: 3) joint is 34396.5N and occurs at time 0.0151 seconds. We will export this force to the Stress Analysis environment.

Export motion loads

7. Tick in the **Export to FEA** column at 0.0151 seconds to export loads at this time frame

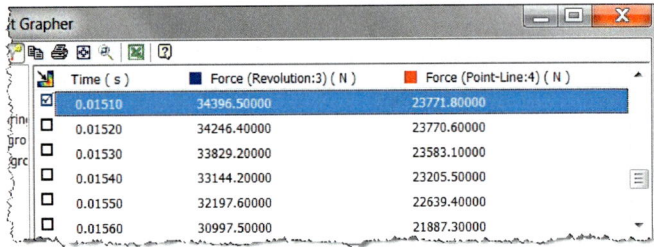

8. Repeat step 6 to 7 for Force (Point-Line: 4)

The maximum value for Force (Point Line:4) joint is 23709.2N and occurs at time 0.0066 seconds.

9. Close **Output Grapher**

10. Select **Export to FEA**

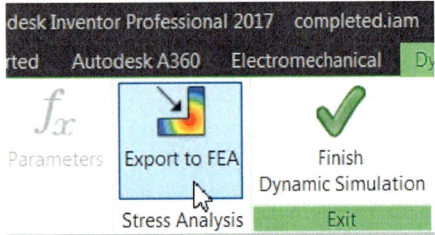

CHAPTER 13
DP12 – Multiple Motion Load Transfer

11. Select Connecting Rod > Click **OK**

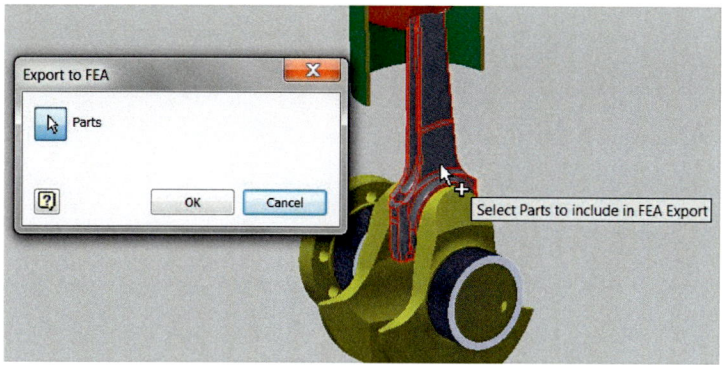

12. Select the face, as shown, to transfer the reaction loads of Joint 3 to this face

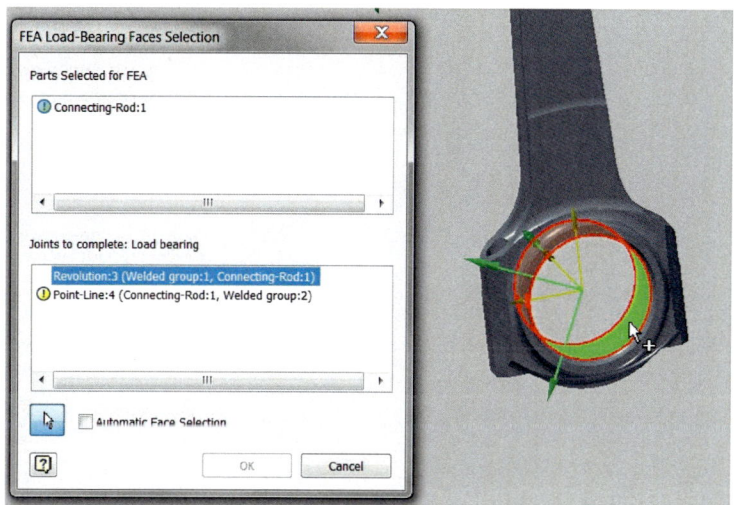

13. Select Joint 4 in the dialogue box > Select face on the other side of connecting rod

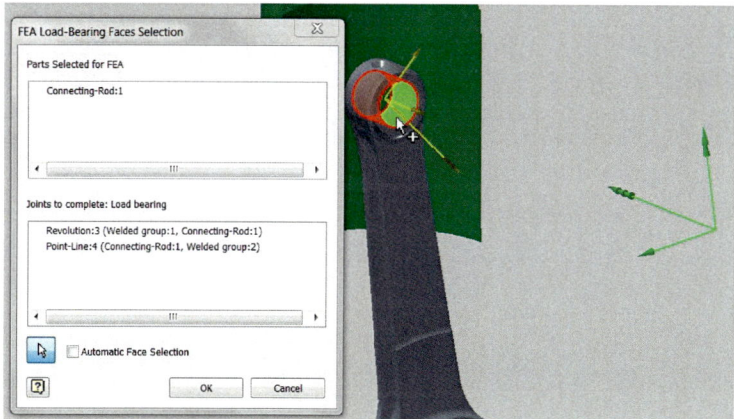

14. Click **OK** > Select **Finish Dynamic Simulation**

CHAPTER 13
DP12 – Multiple Motion Load Transfer

15. Select **Environments** tab > Select **Stress Analysis**

16. Select **Create Study**> Specify **Conrod-Analysis** for Name > Select **Motion Loads Analysis** > Select **0.0151** time step > Click **OK**

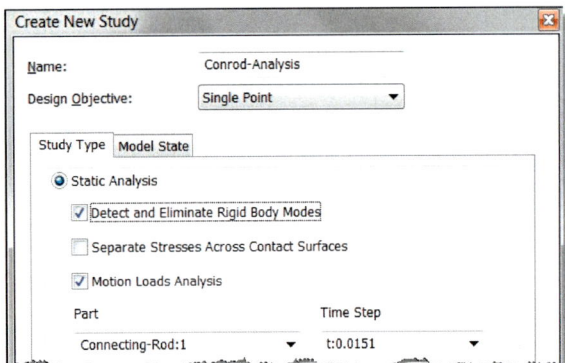

The following loads will be created.

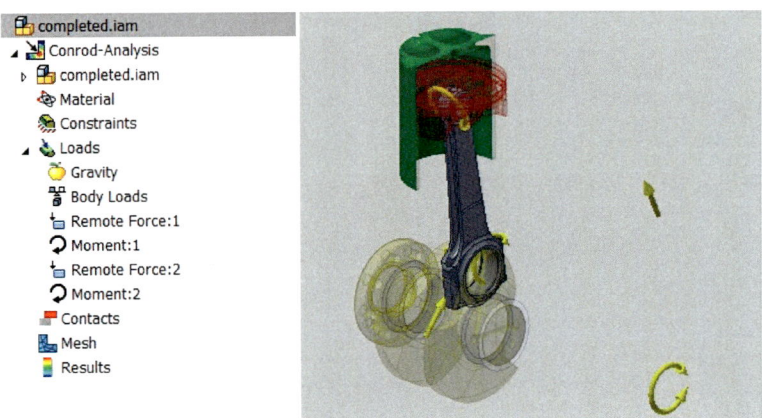

17. Select **Mesh View**

Run simulation and analyze

18. Select **Simulate** > Select **Run**

CHAPTER 13
DP12 – Multiple Motion Load Transfer

19. Select **Actual** from **Adjust Displacement Display**.

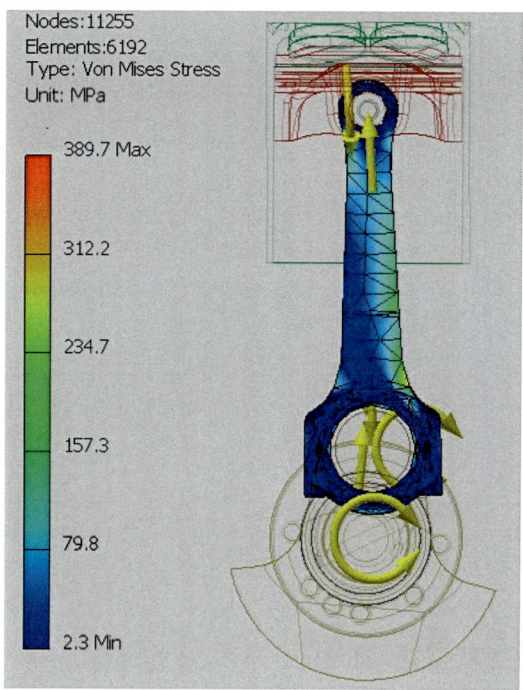

Analyze results

Although we have performed a stress analysis, the motion loads transferred from the top of the connecting rod are not correct as they have induced a moment not acting directly through the center of the connecting rod.

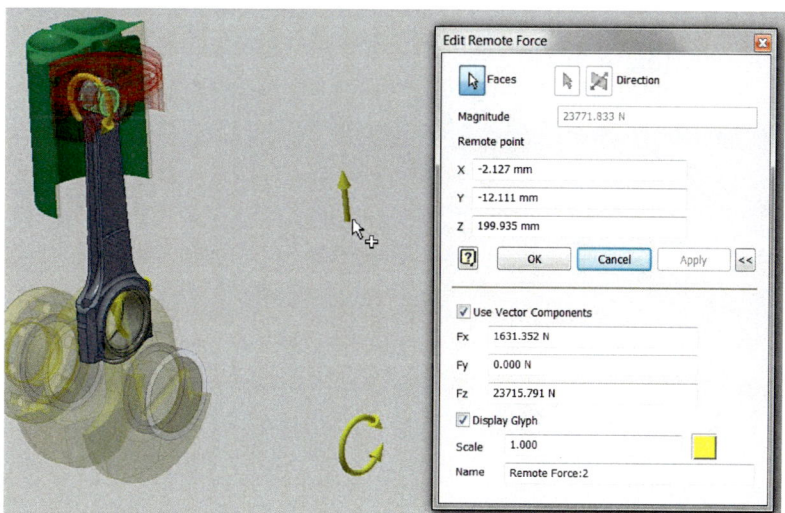

So, we need to alter this to see whether the results change.

20. Select **Finish Stress Analysis**

21. Select **Environments** tab > Select **Dynamic Simulation**

CHAPTER 13
DP12 – Multiple Motion Load Transfer

22. Select **Construction Mode**

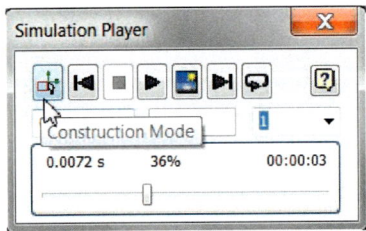

23. Right Click **Point-Line:4** joint > Select **Edit**

24. For Component 1 Origin > Reselect point on conrod as shown > Click **OK**

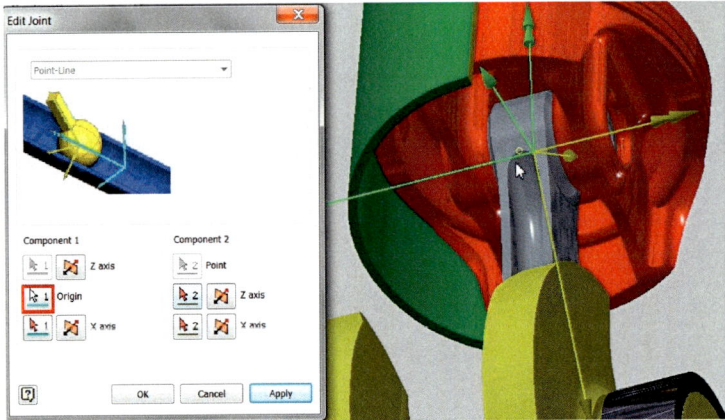

25. Play **Simulation** > Select **Construction Mode** > Select **Finish Dynamic Simulation**

26. Select **Environments** tab > Select **Stress Analysis**

27. Right Click **Loads** > Select **Update**

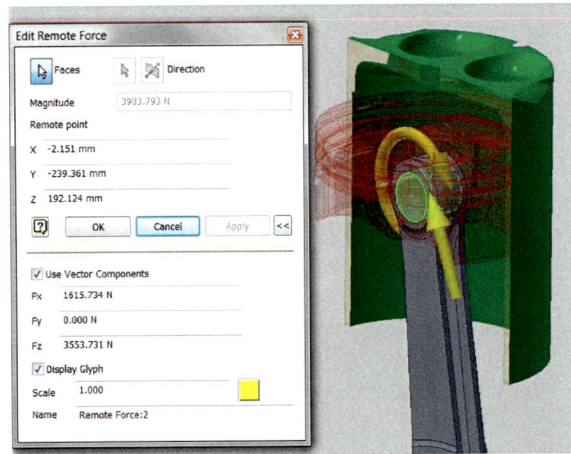

The force has now moved in-line with the connecting rod instead of being offset

CHAPTER 13
DP12 – Multiple Motion Load Transfer

28. Select **Simulate** > Select **Run**

29. Select **Actual** from **Adjust Displacement Display**

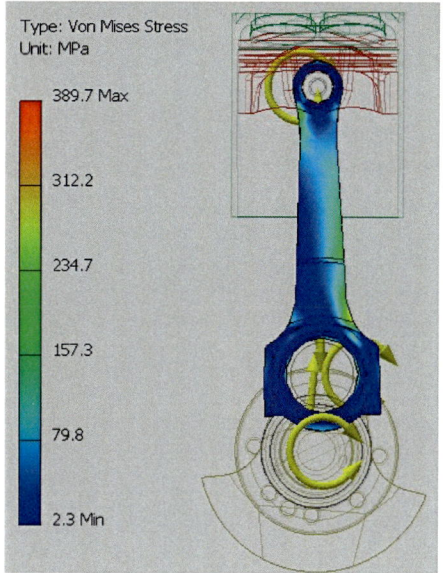

📝 Even though the results did not change, you should be aware of the position of joints and their potential impact on the results.

Perform automatic convergence of results

Next, we need to determine whether the results have converged.

30. Select **Convergence Settings**

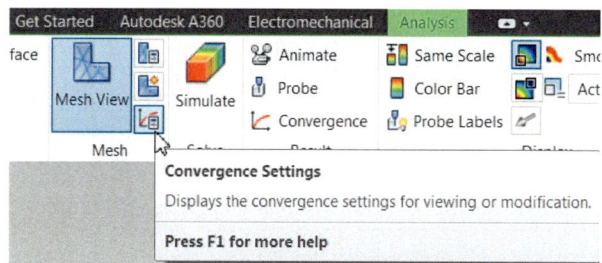

31. Specify 3 **Maximum number of h refinements** > Click **OK**

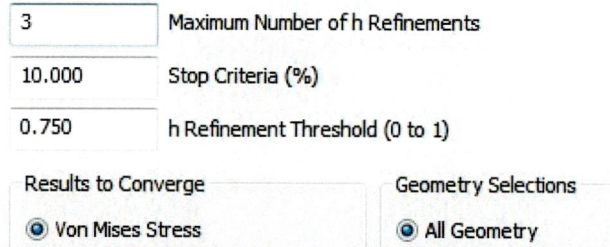

SECTION 4 - Stress Analysis Design Problems using Motion Loads from Dynamic Simulation

CHAPTER 13

32. Select **Mesh Setting** > Specify **0.01** for Average Element Size

33. Select **Simulate** > Select **Run**

34. Select **Convergence Plot**

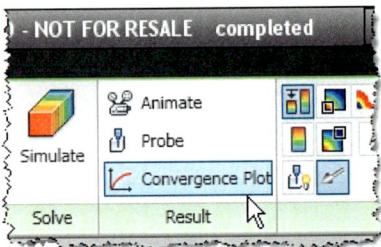

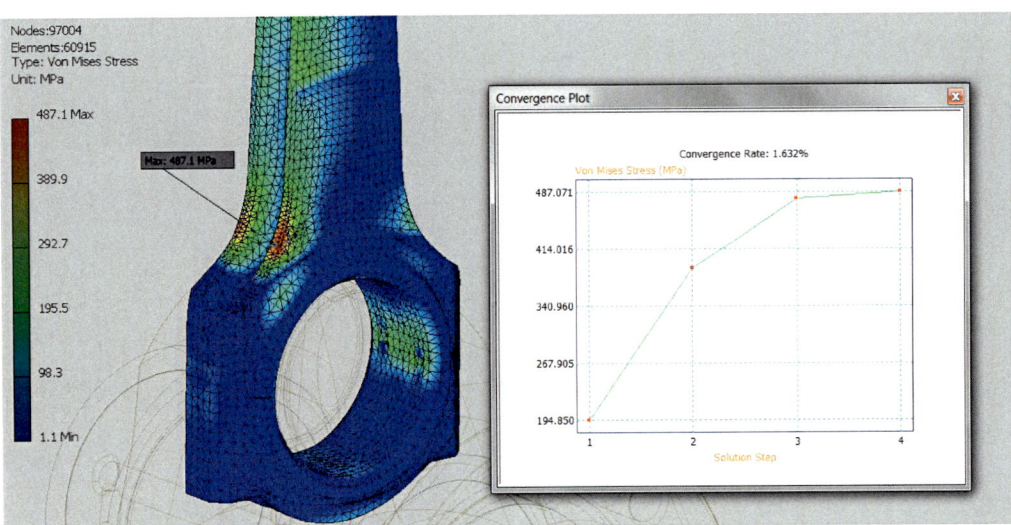

The convergence plot shows that the convergence has been achieved.

Further Exercise

Now, repeat the above steps for the motion load transferred at time step 0.0066s and see whether the safety factor changes.

35. Close File

Section 5 - MODAL ANALYSIS *Design Problems* using SOLID ELEMENTS

CHAPTER 14
DP13 – Modal Analysis

DP13 – Modal Analysis

Modal Analysis of TV Camera Arm attached to Helicopter
(Design Problem courtesy of Aerospace Design Facilities Ltd)

Key features and workflows introduced in this design problem

	Key Features/Workflows
1	Modal shapes and natural frequencies
2	Modal optimization

Introduction

Aerospace Design Facilities Ltd, based in the UK, is a European Aviation Safety Agency (EASA) FIC approved design organization for both helicopters and fixed wing aircraft. Aerospace Design Facilities Ltd also supplies bespoke design and manufacturing services to the film industry. One typical example of their work is designing camera mounts to be placed on helicopters, as shown below.

A major consideration during the design of a camera mount on helicopters is the need to ensure that the vibrations produced by the dynamics of the airframe (rotating components) are not amplified. Generally, the camera systems have been designed to be either hard mounted (i.e. they can cope with the amplitude and frequencies) or attached via an isolation mount. The basic design of the structure to support the camera must be evaluated for its natural frequency response with the camera system installed, and without if the structure is to be flown without a camera system attached.

CHAPTER 14
DP13 – Modal Analysis

The camera arm design is attached to a helicopter having a three-bladed main rotor with a nominal speed of 393rpm. Therefore, the dominant frequency will be **393 rpm / 60s = 6.55**Hz

And as there are 3 rotor blades, there will be 3 passes of the blade in one revolution producing a further dominant frequency of **6.55 Hz x3 = 19.65**Hz

The design of the camera mounts needs to cope with the structural aspects of aerodynamic crash loads; however, the first part of the analysis should be an evaluation of natural frequencies.

Although there are many other considerations involved with this design, this chapter will only investigate two of the natural frequencies that need to be avoided during the design of this camera mount:

Frequency 1 (R1) = **6.55**Hz, Frequency 2 (R3) = **19.65**Hz

The major design restrictions for the camera mount are as follows;

1. The position of the fixing points for the camera mount and the camera are fixed.
2. The maximum weight of the design, including camera, should not exceed 50Kg.
3. The camera offset position relative to the neutral axis of the camera arm is restricted by clearance to both ground and helicopter. In an ideal situation, the position of the centre of gravity of the camera needs to be in line with the neutral axis of the mount arm to minimize vibration.

Workflow of Design Problem 13

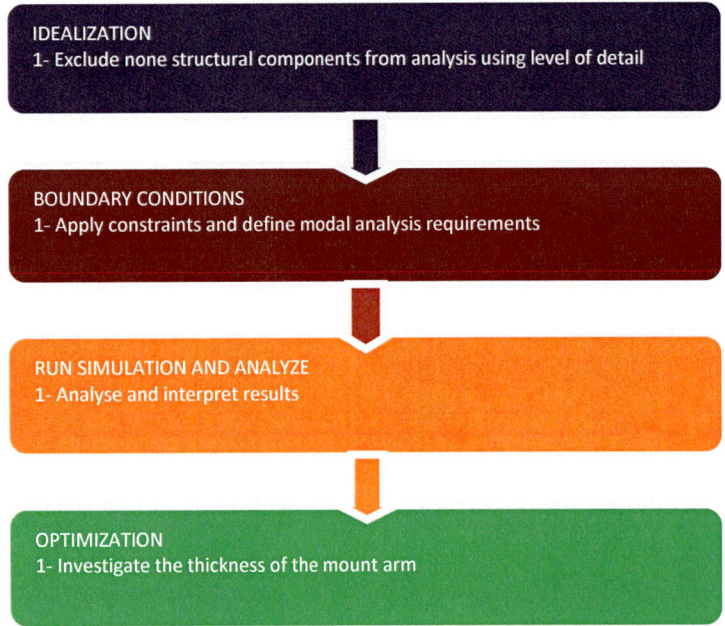

Idealization

The main weight of camera mount assembly comprises the camera (30.5kg) and mount design. The mass of the fasteners is small and to simplify the analysis further all fasteners and associated

CHAPTER 14
DP13 – Modal Analysis

components are excluded from the simulation. Furthermore, the model of the camera and connecting plate has been simplified by suppressing radii, holes, etc. All this idealization of the camera mount is saved as a level of detail, avoiding the need to suppress non-key components and features in the Stress Analysis environment. Two levels of detail have been created: one without the camera and the second with the camera. This will allow us to analyze and compare the modal shape, including natural frequencies, of both models. Initially we will have a look at the natural frequencies of the arm.

1. Open Mount Assembly.iam

Boundary conditions

2. Select **Environments** tab > Select **Stress Analysis**

3. Select **Create Study**> Specify **Arm** for Name > Select **Modal Analysis** > Select **4** for Number of Modes > Select **Enhanced Accuracy**

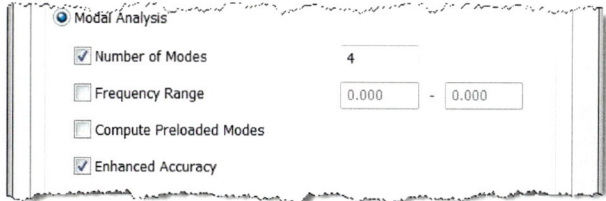

4. Select **Model State** tab > Select **Arm** for **Level of Detail** > Click **OK**

5. Select **Fixed Constraints** > Select the face as shown > Click **OK**

CHAPTER 14
DP13 – Modal Analysis

6. Select **Pin Constraints** > Select the two faces as shown > Click **OK**

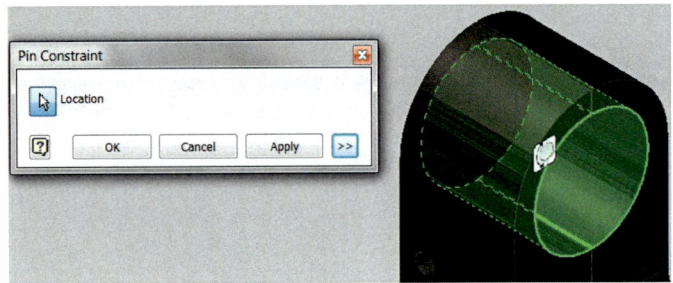

7. Select **Automatic Contacts** to create contacts between components

8. Select **Manual Contact** > Select faces as shown > Click **Apply**

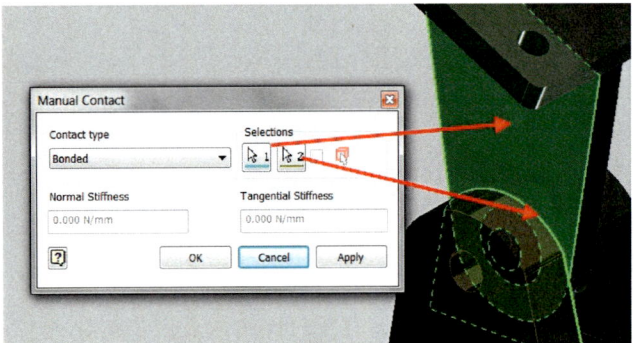

9. Repeat Step 8 for faces on other side of mount > Click **Apply**

10. Select the two faces to connect the tubes together > Click **OK**

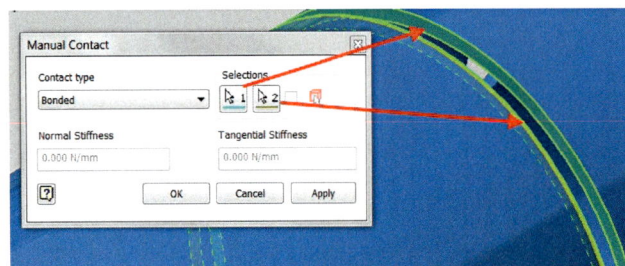

In total 8 contacts will be created

CHAPTER 14
DP13 – Modal Analysis

11. Select **Mesh Settings** > Specify **0.02** for Average Element Size > Check **Create Curved Mesh Elements** > Uncheck **Use part based measure for Assembly mesh** > Click **OK**

12. Select **Mesh View**

 Use a relatively small mesh size to produce a more accurate modal analysis.

Run Simulation and Analyze

13. Select **Simulate** > Select **Run** > Unselect **Mesh View** > Deselect **Boundary Conditions**

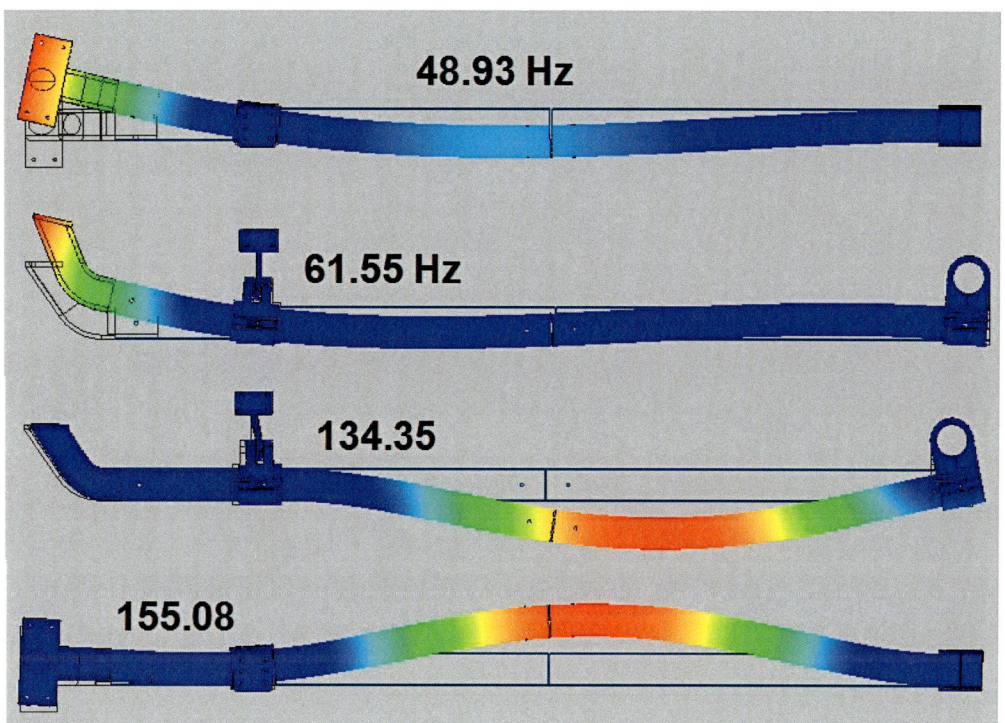

These are the first four modes, defined by the modal shape and natural frequencies, of the arm without the camera. It is important to note that all calculated frequencies are much higher than the R1 and R3 frequencies, which means that the arm without the camera will produce minimal vibration under normal helicopter operating conditions.

Now we will see the effect of adding the camera to the arm and see the first four modes again.

14. Right click **Arm** > Select **Copy Study**

15. Right click **Arm:1** > Select **Edit Study Properties** > Specify **Arm-with-Camera** for Name > Select **Model State** > Select **Arm-with-Camera** for Level of Detail > Click **OK**

16. Right click **Contacts** > Select **Update Automatic Contacts**

 Two more contacts will be created between the camera assembly and arm; ten in total.

CHAPTER 14
DP13 – Modal Analysis

17. Select **Mesh View**

18. Select **Simulate** > Run **Simulation** > Unselect **Mesh View**

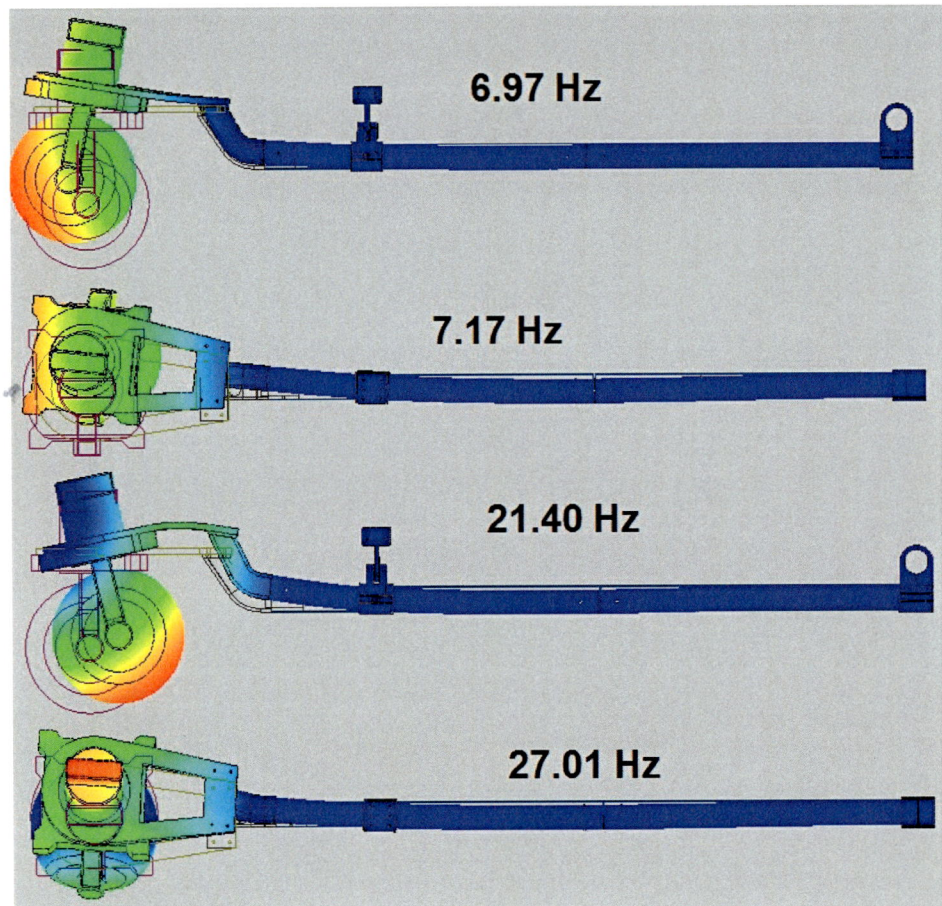

We can now clearly see that the fundamental frequency (Mode 1) has significantly reduced from 48.93 Hz to 6.97 Hz, and this applies to all other three other modes as well. Also, it is important to note that Mode 1 frequency is very close to 6.55 Hz, rotor speeds. This means that we need to alter this mode 1 frequency.

This can be achieved in a number of ways including specifying different material properties, increasing the tube thicknesses, moving the mount positions, and altering geometry of swan neck part to move the position of the center of the gravity of camera in line with the neutral axis of the tubes. Some of these options are limited by the camera ground clearance, interference with the helicopter airframe, and the overall weight of the assembly.

Here, we will pursue the option of increasing the thickness of the arm to alter the natural frequencies.

 Young's modulus, density and Poison's ratio are the only material properties taken into account when performing a modal analysis.

CHAPTER 14
DP13 – Modal Analysis

Optimization

To change tube thicknesses we can either go back into each component or change the sketches, or alternatively we can use parametric optimization within stress analysis to see the effect of tube thicknesses. The latter option is more efficient and, depending on results, can allow the ability to replace and update existing model parameter values with the new stress analysis parameters.

19. Right click **Arm-with-Camera:1** > Select **Edit Study Properties**

20. Change Design Objective to **Parametric Dimension**

21. Select **Simulate** > Select **Run,** this will update results

22. Right click the **Tube Forward 2071-01:1** Part > Select **Show Parameters** > Check **Tube_thickness** user parameter > Click **OK**

23. Right Click the **Tube Rear 208-01:1** Part > Select **Show Parameters** > Check **Tube_ thickness** user parameter > Click **OK**

24. Right click **Swan Neck:1** Part > Select **Show Parameters** > Check **Tube_thickness** user parameter > Click **OK**

25. Select **Parametric Table** > Add **Mass Design Constraint**

26. Specify the following values for Tube_ thicknesses

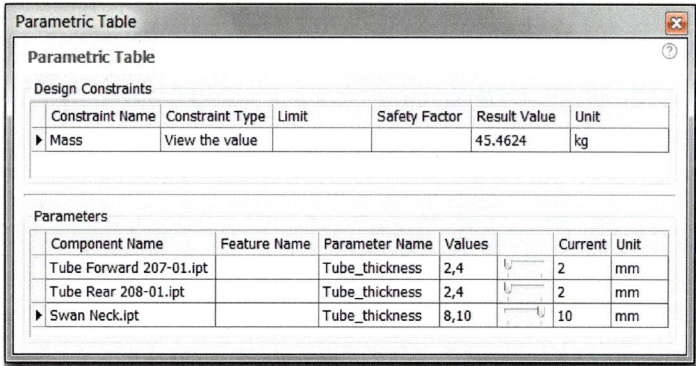

We are going to increase the main tubes of the camera mount assembly from 2 to 4. The Swan neck component is attached to inside of the tubes and, to avoid interference, will need to reduce its thickness by the same amount of (2mm).

27. Set the **Current Values** for each parameter as shown

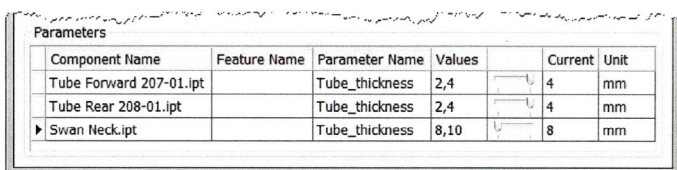

SECTION 5 - Modal Analysis Design Problems using Solid Elements

CHAPTER 14
DP13 – Modal Analysis

28. Right Click in any of the rows > Select **Generate Current Configuration** >

29. Select **Simulate** > Change study to **Current configuration only** > Select **Run**

This will analyze model based on current values set by the user, with the aid of the slider

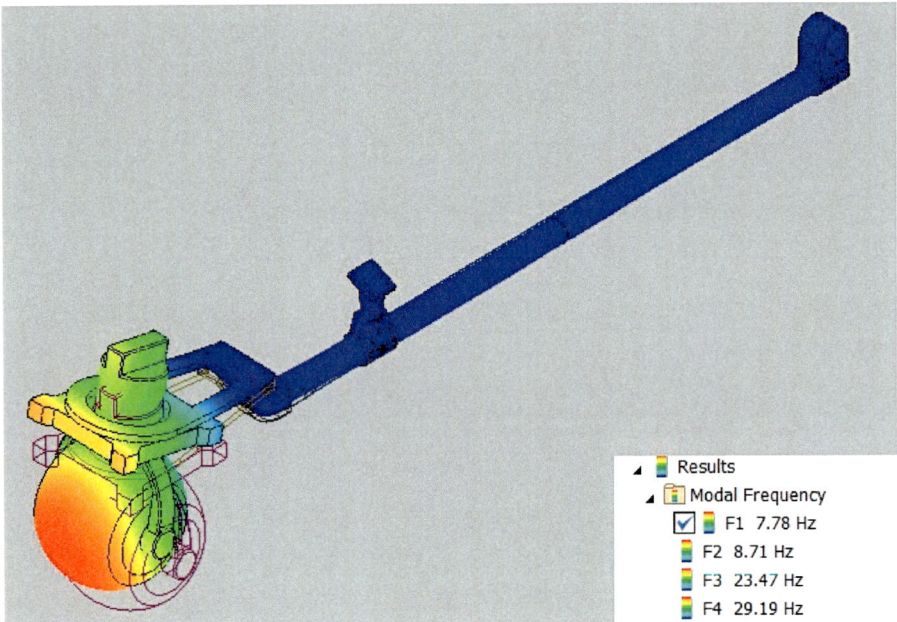

We can clearly see that the frequencies have increased by doubling the wall thickness of the tube and the mass of 47.8472kg, from within the parametric table, is below the 50 kg limit. The frequencies can be further enhanced by making the tube even thicker or even change to a stronger material

30. Close File

Section 6 -
FRAME ANALYSIS
Essentials
& Design Problems
using BEAM ELEMENTS

CHAPTER 15
The Frame Analysis Environment

The Frame Analysis Environment

Frame Analysis Overview

Frame Analysis is associated with analysing large structures mainly comprising of uniform cross-section channels/frames. Typical examples include bridges, structural platforms, towers etc. Some examples are illustrated below.

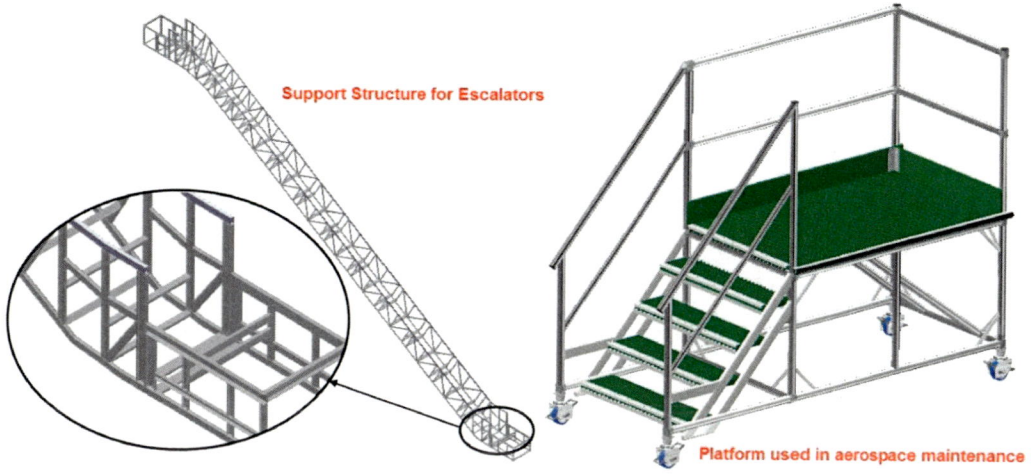

Frame Analysis, within Autodesk Inventor Professional, allows to define criteria for static and modal analysis, including prestressing. In addition, frame analysis uses beam elements instead of the 3D tetrahedron and thin elements used within the stress analysis environment.

A simple beam element comprises of two nodes, one at each end, and has three translational and three rotational degrees of freedom (DOF); six in total.

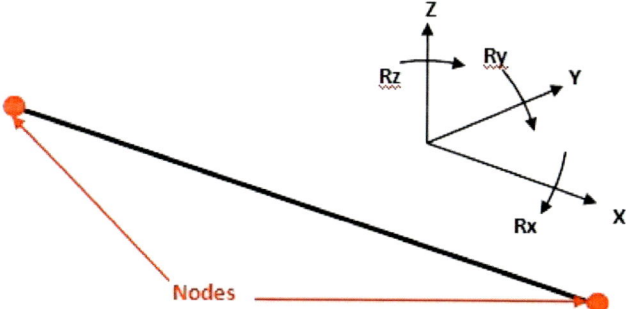

One major benefit of using beam elements over solid tetrahedron elements is faster analysis times. This can be demonstrated by the following example in which a beam is fixed at one end and a load of 1000 N applied at the other end.

CHAPTER 15
The Frame Analysis Environment

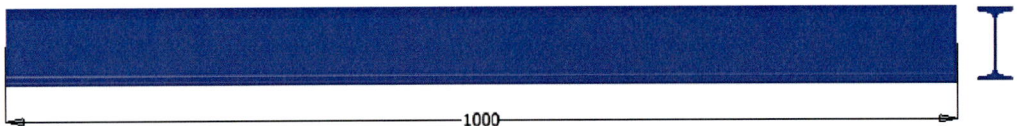

The results of both stress and frame analysis are summarized below (the results are dependent on factors such as computer speed).

	Displacement (mm)	Stress (max) (MPa_	Mesh-time* (s)	N° of elements	Analysis-time (s)
Stress Analysis	1.970	53.32	8	5780	6
Frame Analysis	1.949	51.46	1	10	1
Theoretical Results	1.949	51.46	-	-	-

*A default mesh of 0.1 Average Element Size was used within the Stress Analysis environment.

These results illustrate that a simple structure, such as an I-beam, can have a significant impact on the model sizes and analysis times. For this simple reason it is normal practice to analyse a thin structure, with uniform cross-section, with beam elements. Another advantage of using beam elements is that there is no stress singularities/stress concentrations to overcome. These stress concentrations are probably the cause for slight difference in the stress results (less than 5%).

Frame Analysis Workflow

The process of creating an analysis (both stress and modal) involves four core steps:

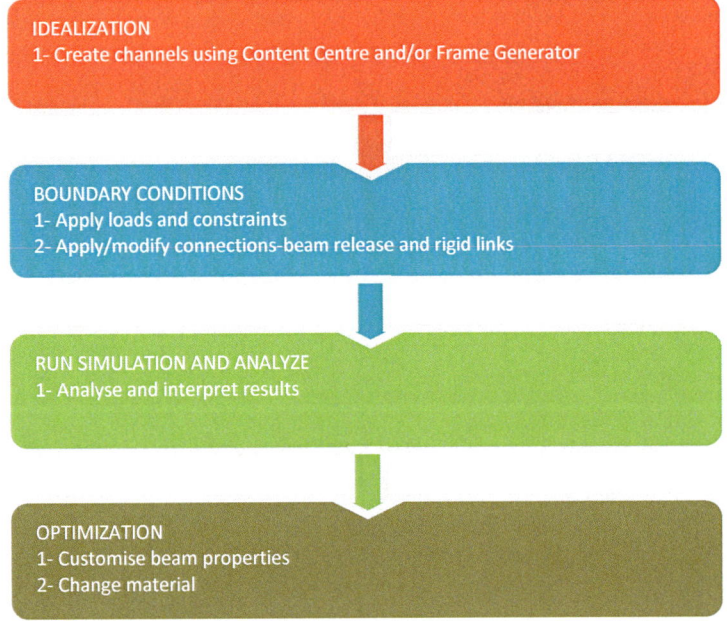

SECTION 6 - Frame Analysis Essentials and Design Problems using Beam Elements

CHAPTER 15
The Frame Analysis Environment

Frame Analysis User Interface

Frame Analysis can only be accessed from the Assembly environment via either the Environments or Design tab.

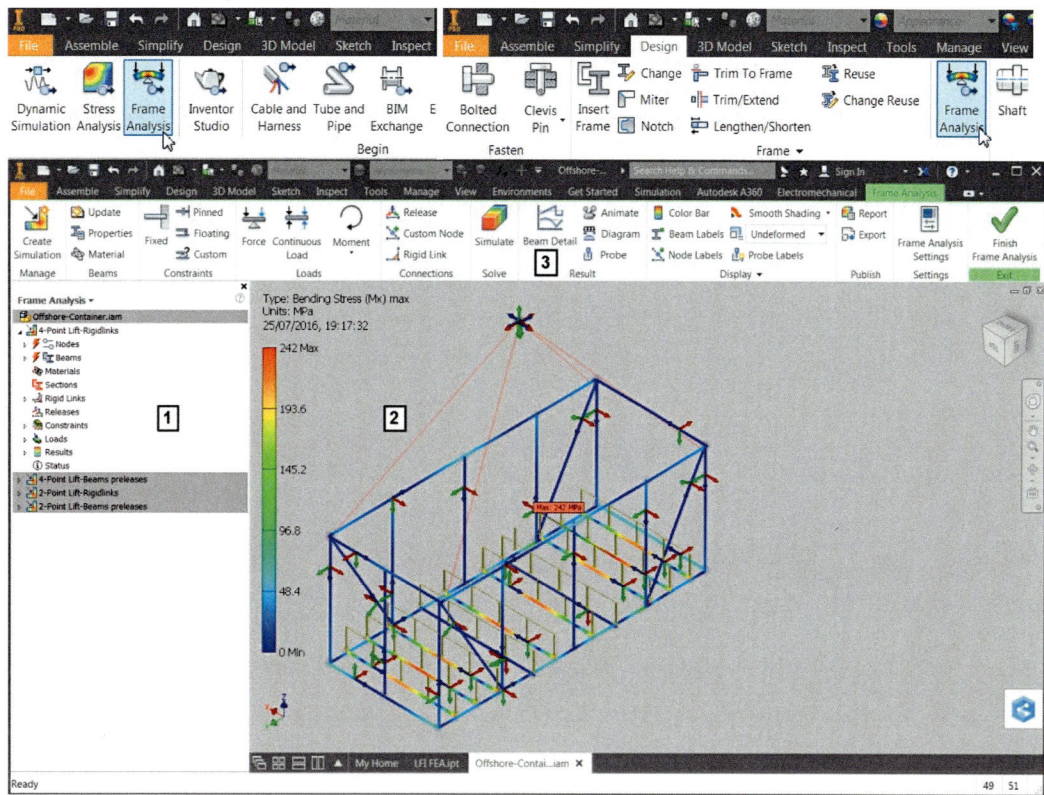

1. Frame Analysis Browser
2. Frame Analysis Graphic Window
3. Frame Analysis Panel

Frame Analysis Browser

Displays part and assembly data, boundary conditions and results in a hierarchical view with nested levels of features and attributes information. You can:

- Copy whole simulations or simulation objects between simulations.
- Right-click on a node for context menu options.
- Expand the folders, select the nodes, and see the selection cross-highlight in the graphic region.

Frame Analysis Graphic Window

Displays the model geometry and simulation results. Updates to show current status of the simulation, including applying boundary conditions and loads with the help of view manipulation tools.

CHAPTER 15
The Frame Analysis Environment

Dynamic Simulation Tab	Workflow Stage	Description
Create Simulation — Manage	Step 1	**Create Simulation** — Here you decide whether you need to create a stress or modal analysis.
Update / Properties / Material — Beams	Step 4	**Beams** — Modify beam properties and materials to experiment with.
Fixed / Pinned / Floating / Custom — Constraints		**Constraints** — Represent how parts and assemblies are constrained to represent reality.
Force / Continuous Load / Moment — Loads	Step 2	**Loads** — Represent the external forces that are exerted on a component. During normal use, the component is expected to withstand these loads and continue to perform as intended.
Release / Custom Node / Rigid Link — Connections		**Connections** — Here you can manually create new nodes and rigid links. Also perform beam release to remove moments at beam ends.
Simulate — Solve		**Solve** — Run the simulation to analyze results as a consequence of defining materials, constraints and loads
Beam Detail / Animate / Diagram / Probe — Result	Step	**Results** — View the stress and deformation results to provide an informed decision regarding whether the component will function under the defined loads and constraints.
Color Bar / Smooth Shading / Beam Labels / Undeformed / Node Labels / Probe Labels — Display	-	**Display** — Modify color plots including displaying maximum and minimum values
Report / Export — Publish	-	**Publish** — Generate an html report of the results to share
Frame Analysis Settings — Settings	-	**Settings** — Predefine initial settings including contact tolerance and other general settings

CHAPTER 15
The Frame Analysis Environment

Frame Analysis Panel

Manage tab

This is the first step in creating a frame analysis study.

Create Simulation

Here you can define whether you want to carry out a static analysis or modal analysis, – Including the option of selecting different levels of representations.

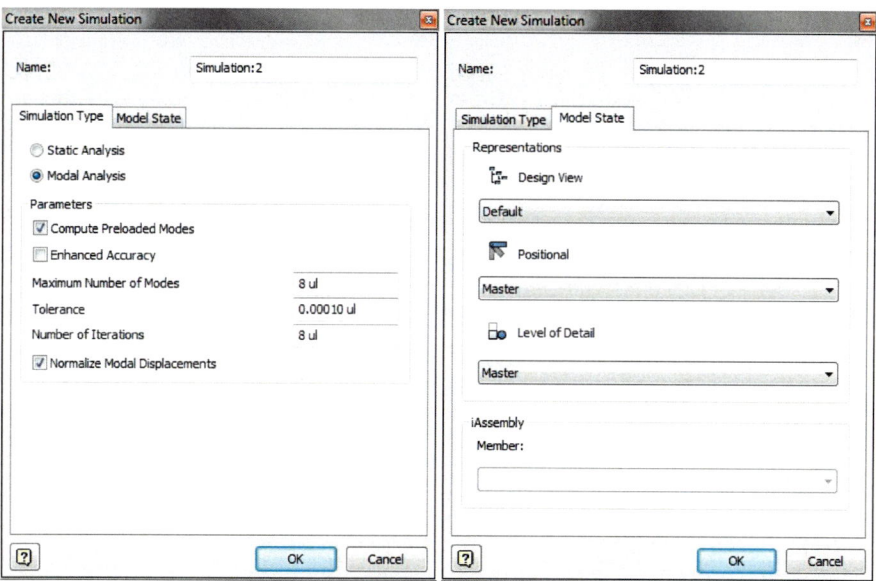

Simulation Type – Here you define whether a stress or modal analysis is to be carried out.

Model State – For an assembly you can choose any design view, positional view and level of detail on which to perform the analysis.

Parameters (modal analysis only) – When performing modal analysis, there are three settings that can be defined.

Enhanced Accuracy – Select this option if you want to increase accuracy of solution and verify results.

CHAPTER 15
The Frame Analysis Environment

Compute Preloaded Modes – This is checked by default and calculates the modes of the model when in the loaded condition. Modes under the preloaded condition tend to have higher natural frequencies than models that are not preloaded.

Maximum Number of Modes – This calculates the number of modes, including modal shape and natural frequencies, required; the default is set to 8.

Tolerance – Here you can define the accuracy of the results required. The iterative solver goes through a repetitive analysis until the difference in the results is within this tolerance setting.

Number of Iterations – Here you define the number of repetitive analysis required. The default value is set to 10.

Normalize Modal Displacements – This option is normally preselected and changes the scale of the results so they are more visually presentable, especially the deformation scale. Note the displacement results are not actual and are just only for visual purposes.

Beams tab

 Update
 Properties
 Material

Beams

Update
This becomes active when the model has been changed, for example in the assembly environment, and thus requires an update.

Properties
Normally most components will have their materials assigned within the Part environment, thus removing the need to assign material, as they will come across directly from the Part environment.

CHAPTER 15
The Frame Analysis Environment

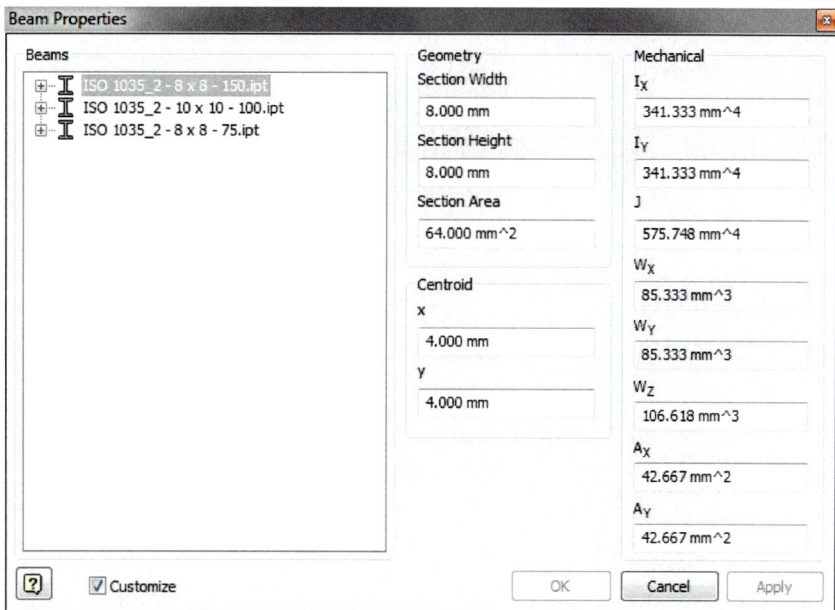

Geometry – The width and height are the overall dimensions of the cross-section of the beam; for example, a diameter of 10mm will have a width and height of 10mm. The area is the true cross-section area of the beam.

Centroid – The position of the centroid with reference to the beam coordinate system.

Mechanical – These values provide details of the second moment of area (I_x, I_y), polar second moment of area (I_z), section modulus (W_x, W_y, W_z) and Shear Stress (A_x, A_y).

Below are two examples of simple shapes with their associated cross-sectional mechanical properties.

	2nd Moment of Area	Section Modulus
Circle (diameter D)	$\dfrac{\pi D^4}{64}$	$\dfrac{\pi D^3}{32}$
Rectangle (b × d)	$\dfrac{bd^3}{12}$	$\dfrac{bd^2}{6}$

Material

The materials of the beams are normally pre-assigned when you create frames using Frame Generator and Content Centre.

CHAPTER 15
The Frame Analysis Environment

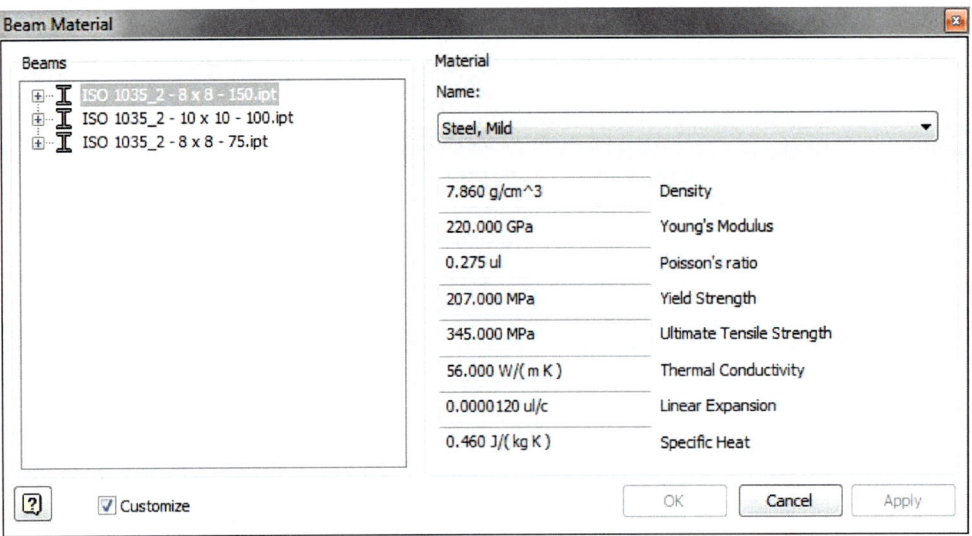

If the material is inadequately defined then the simulation will not run and an error message will be displayed in the Status folder within the browser. The material can be changed within Frame Analysis using the Customize button.

 Customize will not let you alter the material properties including density, young's modulus etc.

Constraints tab

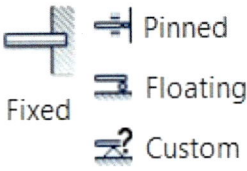

Constraints

Constraints can be created by either using the heads up display (HUD) or constraints dialogue box, as illustrated below.

 When a beam is selected, to place any constraint, a node is automatically created that connects the constraint to the beam.

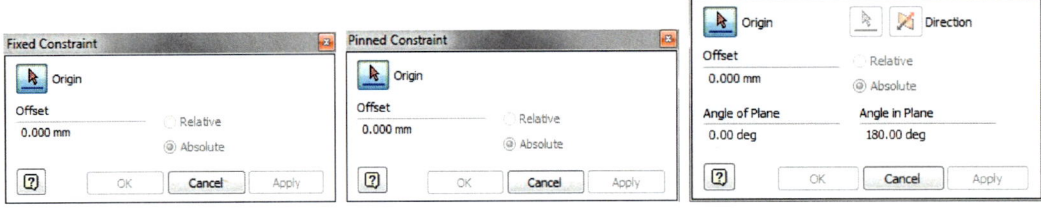

Fixed constraint

Fixed constraint removes all translation and rotational degrees of freedom of the selected node or beam. Both nodes and beams can be selected to specify the origin. The Offset parameter will only be activated if a beam is selected to define Origin. The Offset can be specified either in absolute or relative values. A value of 0.5, when Relative is selected, will place the constraint in the middle of the beam. Fixed constraints simulate bolted and welded connections as illustrated below.

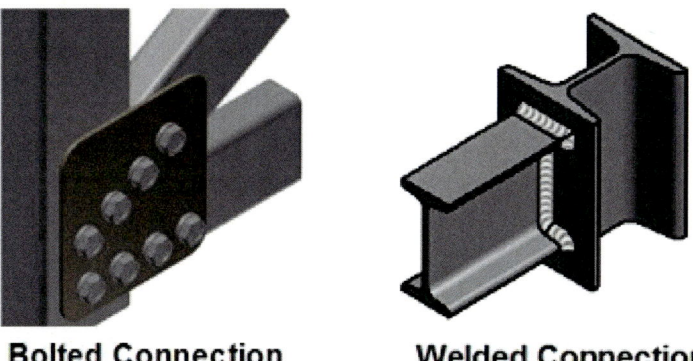

Bolted Connection **Welded Connection**

Pinned constraint

Pinned Constraint only removes all rotational degrees of freedom of the selected node or beam. Both nodes and beams can be selected to specify the Origin. The Offset parameter will only be activated if a beam is selected to define Origin. The offset can be specified in either absolute or relative values. An absolute value of 100 mm will place the constraint in the middle of a 200 mm beam. Pin constraints simulate hinge and pin-hole connections as illustrated below.

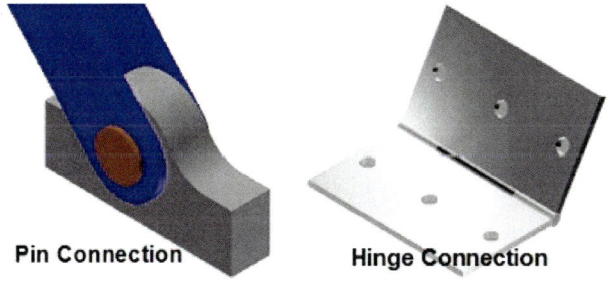

Pin Connection **Hinge Connection**

 A single pin-type constraint will behave more like a spherical joint/constraint, as it has three degrees of rotation. However, in most applications there will be more than one constraint and in such circumstances the constraint will behave more like a pin constraint, as its rotational degrees of freedom will be restricted.

Floating pinned constraint

Floating Pinned Constraint restricts rotation and translation in one plane only for a selected node or beam. Both nodes and beams can be selected to specify the Origin. Additionally, the direction can be specified by selecting work axes, work planes or beam. The Offset parameter will only be activated if a beam is selected to define the Origin. The Offset can either be specified in absolute or relative values. An absolute value of 100 mm will place the constraint at one-third of the length of a 300 mm beam. Floating pinned constraints simulate rollers, wheels and smooth surface-type joints, as illustrated below.

CHAPTER 15
The Frame Analysis Environment

The table below is a summary of the degrees of freedom which are restrained depending on the type of constraint used.

		Translational d.o.f			Rotational d.o.f		
		X	Y	Z	Rx	Ry	Rz
1	Fixed support	√	√	√	√	√	√
2	Pinned connection	√	√	√			
3	Floating support *		√		√		√

CHAPTER 15
The Frame Analysis Environment

Below is a summary of the types of results available, including reactions and moments, depending on the type of standard constraint used.

		Reacting Forces			Reacting Moments		
		Rx	Ry	Rz	Mx	My	Mz
1	Fixed support	√	√	√	√	√	√
2	Pinned connection	√	√	√			
3	Floating support *		√				

* Fixed and loaded in a plane normal to the Y-axis

Custom constraint

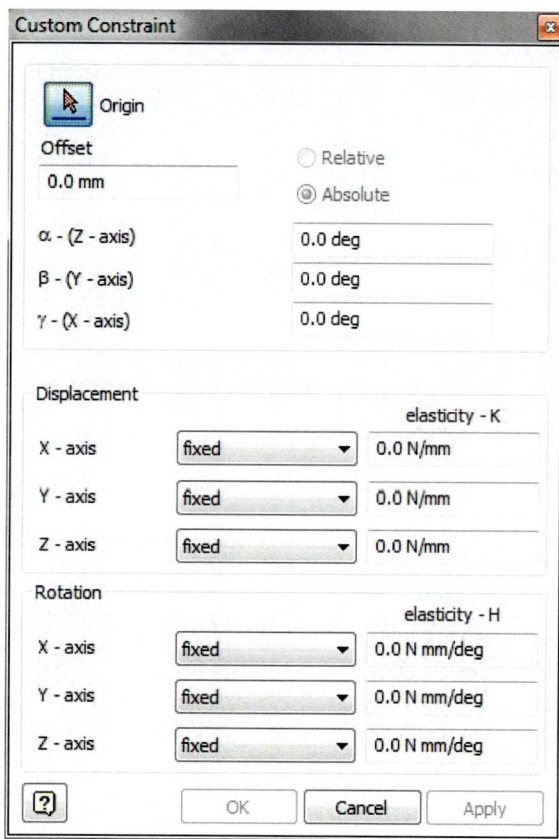

Custom constraint is the only constraint that allows control of its six degrees of freedom: For example, a custom constraint could be used to define a pin constraint by fixing the three degrees of translation only. Custom constraint also allows the specification of stiffness (elasticity), enabling simulation of rubber bushing type connections.

Below are the details of all the options:

α - (Z-axis) – Specify the angle of constraint rotation about the Z axis.
β - (Y-axis) – Specify the angle of constraint rotation about the Y axis.
γ - (X-Axis) – Specify the angle of constraint rotation about the X axis.

CHAPTER 15
The Frame Analysis Environment

Fixed - Means that the joint behaves like a fixed constraint

Uplift none - Means that the degree of freedom (rotation and displacement) is free and not restricted.

Uplift+ - Means that the degree of freedom (rotation and displacement) is free only in the positive direction with respect to the beam coordinate system (local).

Uplift- - Means that the degree of freedom (rotation and displacement) is free only in the negative direction with respect to the beam coordinate system (local).

Refer to the image below to see the consequences of changing uplift settings.

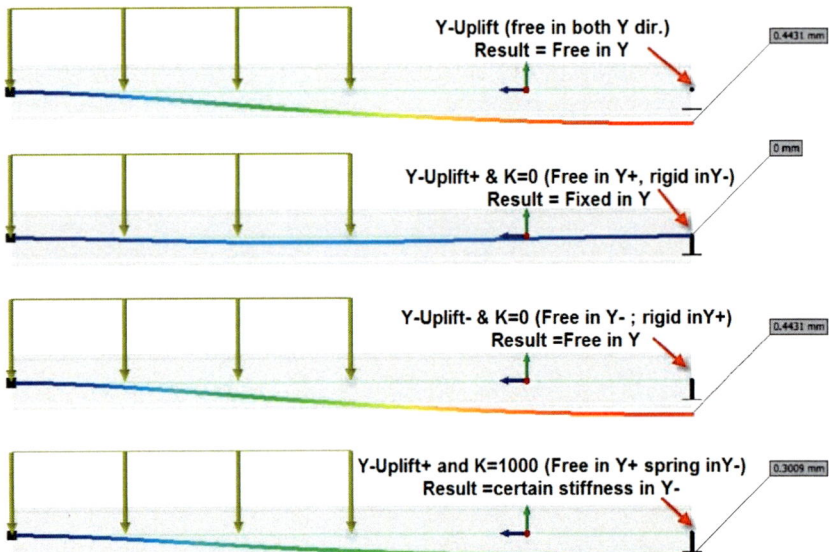

Loads tab

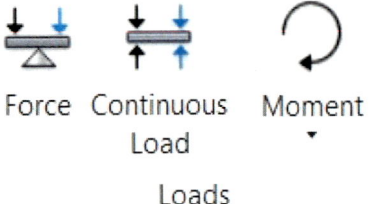

Loads

Force

To fully define a force, an origin, magnitude, and direction are required. Direction can be specified by selecting either the beam or axis. Alternatively, the direction can be specified by specifying Angle of Plane and Angle in Plane, where Angle of Plane rotates the XY plane of where the load is defined and Angle in Plane defines the angle of force from the Z axes. The Offset is only available if the beam is both selected and can be defined in absolute and relative values; for example, a relative value of 0.5 will place the force in the middle of the beam.

CHAPTER 15
The Frame Analysis Environment

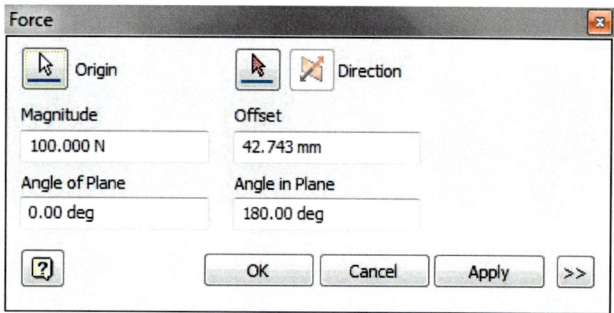

Below is an example of force being defined using **Vector** values.

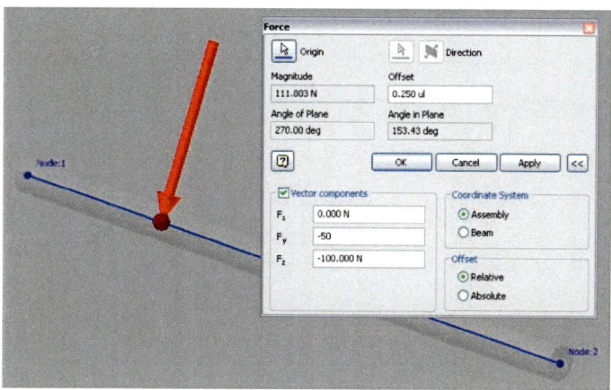

Continuous load

To fully define a continuous load, an origin, magnitude and direction are required. Direction can be specified by selecting either the beam or axis. Alternatively, the direction can also be specified by specifying Angle of Plane and Angle in Plane, where Angle of Plane rotates the XY plane of where the load is defined and Angle in Plane defines the angle of force from the Z axes.

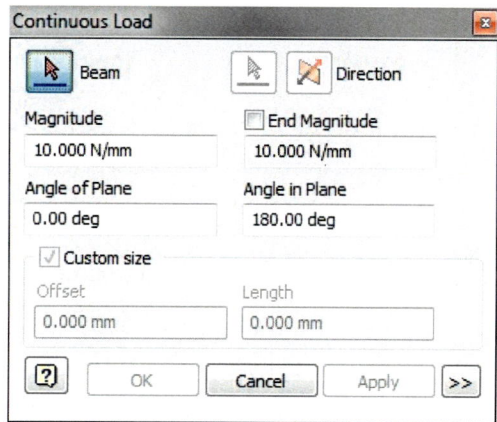

A variable load can be defined by enabling End Magnitude, and specifying two different Magnitude values.

CHAPTER 15
The Frame Analysis Environment

Below is an example of a continuous load being defined using the heads up display (HUD)

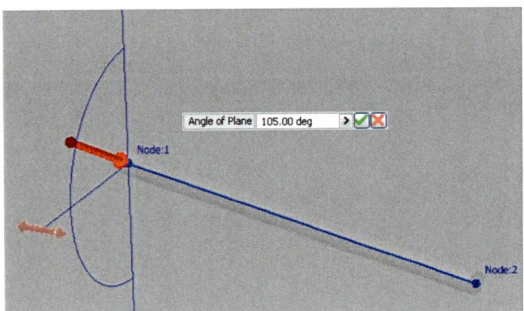

Moment

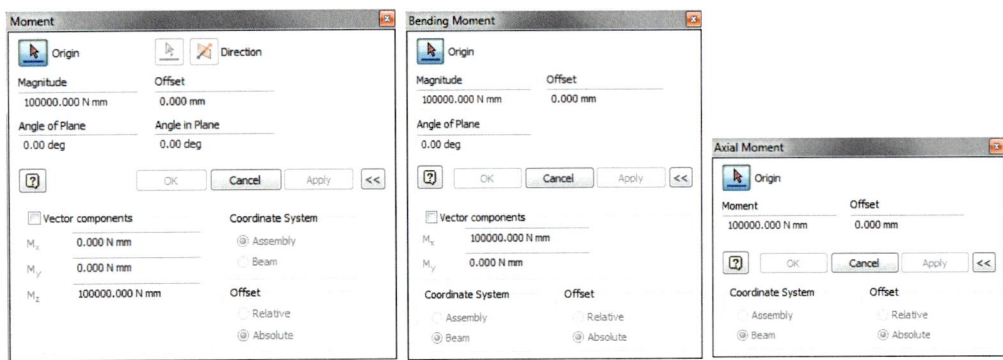

Moment (general)

To fully define a general moment, an origin, magnitude, and direction are required. Direction can be specified by selecting either the beam or axis, including specifying moment in the beam. Alternatively, the direction can be specified by specifying Angle of Plane and Angle in Plane, where Angle of Plane rotates the XY plane of where the moment is acting and Angle in Plane defines the angle of moment from the Z axes. The offset is only available if the beam is selected and can be defined in absolute and relative values; for example, a relative value of 0.5 will place the force in the middle of the beam.

Bending and axial moment can also be defined by using general moment. Below is an example of a bending moment being created using HUD.

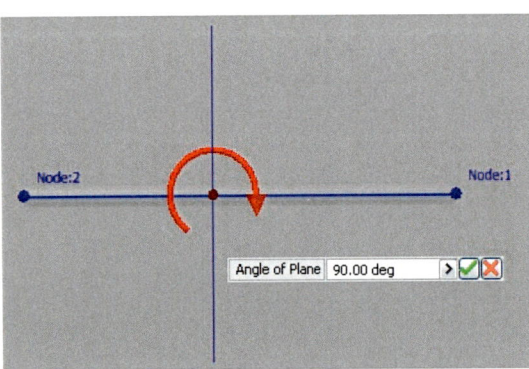

CHAPTER 15
The Frame Analysis Environment

Bending Moment

Creates a bending moment on the selected beam and is applied in the plane parallel to the beam axis. It works in the beam coordinate system only and requires fewer input values than the general Moment dialogue box

Axial Moment

Create an axial moment on the specified beam and is applied in the plane perpendicular to the beam axis. It works in beam coordinate system only and, again, requires fewer input values than the general Moment dialogue box.

Example 1 – Cantilever model results compared with hand calculations

The following example is of a cantilever loaded at one end and fixed at the other.

The beam, made out of mild steel (E = 220 GPa), is 200 mm long and 10 mm diameter. With a 100 N load applied, the maximum deflection and bending Stress are 2.469 mm and 203.7 MPa, respectively.

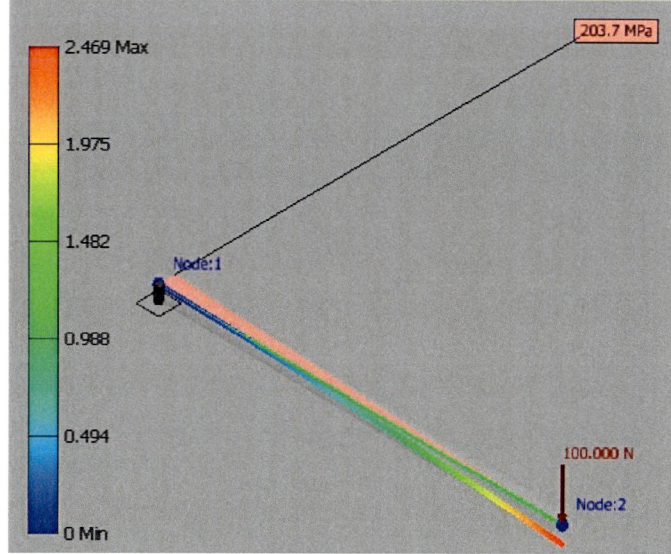

As a comparison, the maximum deflection and bending stress based on theoretical results, using the following formulae, are 2.469 mm and 203.7 MPa, respectively.

CHAPTER 15
The Frame Analysis Environment

Maximum Deflection = $WL^3/3EI$

Where;

W is load
L is length
E is Young's modulus
I is second moment of area

I for a circle is

$\pi D^4/64 = \pi * 0.01^4/64 = 4.908 \times 10^{-10}$

Based on the classical bending stress formula

$$\frac{M}{I} = \frac{\sigma}{y}$$

Maximum Deflection = $100 \times 0.2^3 / 3 \times 220 \times 10^9 \times 4.908 \times 10^{-10} = 0.002469$

Where:

M is Max bending moment = F x L = 100x0.2 = 20 Nm
σ is Max Stress
y is distance of neutral axis

Maximum σ = 20 x 0.005/4.908 x 10^{-10} = 203.7 x 10^6 N/m²

TRY IT! – Open Singlebeam.iam

Example 2 – Simply supported beam created with custom constraint

The model used here is the same as in Example 1, except that it is simply supported by pinned constraints at either end, with a load applied in the middle.

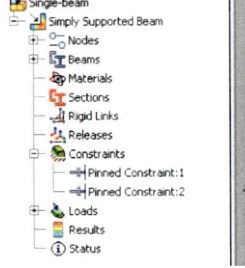
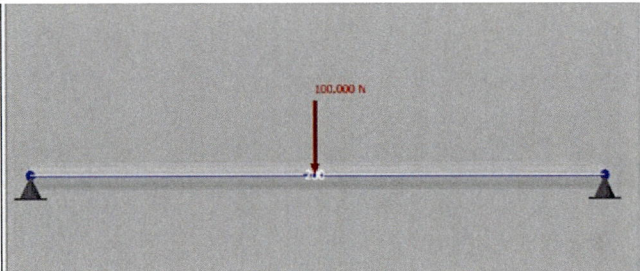

CHAPTER 15
The Frame Analysis Environment

With a 100 N load applied, the maximum deflection and bending Stress are 0.1543 mm and 50.93 MPa, respectively.

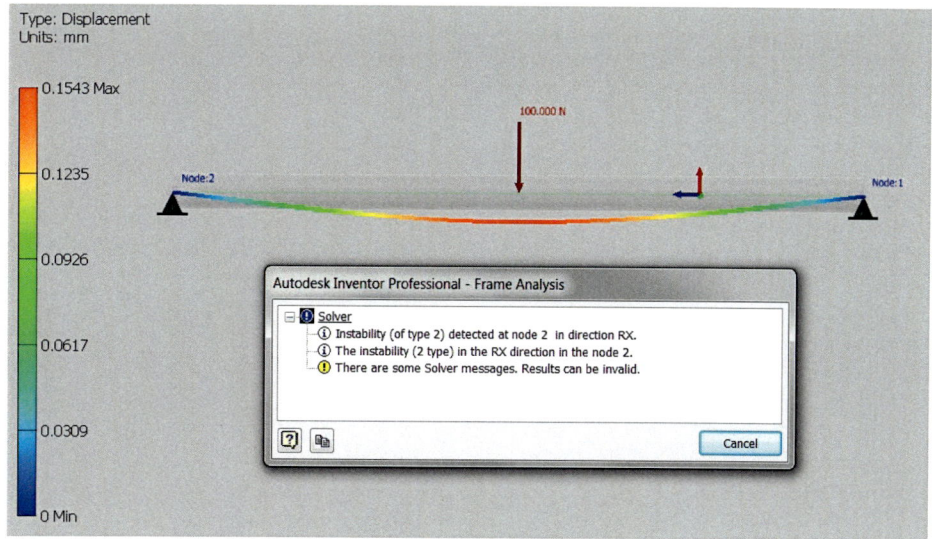

Although the results are correct based on the theoretical results, a warning appears detailing that the beam is free to rotate about its axis. This is due to the fact that applying a second pinned constraint on the other end of the beam has restricted the Y and Z (global) rotational degrees of freedom of both constraints. However, none of the constraints restrict motion about the axis of the beam.

To avoid the warning, we can replace one of the pinned constraints with a custom constraint, with all displacements and rotation about the axis of the beam fixed.

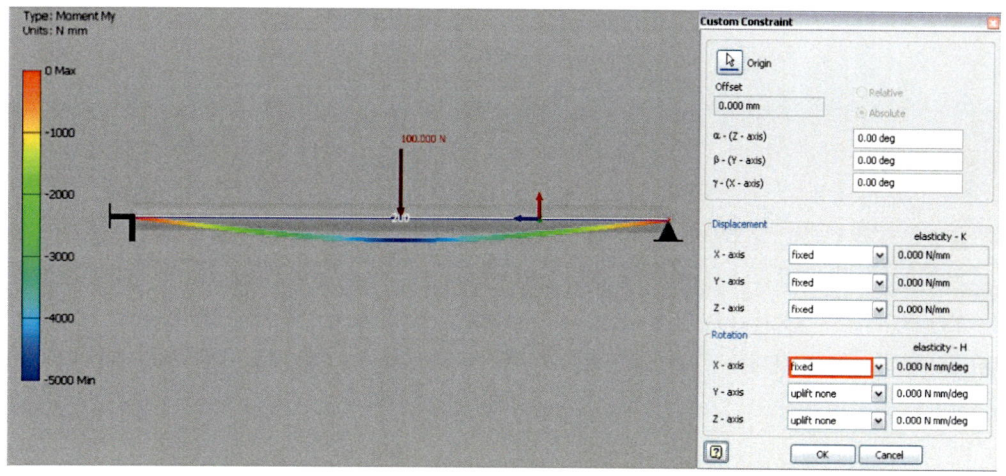

TRY IT! – Open Singlebeam.iam

SECTION 6 - Frame Analysis Essentials and Design Problems using Beam Elements

CHAPTER 15
The Frame Analysis Environment

Connections tab

 Release

 Custom Node

 Rigid Link

Connections

Release

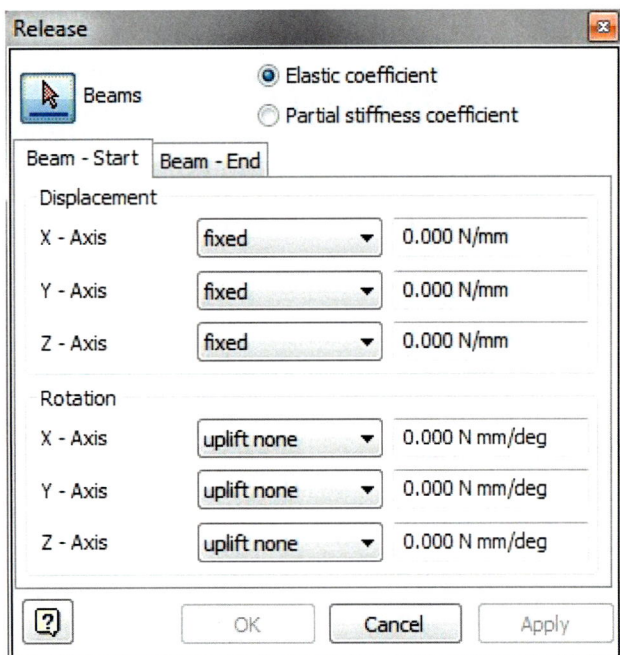

Beam release allows the release of rotational and translational degrees of freedom in beam connections that have been created automatically; by default, beam end connections are rigid. For example, by releasing the rotational degrees of freedom; the fixed connection will convert to a pinned connection at the beam ends, thus removing moments in the beam. Refer to the beam release example. In addition to releasing degrees of freedom, elastic coefficients can also be specified to create stiffness at the beam ends, enabling some flexibility at the connections. When Partial stiffness coefficient is selected, value of 1.0 will mean no release and a value of 0 will mean maximum release.

 When there are two or more adjoining beams, one of them should be fixed without a release at that beam end, as constraint already contains information about boundary conditions of adjoining beam.

While editing, the beam coordinate systems is displayed near the start or end of the beam.

Fixed - Means that the joint behaves like a fixed constraint.

CHAPTER 15
The Frame Analysis Environment

Uplift none - Means that the degree of freedom (rotation and displacement) is free and not restricted.

Uplift+ - Means that the degree of freedom (rotation and displacement) is free only in the positive direction with respect to beam coordinate system (local).

Uplift- - means that the degree of freedom (rotation and displacement) is free only in the negative direction with respect to beam coordinate system (local).

Example 3 – Releasing moments in Structure using Beam Release

In this example, the following frame is loaded as shown.

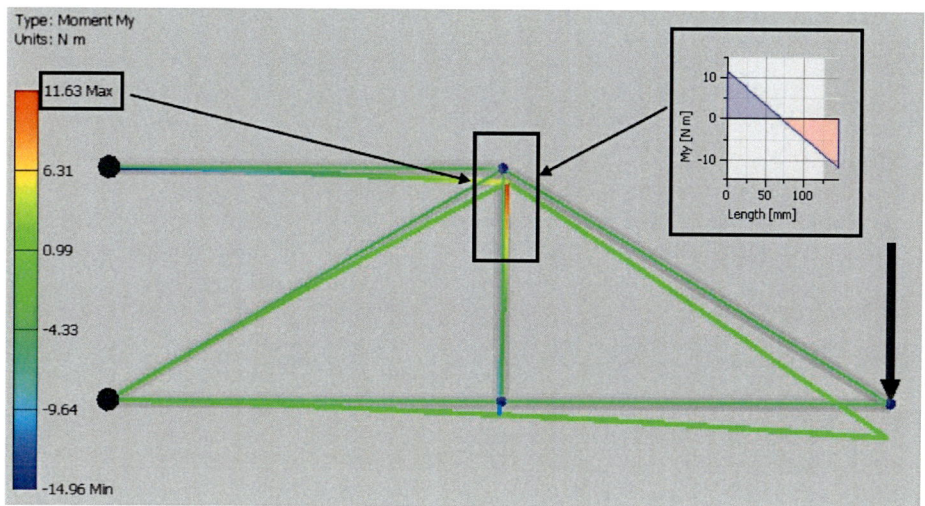

The maximum bending in the vertical member is 11.63 Nm and, again, this is due to the frame member not having any rotational degree of freedom at beam ends. This can be achieved by using the beam release command.

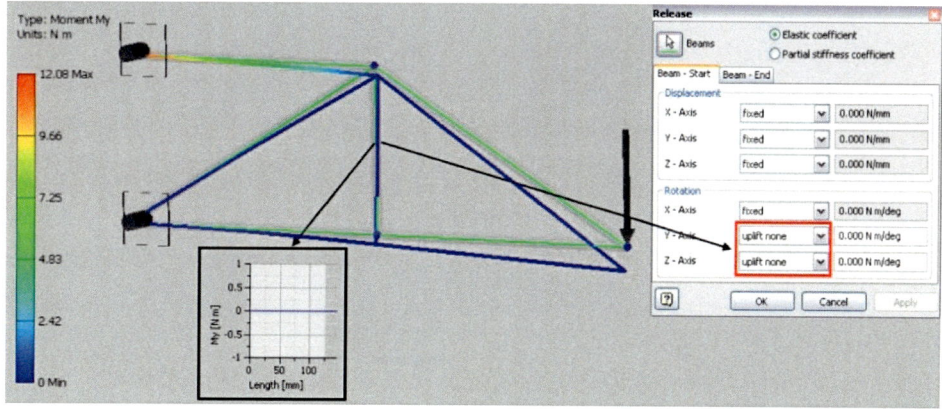

As we can see, by releasing rotation in the y and z axes for both ends of the beam has resulted in zero moment in the beam.

CHAPTER 15
The Frame Analysis Environment

> Releasing rotational degrees of freedom of the rigid link about y axis would have also sufficed to remove moments.

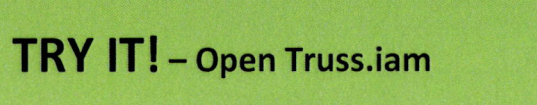

Custom Node

Custom nodes can be created anywhere along a beam and can be used to place forces and create rigid links. They are not graphically different from automatically converted nodes in the browser. However, we can assign different color in the Frame Analysis Settings.

Rigid link

Rigid links are used to join disconnected beams together. A rigid link comprises of a parent node and a child node. All displacement and rotations of the parent node are passed on to the child node; for example, compatibility between both nodes is maintained by the parent node. Displacements and rotations defined for a rigid link can be changed; for example, the Rigid Link setting below will maintain translation and rotation between the parent and child nodes.

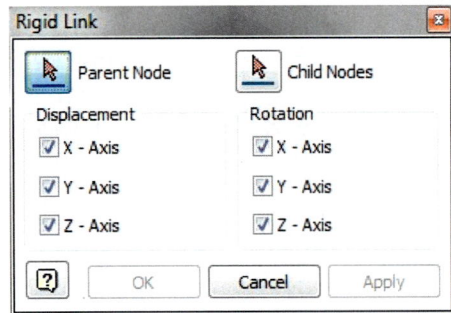

> Rigid links only act between nodes.

> Rigid links are only defined in assembly coordinate systems.

> Rigid links requires two nodes: one parent and one child.

CHAPTER 15
The Frame Analysis Environment

Below is an example of how two simple beams are connected together using rigid links.

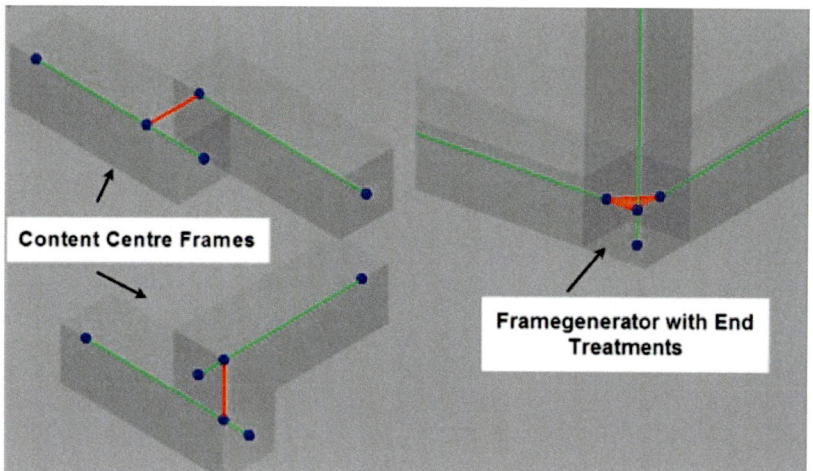

 Use Frame Generator to create frames without end treatments, as this will remove the need for the creation of rigid links.

Below is an example of how four beams with end treatments, using Frame Generator, are connected with rigid links.

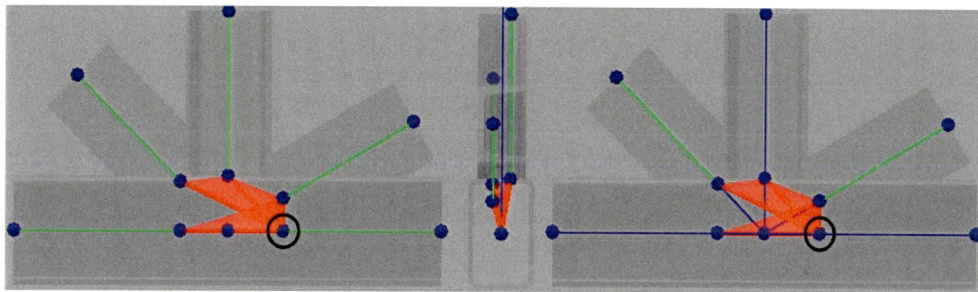

 A parent node is the one in which all rigid links have a common connection point.

The blue lines are the sketch line used to create offset frames using Frame Generator and the green lines are the beam elements created in Frame Analysis based on the true neutral axis of the beam. Therefore, it is important to note that the beams elements are not necessarily created on the same axis on which the frames were originally created, with the exception of, for example, circular and square members.

 Further information on how rigid links are connected between beams is available from the Autodesk Inventor Help file.

SECTION 6 - Frame Analysis Essentials and Design Problems using Beam Elements

CHAPTER 15
The Frame Analysis Environment

Example 4 – Simple frame in which beams are connected without using rigid links

The following support frame example is loaded at one end and fixed at the other end. Further, the example is created using Frame Generator with no end treatments. The deformation results show a maximum deflection of 2.035 mm and a maximum normal stress of 118.8 MPa.

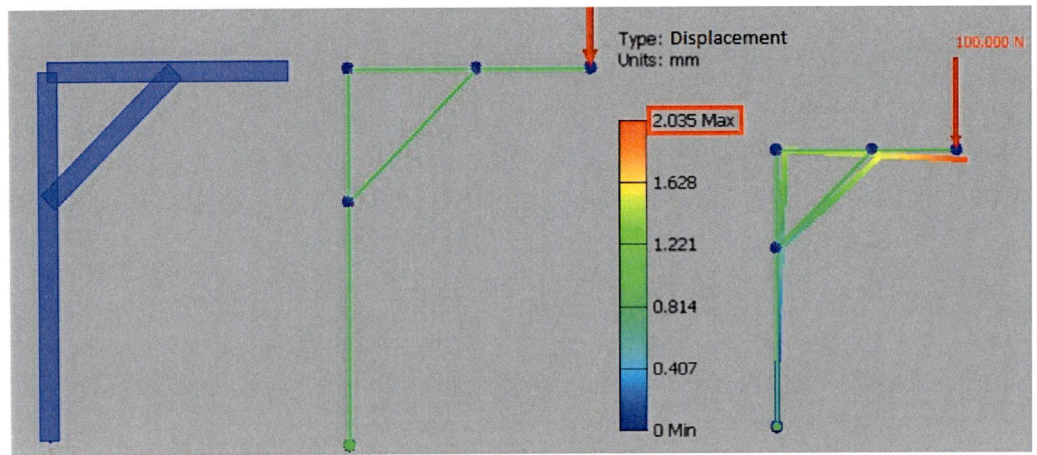

TRY IT! – Open Simple-Frame.iam

Example 5 – Frame Generator in which beams are connected using rigid links

Now the same example created with frame generator and with end treatments is simulated again.

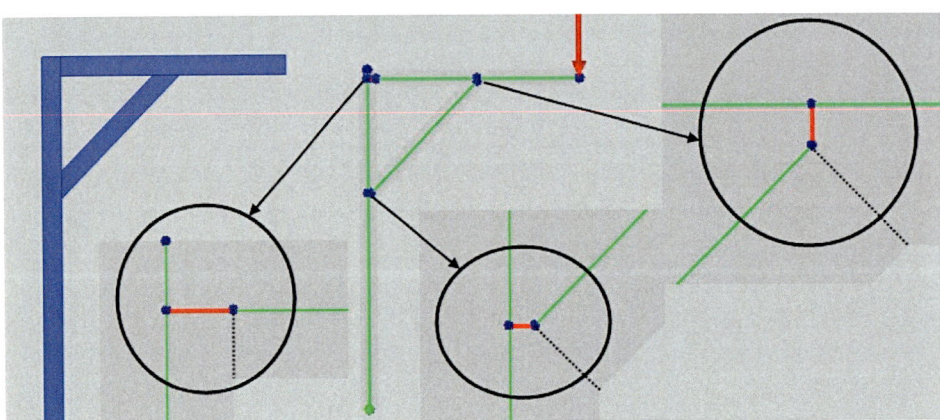

The immediate difference, even before we run the analysis, is the creation of the red rigid links. These links are automatically created and join the disconnected beams, due to trimming. The beams are extracted based on the neutral axis position and their length are defined by the intersection of longest face on the solid beam with a plane perpendicular to the neutral axis (see above). As a result of this, the rigid links are created between the beam elements using the shortest possible distance. However, the difference in the results is negligible as the maximum deformation and stress is 2.039 mm and 118.8 MPa, respectively.

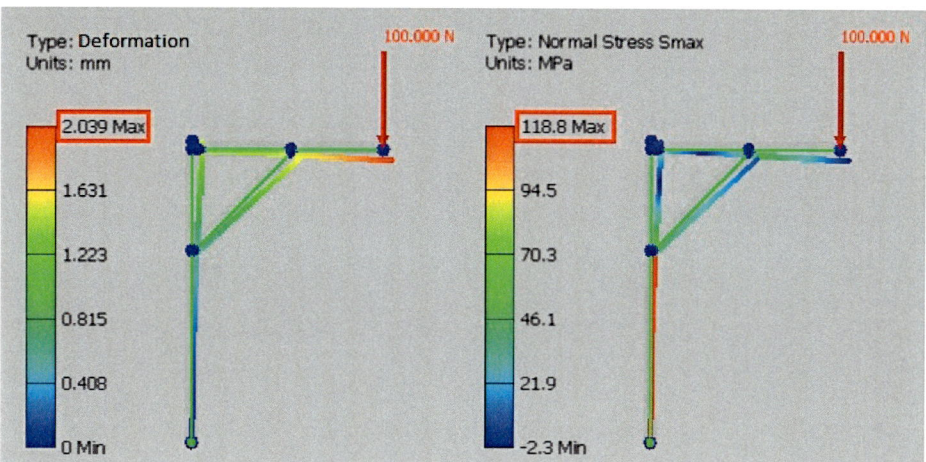

The reason for this similar result is that cross-section of the beam is very small compared to the length of the beam. In most structural applications this will always be the case, hence the reason for using beam elements rather than solid elements.

If the example is further analyzed, the beam connecting the horizontal and vertical beam is shown to have moments as shown below.

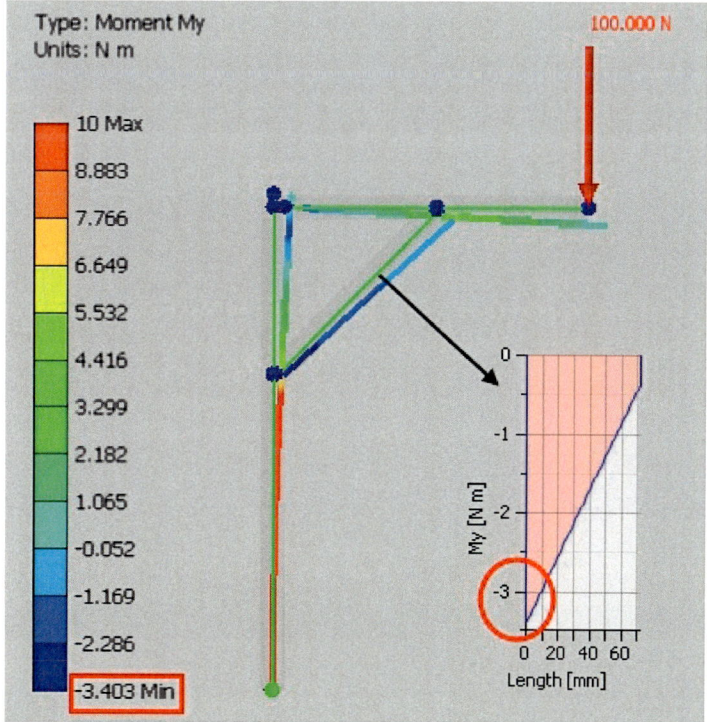

CHAPTER 15
The Frame Analysis Environment

The reason for these moments is that the beam is completely fixed/welded at the ends. To remove moments at the end of the beam, the rotational degrees of freedom of the rigid links connecting the beams can be released.

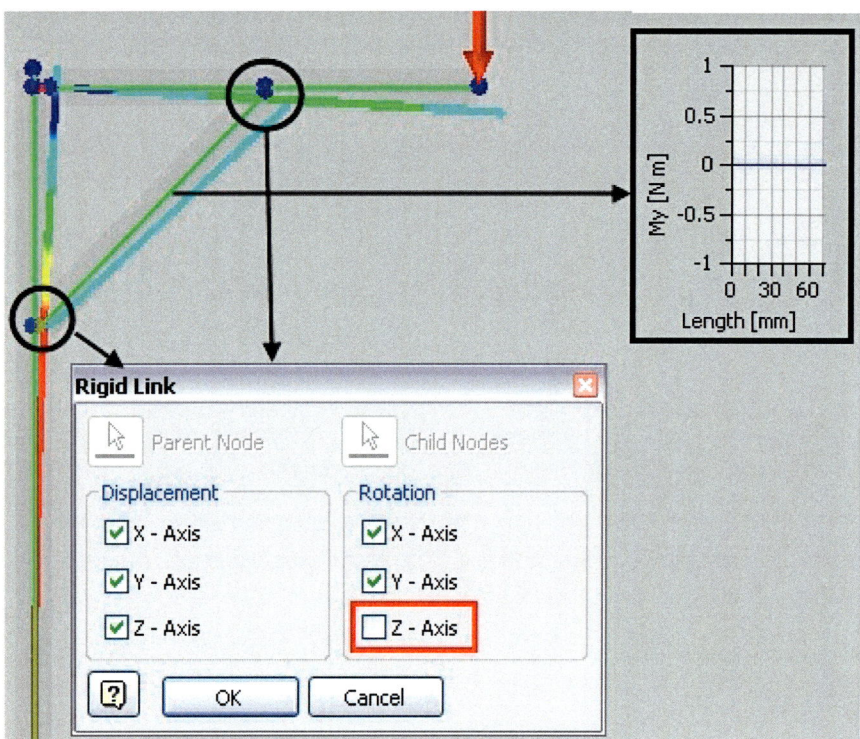

Rotation about the Z-axis (global coordinate system) is released and as thus removes moments completely in the beam. The stress now induced in the beam is completely due axial loading and not bending.

TRY IT! – Open Simple-Framegenerator.iam

CHAPTER 15
The Frame Analysis Environment

Result tab

Beam detail

Beam Detail allows quick analysis of the details of the results for selected beams including maximum bending and forces.

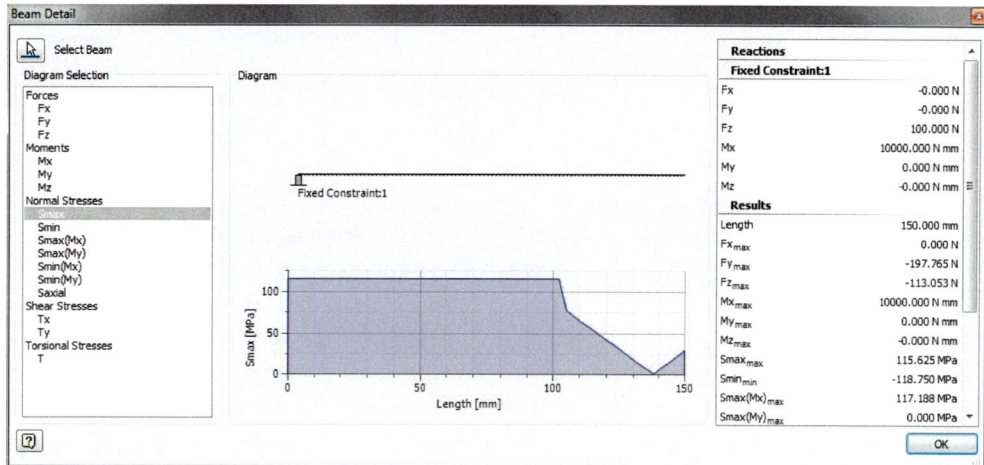

Animate

Creates a video file of the animation.

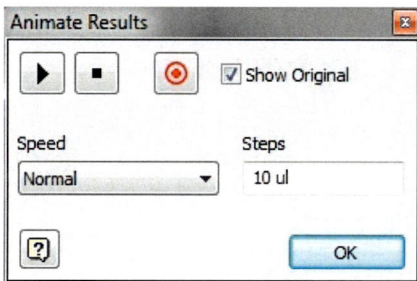

If Show Original is selected then the original model shape is visible during animation playback. On the other hand, if the option is not selected, the original wireframe is presented as an overlay on the deformed model. This option is checked by default.

 For a smoother display, increase the number of steps. You can specify any value between 1 and 100.

CHAPTER 15
The Frame Analysis Environment

Diagram

Plots specific results, as diagrams, on beam models, result types include maximum forces and moments.

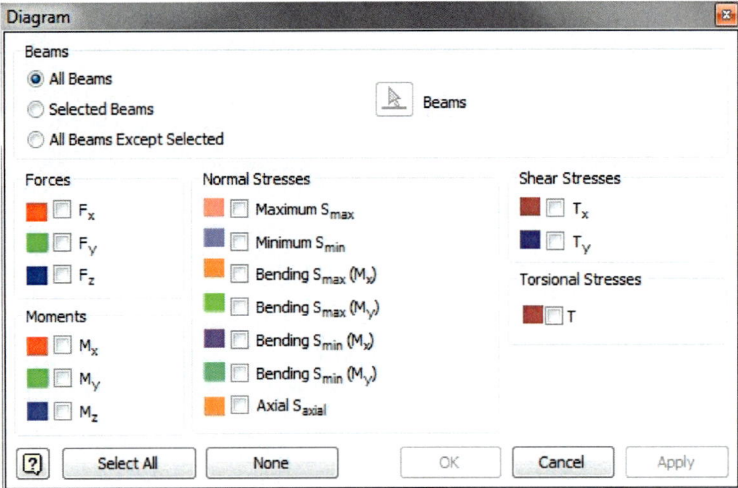

Multiple diagrams can be applied at the same time for the selected beam. The diagrams are plotted according to the beam local coordinate system and on the undeformed beams. The graphs that would normally be displayed along the beam axis are displayed along Y or Z axis of the beam coordinate system (in plane XY or XZ).

The complete list of result display available are shown below.

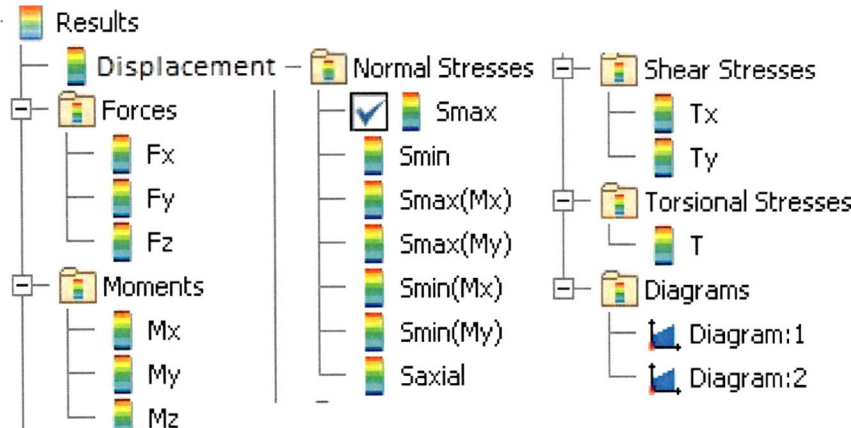

Smax is the worst case stress that includes both tensile bending stress Smax(Mx) and Smax(My) and axial stress Saxial.

CHAPTER 15
The Frame Analysis Environment

The following shows a diagram of the structural beam model.

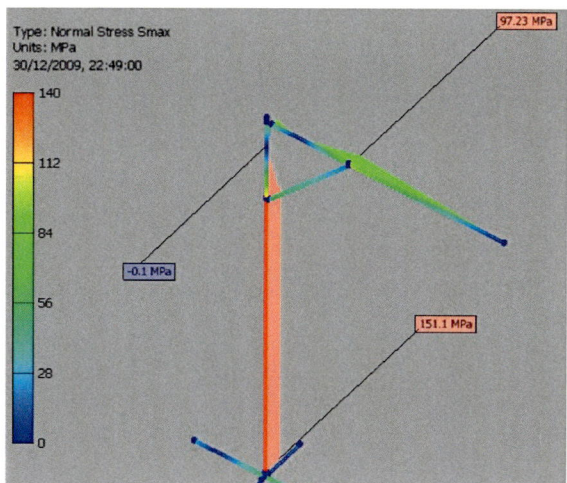

Probe

Allows users to create probe labels at user specified locations.

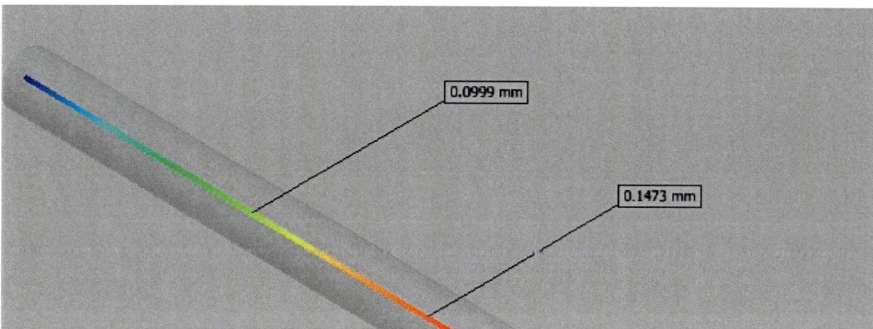

Display tab

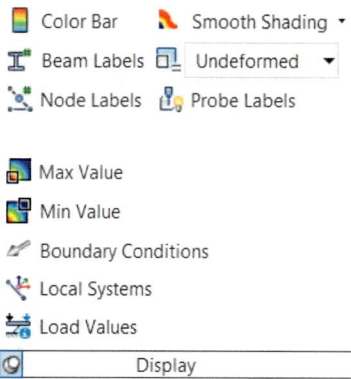

Color bar

The Color Bar is probably the most important tool within the Display panel and, when effectively used, can help with the understanding of results with ease. It can be displayed in various locations

CHAPTER 15
The Frame Analysis Environment

in the graphic window using the Position setting. The maximum and minimum threshold values can be altered by unchecking the Maximum and Minimum values.

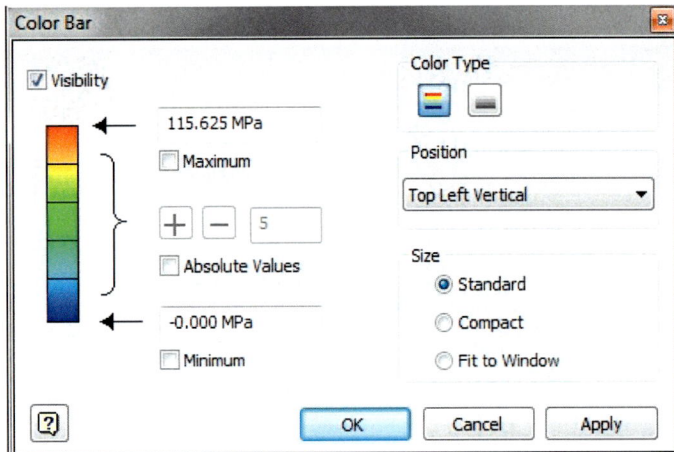

Absolute Values, when checked, displays all result values in absolute values and the color bar reflects those values.

 The numbers of the color legend can only be changed when Contour Shading is selected. Smooth Shading by default will use Maximum.

Beam and node labels

These help with visually identifying specific nodes and beams by displaying labels, as illustrated below.

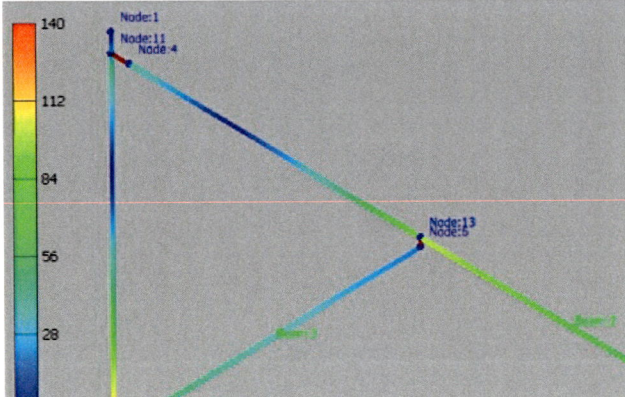

CHAPTER 15
The Frame Analysis Environment

251

Display results

Here you can decide whether you want display smooth, contour and no results display.

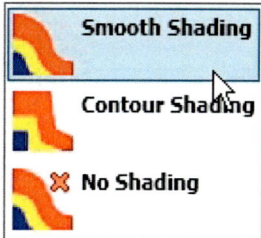

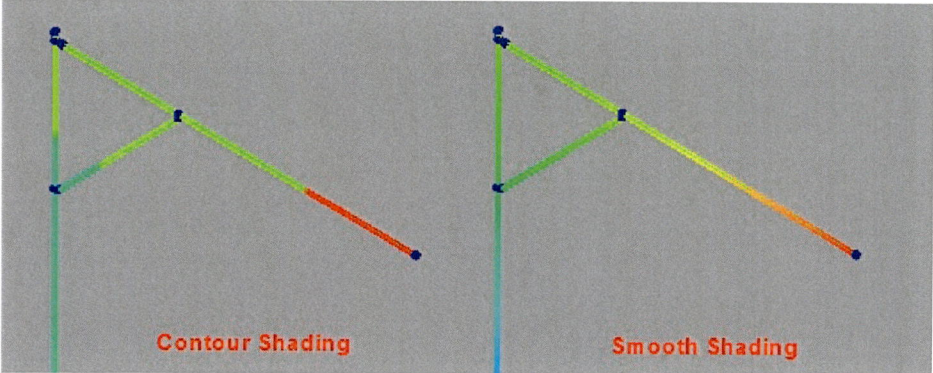

Probe Labels

Displays the user defined locations.

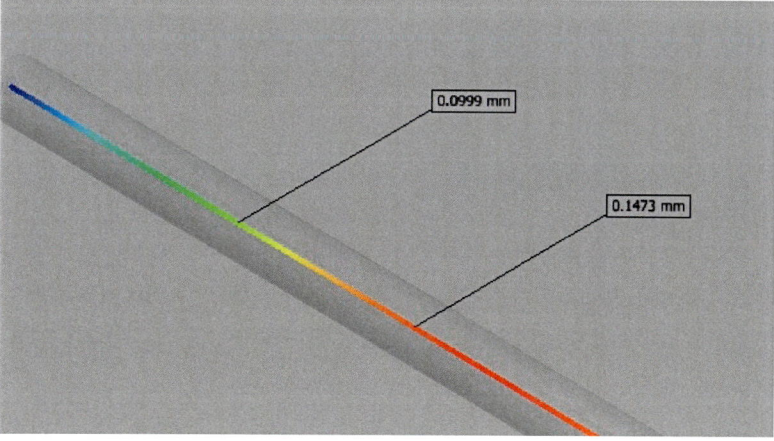

CHAPTER 15
The Frame Analysis Environment

Adjust displacement display
Here you can adjust the scale of the results, particularly useful when animating results.

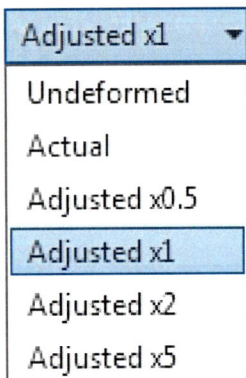

Max and min values
Displays the maximum and minimum values, for the selected results type, aiding in locating their positions on the model, as illustrated below.

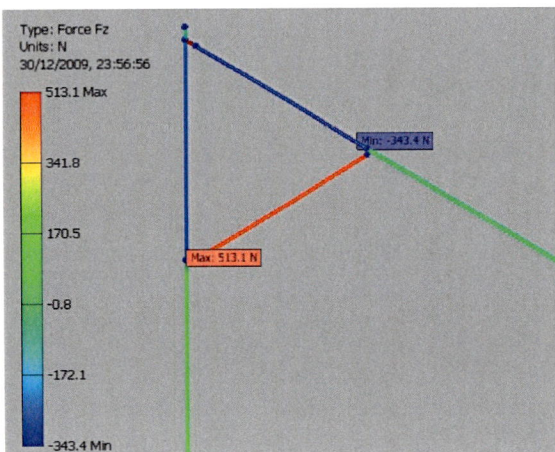

CHAPTER 15
The Frame Analysis Environment

Boundary conditions
Displays all the loads and constraints applied on the model.

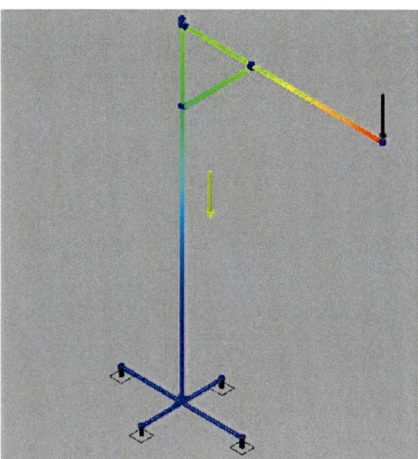

Local systems
Displays the local coordinate system for all beams.

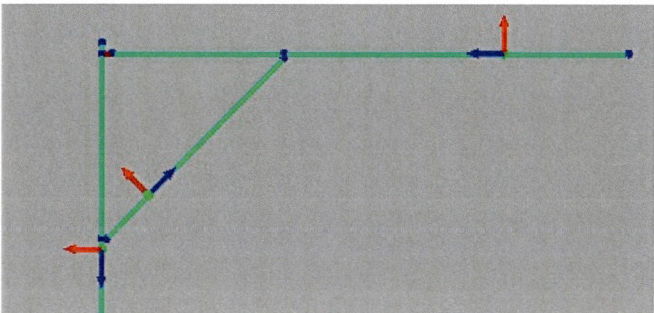

Load values
Displays load value associated with all the loads applied on the model.

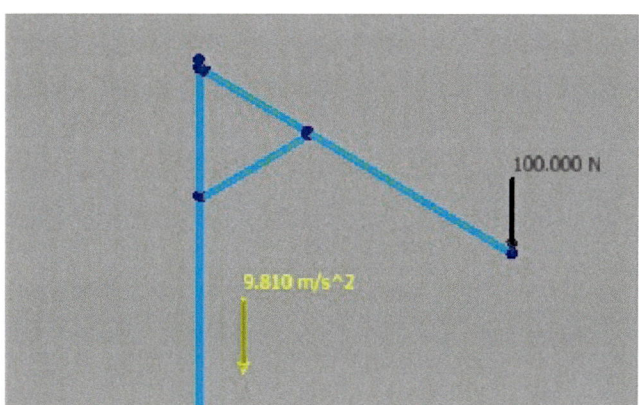

Boundary conditions need to be active in order to be able to see load values.

CHAPTER 15
The Frame Analysis Environment

Publish tab

 Report

 Export

Publish

Report

Autodesk Inventor – in addition to standard html format – now lets you create reports in mhtml (single web page) and rich text formats (word documents), making it very easy to customize the reports to specific requirements.

 Microsoft Word is required to generate the RTF file.

In addition to being able to customize settings using the General, Properties and Simulation tabs from the Report Generator dialogue box, there are now more settings within the Format tab.

Use Dynamic Content - Select this to include size buttons for image width and buttons that you can click to collapse or expand the associated sections.

 Not available for the RTF format.

Create OLE Link - Select to create an OLE link from the model browser to the report. The report icon displays under the Third Party folder in the model browser. To edit the report, double-click the icon or right-click and select Edit.

CHAPTER 15
The Frame Analysis Environment

Export

Autodesk Inventor also allows to export frame analysis data to Autodesk Robot Structural analysis data in RTD file format.

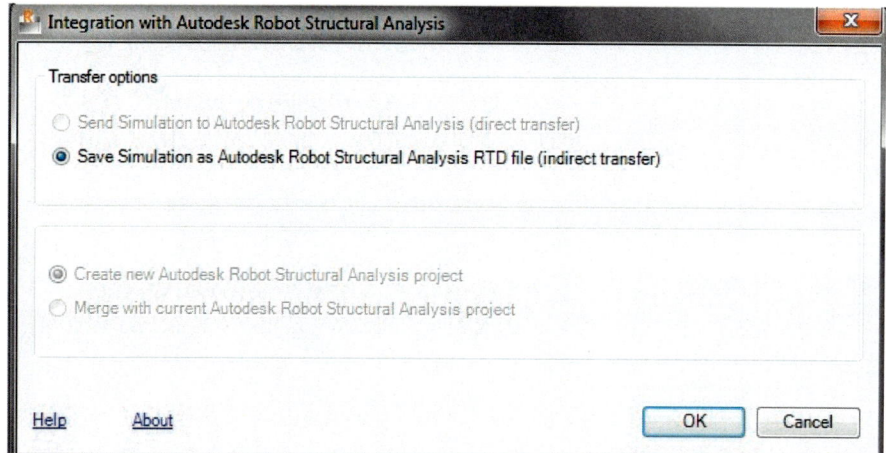

 Only available if an active Robot Structural Analysis license is installed.

The RTD file contains all defined loads, constraints, rigid links, releases, beam materials and beam sections.

The following export options are available:

- Save the simulation as an RTD file.

- Send Simulation to Autodesk Robot Structural Analysis – Directly creates a calculation model in Autodesk Robot Structural Analysis based on the current frame analysis data in Autodesk Inventor.

- Create New Autodesk Robot Structural Analysis project.

- Merge with current Autodesk Robot Structural Analysis project.

 Further details on Export are available in Autodesk Inventor Help menu.

CHAPTER 15
The Frame Analysis Environment

Frame Analysis Settings tab

Frame Analysis Settings

Settings

Allows the predefinition of settings for current and preceding analyzes.

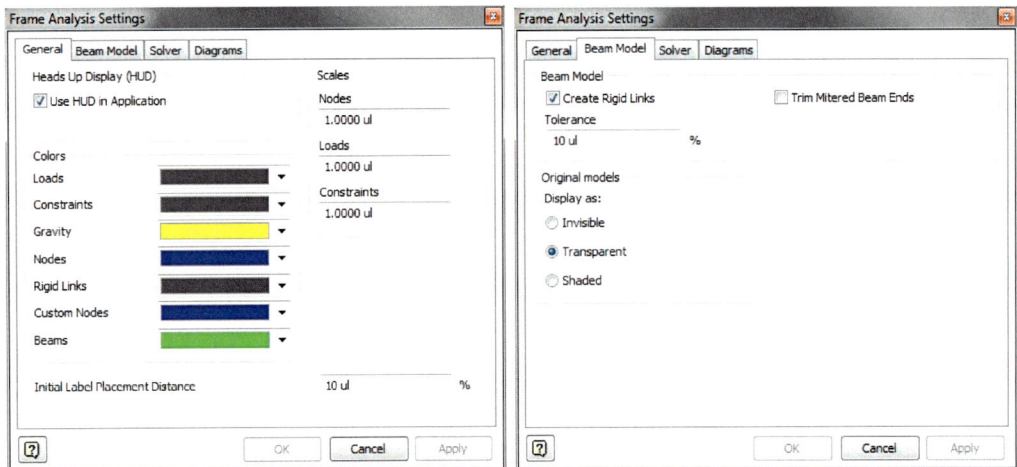

Use HUD in Application – Checked by default. Uncheck if you want to use the dialogue boxes for editing and creating boundary conditions etc.

 While creating boundary conditions, with HUD active, you can right-click and select More Options. This will allow you to edit using dialogue boxes.

Colors – Here you can define specific colors for loads constraints, nodes etc.

Scales – Here you can alter the visual scale of the nodes, loads and constraints.

Beam Model – This is the tolerance that dictates whether a rigid link will be created between the beams that are not connected. The default value is 2%. When the distance between two beams is smaller than the sizes of sections multiplied by this tolerance, a rigid link connection is created via the shortest distance between nearest nodes. You can specify any value between -100% and 500%, with a negative value meaning that the beams will be connected at the location where they overlap.

Rigid Links - If selected will create rigid links between beams that have gaps.

Trim Mitered Beam Ends - When selected, the overlaps are trimmed during automatic model conversion

CHAPTER 15
The Frame Analysis Environment

Original Models – Hear you can define how the original models appear in frame analysis. By default, the original models are set to transparent.

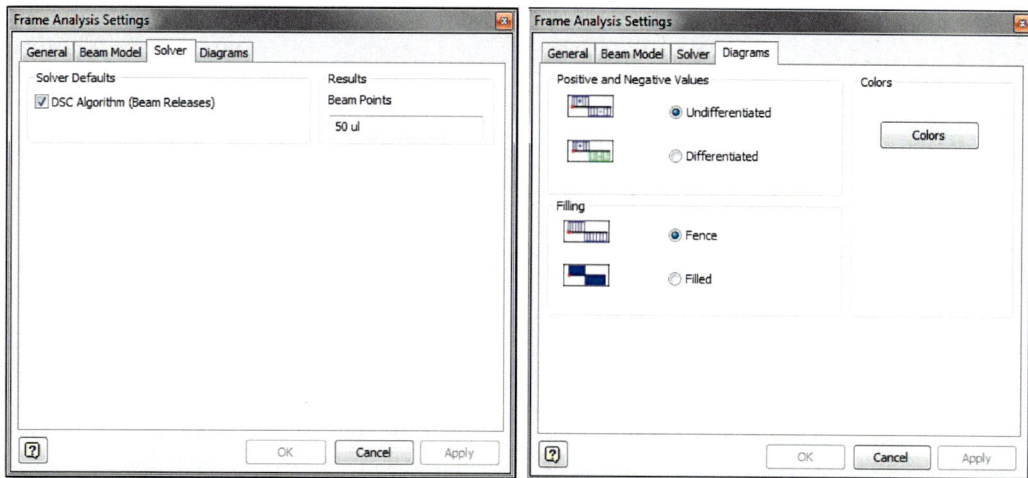

Solver Defaults - DSC Algorithm (Beam Releases) should be checked if the structure contains beam releases. The algorithm carries out the following operations:

1. A new node is generated in the structure (during the structure model generation).
2. The input element with the release is modified in such a way that the new node takes the place of the old one in the element (the old node remains in other structure elements).
3. Between the old and the new node, the program creates the so called DSC element; see the image on the next page.

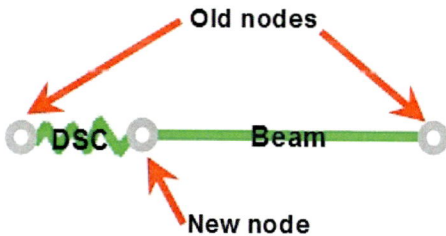

Results – Here you can specify number of beam points that are calculated by solving; this basically splits the beam into smaller linear beam elements. Any value between 5 and 1000 can be specified, with 50 being the default.

Positive and Negative Values – Can specify how positive and negative values are visually displayed.

- **Undifferentiated** – No differentiation between positive and negative values.
- **Differentiated** – Shows positive and negative values.

Filling – Here you can specify how the diagrams will be filled.

- **Fence** – Uses a fence-style shading to display the diagram.
- **Filled** – Displays the diagram as completely shaded/filled.

Colors – Select to change the colors of loads and stresses displayed in the graphic diagrams.

CHAPTER 15
The Frame Analysis Environment

DP14 – Frame Analysis Using Content Centre Structures

Structural design of Aerospace Maintenance Platform
(Design Problem Courtesy of Planet Platforms Ltd)

Key features and workflows introduced in this design problem

	Key Features/Workflows
1	Content center frames converted to beam elements
2	Tolerance settings – used to create rigid links automatically
3	Pinned constraints and continuous loading
4	Change material and beam properties

Introduction

Planet Platforms, established since 1977, is a leading manufacturer and distributor of work place access solutions. Ranging from podium steps to award-winning intelligent platforms, their access solutions have been keeping people safe for the past 30 years. Through a process of communication, site surveys, CAD rendered visuals and proven manufacturing, Plant Platform delivers the end result - a platform that is safe, reliable and perfectly suited for the application.

Some of their prestigious clients include Rolls Royce, Thomas Cook, the Orient Express, the Royal Albert Hall, ICI Chemicals, Shell Offshore and the National Trust

CHAPTER 16
DP14– Frame Analysis Using Content Centre Structures

Above is a picture of platform that is used by Rolls Royce personal to carry out essential maintenance work. The platform is constructed from mild steel and is to be designed such that the platform, including steps, can withstand the load of two people including their maintenance equipment and other essential components.

To this effect a total load of 250Kg will be used to determine;

1. The maximum bending stress in the platform under normal operating conditions.
2. The maximum deflection in the platform.
3. The factor of safety (F.O.S).

With

4. Maximum deflection not to be above 5 mm.
5. Minimum F.O.S of 4.
6. Material construction to be limited to aluminum or mild steel
7. Frame tube construction to be used from Standard ISO Content Centre

CHAPTER 16
DP14 – Frame Analysis Using Content Centre Structures

Workflow of Design Problem 14

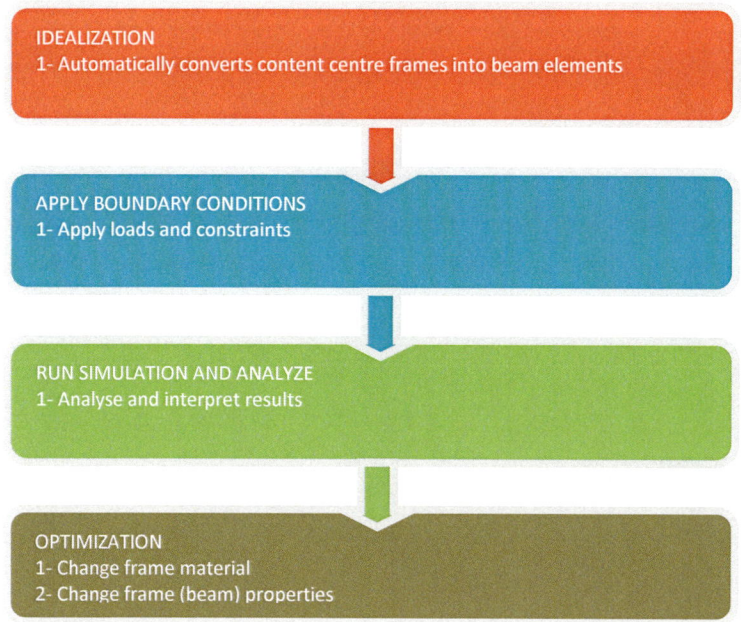

IDEALIZATION
1- Automatically converts content centre frames into beam elements

APPLY BOUNDARY CONDITIONS
1- Apply loads and constraints

RUN SIMULATION AND ANALYZE
1- Analyse and interpret results

OPTIMIZATION
1- Change frame material
2- Change frame (beam) properties

Idealization

Frame Analysis will automatically convert frames/channels created from both Content Centre and Frame Generator. All other components will be not be converted and therefore are not included in the analysis. Note: if neither Content Centre nor Frame Generator is used to create any content then no frame or channels will be idealized into beam elements.

1. Open Platform.iam

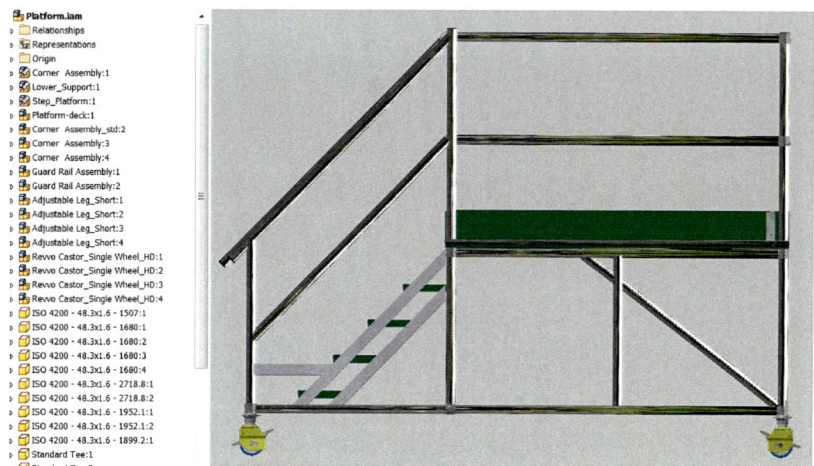

Now we can begin the second stage of the analysis of applying boundary conditions.

Boundary conditions

2. Select **Environments** tab > Select **Frame Analysis**

SECTION 6 - Frame Analysis Essentials and Design Problems using Beam Elements

CHAPTER 16
DP14– Frame Analysis Using Content Centre Structures

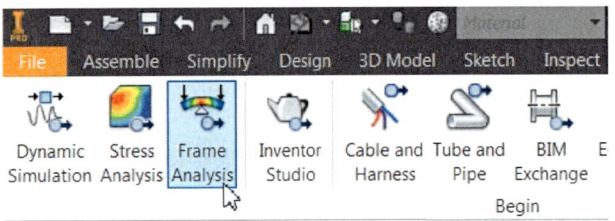

3. Select **Create Simulation** > Select **Model State** tab > Select **Main-Structure** for Level of Detail > Click **OK**

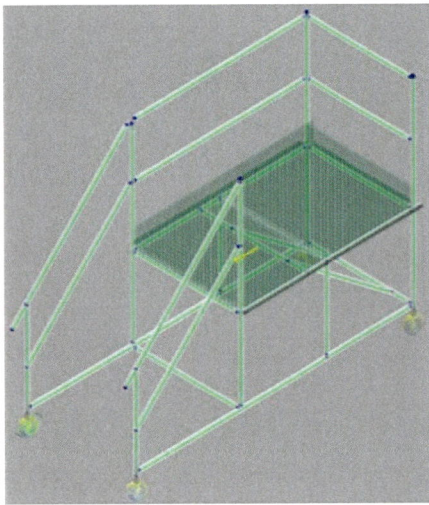

This will idealize all the content center frames into beam elements excluding all the remaining parts/assemblies from the analysis (shown transparently).

It is also important to note that as the frames where connected via tee-connectors, which are not included in the analysis, there will be gaps between the ends of the beams as shown below.

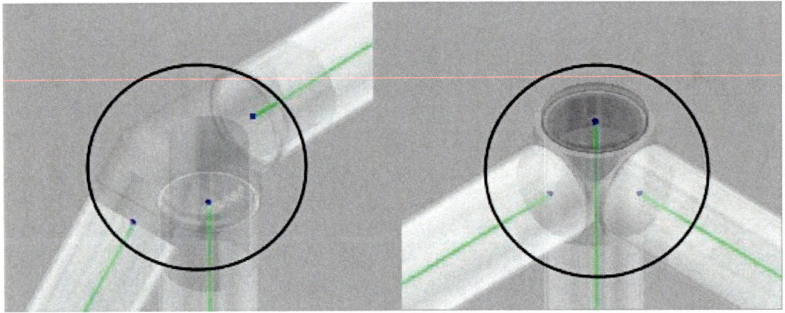

To connect these beams via rigid links, the tolerance needs to be increased.

4. Select **Frame Analysis Settings** > Select the **Beam Model** tab > Change **tolerance** setting from 2% to 50% > Click **OK**

5. Select **Update**

CHAPTER 16
DP14 – Frame Analysis Using Content Centre Structures

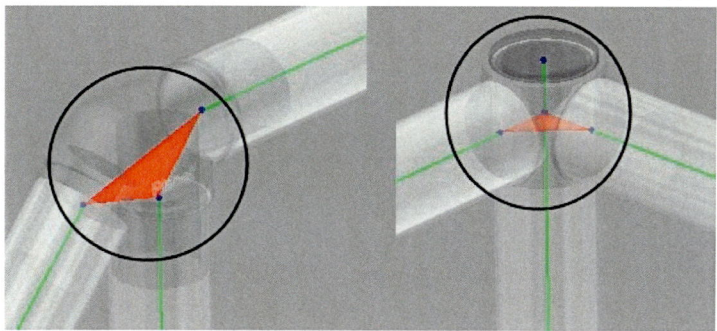

All the beams at the tee connections are now connected via rigid links. This can be verified by simply looking at all the connection points. For large models this can be tedious and, hence, in these situations it would be quicker to do a modal analysis to check whether all beams are connected by analyzing the deformation results. The gravity is acting in the wrong direction so first we need to specify gravity to act downwards.

6. Right click **Gravity** in the browser > Select **Edit** > Change **Direction** to positive X direction > Click **OK**

Next, we are going to apply the constraints and loads so we can determine the structural integrity of the platform when carrying two people with necessary maintenance equipment.

7. Select **Pinned Constraint** > Right click > Select **More Options** > Select node at the bottom near the wheels to define **Origin** of the constraint > Select **Apply**

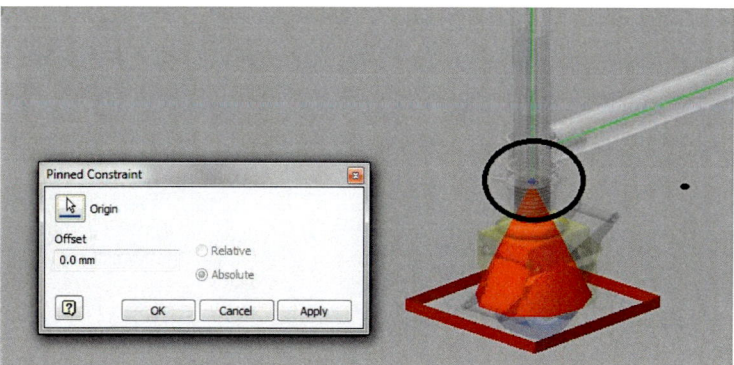

CHAPTER 16
DP14– Frame Analysis Using Content Centre Structures

8. Repeat step 7 for creating pinned constraint at the other three wheels > Click **OK** once the last node has been selected.

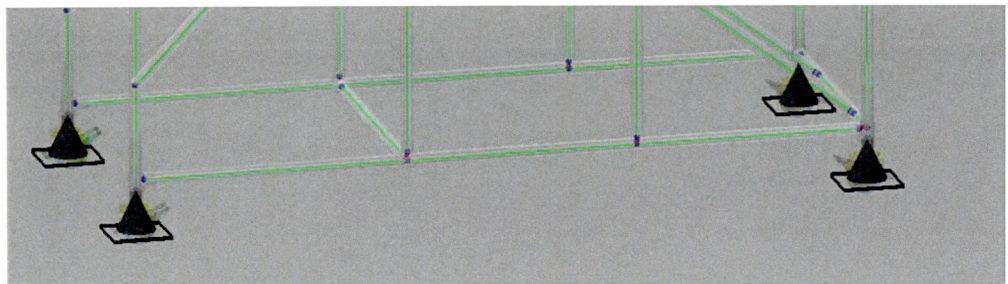

The platform needs to withstand the load of two maintenance workers, including the weight of the tools, components etc. This equates to a weight of 125Kg/person. So the total load the platform needs to withstand is 2500 Kg, using a value of 10 m/s² for gravity.

$$Total\ Load = Weight\ of\ person\ x\ number\ of\ people\ x\ gravity$$

As the platform deck is supported by the frames directly beneath it, this load will be distributed evenly across all these frames. The load we will use is the continuous load N/mm .To calculate this value, we need to determine the total length of all the frames directly supporting the platform deck and then divide the total load by the total length of the frames. This will be a good estimate to determine the weight of the two people, in the absence of the platform deck not being analyzed.

$$Continuous\ Load = \frac{2500}{6.6} = 378N/m = 0.378N/mm$$

9. Select **Continuous Load** > Right click > Select **More Options** > Select beam as shown > Specify **0.378N/mm** for load value > Select **Apply**

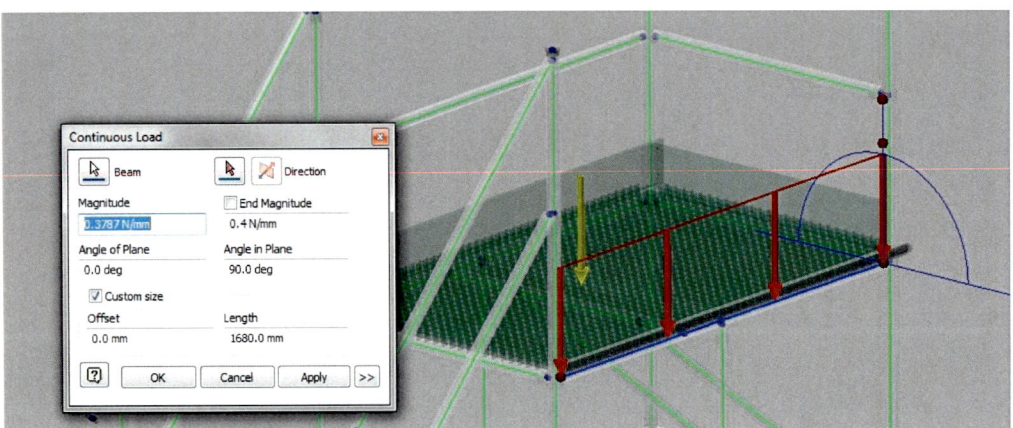

CHAPTER 16
DP14 – Frame Analysis Using Content Centre Structures

10. Repeat step 9 for the other four beam elements directly under the platform deck > Click **OK**

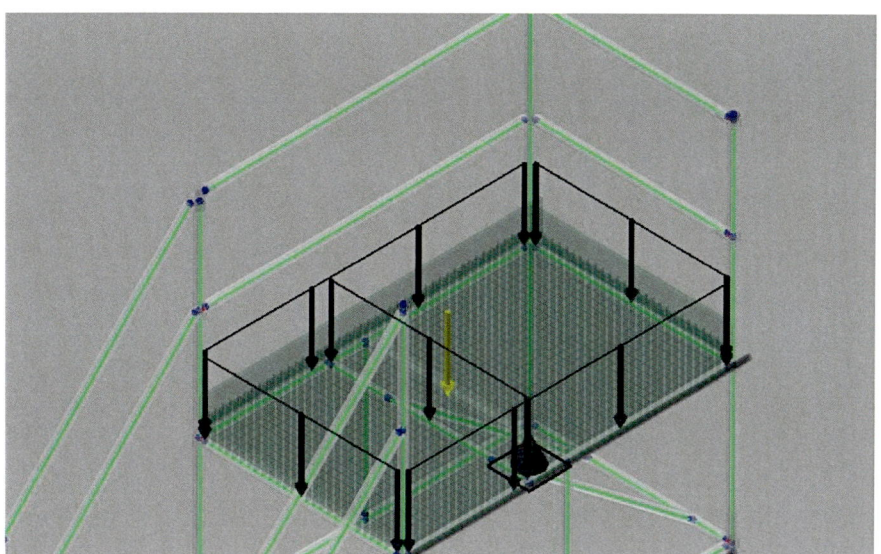

📝 There should be five Continuous loads in the browser.

Run simulation and analyze

11. Select **Simulate**

12. Select **Adjust x 1** from Adjust Displacement Display > Select **Smax Normal Stress**

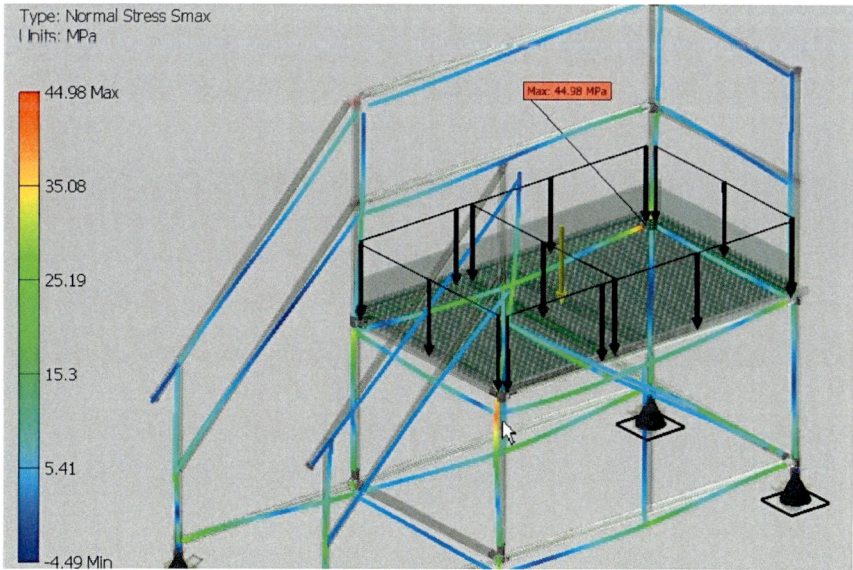

There are two maximum stresses, one at the front, illustrated by the arrow, and one at the back, shown by max value, the maximum deflection being 1.463 mm. We will now reanalyze the platform but this time will include additional steps and see whether they have an effect on the overall structural integrity of the platform.

CHAPTER 16
DP14– Frame Analysis Using Content Centre Structures

13. Right click **Simulation:1** > Select **Copy Simulation**

14. Right click **Simulation:2** > Select **Edit Simulation**

15. Select **Model State** tab > Select **Master** for **Level of Detail**

📝 The warning refers to that the model may need to be updated

16. Click **OK** > Cancel Warning

📝 The warning refers to that some beam elements have a zero value for torsional modulus

17. Select **Frame Analysis Settings** > Select **Beam Model** tab > Select **Invisible** for the original models not included in the analysis > Click **OK**

18. Select **Simulate** to rerun the analysis again.

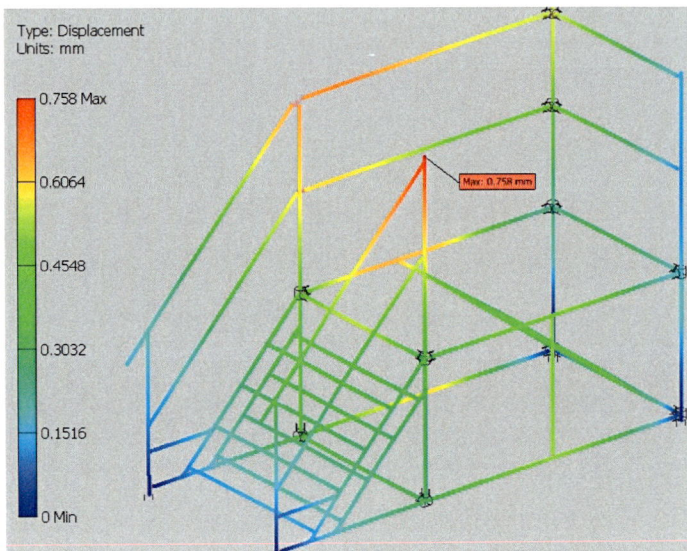

The maximum deflection has reduced by half to 0.758 mm

19. Select **Smax Normal Stress** > Select **Color Bar** > Unselect **Maximum Value** > Specify **30** > Unselect **Minimum Value** > Specify **0** > Click **OK**

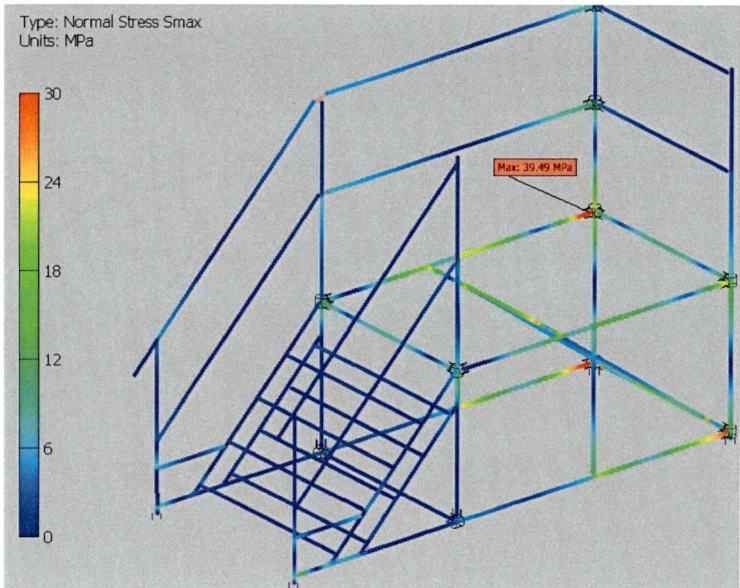

Although the maximum stress value has reduced, it is worth noting that the stress due to bending at the front has considerably reduced by adding the steps structure. We can now confidently say the steps structure is fundamental to the structural integrity of the platform. You will also note that the axial, shear, torsional stresses are insignificant compared to the stresses caused by bending. This can be investigated by looking at different stress plots using axial, torsional, and shear stress results. Based on the maximum stress value the minimum factor of safety is

$$\textbf{Factor of Safety} = \frac{\text{Yield Stress}}{\text{Operationl Stress}} = \frac{207}{39.27} = \textbf{5.27}$$

This meets the minimum design F.O.S of **4**.

Optimization

As the structure is made from mild steel, we would like to investigate the platform being constructed from aluminum. In Frame Analysis, it is very easy to multi-select all frames and override material specified within Content Centre. This is ideal to check the suitability of different materials before changing the material via Content Centre – which can be tedious, especially when you have a lot of frames/components.

20. Right Click **Simulation:2** > Select **Copy Simulation**

21. Select **Material** from the **Beams** panel

CHAPTER 16
DP14– Frame Analysis Using Content Centre Structures

22. Highlight all beams > Select **Customize** > Change **Material** to **Aluminium-6061** > Click **OK**

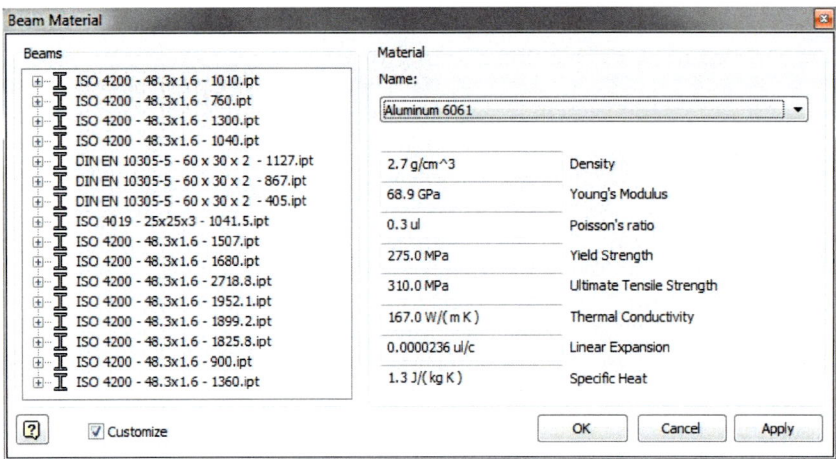

23. Select **Simulate** > Select **Color bar** > Unselect **Maximum** value > Specify **1** > Click **OK**

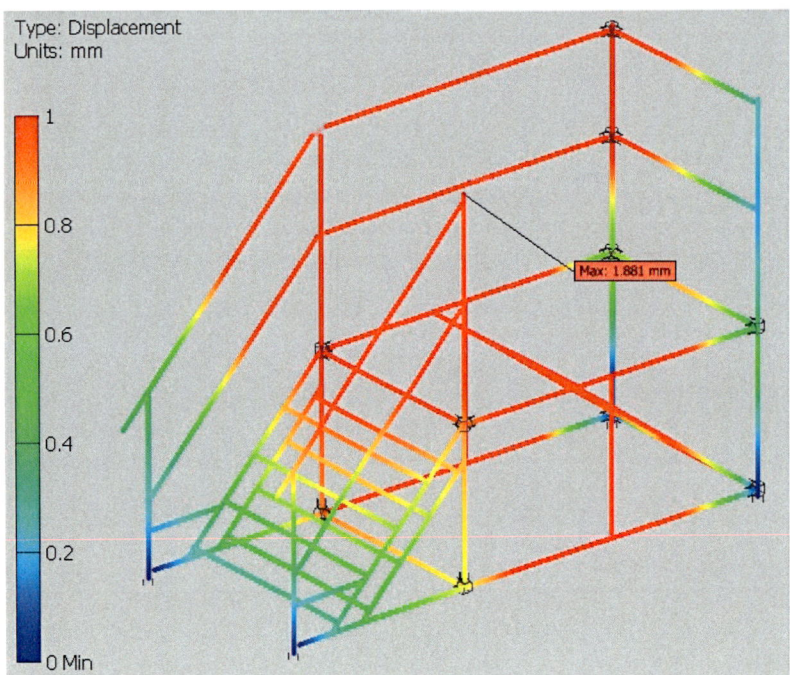

The max deflection has more than doubled to 1.881 mm; this is due the fact that aluminum is more flexible than steel. Although the deflection has increased, it is negligible and insignificant in terms of the overall dimensions of the platform. Another thing to note that maximum stress has reduced slightly to 34.62MPa because aluminum has a higher yield stress value. The F.O.S. now becomes

$$\textbf{\textit{Factor of Safety}} = \frac{\text{Yield Stress}}{\text{Operationl Stress}} = \frac{275}{34.62} = \textbf{7.94}$$

CHAPTER 16
DP14 – Frame Analysis Using Content Centre Structures

As the factor of safety is almost twice the design F.O.S, a value of 4, we will investigate using a smaller tube with twice the thickness; tube ISO 4200 33.7 X 3.2. Here, we will consider overriding the key mechanical properties of the original tube with those of the proposed tube as illustrated below.

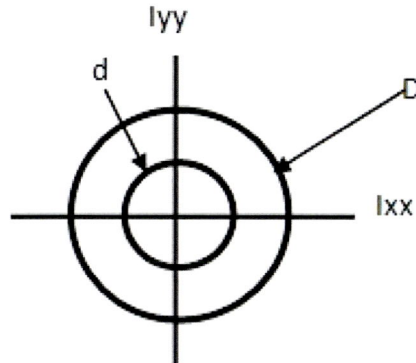

Note calculations are in mm for the following:-

$Area = \pi(D^2-d^2)/4$ & $Ixx = Iyy = \pi(D^4-d^4)/64$ & $Ixx + Iyy = Izz$

$Area = \pi(33.7^2-27.3^2)/4 = 306.619 \text{mm}^2$

$Ixx = Iyy = \pi(D^4-d^4)/64 = \pi(33.7^4-27.3^4)/64 = 36046.565$

We will override the default values with the above to represent new tube ISO4200 33.7X3.2, in addition to the Centroid (16.85mm) and Wz values.

24. Right Click **Simulation:3** > Select **Copy Simulation**

25. Expand the Beams node > Select beams 1 to 27 > Right Click > Select **Beam Properties**

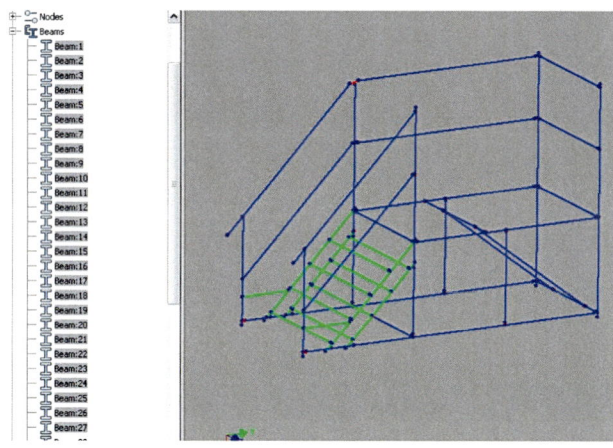

We are not including the step structure as they are constructed from box sections and not tubes.

CHAPTER 16
DP14– Frame Analysis Using Content Centre Structures

26. Highlight all beams > Select **Customize** > Specify new calculated values > Click **OK**

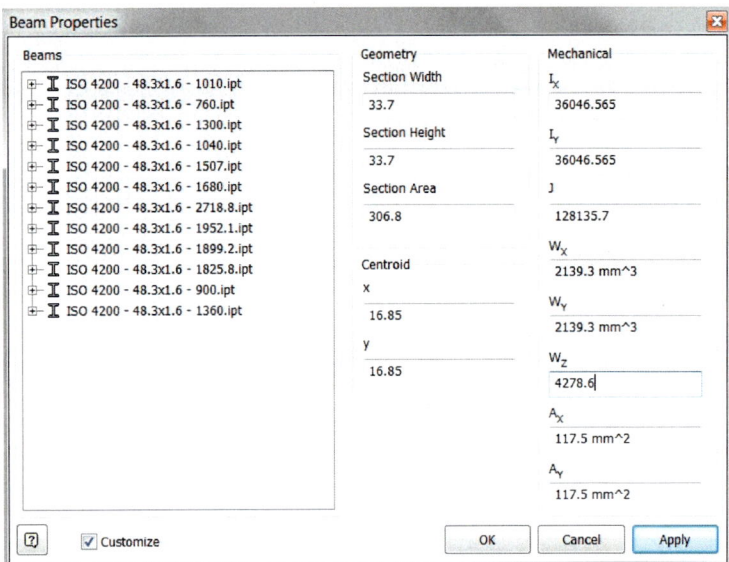

📝 Will leave Ax and Ay values as we are only interested in the maximum stress due to bending

27. Select **Simulate** > Accept warning

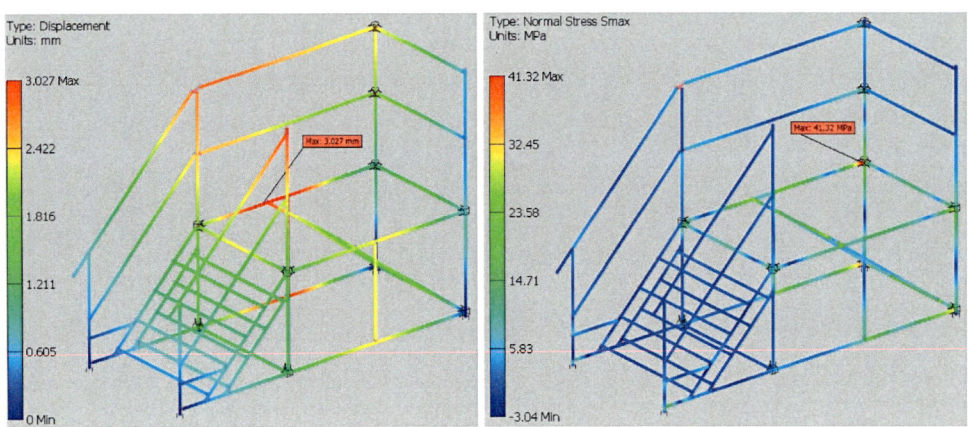

The results show that the deflection has increased to 3.027 mm and maximum stress to 41.32 MPa. Value may differ slightly. Now taking this new value the F.O.S. is

$$\textbf{Factor of Safety} = \frac{\text{Yield Stress}}{\text{Operationl Stress}} = \frac{275}{41.32} = \textbf{6.65}$$

As both value are within the specified design criteria we can safely replace the existing tubes ISO 4200 43.8 X 1.6, with tube ISO 4200 33.7 X 3.2.

28. Close File

DP15 – Frame Analysis Using Frame Generator Structures

Analysis of an Escalator Support Structure
(Design Problem courtesy of KONE plc)

Key features and workflows introduced in this design problem

	Key Features/Workflows
1	Frames, created using Frame Generator, converted to beam elements
2	Tolerance settings – used to create rigid links automatically
3	Custom constraints and multiple forces
4	Beam diagram, detail and scales

Introduction

KONE plc is a world's leading manufacturer of escalators and caters for various markets including retail, infrastructure, leisure and offices. Retail markets include supermarkets and shopping malls, whereas the Infrastructure market serves underground tubes, train stations and airports. Kone support their customers every step of the way, from design, manufacturing, and installation to maintenance and modernization.

CHAPTER 17
DP15– Frame Analysis Using Frame Generator Structures

Above is a picture of a typical passenger escalator, within a shopping mall. The escalator design goes through intensive tests to make sure they are safe. A typical requirement in escalator design is to make sure that the support structure, holding the escalator, can hold the weight of passengers and key components including steps and balustrade etc.

In this example we will determine the strength of the structure in relation to the weight of the structure, passengers and balustrade;

1. The structure weight is based on density of material, which is mild steel.
2. For the passenger load, a value of 200kg or 2000N will be used.
3. The weight of the balustrade will be applied as a continuous load of 1.2N/mm.

Note: In practice a typical escalator can go through up to thirty different load cases to fully validate the designs.

The design requirements are:

4. Maximum deflection not to exceed 3mm
5. Minimum factor of safety (FOS) to be 4

CHAPTER 17
DP15– Frame Analysis Using Frame Generator Structures

Workflow of Design Problem 15

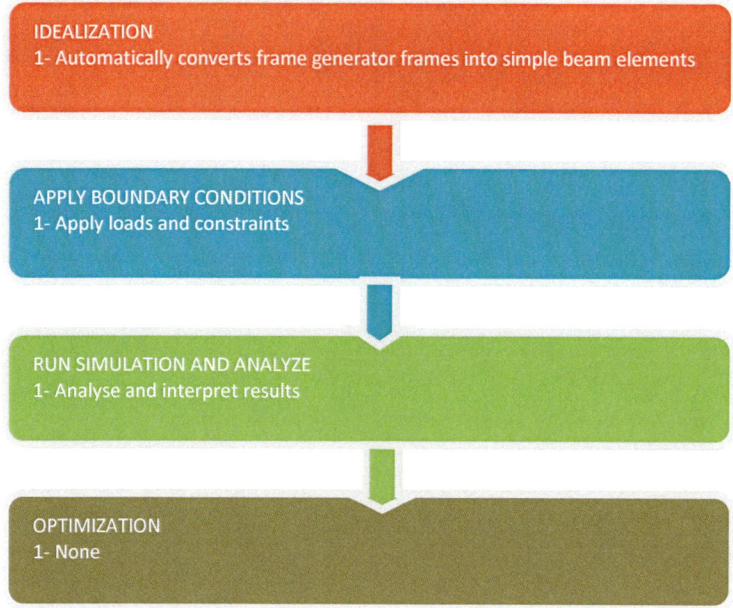

Idealization

As mentioned in the previous example, idealization is done automatically by converting frames created by Frame generator and Content Centre into simple line beam elements. It is important to note, however, that frame analysis cannot be used if neither Content Centre nor Frame Generator are used to create the frames and channels, as frame analysis will have nothing to analyze.

1. Open Kone.iam

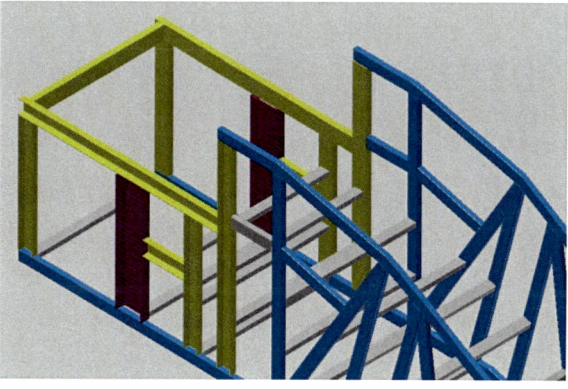

Now we can begin the second stage of the analysis of applying boundary conditions.

SECTION 6 - Frame Analysis Essentials and Design Problems using Beam Elements

CHAPTER 17
DP15– Frame Analysis Using Frame Generator Structures

Boundary conditions

2. Select **Design** tab > Select **Frame Analysis**

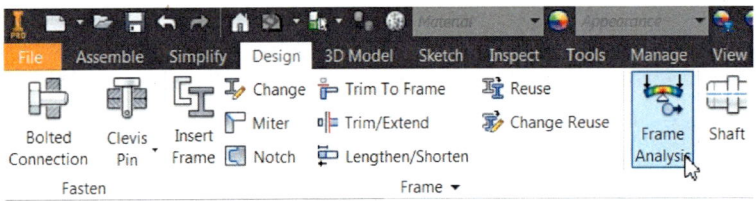

3. Select **Create Simulation** > Click **OK**

💡 Modal analysis is a very quick way to easily investigate unconnected beams, especially when the model has a large number of beams. This will help in identifying the need to create rigid links manually or automatically by increasing the beam model tolerance.
Note only constraints are required to run a modal analysis.

4. Select **Frame Analysis** Settings > Change Rigid Links color to **red** > Change scale of **Nodes** to 1 > Change scale of **Constraints** to 1 > Click **OK**

In the following steps, fixed constraints will be applied to top end of the escalator structure.

5. Select **Fixed Constraint** > Right click > Select **More Options** > Select parent node as shown > Select **Apply**

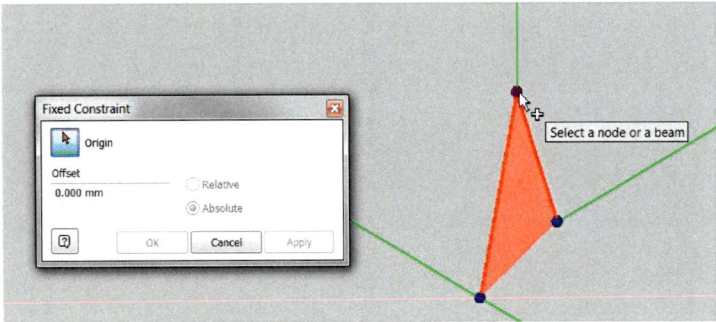

6. Repeat step 5 to apply more constraints on the other locations defined below.

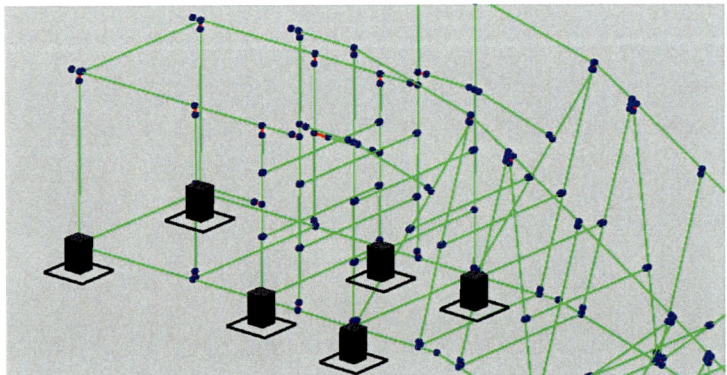

SECTION 6 - Frame Analysis Essentials and Design Problems using Beam Elements

CHAPTER 17
DP15– Frame Analysis Using Frame Generator Structures

Now we need to apply floating pin constraints at the V frame junctions as indicated below

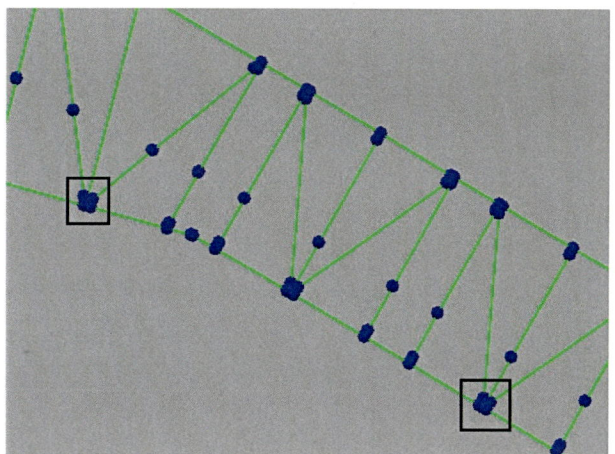

The constraints are to be applied at each alternating V junction on both sides of the structure on the incline of the escalator support structure.

7. Select **Floating Constraint** > Right Click > Select **More Options** > Select **Nodes**

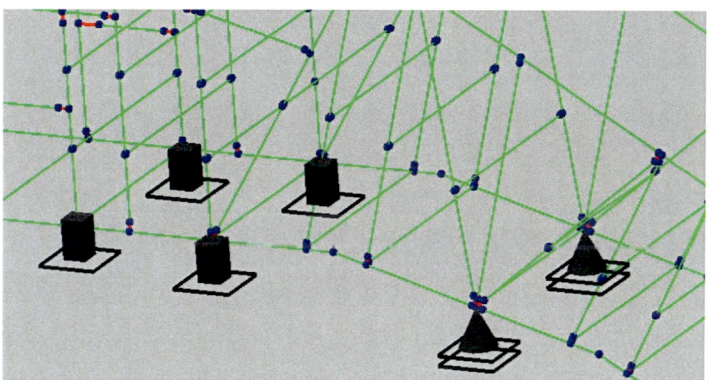

8. Repeat step 7 for the following locations

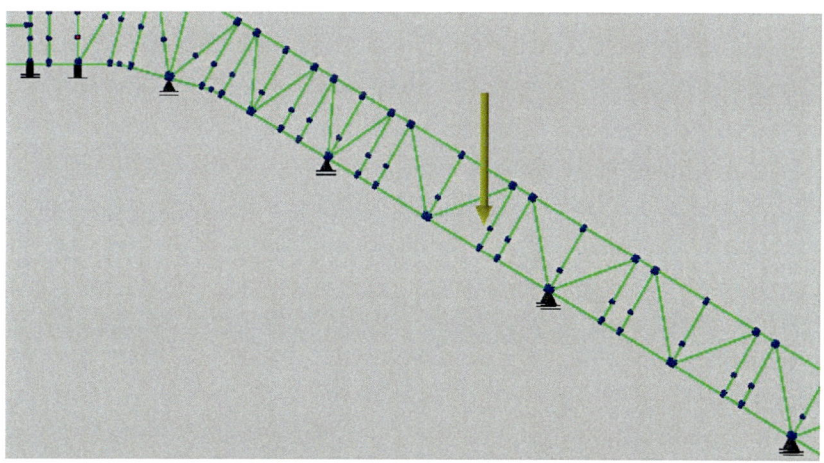

SECTION 6 - Frame Analysis Essentials and Design Problems using Beam Elements

CHAPTER 17
DP15– Frame Analysis Using Frame Generator Structures

9. Continue to repeat step 7 at the following locations

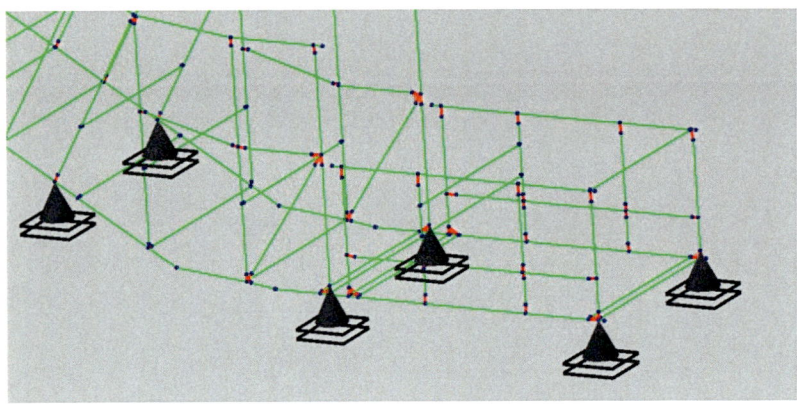

As all constraints have now been applied, the loads need to be defined on the support structure.

The first load to be taken into account is of the balustrade weight, as shown above, which will be applied as a continuous load of 1.2 N/mm.

10. Select **Continuous load** > Right click > Select **More Options** > Specify **1.2** N/mm for Magnitude > Select the beam as shown > Select **Apply**

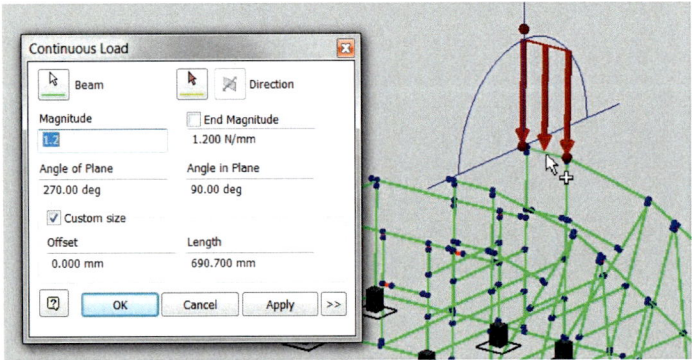

CHAPTER 17
DP15– Frame Analysis Using Frame Generator Structures

11. Repeat step 10 until all beams on the top, on both sides, have been selected as shown below > Click **OK**

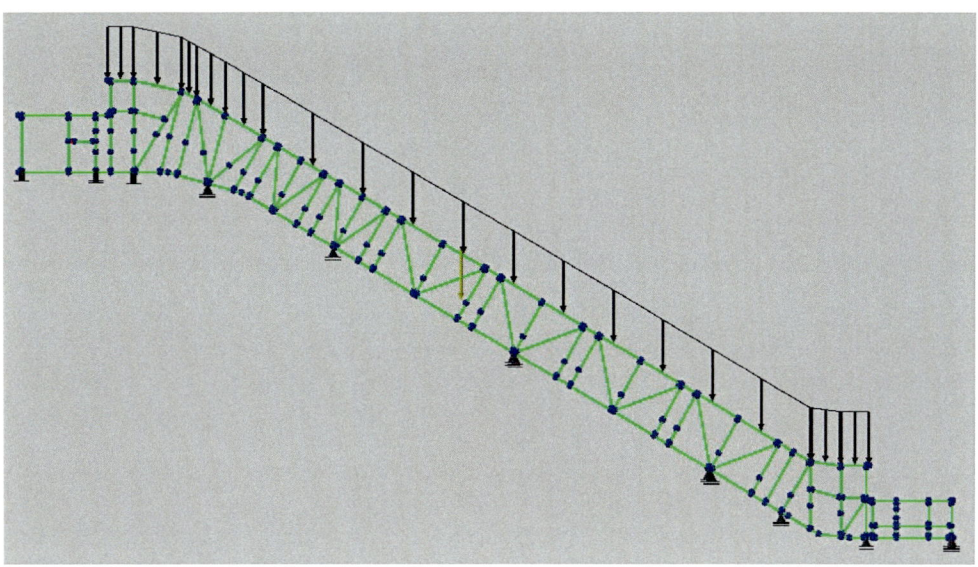

Run simulation and analyze

12. Select **Simulate** > Cancel Warning

13. Select **Display** > Deselect **Boundary Conditions** > Select **Maximum Value**

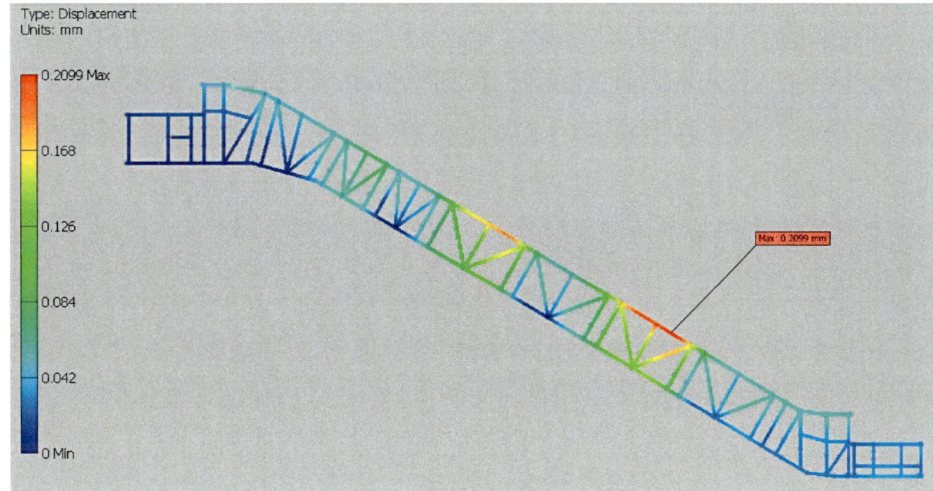

The maximum deflection is only 0.2 mm under the balustrade load and is well below the limit. We will next look at the maximum bending stress in the structure.

14. Select **Frame Analysis** Settings > Change scale of **Nodes** to 0.1 > Click **OK**

CHAPTER 17
DP15– Frame Analysis Using Frame Generator Structures

15. Select **Smax Normal Stress** > Select **Color Bar** > Unselect **Maximum Value** > Specify **6** as new **Maximum Value** > Select **Absolute Values** > Click **OK**

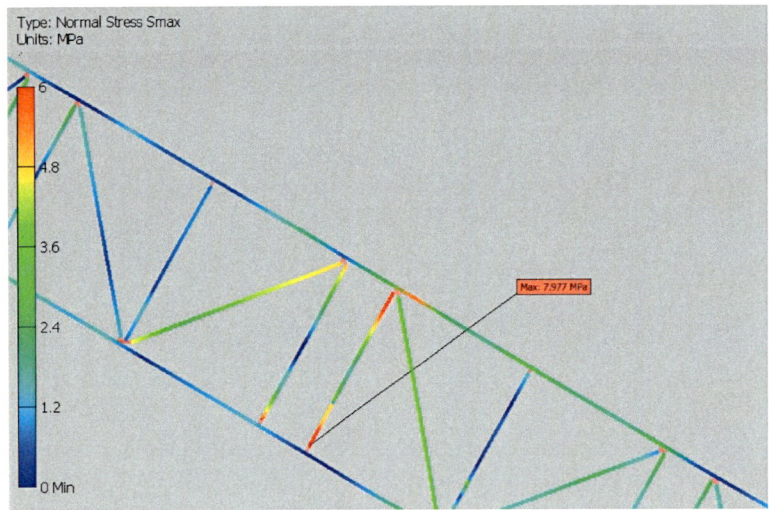

Maximum stress is 7.977 MPa

Next, we are going to look at the bending Stresses across the lower long beam of the escalator.

16. Select **Diagram** > **Activate Selected Beam** > Select the beam as shown > Select **Maximum Smax** > Click **OK**

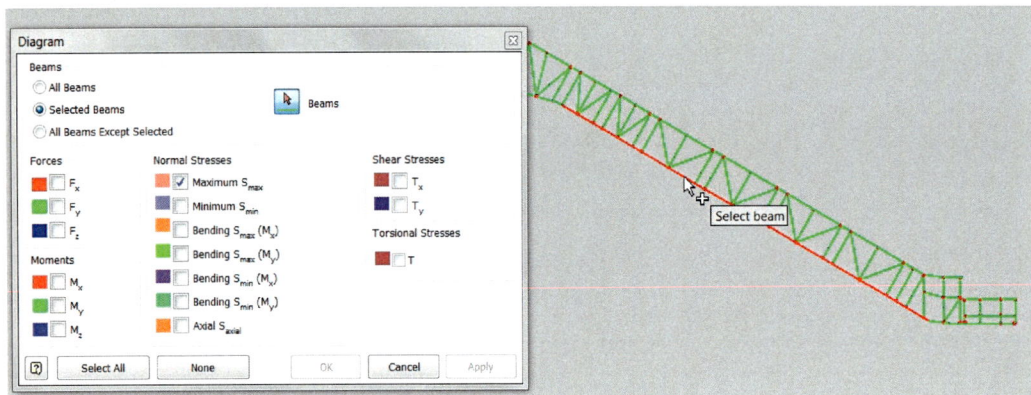

17. Select **Frame Analysis Settings** > Select **Diagrams** tab > Select the **Differentiated** and **Filled** option > Select **Colors** > Select **Red** for **Smax** > Click **OK** twice

CHAPTER 17
DP15– Frame Analysis Using Frame Generator Structures

18. Right Click **Diagram:1** > Select **Diagram Scales** > Change **Normal Stresses** to 0.00500 MPa/mm > Click **OK**

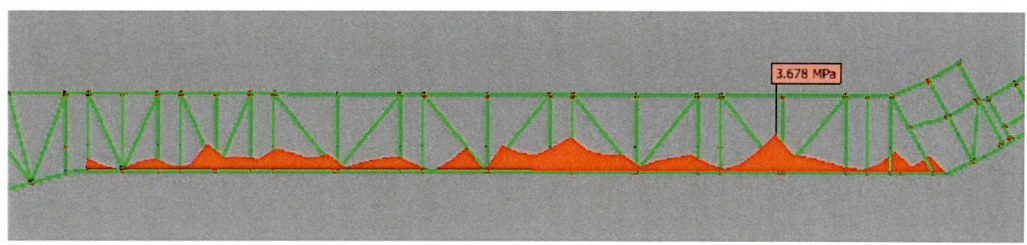

📝 Value may differ slightly as this down to selection of nodes for constraints, as they may be in slight different location when clicked.

💡 Beam Detail will provide a more comprehensive summary of results, including the reactions of the selected beam.

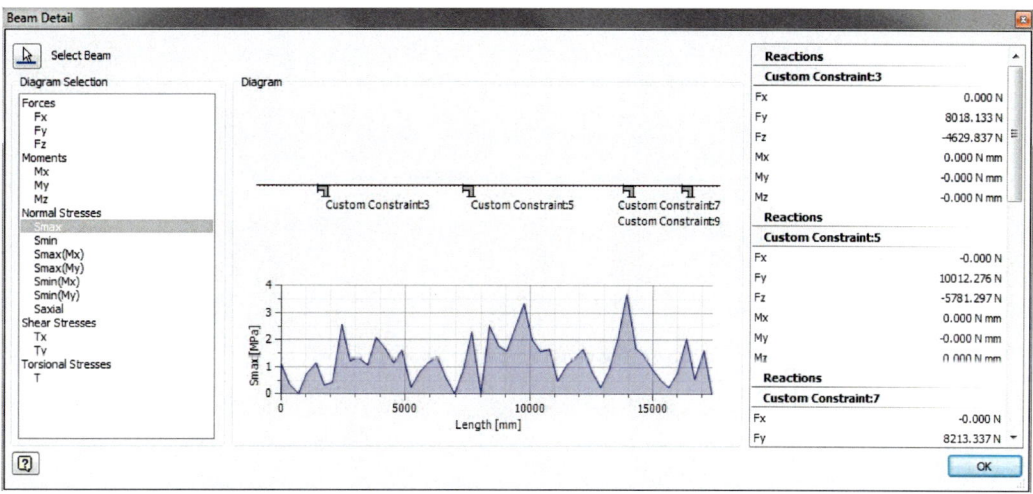

A typical escalator analysis can have up to 30 load cases, including passenger and step load cases. To analysis of all these load cases is beyond the scope of this exercise and therefore only the passenger load case will be considered in addition to the balustrade weight (including the weight of the escalator structure). Each step of the escalator needs to carry two people, including any extra weight that they may be carrying, for example shopping goods etc. Therefore, the weight to be used for the purposes of analysis is 200 kg (or 2000 N) per person.

SECTION 6 - Frame Analysis Essentials and Design Problems using Beam Elements

CHAPTER 17
DP15– Frame Analysis Using Frame Generator Structures

The load of the passenger is transferred to structure via escalator tracks, as shown below.

The tracks are positioned 200 mm from the sides and therefore the forces need to be applied on the cross members 200 mm offset from either end. The length of these cross member is ≈ 1540 mm, which means the values for offsetting the forces will be 200mm and 1340mm.

19. Right Click **Simulation:1** > Select **Copy Simulation**

20. Select **Force** > Right click > Select **More Options** > Select **2000** for Magnitude > Select beam as shown > Select **1340** mm for **Offset** > Select **Apply**

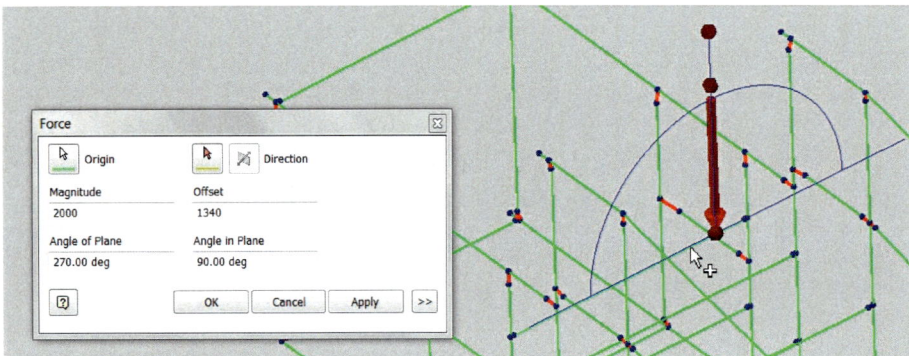

21. Select same beam again > Select **200** mm for **Offset** > Click **Apply**

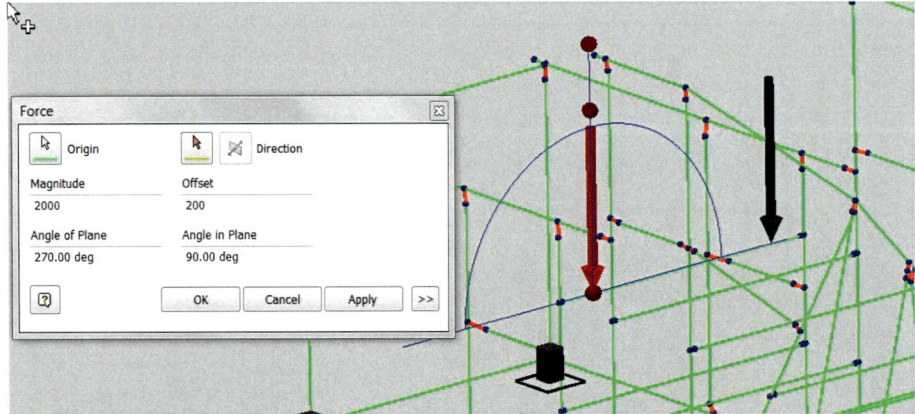

CHAPTER 17
DP15– Frame Analysis Using Frame Generator Structures

22. Repeat steps **20-21** for all cross member beams on the escalator

📝 60 forces in total are created

📝 The forces on the incline are @ 30° to the vertical such as Angle of Plane is 240°

📝 The eight forces (4 on each side of the beam) on the top between the horizontal and the incline, as shown below, have an Angle of Plane value of 255°

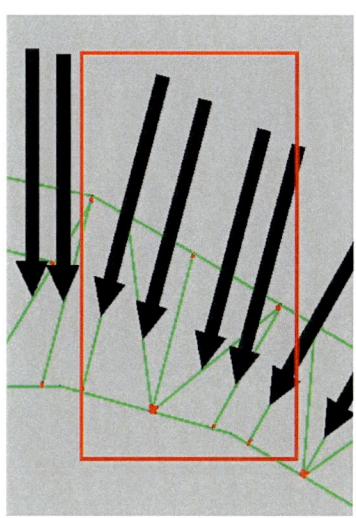

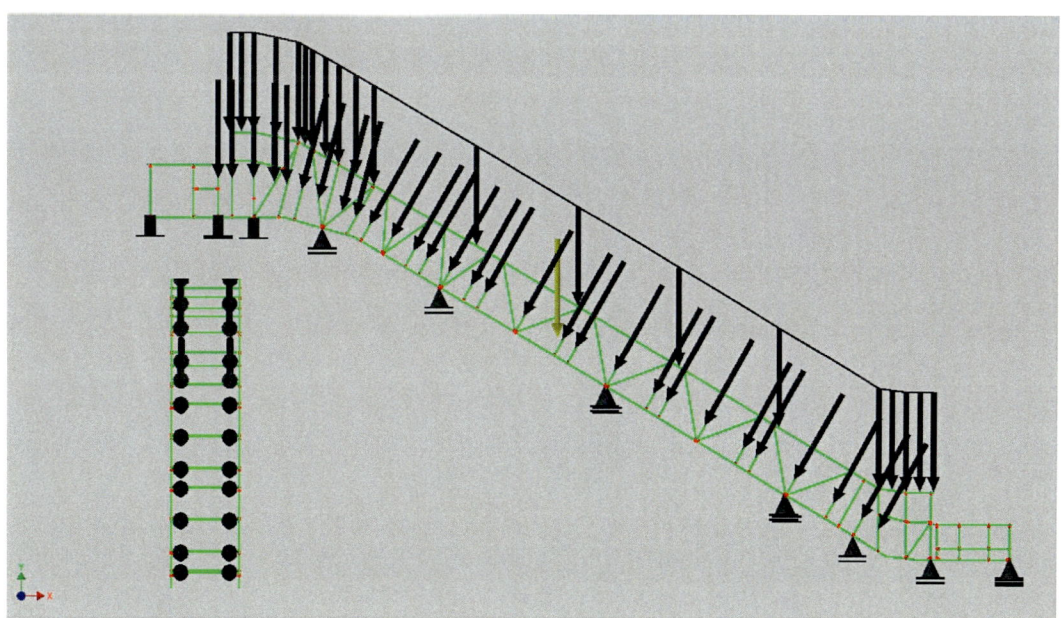

CHAPTER 17
DP15– Frame Analysis Using Frame Generator Structures

23. Select **Simulate** > Cancel **Warning**

The maximum value has now increased from 0.2 mm to 0.9942 mm.

24. Select S_{max} **Normal Stress** > Select **Color Bar** > Unselect **Maximum Value** > Specify **15** > Select **Absolute Values** > Deselect **Boundary Conditions** > Click **OK**

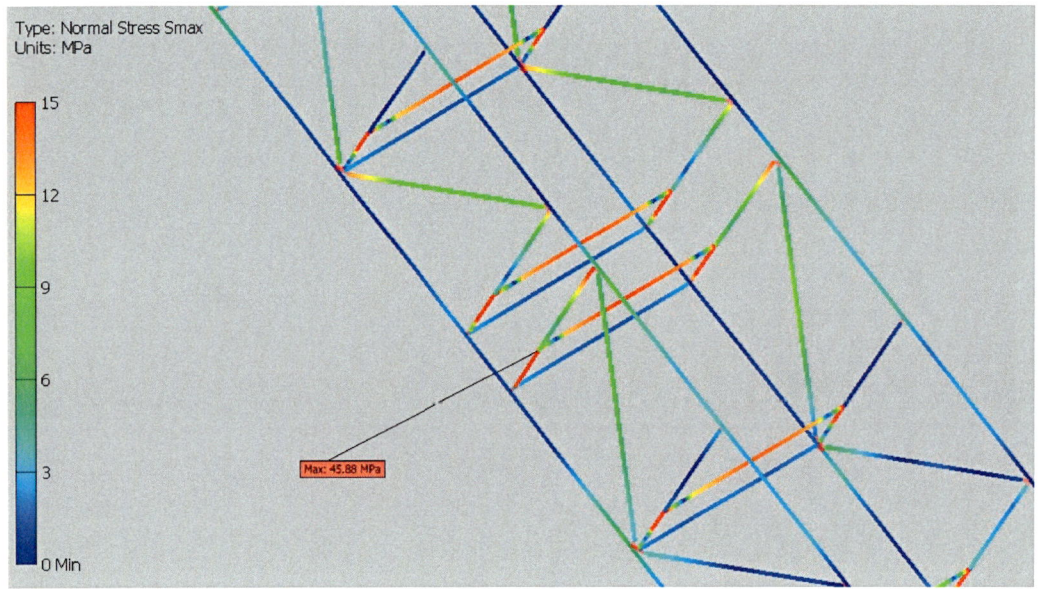

The maximum stress value has increased from 7.977MPa to 45.88 MPa. Based on this new value the minimum safety factor is

$$Factor\ of\ Safety = \frac{\text{Yield Stress}}{\text{Operationl Stress}} = \frac{207}{45.88} = 4.5$$

A typical escalator, as mentioned earlier, will go through several more load case analyses.

25. Close File

CHAPTER 18
DP16– Frame Analysis Using Frame Advance Settings

DP16 – Frame Analysis Using Advance Settings

Analysis of an Offshore Container
(Design Problem courtesy of Swire Oilfield Services Ltd)

Key features and workflows introduced in this design problem

	Key Features/Workflows
1	Beams and beam releases to simulate Slings
2	Modifying and Creating Rigid Links
3	Custom Constraints with Stiffness Properties

Introduction

Swire Oilfield Services, part of the global conglomerate, the Swire group, is the world's largest supplier of specialist offshore cargo carrying units to the global energy industry and is a leading supplier of cargo carrying solutions, modular systems, offshore aviation services and fluid management.

SECTION 6 - Frame Analysis Essentials and Design Problems using Beam Elements

CHAPTER 18

DP16– Frame Analysis Using Advance Settings

Established in 1979, Swire Oilfield Services provides the largest hire fleet worldwide. Its in-house engineering capability allows the company to design and manufacture customized equipment. The company supplies tailored modular workspace systems and services to the marine and energy industries.

Swire Oilfield Services' comprehensive fluid management services save its customers time and money and minimizes health and safety concerns both on and offshore. Through its fully certified and approved offshore aviation services, Swire Oilfield Services plays a crucial role in the efficient operations of offshore helicopters.

Operating in 31 countries, Swire Oilfield Services has a team of over 750 staff in 36 bases around the globe. The company has a presence in all major oil and gas regions with large operations in Northern Europe, The Americas, Africa, Asia Pacific and Australia

Swire Oilfield Services design, manufacture and physically test all of their offshore containers to meet DET NORSKE VERITAS (DNV for short) 2.7.1 Standard. Two of the tests they have to meet is the 4 and 2 Point Lift. Using FEA analysis the primary structure (excluding side wall and floor etc.) of the component is either modeled as shells or beams, in this example we will use beams. To simulate the realistic behavior of the container as much as possible the lifting sets (slings) will be included and again modeled as beams.

In this design problem we will simulate a 4 Point and 2 Lift test for one of Swire's Unit within Inventor Frame Analysis under DNV guidelines. The offshore container needs to lift 65 tonnes and for the purposes of this exercise the material to be used is Mild Steel for the container.

Workflow of Design Problem 16

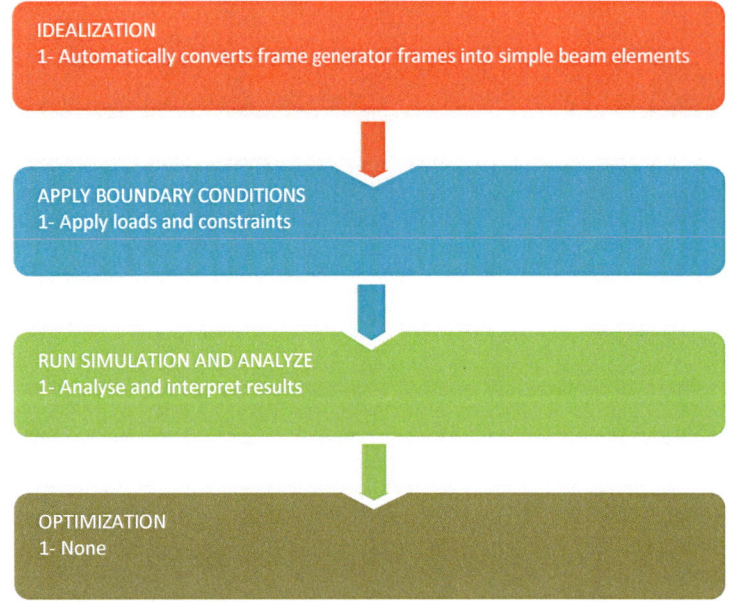

CHAPTER 18
DP16– Frame Analysis Using Frame Advance Settings

Idealization

Idealization is done automatically by converting frames created by Frame generator and Content Centre into simple line beam elements. It is also worth noting that to reduce the complexity of rigid links automatically created is not to perform end treatments, via frame generator, prior to any frame analysis. As such in this example unlike the previous example majority of the frames are overlapping.

1. Open Offshore-Container.iam

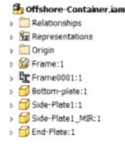

By further examining the model we can see that all frames are overlapping

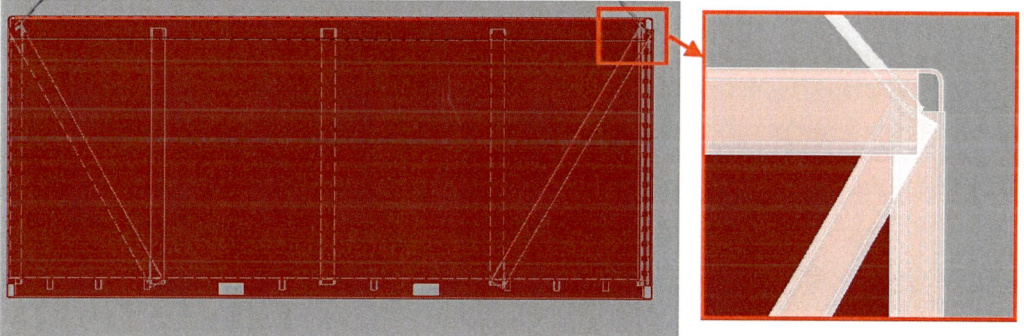

 It's better for frame analysis if you do not perform end treatments using Frame Generator

Now we can begin the second stage of the analysis of applying boundary conditions.

Boundary conditions

2. Select **Design** tab > Select **Frame Analysis**

3. Select **Create Simulation** > For Name specify **4 Point Lift** > Click **OK**

To be able to better see the beams and rigid links created change the visibility of original models from transparent to invisible, via Frame Analysis Settings. Rigid links are created as a result of specifying offset positions when placing content/structures using Frame Generator.

CHAPTER 18
DP16– Frame Analysis Using Advance Settings

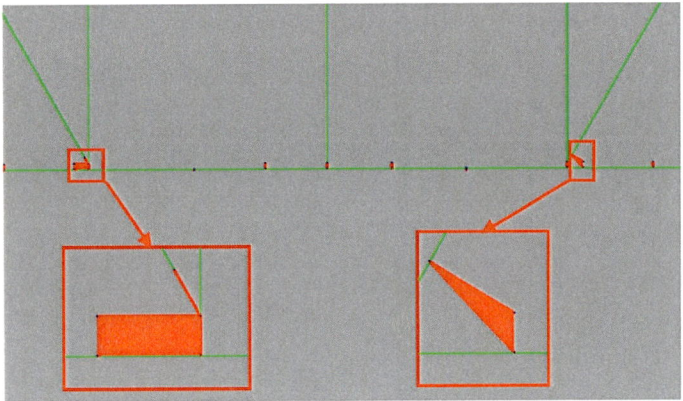

💡 If no offset positions are specified when placing content, via frame generator, then all beam elements will be connected. This also means there will be no gaps between the beams, hence no rigid links will be automatically created, or needed.

The complexity of four of the rigid links created, two on each side, can be simplified by creating them manually, and suppressing the one's automatically created.

4. Select one of the rigid links in the graphics window as illustrated in above image > Right click > Select **Suppress**

Repeat step 4 for the remaining three rigid links. Four Rigid links will now be suppressed in the browser, under the Rigid Links heading. We are going to start to create manual rigid links, in the following steps, starting from the front end (the opening)

5. Select **Frame Analysis Settings** > Change Nodes Scales to **0.5** > Click **OK**

6. Select **Rigid Links** > Select **top node** for Parent and **bottom node** for Child as indicated below > Click **Apply.** A rigid link will be created as shown by the red line below

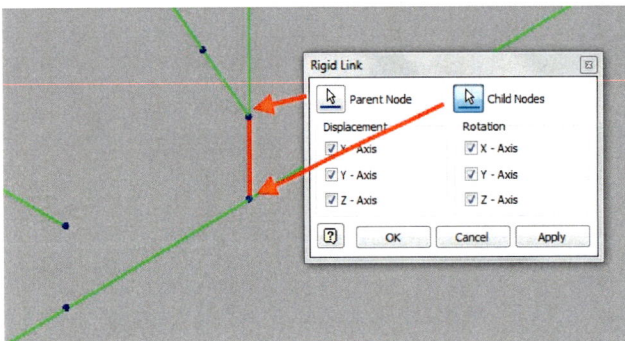

CHAPTER 18
DP16– Frame Analysis Using Frame Advance Settings

7. Now repeat step **6** to connect the two beam nodes in front > Click **Apply**. Another rigid link will be created as shown below

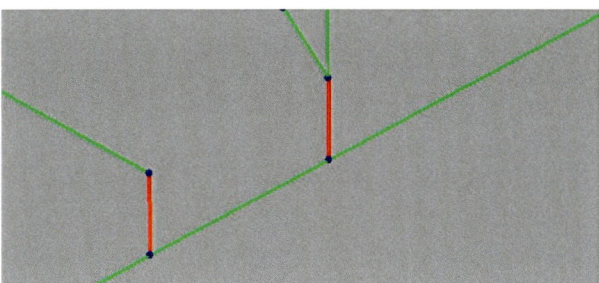

Now repeat step 6 to 7 for the other side. In the following steps we are going to create rigid links towards the back end of the container.

8. Select **top node** for Parent and **bottom node** for Child as indicated below > Click **Apply**. A rigid link will be created as shown by the red line below

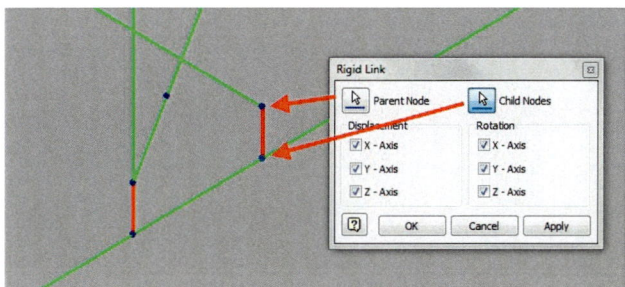

9. Now repeat step 8 for the other side.

The following four simplified rigid links will be created (two on each side)

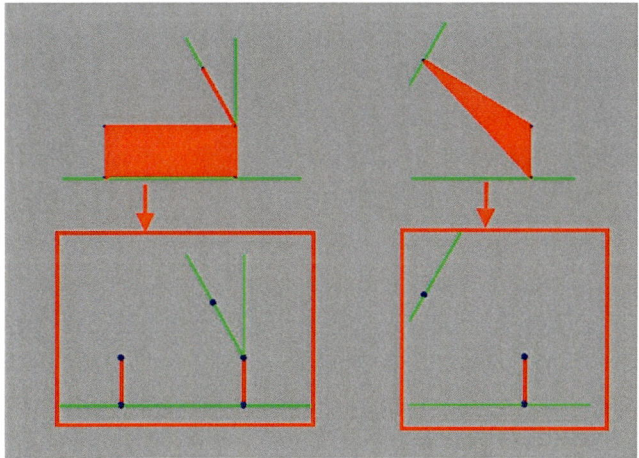

Now modify Gravity to point in the negative Z-direction. Now we are going to specify a pin constraint at top of the slings as in reality the slings are attached via a hook, which will allow rotation.

SECTION 6 - Frame Analysis Essentials and Design Problems using Beam Elements

CHAPTER 18
DP16– Frame Analysis Using Advance Settings

10. Right Click **Gravity** > Select **Edit** > Set Direction to **-Z** > Click **OK**

   Typically when analyzing offshore containers for lifts one is not concerned with the stress and deflections in the slings.

11. Select **Frame Analysis Settings** > Change Constraints Scales to **0.5** > Click **OK**

12. Select **Fixed Constraint** > Select node on top of the slings > Click **Ok**

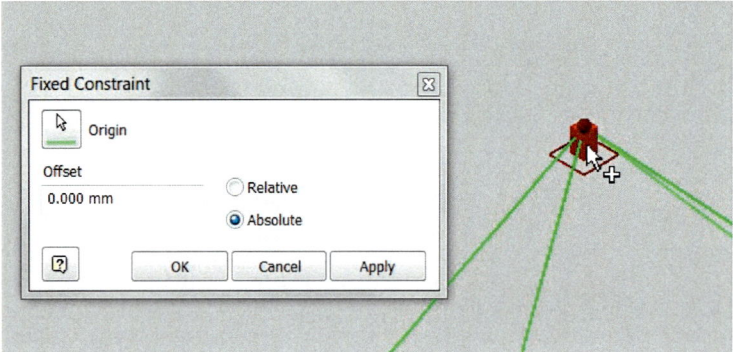

13. Select **Release** from connections panel > Select 1st sling to convert from fixed to pinned ends

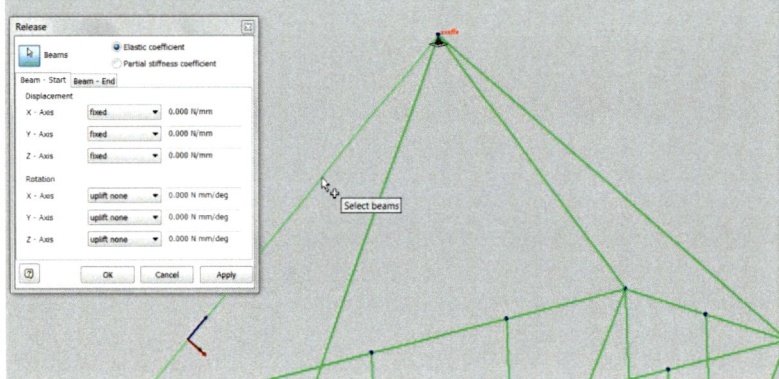

14. Click **OK** > Repeat Step 13 for other 3 slings

CHAPTER 18
DP16– Frame Analysis Using Frame Advance Settings

289

15. Select **Simulate**

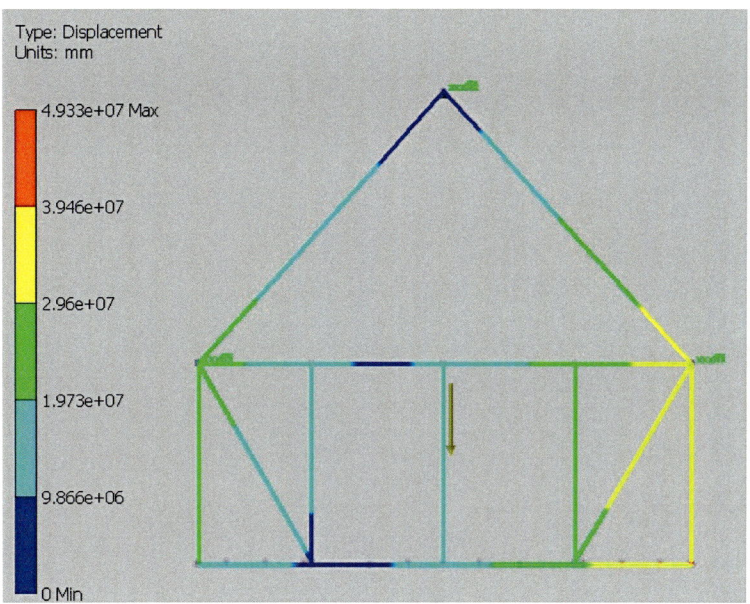

Note there is excessive displacement and this is due to the model being unstable. In the next steps we will make use of custom constraints to stabilize the model.

16. Select **Custom Constraint** > Specify **uplift none** for all displacements and rotations > Specify **100 N/mm** elasticity – K for Displacement X-axis and Y-axis > Select the parent node of the rigid link as shown > Click **Apply**

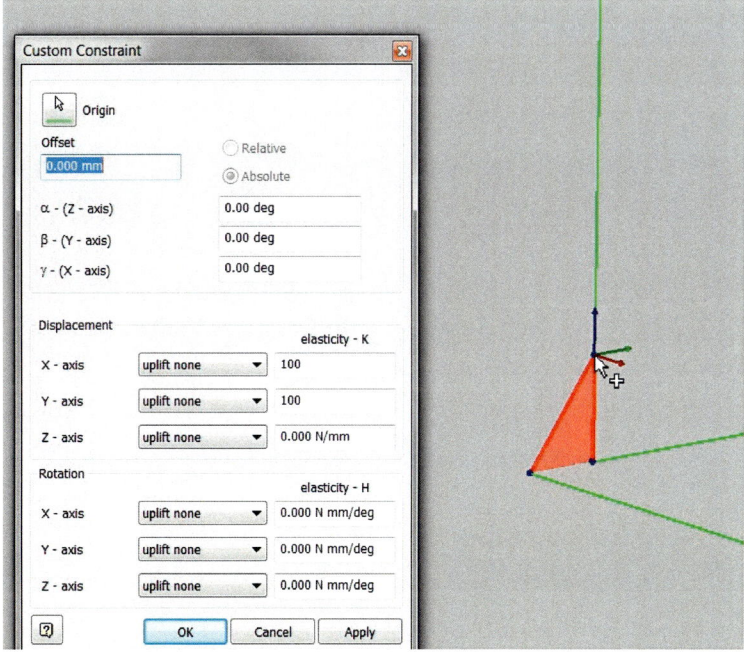

17. Repeat step 16 for the other 3 corners

SECTION 6 - Frame Analysis Essentials and Design Problems using Beam Elements

CHAPTER 18
DP16– Frame Analysis Using Advance Settings

 For Inventor Frame Analysis a value of 100N/mm provides a stable model by restraining two translational directions on all corners of the frame. This technique is widely used when analyzing containers using any FEA software, with the only difference being the value used. You can experiment with different values to simulate physical testing results

18. Select **Simulate**

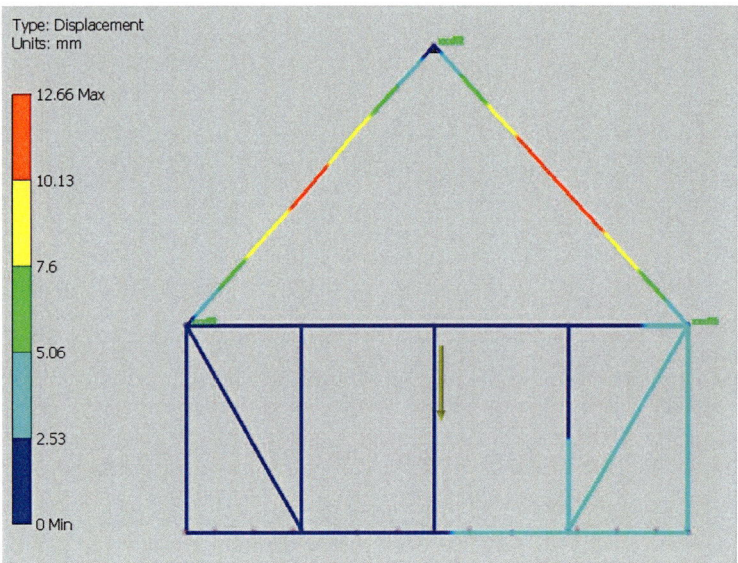

Although the model seems stable we can check whether the custom constraints have an impact on the results. We can check this by looking at the reactions of the constraints.

19. Select **Custom Constraint:1** > Right Click > Select **Reactions**

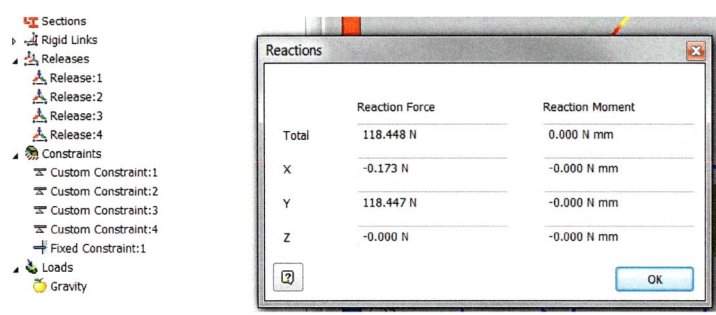

The maximum value 118.447 N in the Y direction is small. Also note the reaction in the Z direction is zero as we did not want to restrain in the direction of the loading. The other custom constraints produce similar reactions.

CHAPTER 18

DP16– Frame Analysis Using Frame Advance Settings

Now we will apply the loads on the container as defined below

Main data for calculations	
Max. gross mass (R)	25000kg
Payload	18500kg
Tare mass	6500kg
Sling leg angle	45°
Enhancement factor	1.104

4 Point Lifting Load

Load on structure   F=(2.5xR)g = (2.5x25000)x9.81 = **613,125N**

2 Point Lifting Load

Load on structure   F=(1.5xR)g = (1.5x25000)x9.81 = **367,875N**

Initially we are going to test the structure using the 4 point lifting load value of 613,125N. As the container at the bottom is supported by 10 cross-members, excluding the outer members, we need to spread this load uniformly across all members using Continuous Load. To calculate this value, we determine the total length of all the frames directly supporting the floor of the container and then divide the total load by the total length of the frames. In this example the length of the frames supporting the floor of the container are 2750mm.

$$\text{Continuous Load} = \frac{613125}{2750 \times 10} = 22.295 \text{ N/mm}$$

20. Select **Continuous load** > Right click > Select **More Options** > Specify **613125/27500** for Magnitude > Select the beam as shown > Select **Apply**

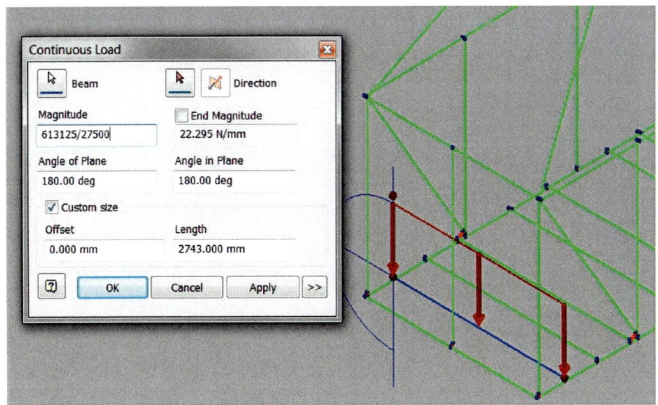

✎ Used a value of 2750mm as an approximate value for the purposes of calculating Load

21. Repeat step 20 until all the other nine beams on the bottom have been selected > Click **OK**

CHAPTER 18
DP16– Frame Analysis Using Advance Settings
Run simulation and analyze

22. Select **Simulate** > Select **Adjusted** x 1 from Adjust Displacement Display

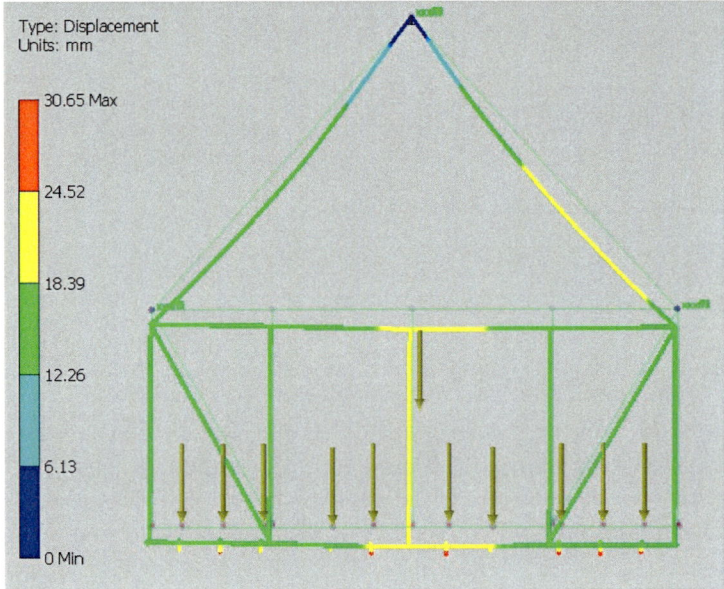

We can see the sling extends by approximately 14-18mm at the ends. There also seems to be some extra movement of the slings somewhere in the middle, most likely due the weight of the slings. The illustration below shows same simulation without gravity.

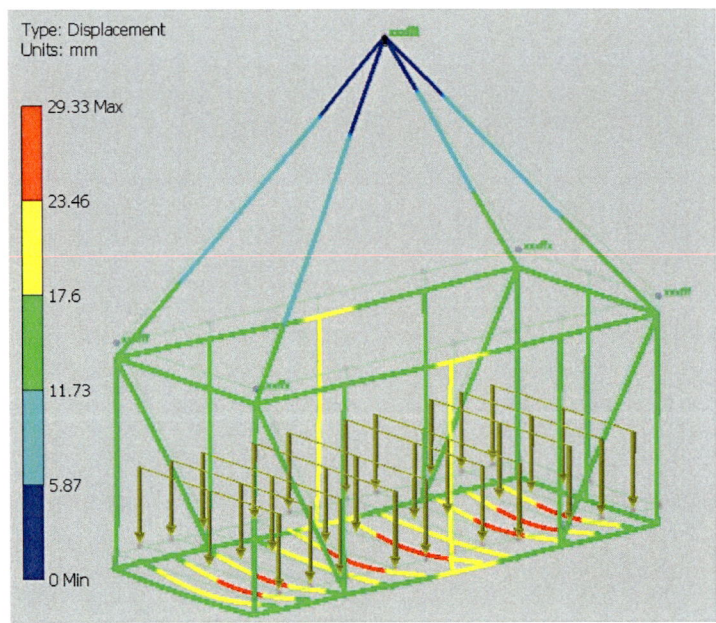

We will continue with the exercise with gravity on.

CHAPTER 18

DP16– Frame Analysis Using Frame Advance Settings

23. Select **Smax Normal Stesses** > Select **Undeformed** x 1 from Adjust Displacement Display > Select **Maximum Value**

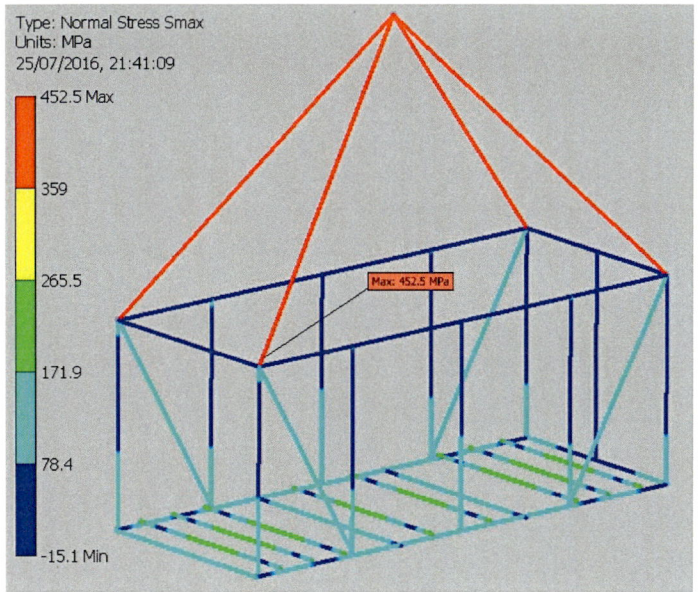

The maximum value of 452.5 MPa is high and is located at slings, for which we are not interested in. We will now change the color bar settings and use probe to better interrogate the results on the container in the next steps.

24. Select **Color Bar** > Unselect **Maximum** value > Specify **250** for maximum value > Select **Absolute Values** > Click **OK**

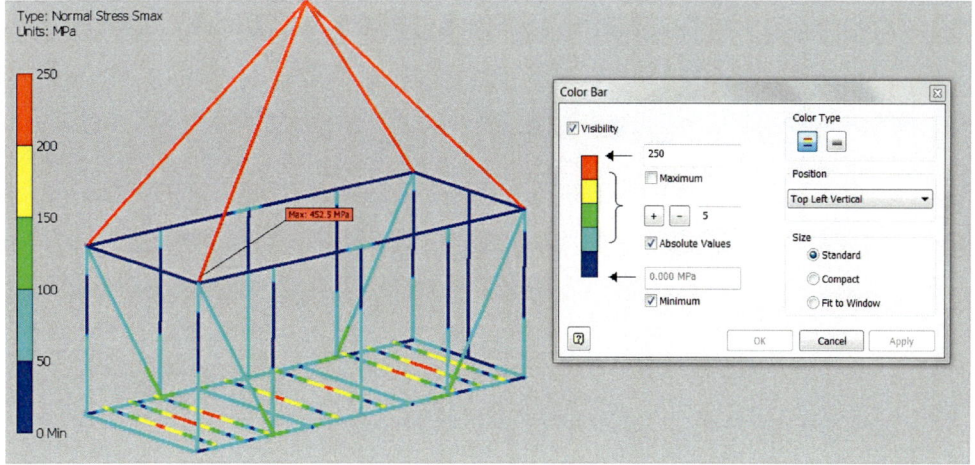

CHAPTER 18
DP16– Frame Analysis Using Advance Settings

25. Select **Probe** > Select beam as shown > Right Click > Select **More Options** > Select **Relative** option > Specify **0.5**

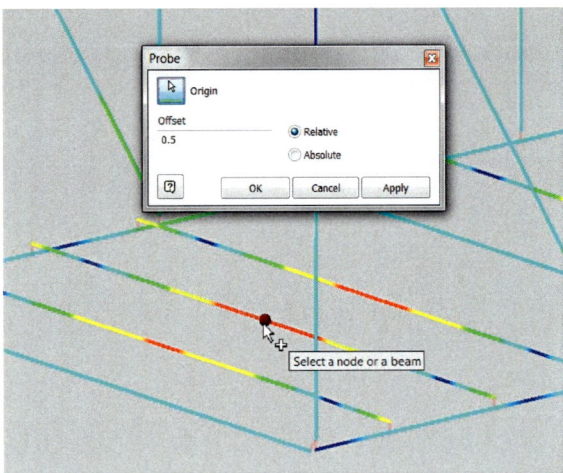

26. Click **OK**

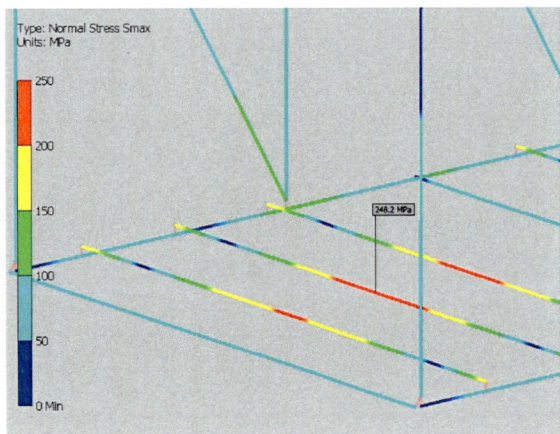

This shows the maximum stress in the container is at the bottom beams and the value is 248.2 MPa and is due to bending stress.

CHAPTER 18
DP16– Frame Analysis Using Frame Advance Settings

27. Select Smax(Mx)

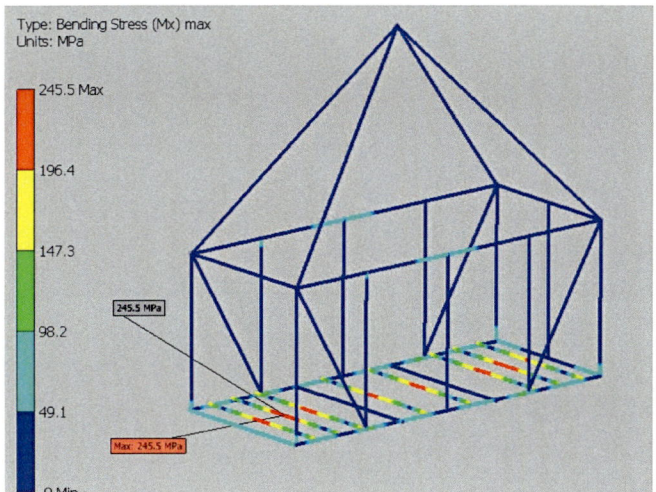

This confirms the stress is the maximum and is due to bending stress. You can also see there is very little bending stress in the slings and this is due to beam releases. The only stress the slings can withstand are axial and is shown below.

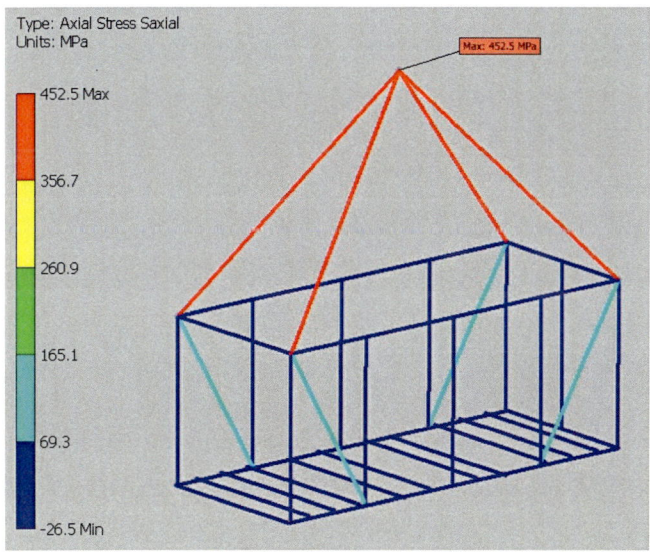

Although in this exercise the material used is mild steel with a yield limit of 207 MPa. In practice the containers are made of material with a high yield limit in the region of 355 MPa. This indicates the maximum tensile bending stress value of 245.5 MPa is below yield.

CHAPTER 18
DP16– Frame Analysis Using Advance Settings

The picture below shows Bending Stress (Mx) value when running the analysis using carbon steel material using material custom option in frame analysis. The maximum value changes slight due to a small difference in the young's modulus value. The only significant value which is different is the yield limit value of 350 MPa and UTS of 420 MPa

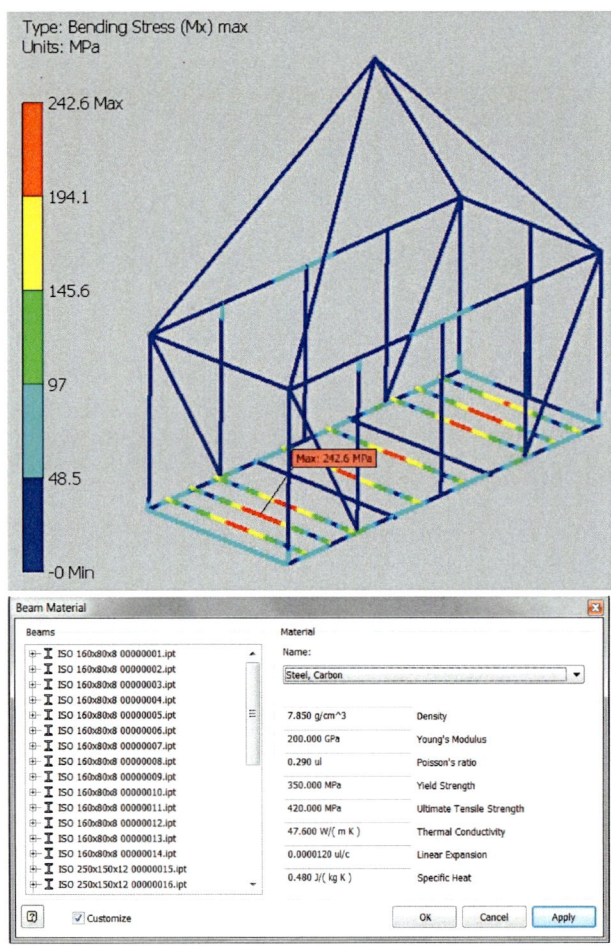

We will continue using Mild Steel for the rest of the exercise. We will now carry out the 2-point analysis.

28. Right Click **4 Point Lift** Simulation > Select **Copy Simulation** > Right Click **4 Point Lift:1** > Select **Edit Simulation** > Specify **2 Point Lift** for Name > Click **Ok**

2-Point Load is 13.377 N/mm

$$\text{Continuous Load} = \frac{367875}{2750 \times 10} = 13.377 \text{ N/mm}$$

CHAPTER 18
DP16– Frame Analysis Using Frame Advance Settings

297

29. Select **Beam:34** and **Beam:36** > Select **Suppress**

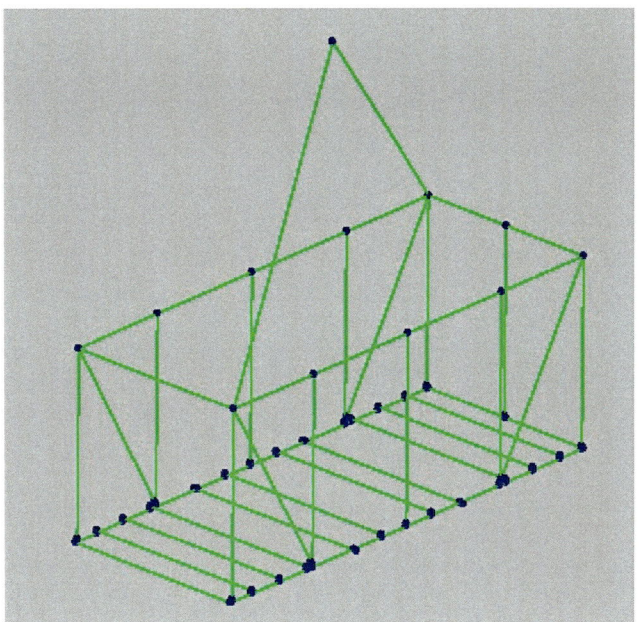

30. Right Click **Continuous Load:1** > Select **Edit** > Change **Magnitude** to **13.377** N/mm > Click **OK**

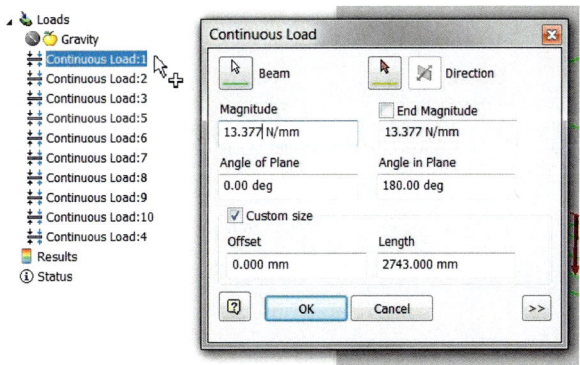

31. Repeat step 30 for all other continuous loads

SECTION 6 - Frame Analysis Essentials and Design Problems using Beam Elements

CHAPTER 18
DP16– Frame Analysis Using Advance Settings

32. Select **Simulate**

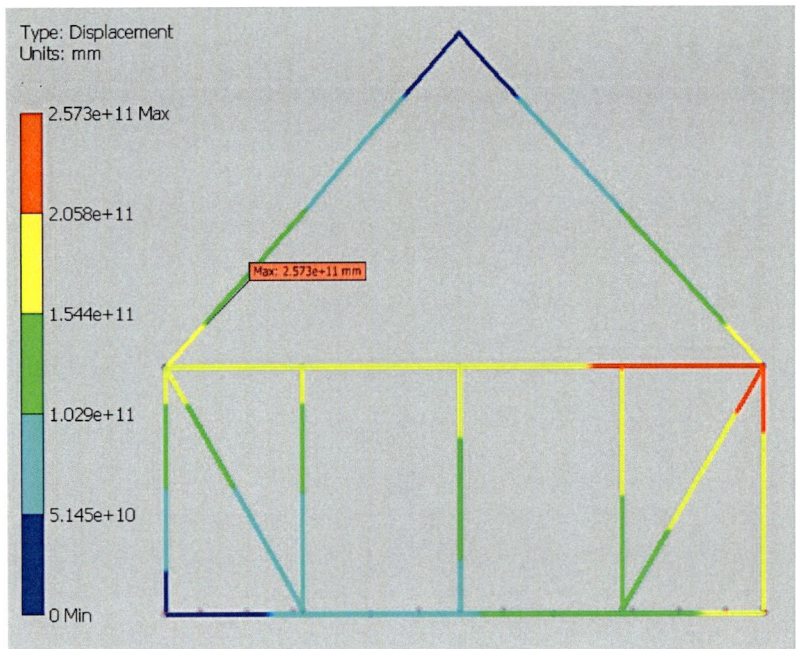

The displacement results seems excessive. This as previously demonstrated can be stabilized using further custom constraints. We will apply a 1 N/mm Elasticity – K value in the 4 corners in the X and Y values instead of 100 N/mm as in step 16 and 17 in an attempt to stabilize the model.

33. Select **Custom Constraint** > Specify Uplift none for all displacements and rotations > Specify **1 N/mm** elasticity – K for Displacement X-axis and Y-axis > Select the parent node of the rigid link as shown > Click **Apply**

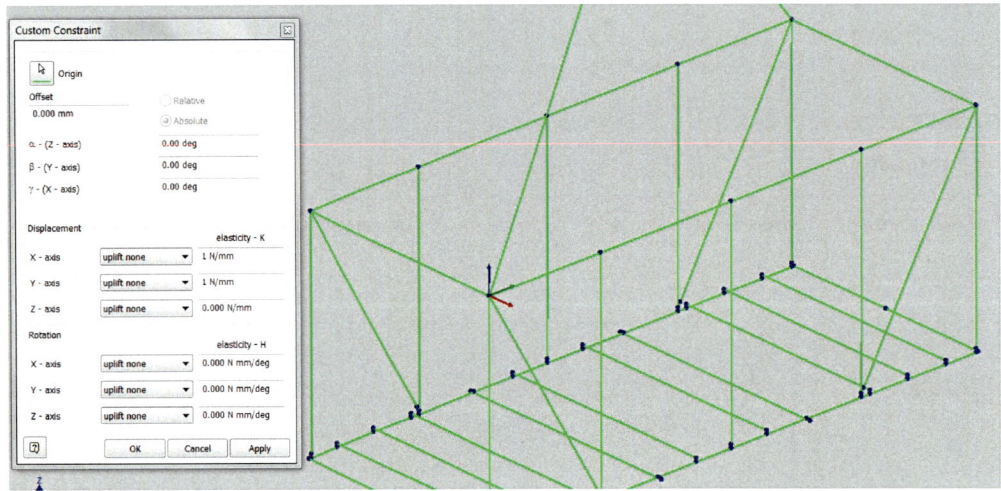

34. Repeat step 33 for the other top 3 corners

CHAPTER 18
DP16– Frame Analysis Using Frame Advance Settings

35. Select **Simulate**

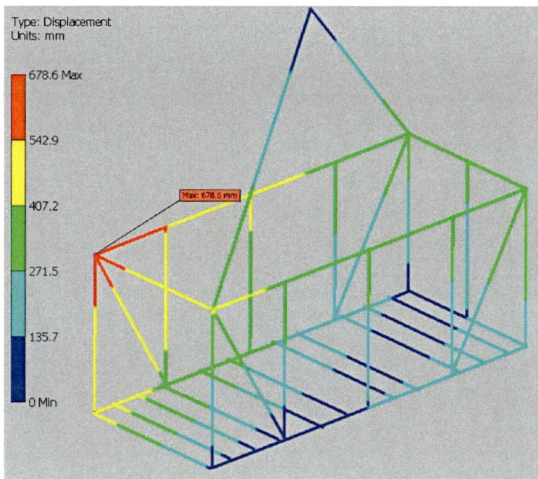

As predicted the model is more stable with displacement value of 678.6mm. The reactions at the custom constraints at the top corners range 500N and 300N which are very small indicating the constraints having minimal impact on the results.

36. Select **Smax Normal Stress** > Deselect **Maximum Value** > Select **Color Bar** > Unselect **Maximum** value > Specify **250** for maximum value > Select **Absolute Values** > Click **OK**

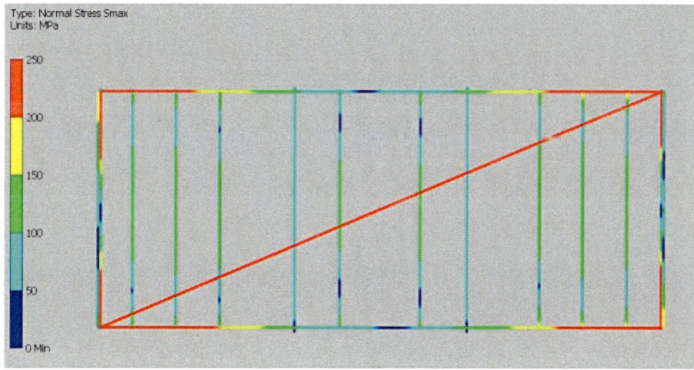

We can see the maximum combined stress is at the corners using probe we can determine the stresses

CHAPTER 18
DP16– Frame Analysis Using Advance Settings

Using probe select the top beams near the corner (not on the corner) and using the relative option select the near the end of the beams specifying either 0.99 or 0.01.

📝 If you select the corner then you may get a lower value of the vertical beam.

Below are the results showing both total stress and max bending stresses.

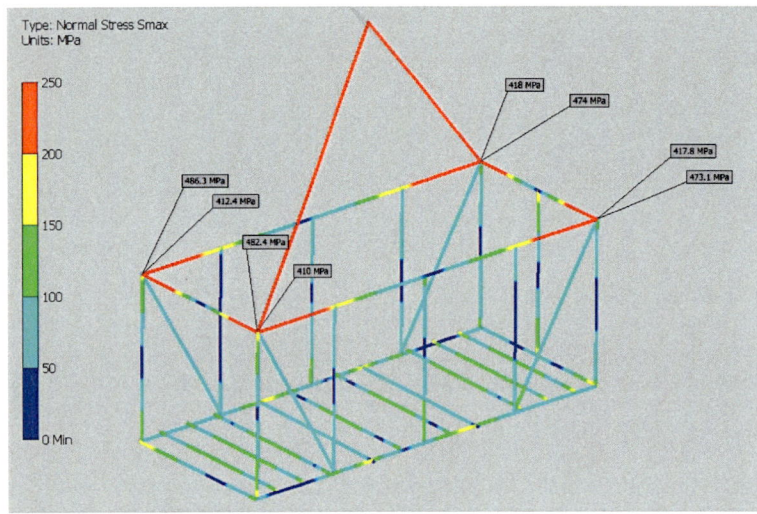

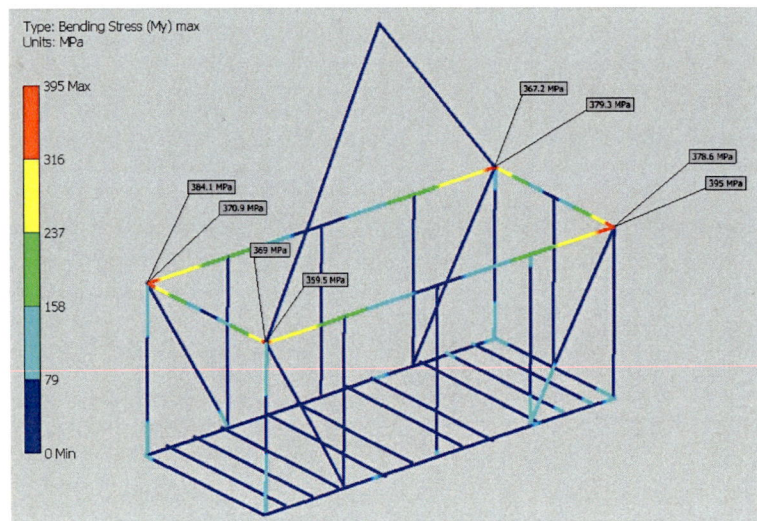

Depending on the UTS value of the material will indicate failure of the container. Let's take Carbon Steel as an example which has a yield limit of 350 MPa and UTS of 420 MPa. Based on the max bending stress values we are below UTS so the container should not completely fail or rupture, as there might be localized permanent deformation at the corners, as stress is higher than yield limit. Bases on Normal Stress Smax the values range from 413 MPa to 490 MPa which indicates stress can be higher than UTS value, indicating complete rupture failure. So here material selection and careful analysis of results becomes critical.

37. Close File

Made in the USA
San Bernardino, CA
12 March 2017